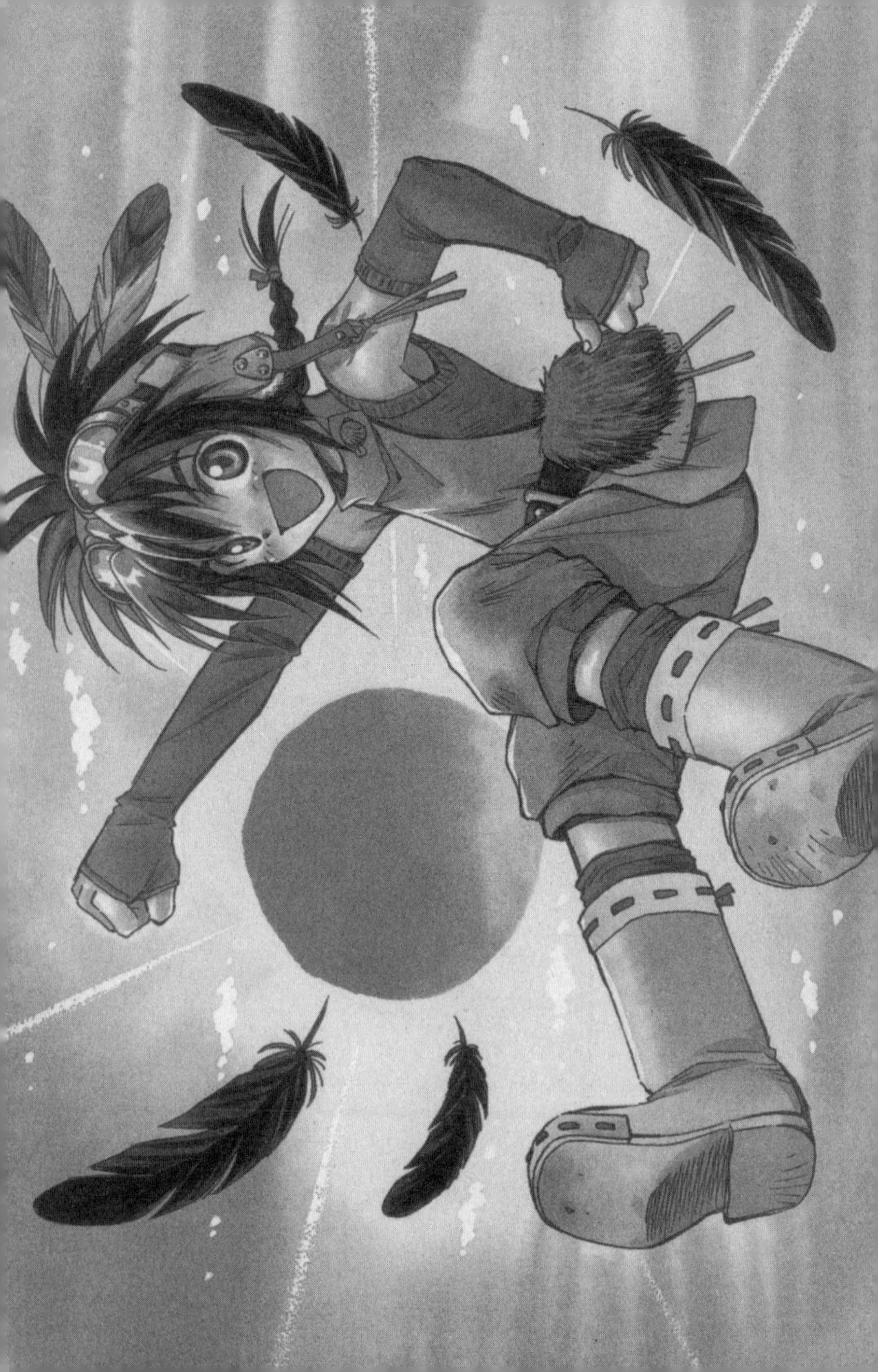

+Anima Vol. 2
Created by Natsumi Mukai

Translation - Alethea Nibley
English Adaptation - Karen S. Ahlstrom
Copy Editor - Peter Ahlstrom
Retouch and Lettering - Camellia Cox
Production Artist - Jennifer Carbajal and Jose Macasocol, Jr.
Cover Design - James Lee

Editor - Troy Lewter
Digital Imaging Manager - Chris Buford
Managing Editor - Vy Nguyen
Production Manager - Elisabeth Brizzi
Editor-in-Chief - Rob Tokar
VP of Production - Ron Klamert
Publisher - Mike Kiley
President and C.O.O. - John Parker
C.E.O. and Chief Creative Officer - Stuart Levy

A ✿ TOKYOPOP® Manga

TOKYOPOP Inc.
5900 Wilshire Blvd. Suite 2000
Los Angeles, CA 90036

E-mail: info@TOKYOPOP.com
Come visit us online at www.TOKYOPOP.com

ISBN: 978-1-4278-0442-6

First TOKYOPOP printing: February 2007
10 9 8 7 6 5 4 3 2 1
Printed in the USA

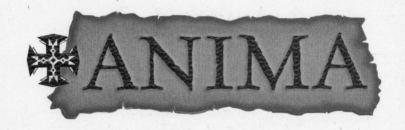

Volume 2
by Natsumi Mukai

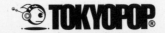

HAMBURG // LONDON // LOS ANGELES // TOKYO

+ ANIMA

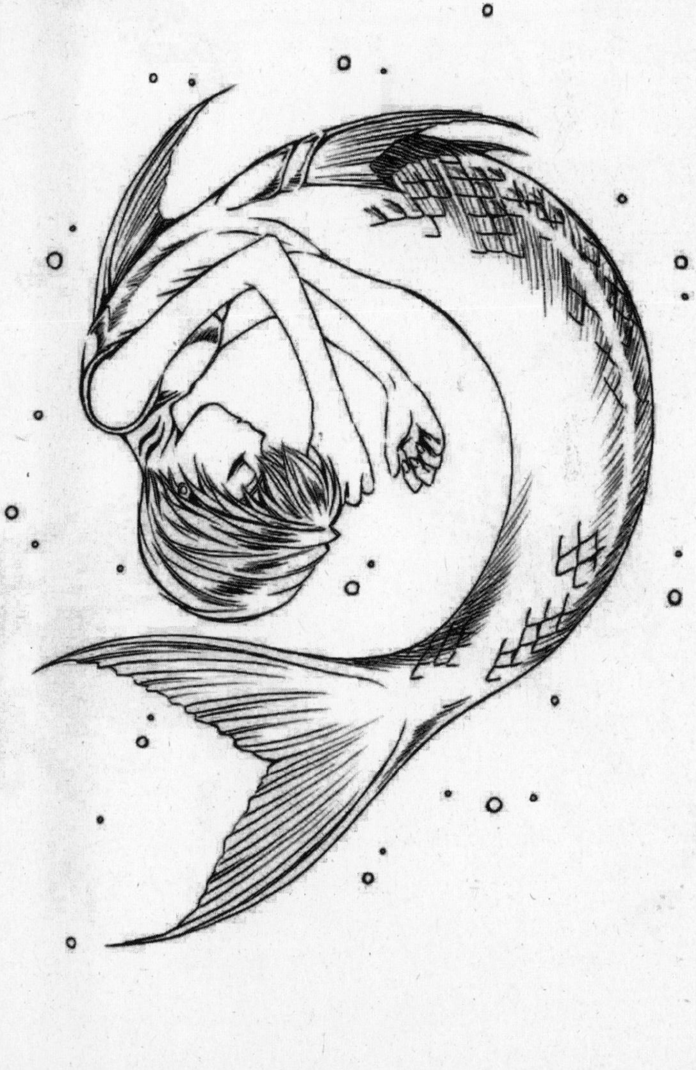

+ANIMA

プラスアニマ

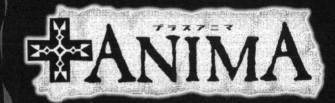

迎夏生
NATSUMI MUKAI

STORY & CHARACTERS

!

At the village of Abon, Cooro and Husky meet Senri, the bear +Anima, who is protecting the village from the Garrison Gang's scheme to dig a gold mine there. After Cooro and the others save the town and their famous plants, Senri joins them as they continue their travels...

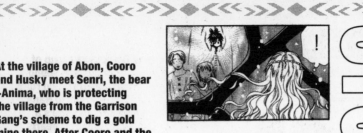

In this world, there are those known as +Anima: humans who have within them the powers of animals. When Cooro (a crow +Anima) stops at a circus during his travels, he meets Husky, a fish +Anima who is performing there. Cooro and Husky escape from the circus and end up traveling together.

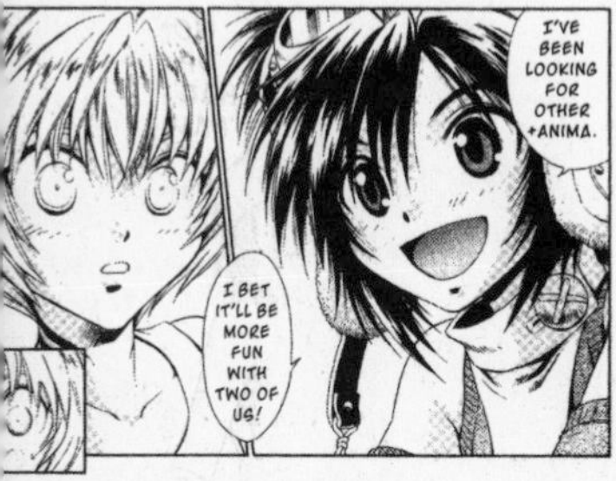

I'VE BEEN LOOKING FOR OTHER +ANIMA.
I BET IT'LL BE MORE FUN WITH TWO OF US!

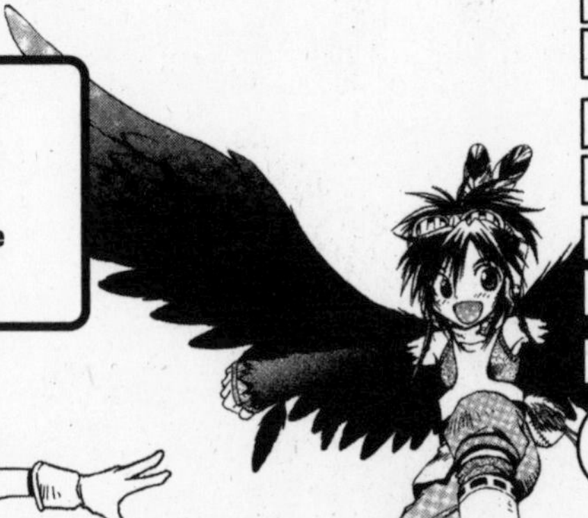

クーロ [Cooro]

Crow +Anima. He spreads his pitch-black wings and soars to the sky...He's always on the lookout for something to eat.

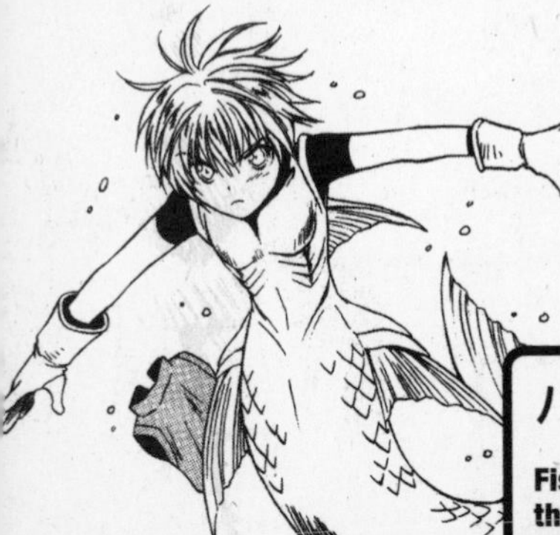

ハスキー[Husky]

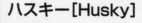

Fish +Anima. He can swim freely through water like a merman. He's a little stubborn, and doesn't like girls.

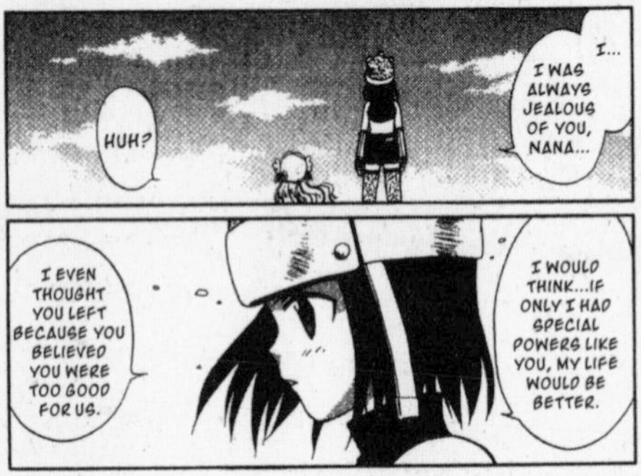
I...
I WAS ALWAYS JEALOUS OF YOU, NANA...
HUH?
I WOULD THINK...IF ONLY I HAD SPECIAL POWERS LIKE YOU, MY LIFE WOULD BE BETTER.
I EVEN THOUGHT YOU LEFT BECAUSE YOU BELIEVED YOU WERE TOO GOOD FOR US.

In the city of Octopus, a group of orphaned children live and support each other in the underground ruins. Among them is a girl named Nana who lives alone because she's a bat +Anima. When Husky's pearls are stolen, we see a glimpse of the problems caused by being different from other humans.

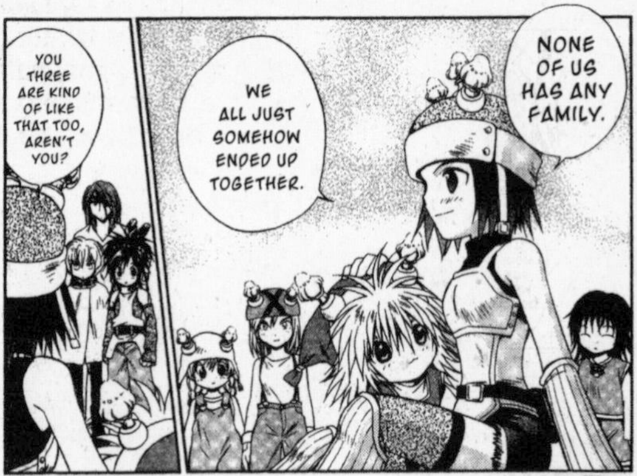
NONE OF US HAS ANY FAMILY.
WE ALL JUST SOMEHOW ENDED UP TOGETHER.
YOU THREE ARE KIND OF LIKE THAT TOO, AREN'T YOU?

Nana wants to travel with Cooro and the others, but Husky, who for some reason hates girls, is against the idea and takes off by himself. After hearing the details of how Nana discovered she was a +Anima, Husky accepts her as a member of the group.

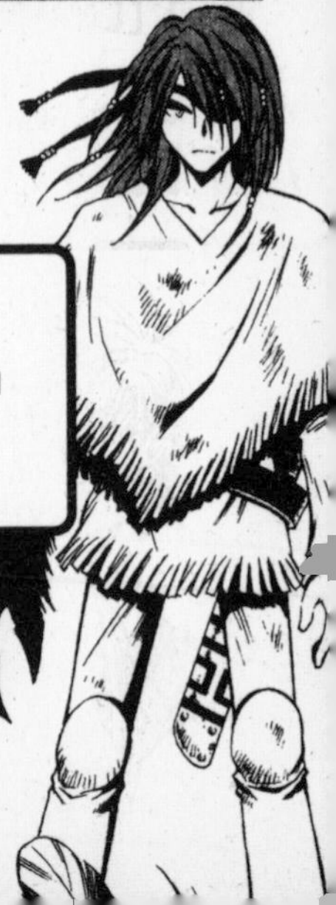

センリ [Senri]

Bear +Anima. His sharp-clawed arm is amazingly strong. He doesn't talk very much.

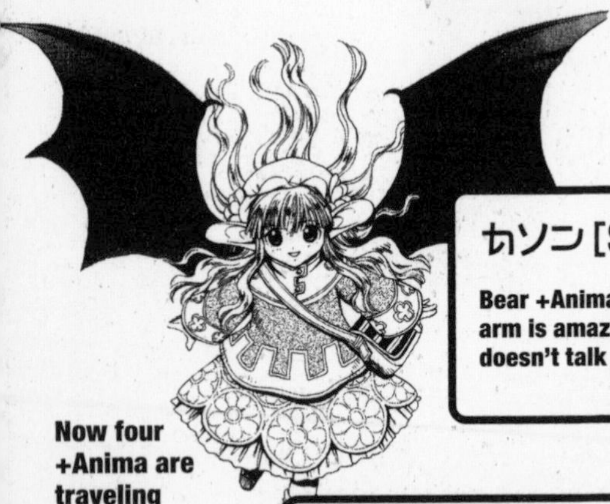

ナナ [Nana]

Bat +Anima. She can fly and has an ultrasonic screech. She loves pretty clothes and is scared of forests at night.

Now four +Anima are traveling together... What adventures await them on their journey?

C O N T E N T S

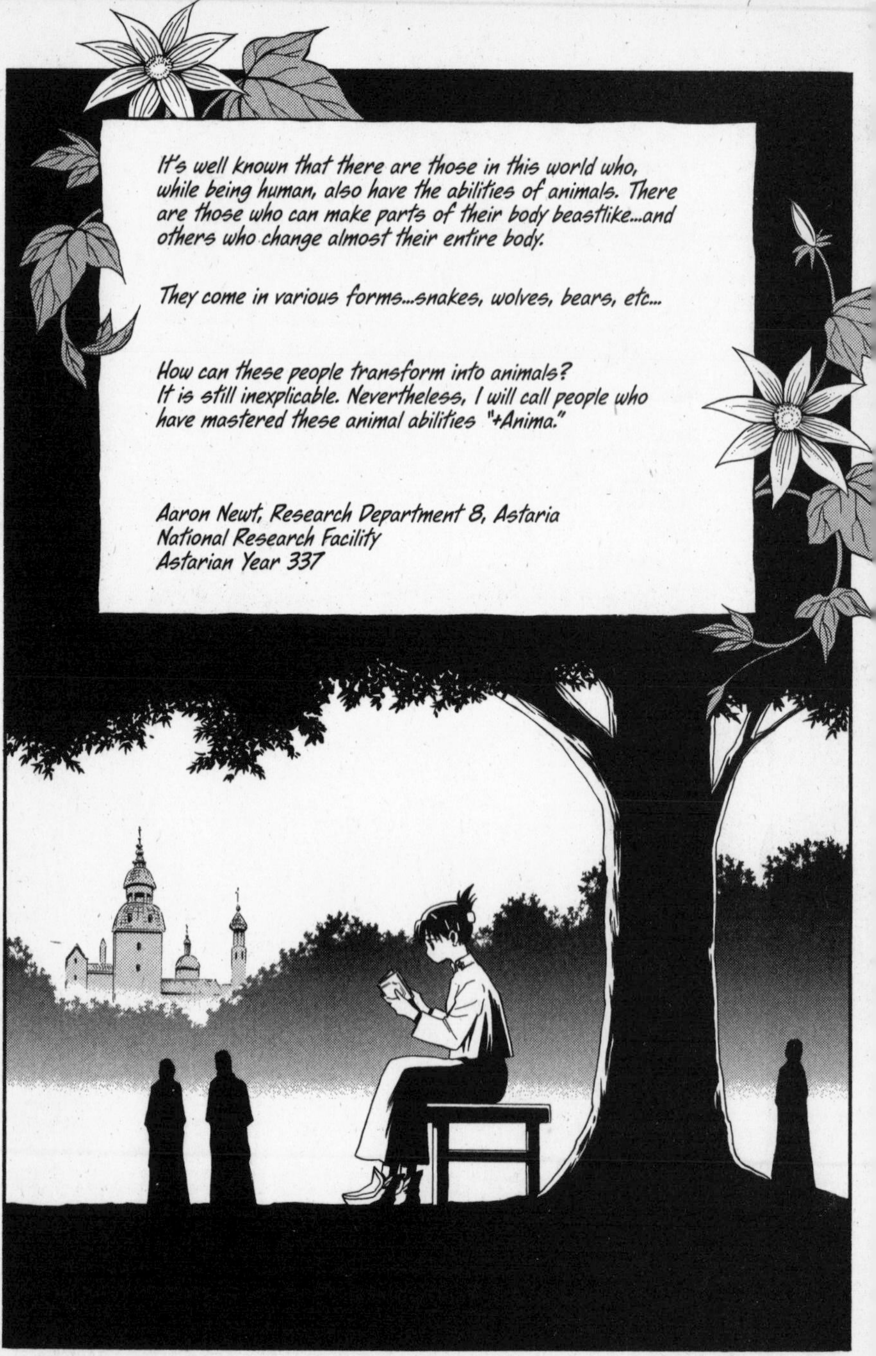
It's well known that there are those in this world who, while being human, also have the abilities of animals. There are those who can make parts of their body beastlike...and others who change almost their entire body.
They come in various forms...snakes, wolves, bears, etc...
How can these people transform into animals? It is still inexplicable. Nevertheless, I will call people who have mastered these animal abilities "+Anima."
Aaron Newt, Research Department 8, Astaria National Research Facility
Astarian Year 337

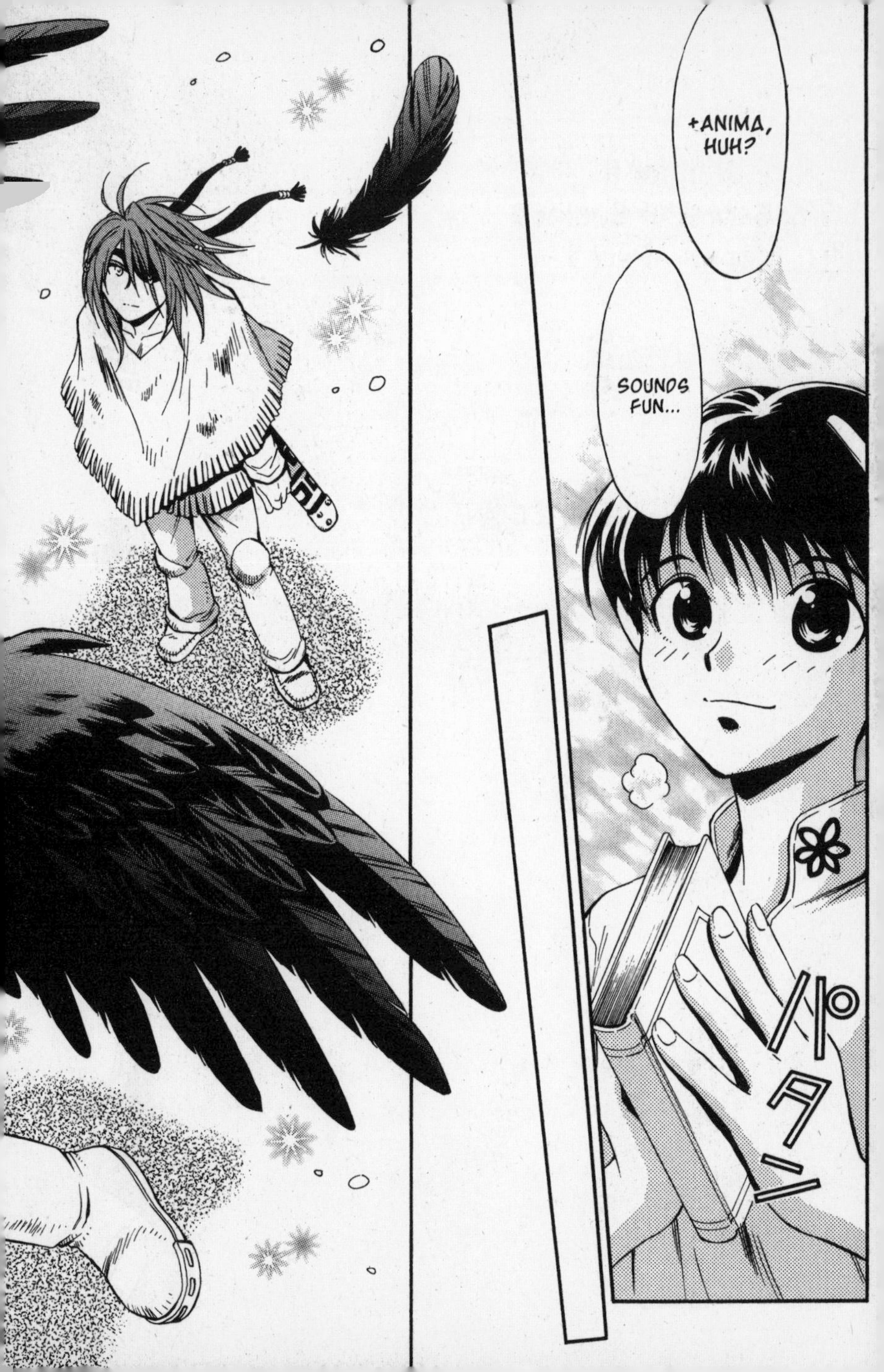
+ANIMA, HUH?
SOUNDS FUN...

Chapter 6
The Secret of Beehive Manor—Part 1

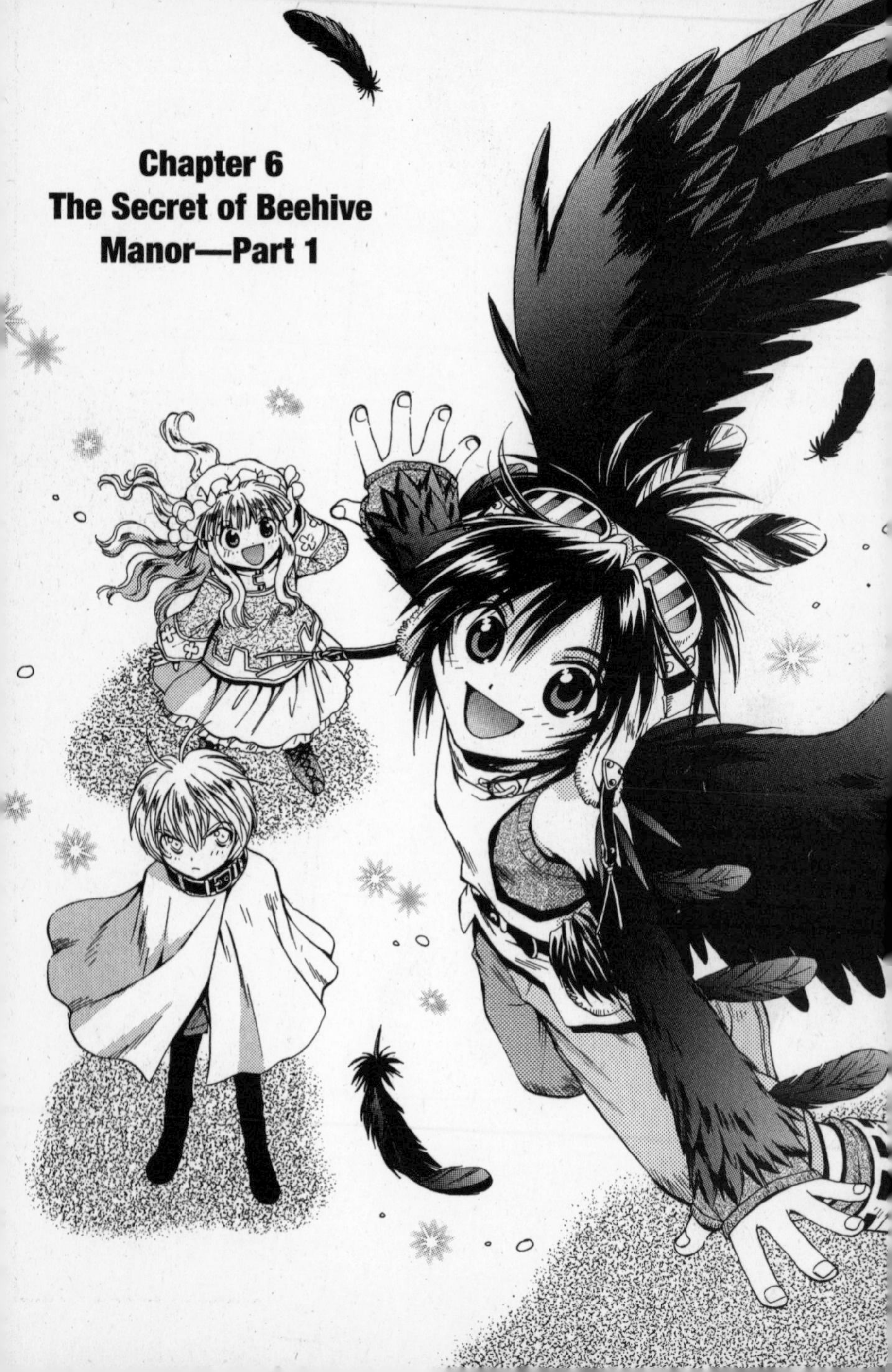

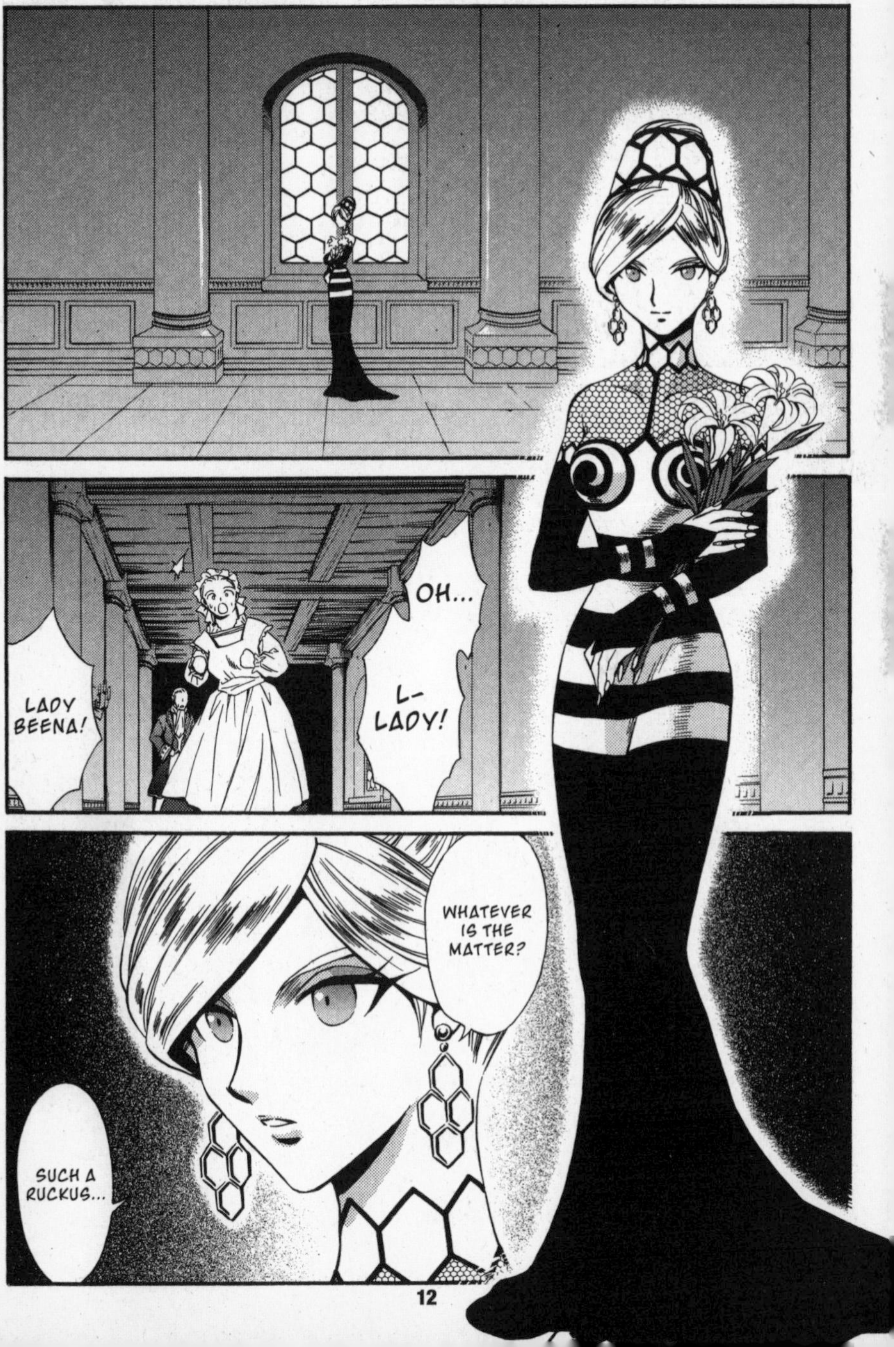
OH...
L-
LADY!
LADY
BEENA!
WHATEVER
IS THE
MATTER?
SUCH A
RUCKUS...

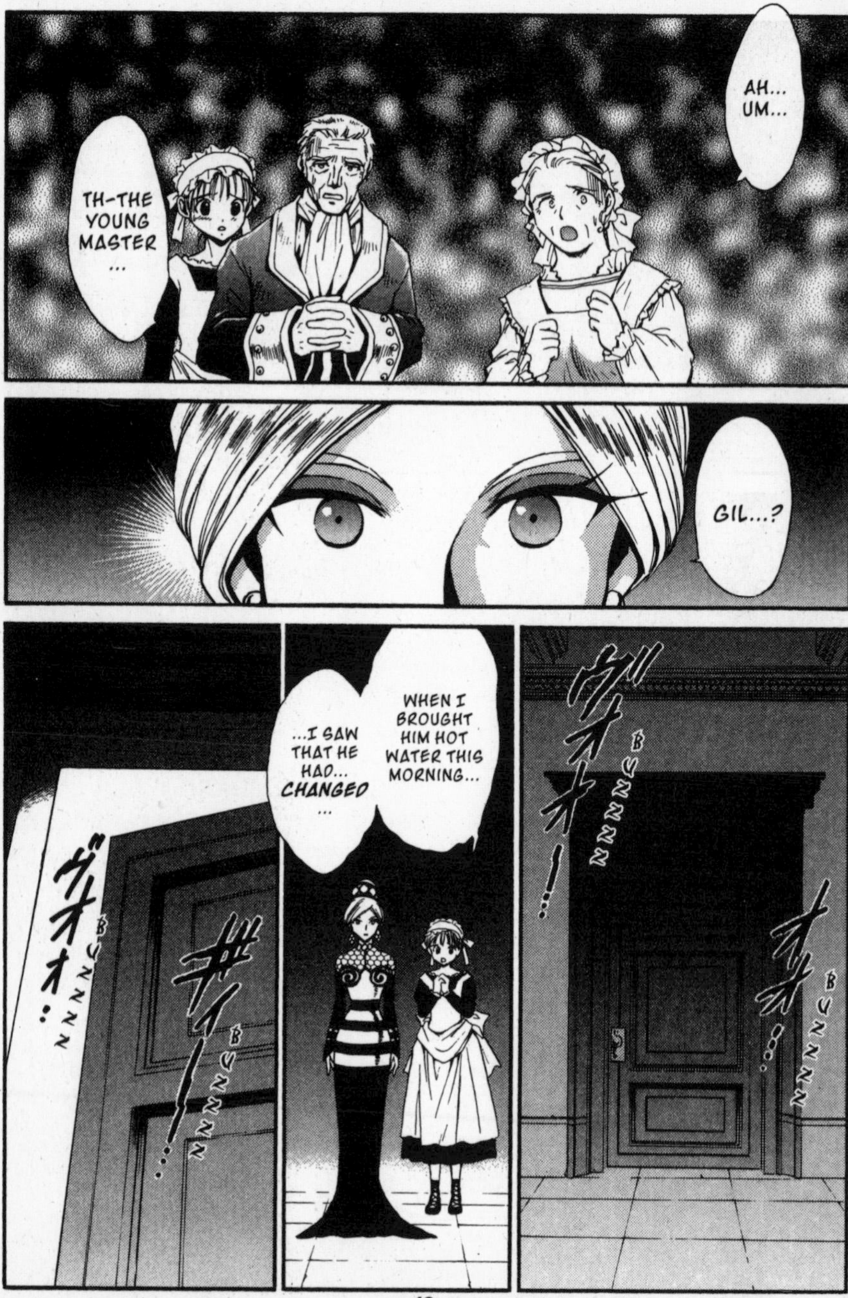
AH... UM...
TH-THE YOUNG MASTER ...
GIL...?
BUZZZZZ
BUZZZZZ
WHEN I BROUGHT HIM HOT WATER THIS MORNING...
...I SAW THAT HE HAD... CHANGED ...
BUZZZZ
BUZZZZZ

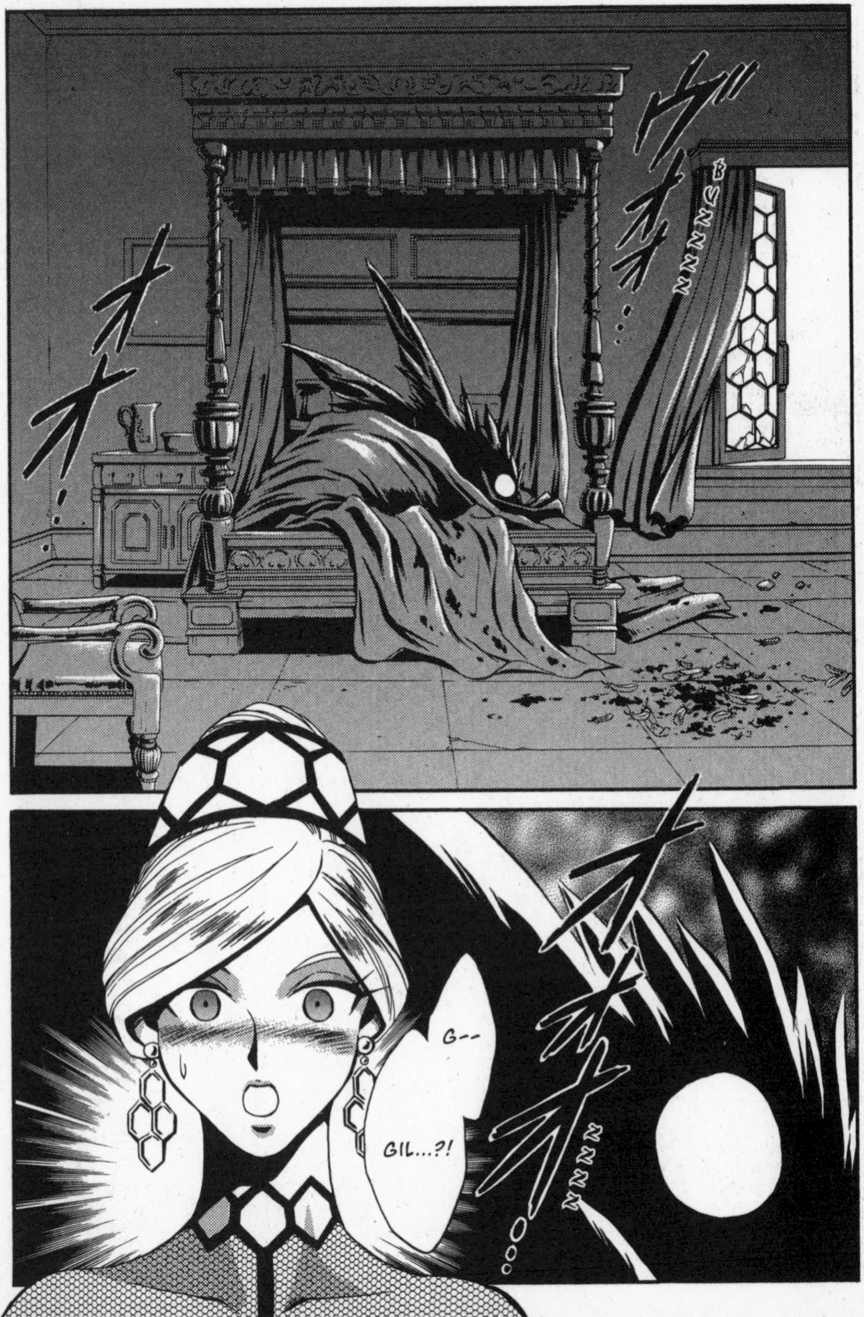
BUNNNN...
G--
GIL...?!
NNNN...

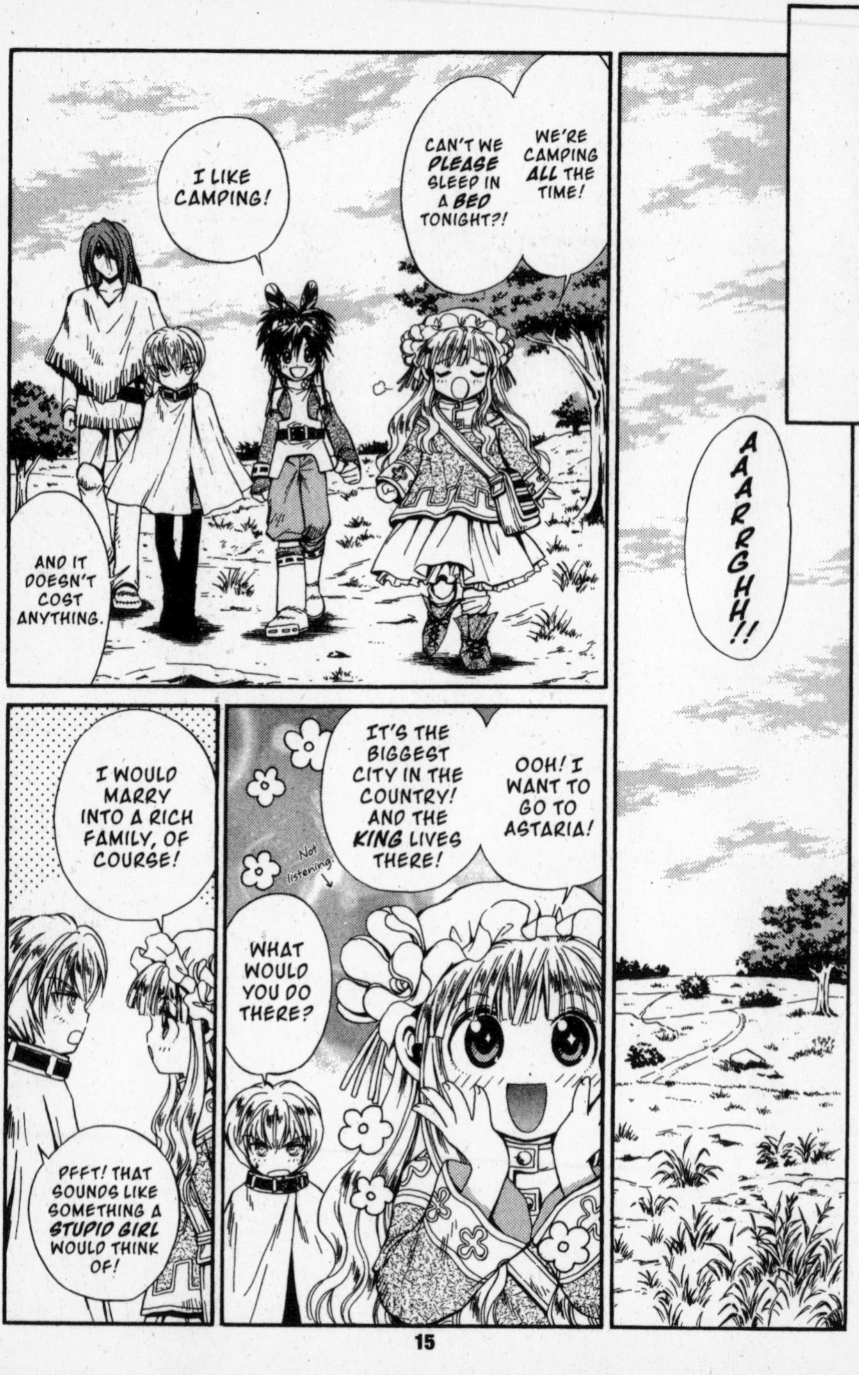
AAARRGHH!!
WE'RE CAMPING ALL THE TIME!
CAN'T WE PLEASE SLEEP IN A BED TONIGHT?!
I LIKE CAMPING!
AND IT DOESN'T COST ANYTHING.
OOH! I WANT TO GO TO ASTARIA!
IT'S THE BIGGEST CITY IN THE COUNTRY! AND THE KING LIVES THERE!
Not listening.
WHAT WOULD YOU DO THERE?
I WOULD MARRY INTO A RICH FAMILY, OF COURSE!
PFFT! THAT SOUNDS LIKE SOMETHING A STUPID GIRL WOULD THINK OF!

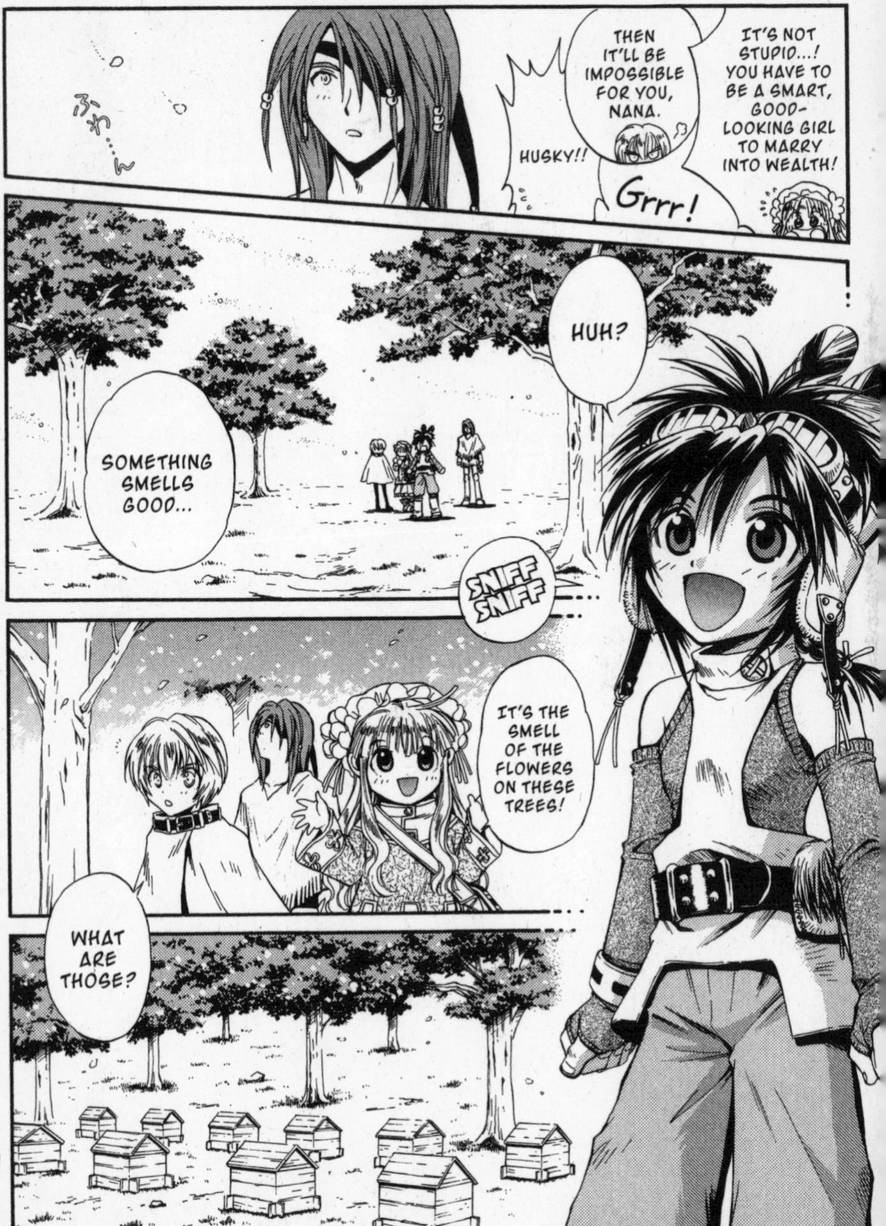
IT'S NOT STUPID...! YOU HAVE TO BE A SMART, GOOD-LOOKING GIRL TO MARRY INTO WEALTH!
THEN IT'LL BE IMPOSSIBLE FOR YOU, NANA.
Grrr!
HUSKY!!
ふわ…ん
HUH?
SOMETHING SMELLS GOOD...
SNIFF SNIFF
IT'S THE SMELL OF THE FLOWERS ON THESE TREES!
WHAT ARE THOSE?

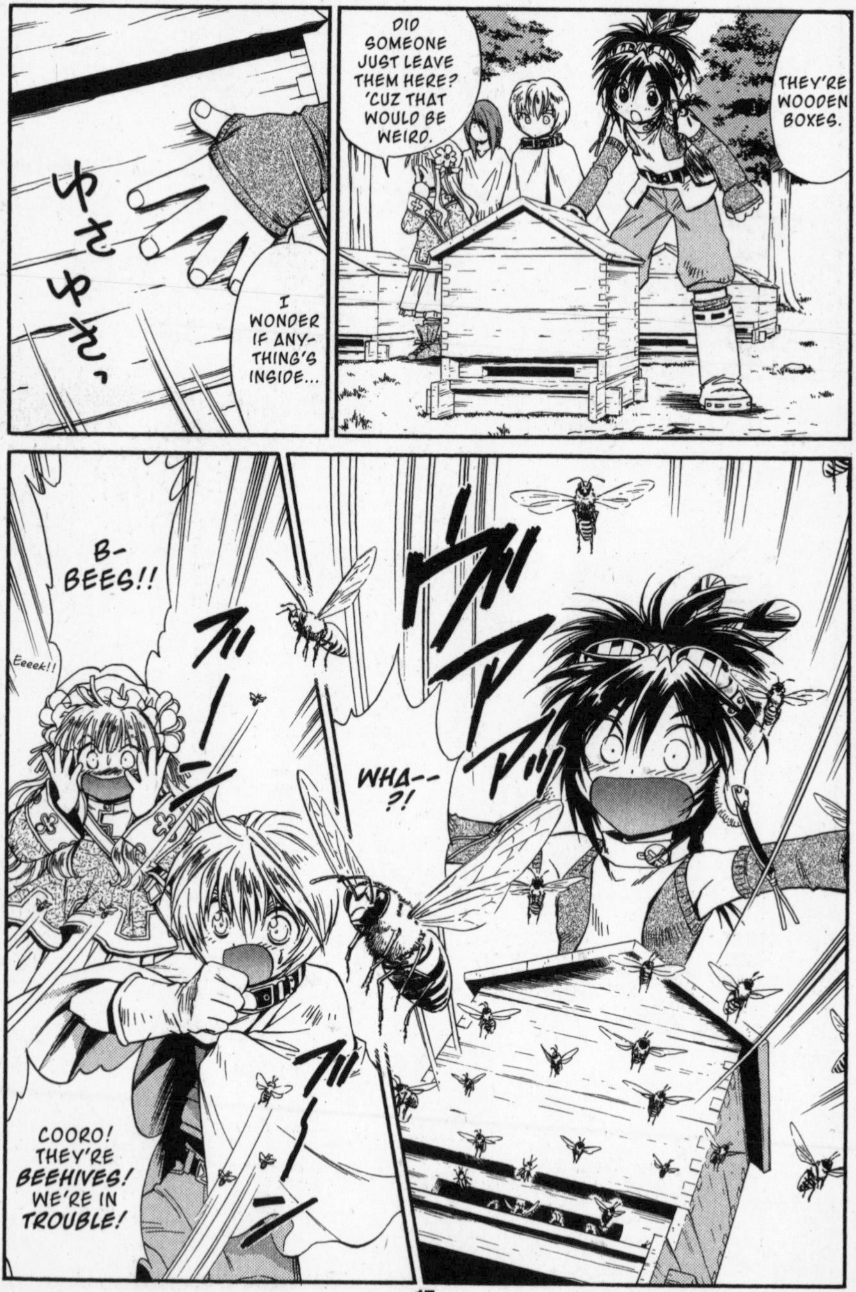
THEY'RE WOODEN BOXES.
DID SOMEONE JUST LEAVE THEM HERE? 'CUZ THAT WOULD BE WEIRD.
I WONDER IF ANYTHING'S INSIDE...
ゆさゆさ
ヴァッ
WHA--?!
B-BEES!!
Eeeek!!
COORO! THEY'RE BEEHIVES! WE'RE IN TROUBLE!

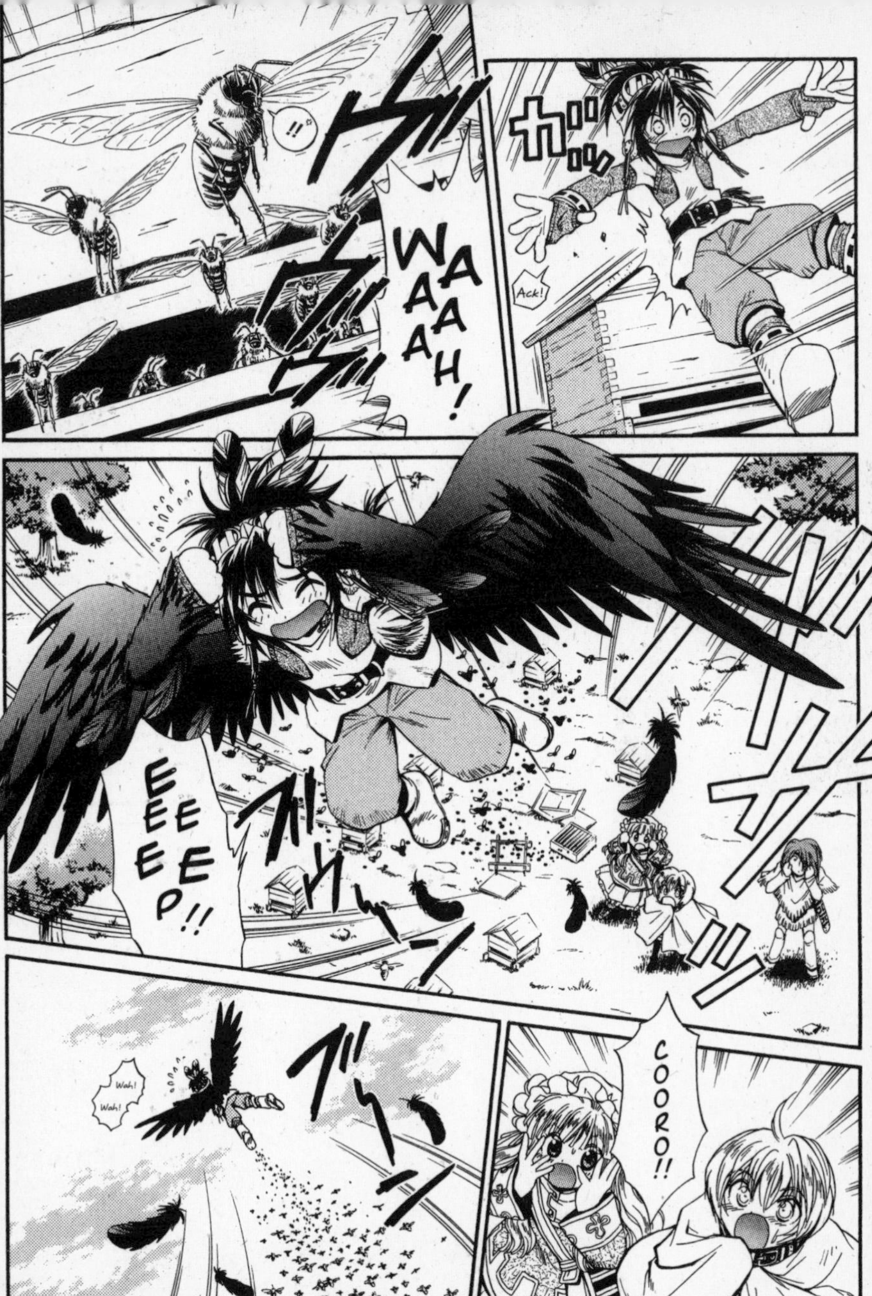
Ack!
!!
WAAAAH!
EEEEEP!!
COORO!!
Wah!
Wah!

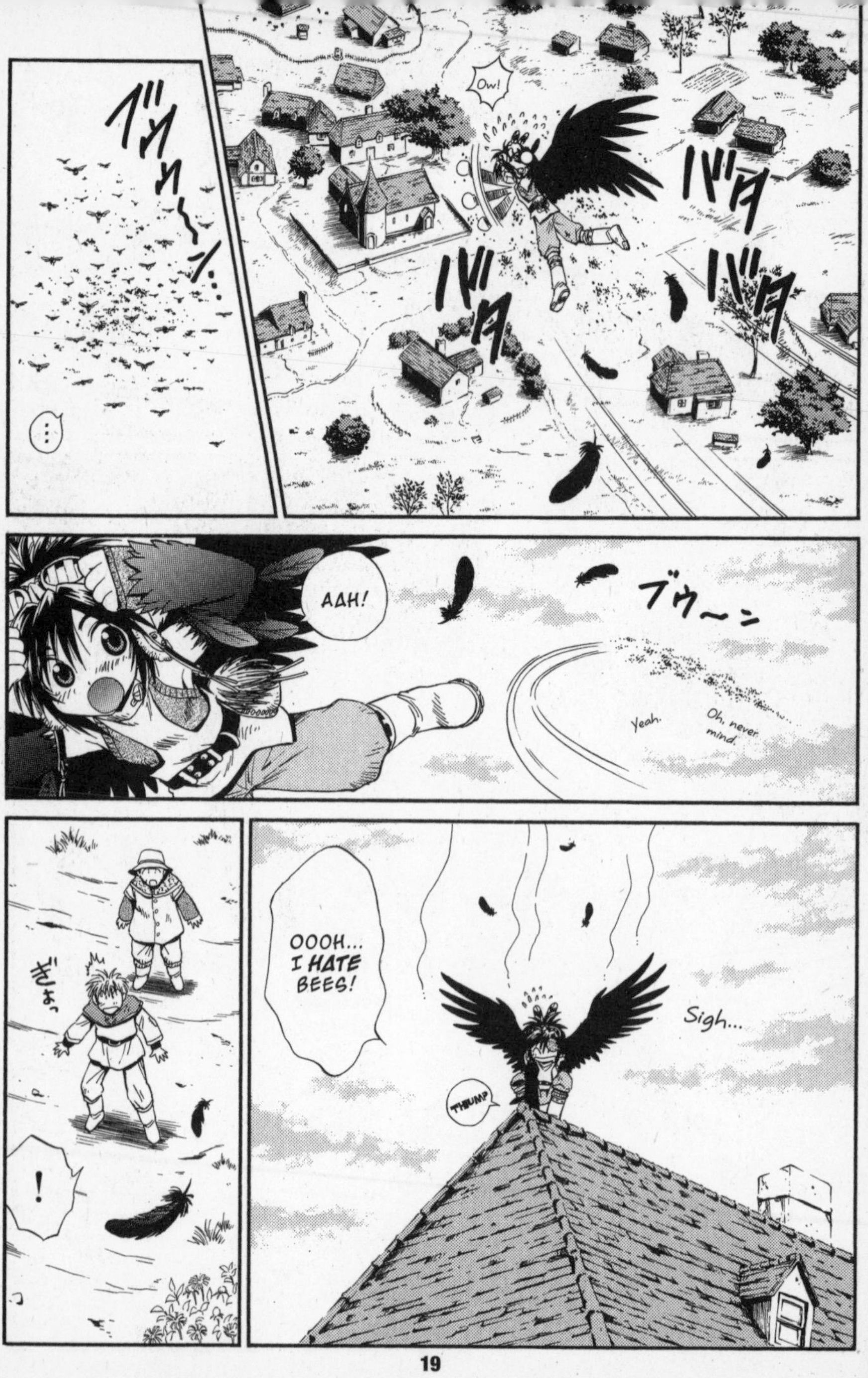
Ow!
AAH!
ブウ～ン
Oh, never mind.
Yeah.
OOOH... I HATE BEES!
Sigh...
THUMP
!

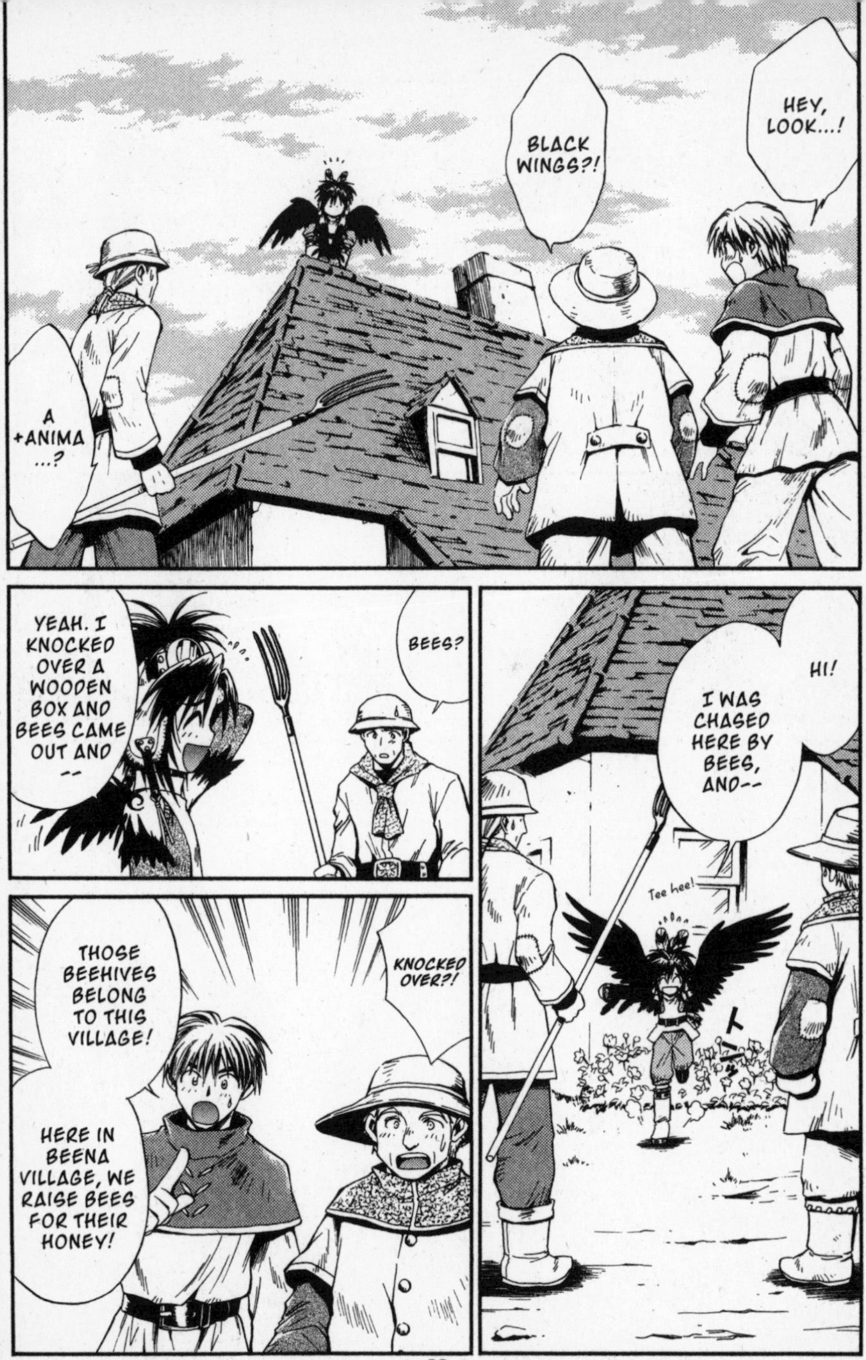
HEY, LOOK...!
BLACK WINGS?!
A +ANIMA ...?
HI!
I WAS CHASED HERE BY BEES, AND--
Tee hee!
BEES?
YEAH. I KNOCKED OVER A WOODEN BOX AND BEES CAME OUT AND --
KNOCKED OVER?!
THOSE BEEHIVES BELONG TO THIS VILLAGE!
HERE IN BEENA VILLAGE, WE RAISE BEES FOR THEIR HONEY!

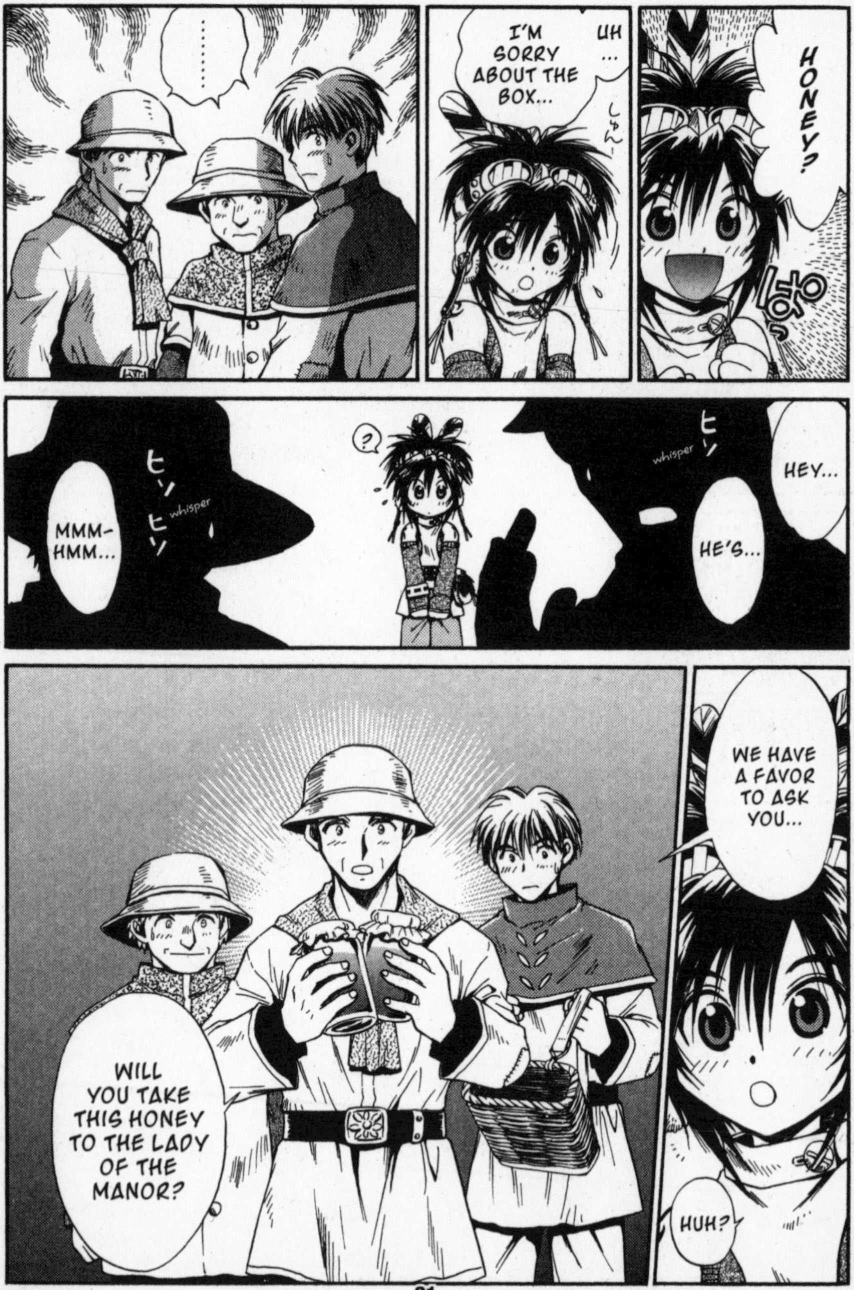
HONEY?
ぱっ
UH...
I'M SORRY ABOUT THE BOX...
しゅん
......
HEY...
HE'S...
ヒソ
whisper
?
MMM-HMM...
ヒソヒソ
whisper
WE HAVE A FAVOR TO ASK YOU...
HUH?
WILL YOU TAKE THIS HONEY TO THE LADY OF THE MANOR?

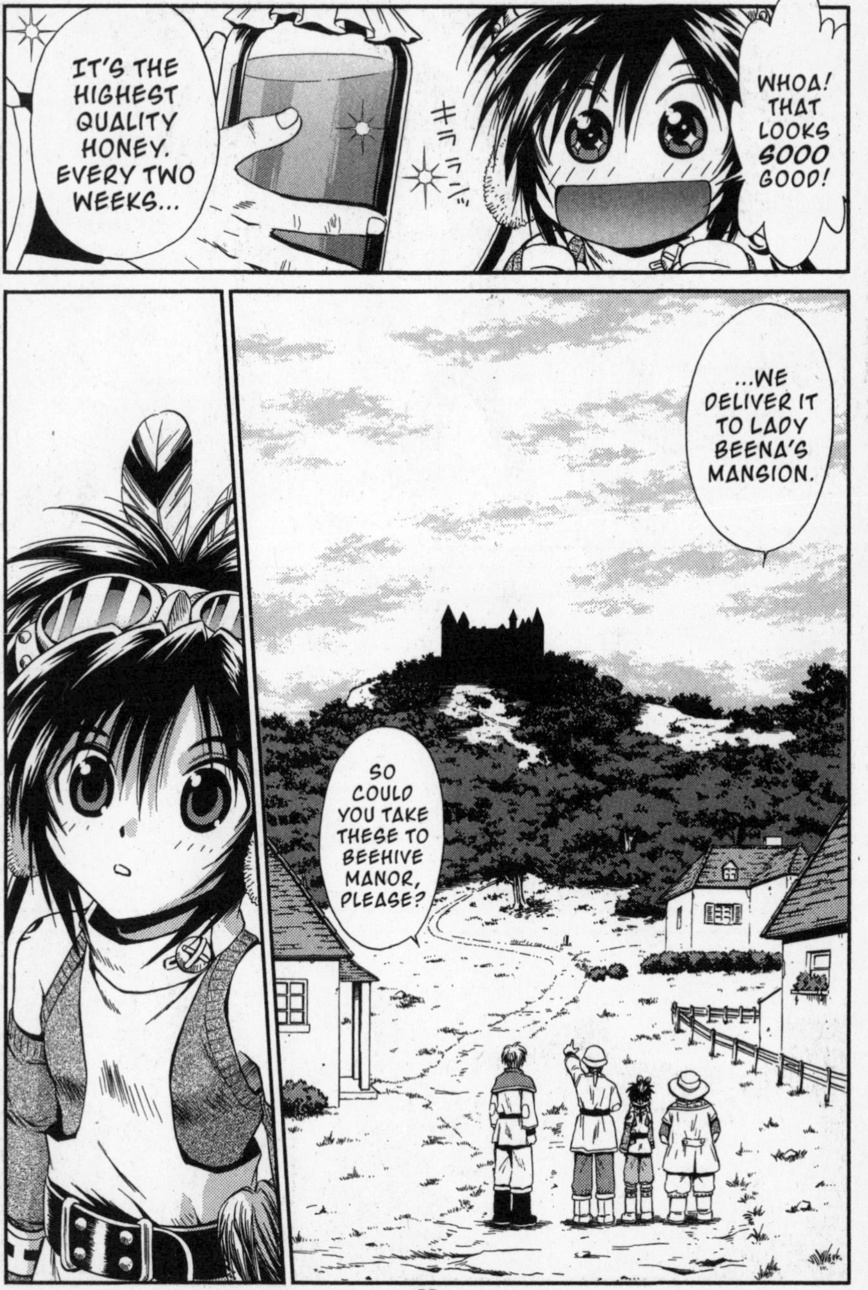
WHOA! THAT LOOKS SOOO GOOD!
IT'S THE HIGHEST QUALITY HONEY. EVERY TWO WEEKS...
...WE DELIVER IT TO LADY BEENA'S MANSION.
SO COULD YOU TAKE THESE TO BEEHIVE MANOR, PLEASE?

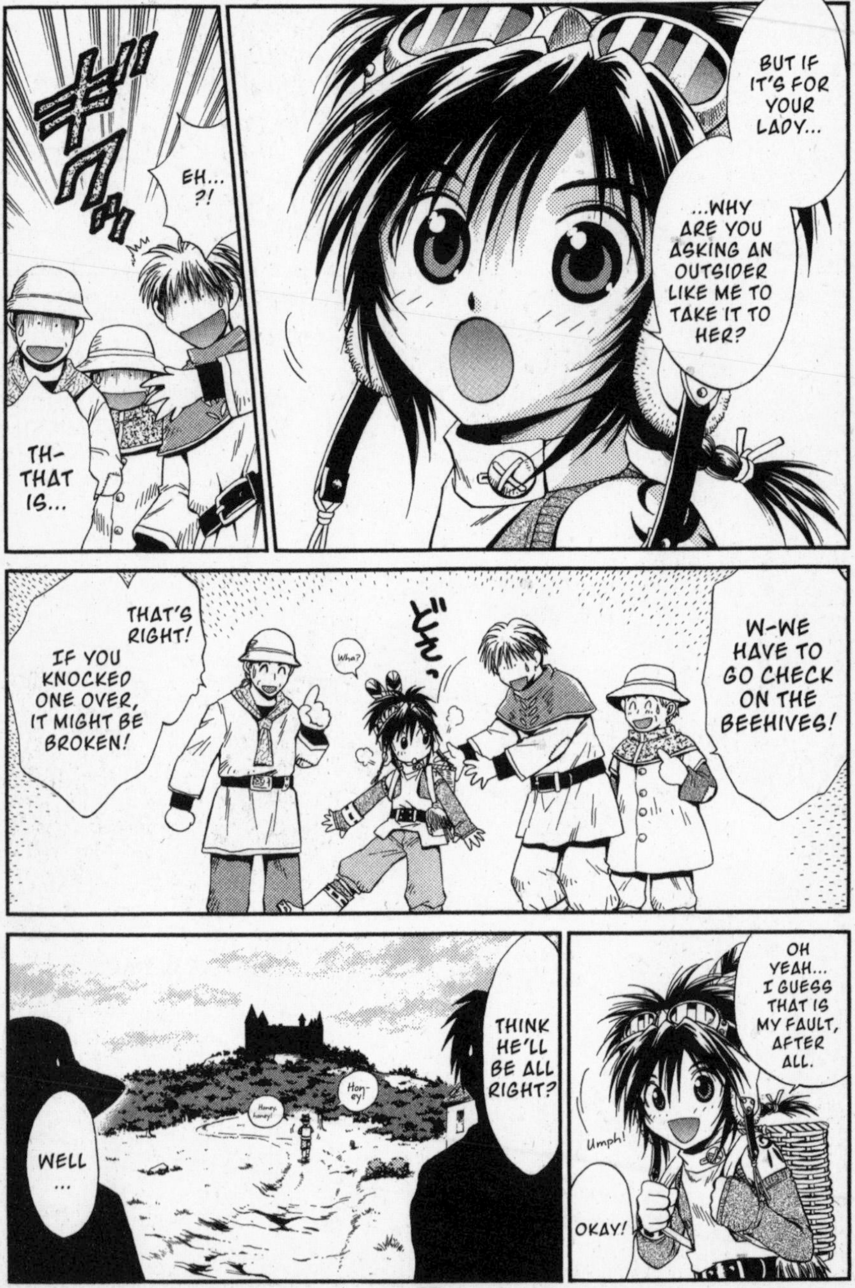
BUT IF IT'S FOR YOUR LADY...
...WHY ARE YOU ASKING AN OUTSIDER LIKE ME TO TAKE IT TO HER?
EH... ?!
TH- THAT IS...
W-WE HAVE TO GO CHECK ON THE BEEHIVES!
Wha?
THAT'S RIGHT! IF YOU KNOCKED ONE OVER, IT MIGHT BE BROKEN!
OH YEAH... I GUESS THAT IS MY FAULT, AFTER ALL.
Umph!
OKAY!
THINK HE'LL BE ALL RIGHT?
Hon- ey!
Honey, honey!
WELL ...

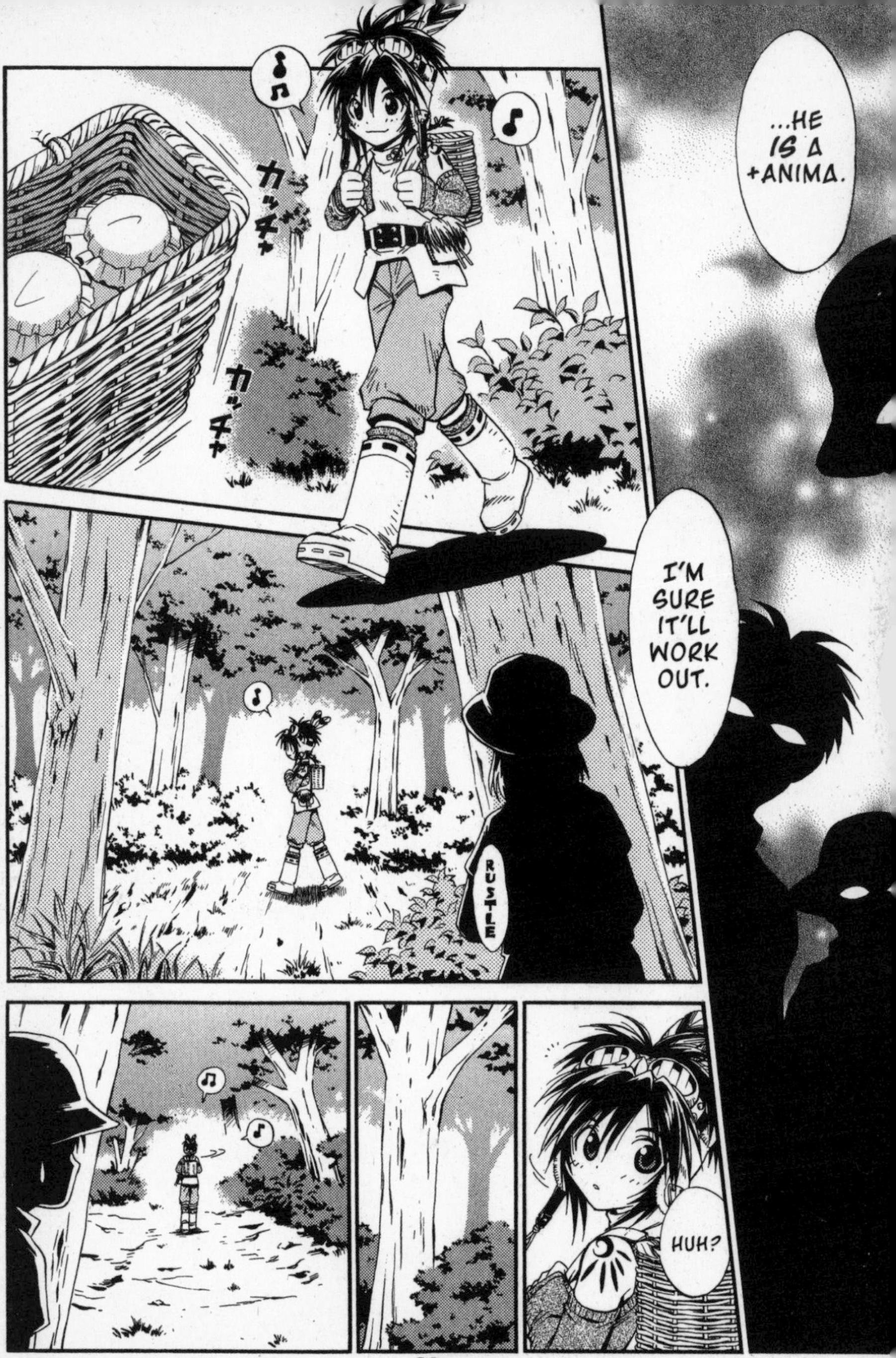
...HE IS A +ANIMA.
I'M SURE IT'LL WORK OUT.
カッチャ
カッチャ
RUSTLE
HUH?

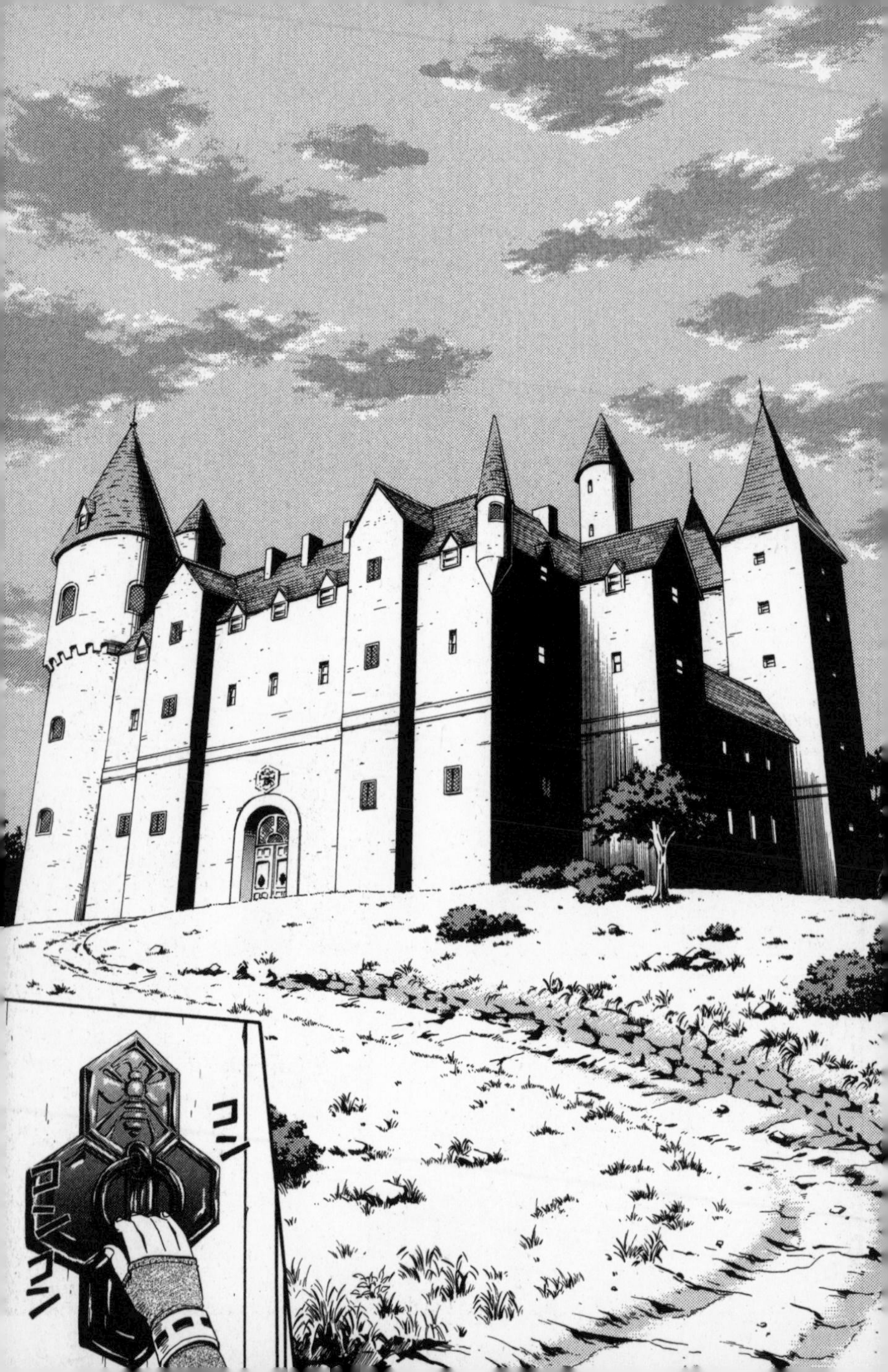
コン
コン

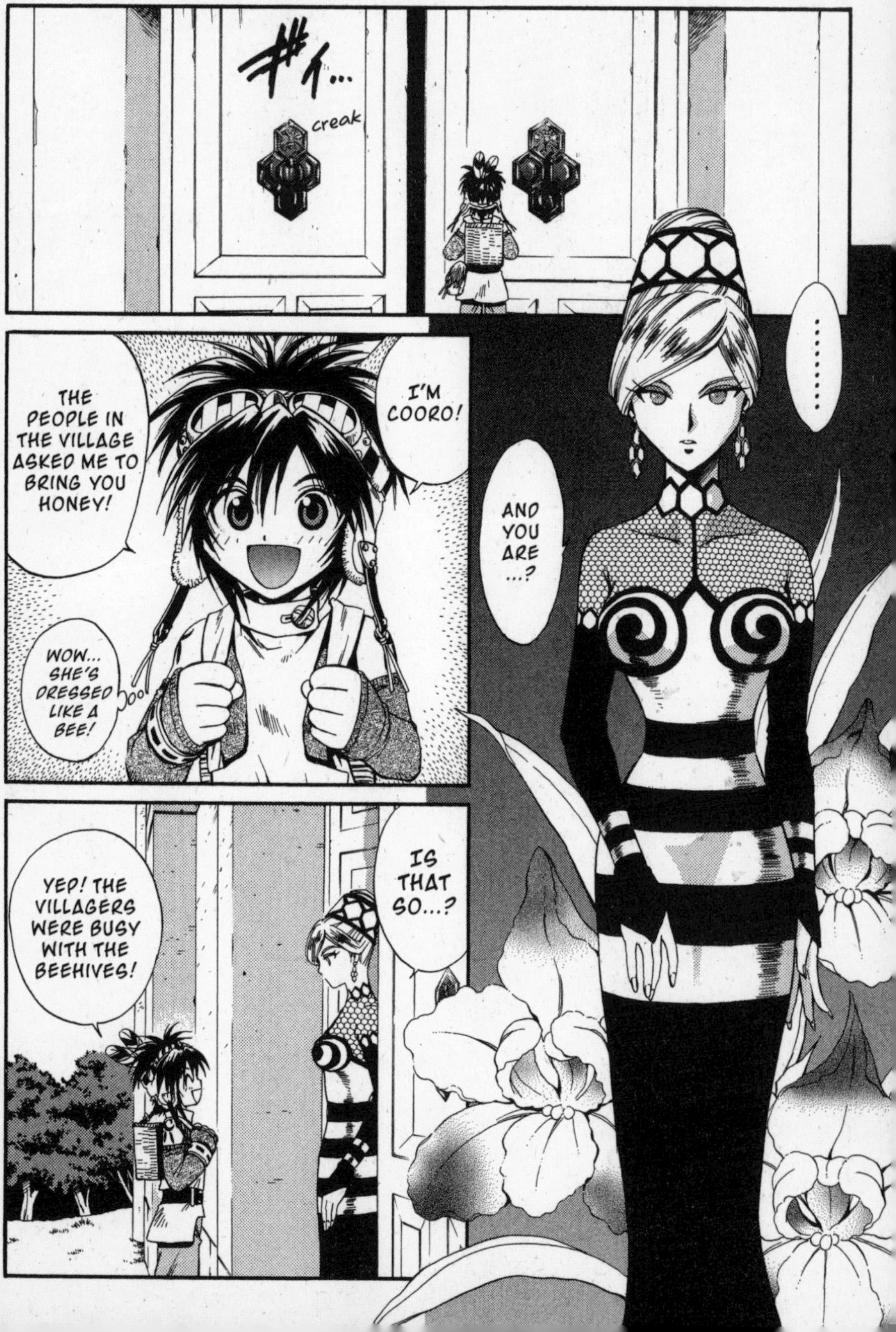

creak
......
AND YOU ARE ...?
I'M COORO!
THE PEOPLE IN THE VILLAGE ASKED ME TO BRING YOU HONEY!
WOW... SHE'S DRESSED LIKE A BEE!
IS THAT SO...?
YEP! THE VILLAGERS WERE BUSY WITH THE BEEHIVES!

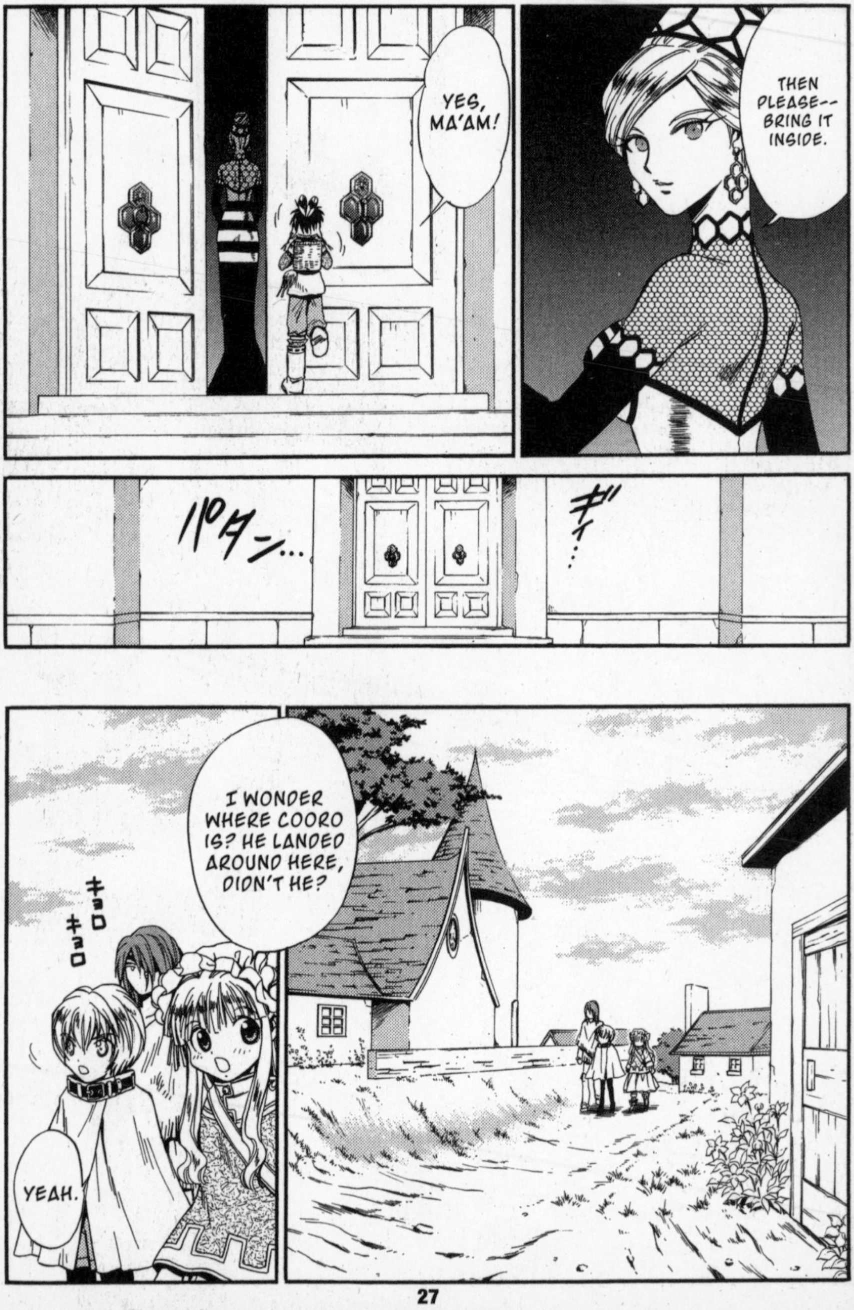
THEN PLEASE-- BRING IT INSIDE.
YES, MA'AM!
ギィ...
パタン...
I WONDER WHERE COORO IS? HE LANDED AROUND HERE, DIDN'T HE?
キョロキョロ
YEAH.

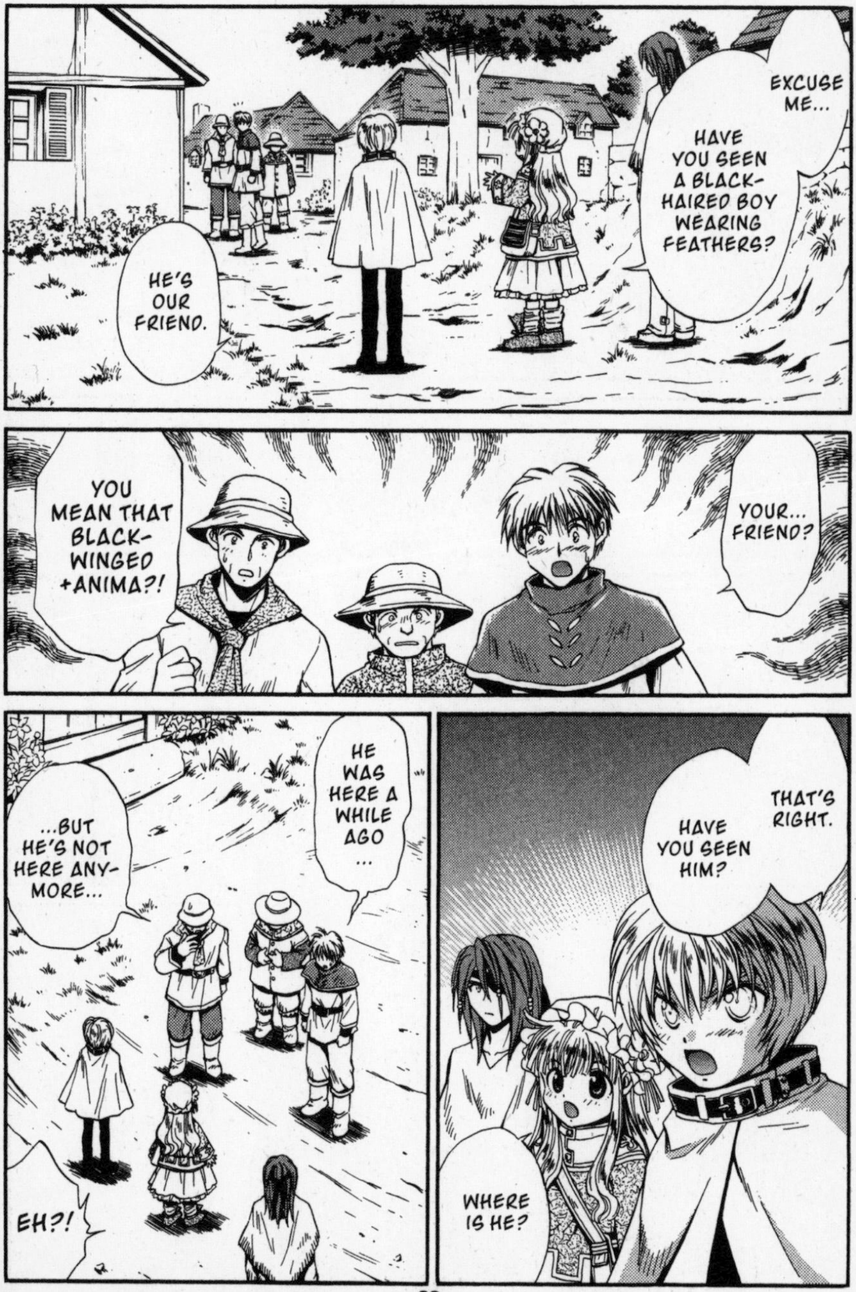
EXCUSE ME...
HAVE YOU SEEN A BLACK-HAIRED BOY WEARING FEATHERS?
HE'S OUR FRIEND.
YOUR... FRIEND?
YOU MEAN THAT BLACK-WINGED +ANIMA?!
THAT'S RIGHT.
HAVE YOU SEEN HIM?
WHERE IS HE?
HE WAS HERE A WHILE AGO...
...BUT HE'S NOT HERE ANYMORE...
EH?!

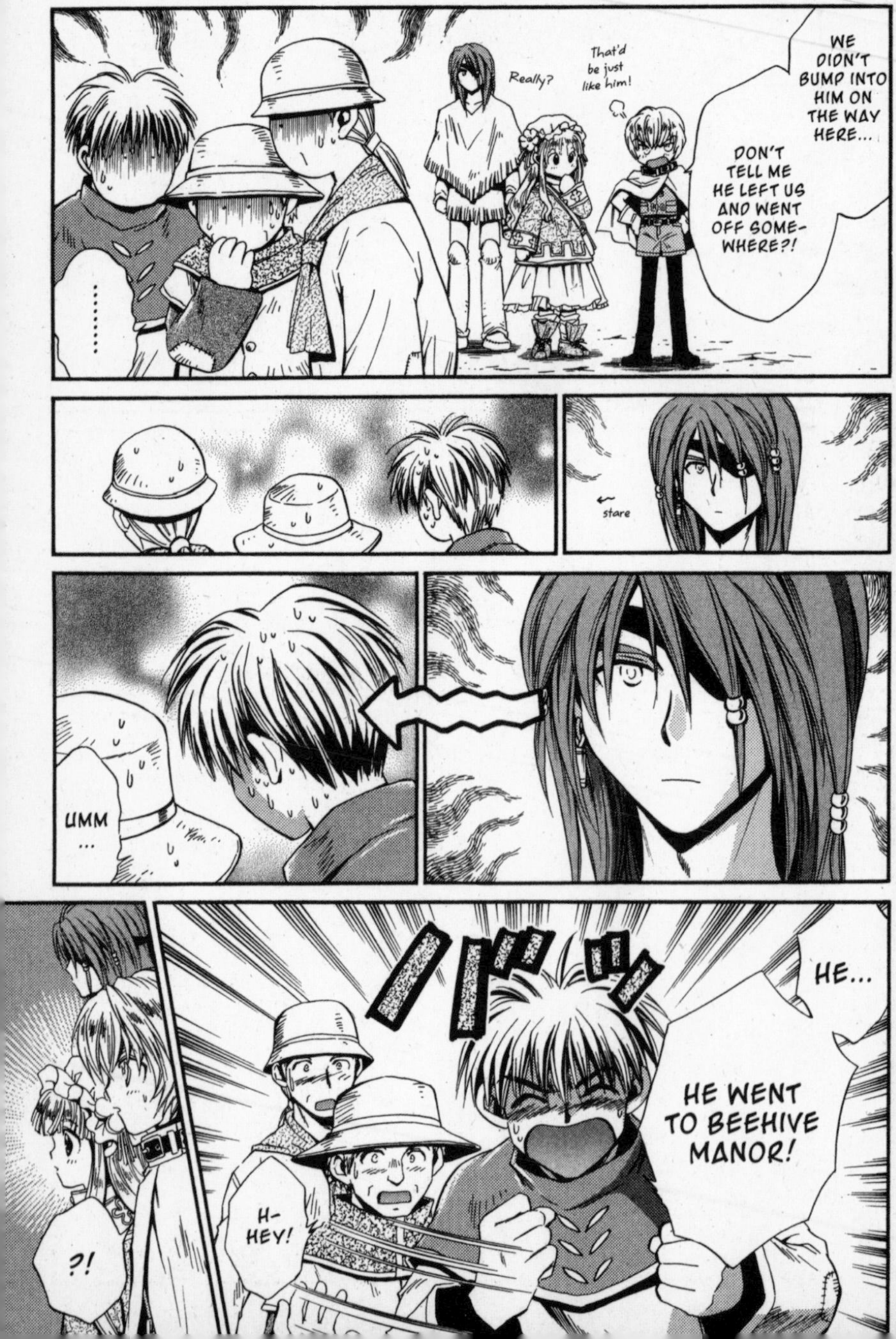
WE DIDN'T BUMP INTO HIM ON THE WAY HERE...
DON'T TELL ME HE LEFT US AND WENT OFF SOME-WHERE?!
That'd be just like him!
Really?
......
stare
UMM ...
HE...
HE WENT TO BEEHIVE MANOR!
H-HEY!
?!

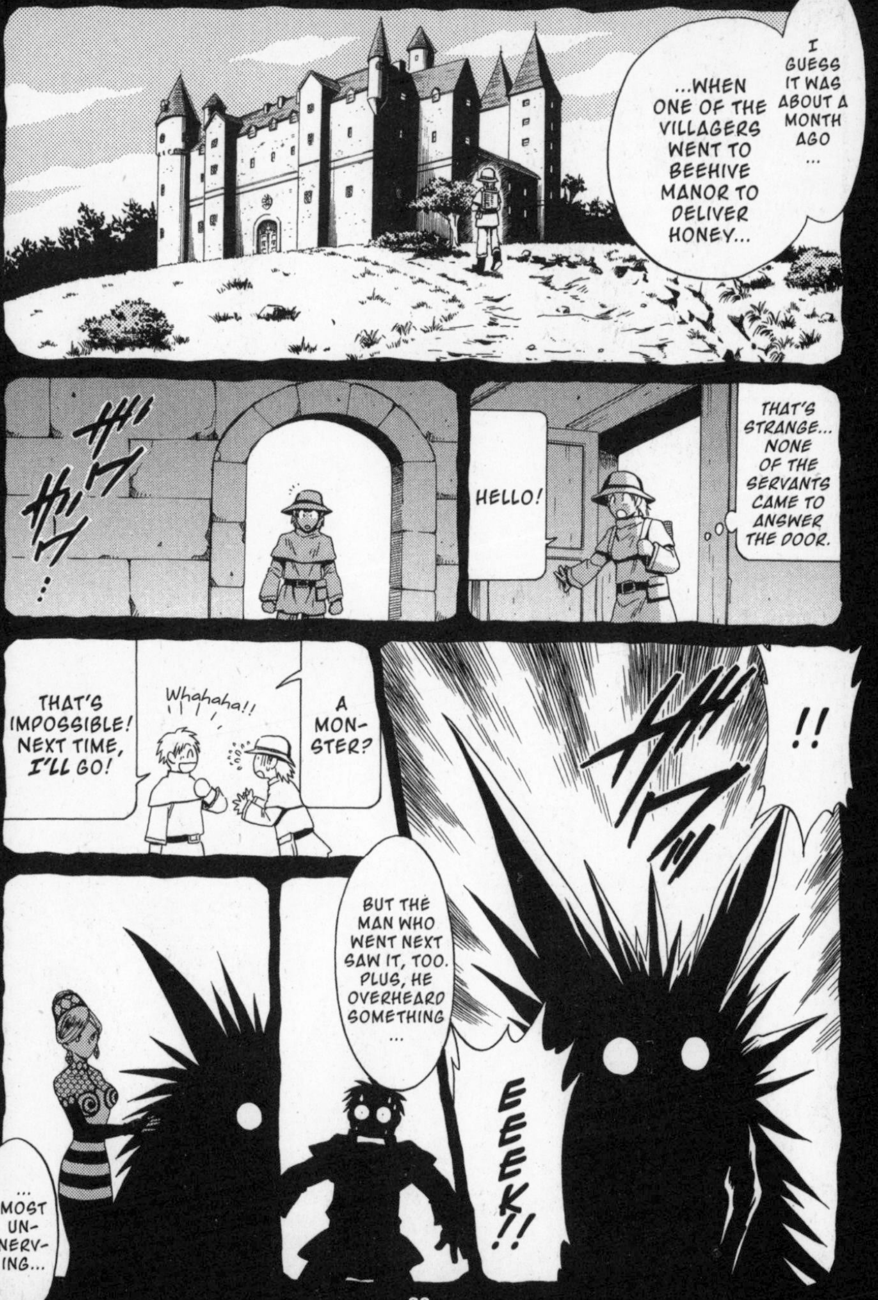
I GUESS IT WAS ABOUT A MONTH AGO ...
...WHEN ONE OF THE VILLAGERS WENT TO BEEHIVE MANOR TO DELIVER HONEY...
THAT'S STRANGE... NONE OF THE SERVANTS CAME TO ANSWER THE DOOR.
HELLO!
ザワ ザワ...
!!
EEEEK!!
A MON-STER?
Whahaha!!
THAT'S IMPOSSIBLE! NEXT TIME, *I'LL* GO!
BUT THE MAN WHO WENT NEXT SAW IT, TOO. PLUS, HE OVERHEARD SOMETHING ...
... MOST UN-NERV-ING...

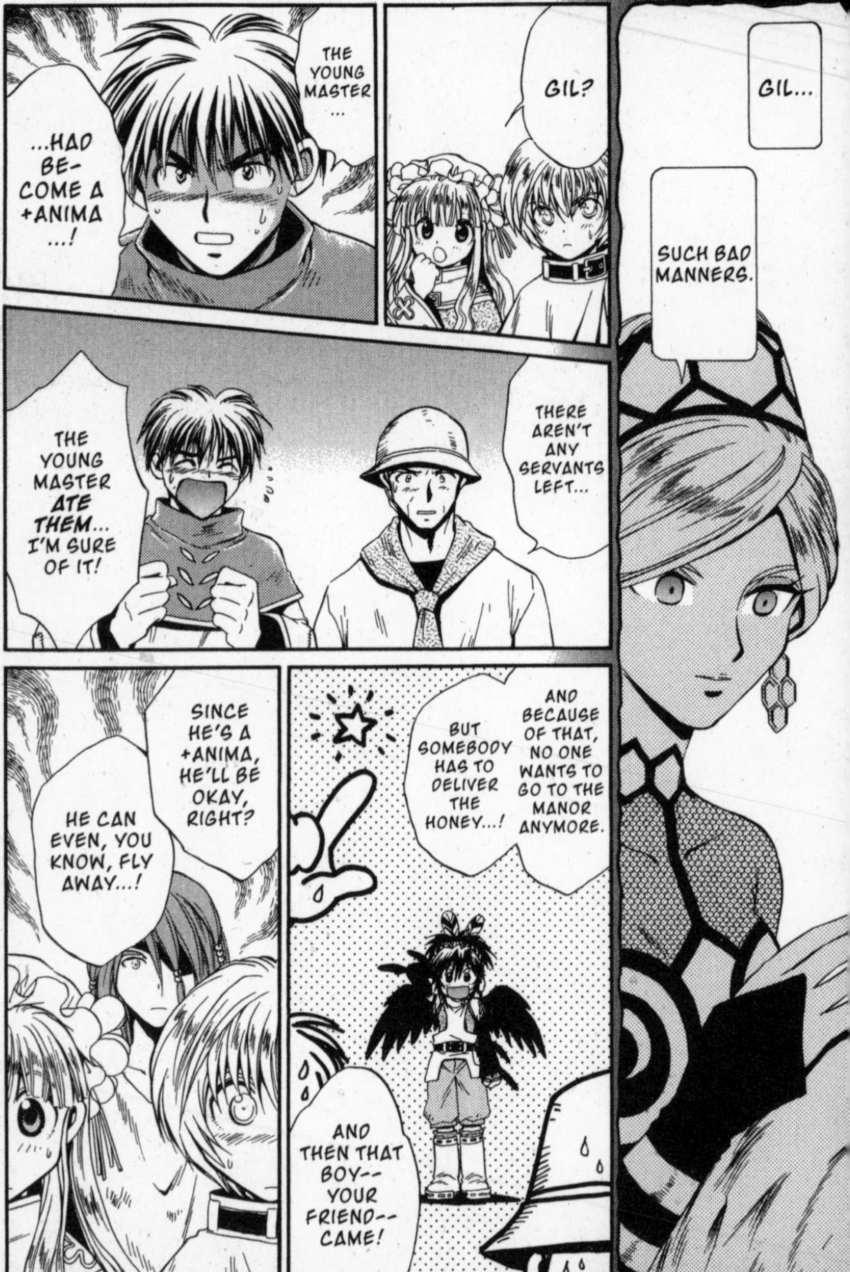
GIL...
SUCH BAD MANNERS.
GIL?
THE YOUNG MASTER ...
...HAD BE- COME A +ANIMA ...!
THERE AREN'T ANY SERVANTS LEFT...
THE YOUNG MASTER **ATE THEM**... I'M SURE OF IT!
AND BECAUSE OF THAT, NO ONE WANTS TO GO TO THE MANOR ANYMORE.
BUT SOMEBODY HAS TO DELIVER THE HONEY...!
AND THEN THAT BOY--YOUR FRIEND--CAME!
SINCE HE'S A +ANIMA, HE'LL BE OKAY, RIGHT?
HE CAN EVEN, YOU KNOW, FLY AWAY...!

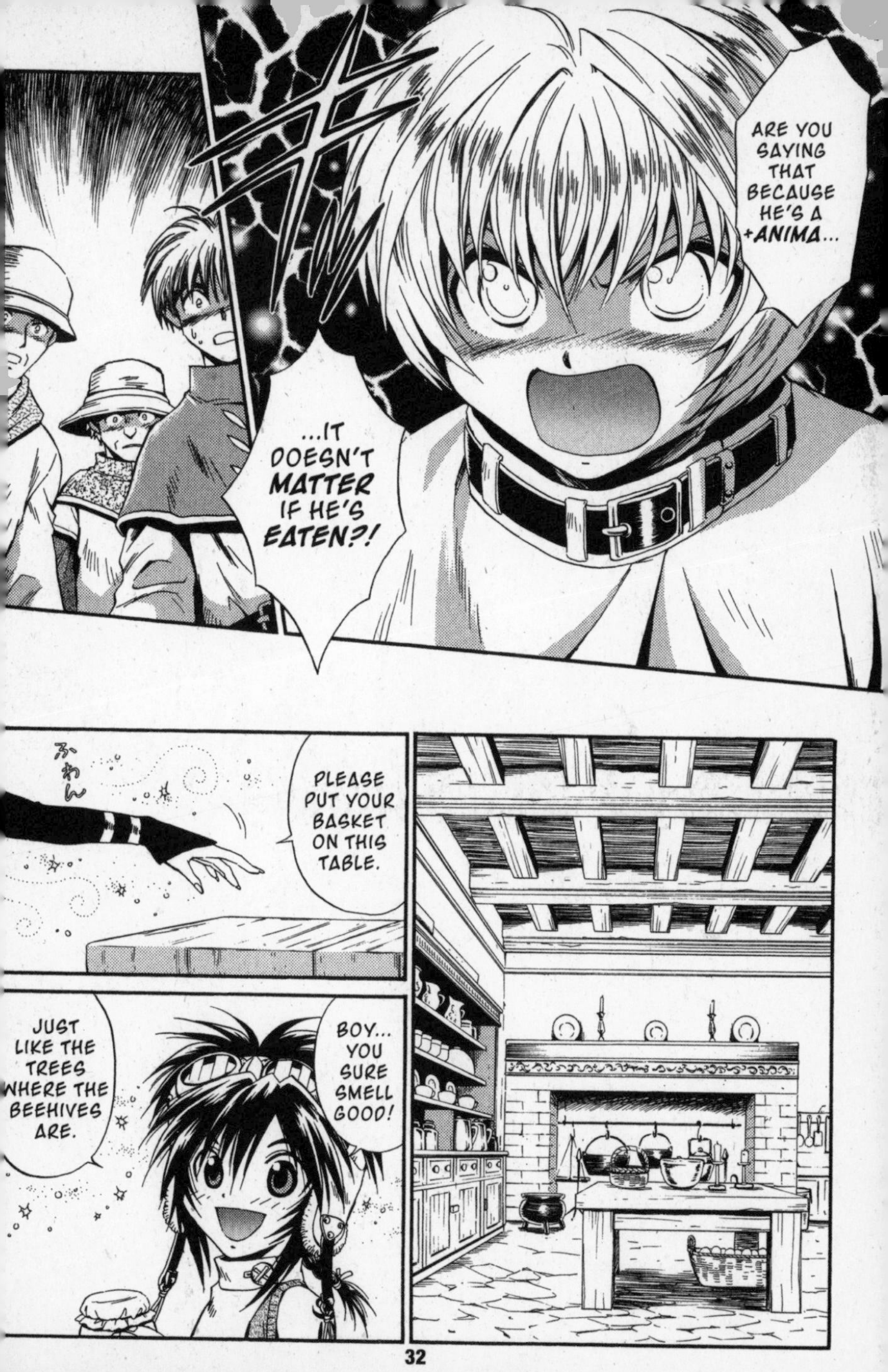
ARE YOU SAYING THAT BECAUSE HE'S A +ANIMA...
...IT DOESN'T MATTER IF HE'S EATEN?!
PLEASE PUT YOUR BASKET ON THIS TABLE.
ふわん
BOY... YOU SURE SMELL GOOD!
JUST LIKE THE TREES WHERE THE BEEHIVES ARE.

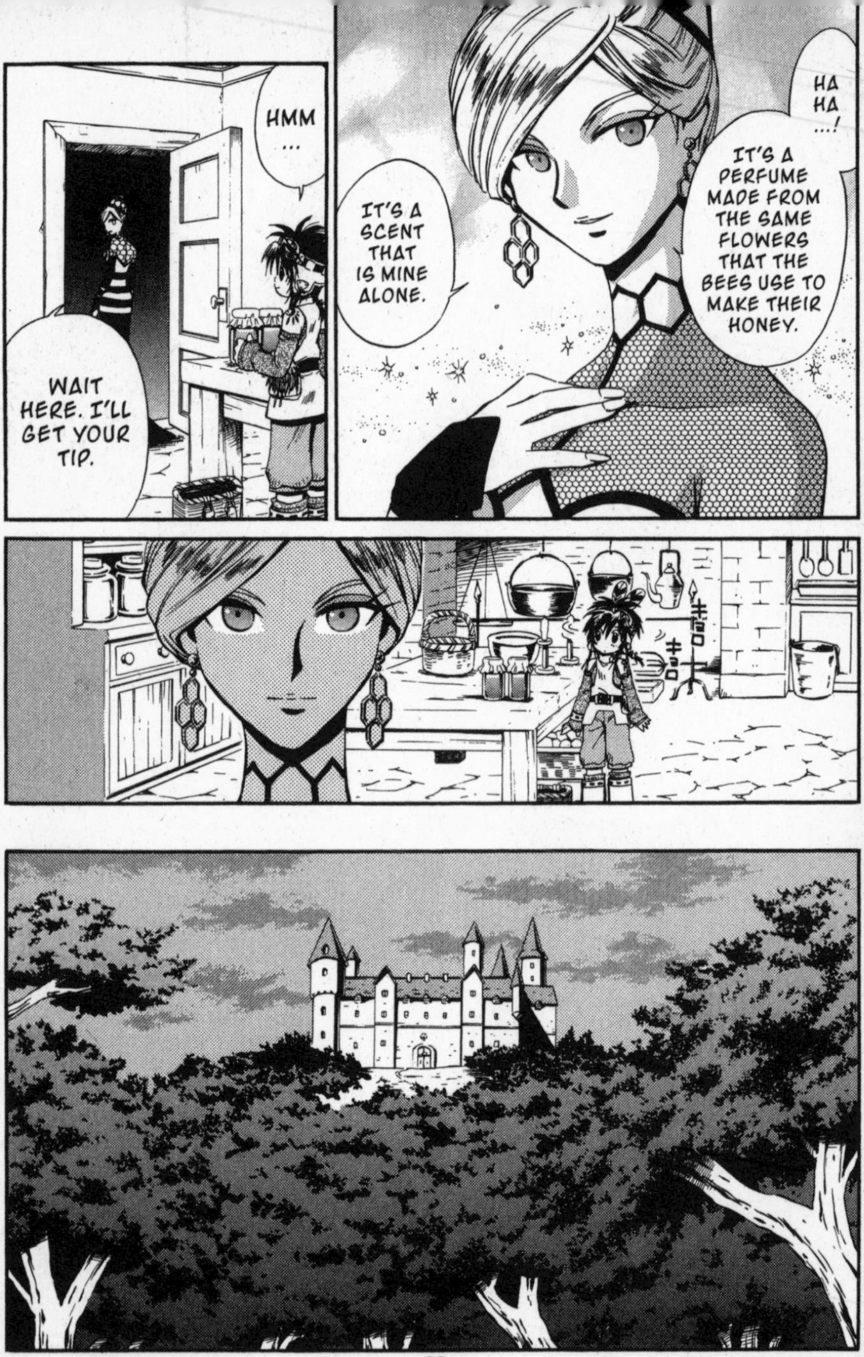
HA HA ...!
IT'S A PERFUME MADE FROM THE SAME FLOWERS THAT THE BEES USE TO MAKE THEIR HONEY.
IT'S A SCENT THAT IS MINE ALONE.
HMM ...
WAIT HERE. I'LL GET YOUR TIP.
キョロ
キョロ

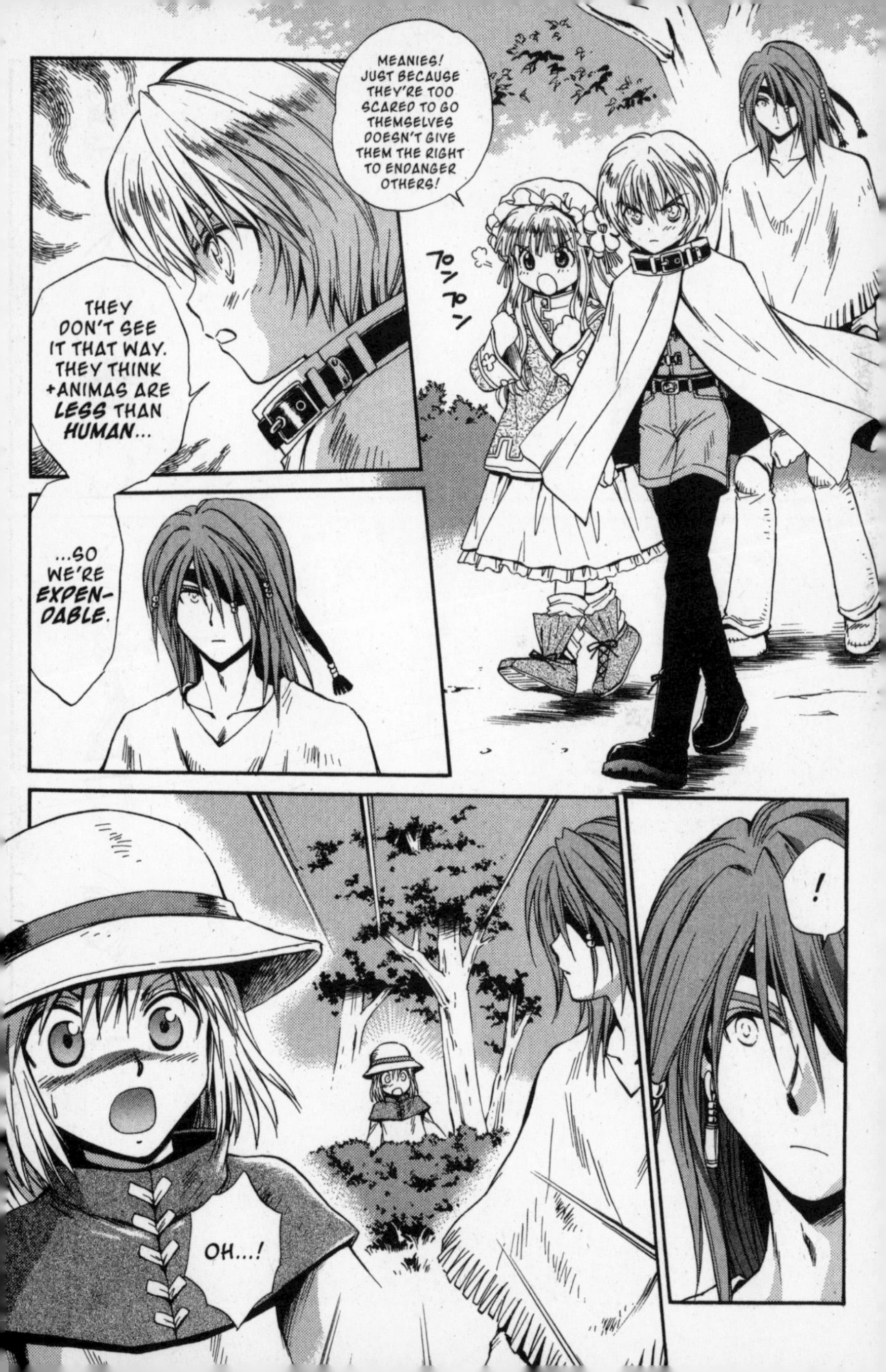
MEANIES! JUST BECAUSE THEY'RE TOO SCARED TO GO THEMSELVES DOESN'T GIVE THEM THE RIGHT TO ENDANGER OTHERS!
プン プン
THEY DON'T SEE IT THAT WAY. THEY THINK +ANIMAS ARE LESS THAN HUMAN...
...SO WE'RE EXPEN-DABLE.
!
OH...!

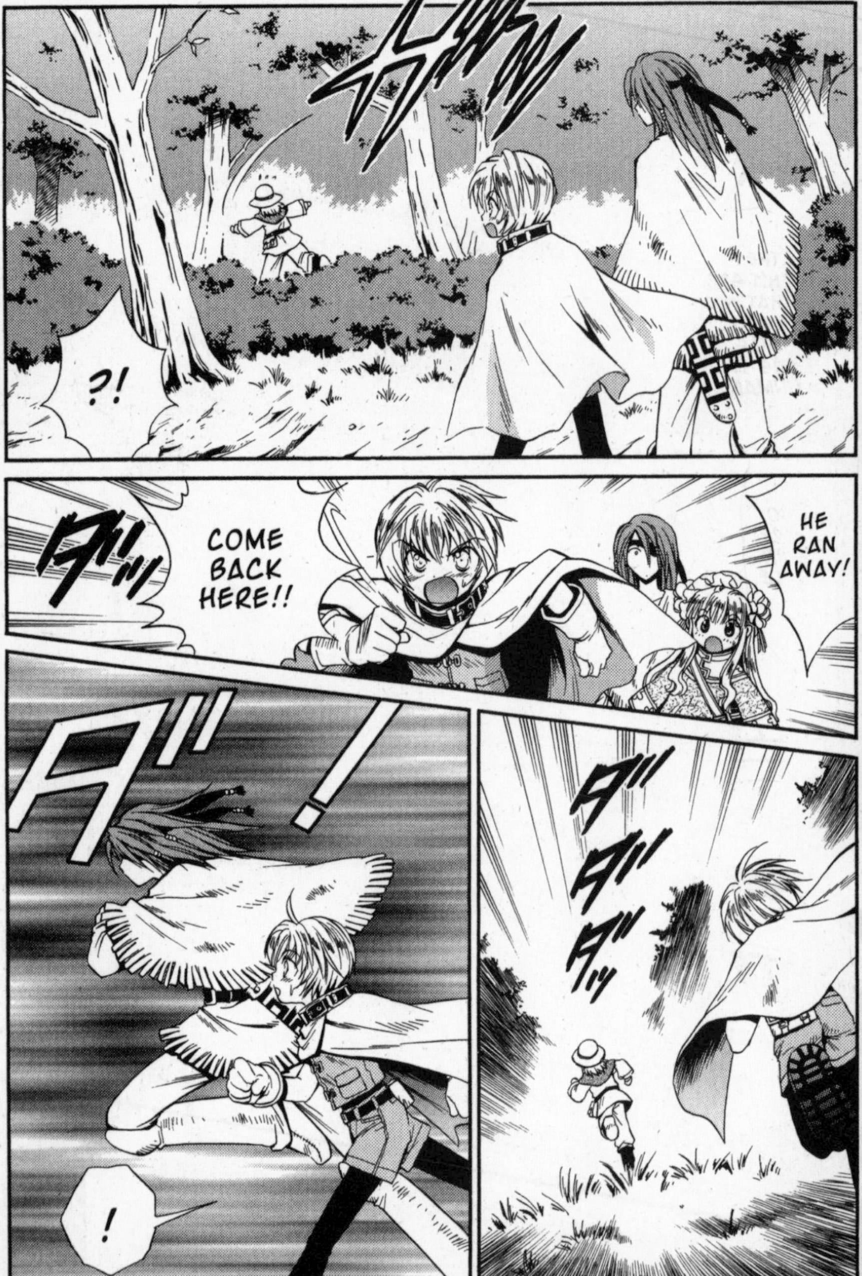
?!
HE RAN AWAY!
COME BACK HERE!!
!

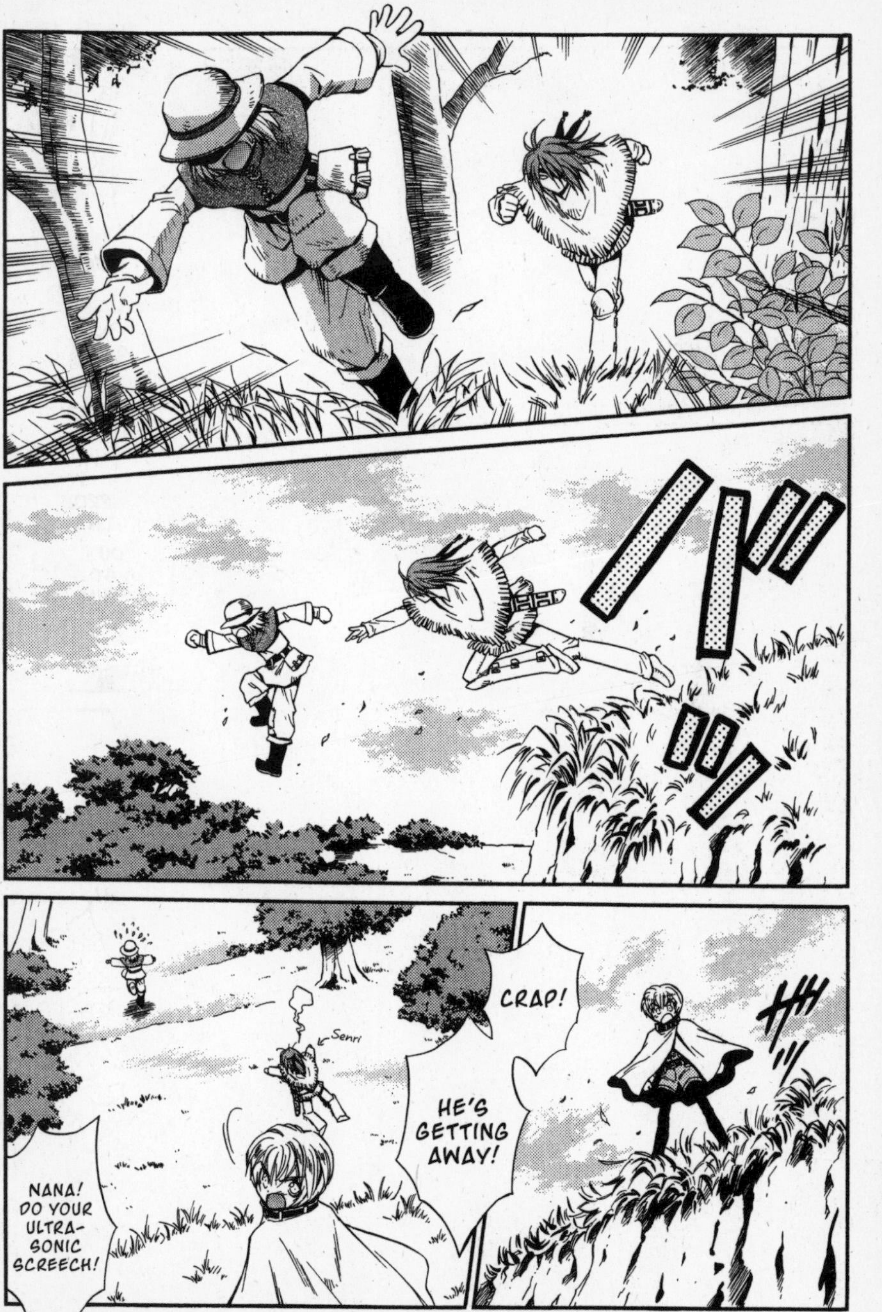
CRAP!
HE'S GETTING AWAY!
Senri
NANA! DO YOUR ULTRA-SONIC SCREECH!

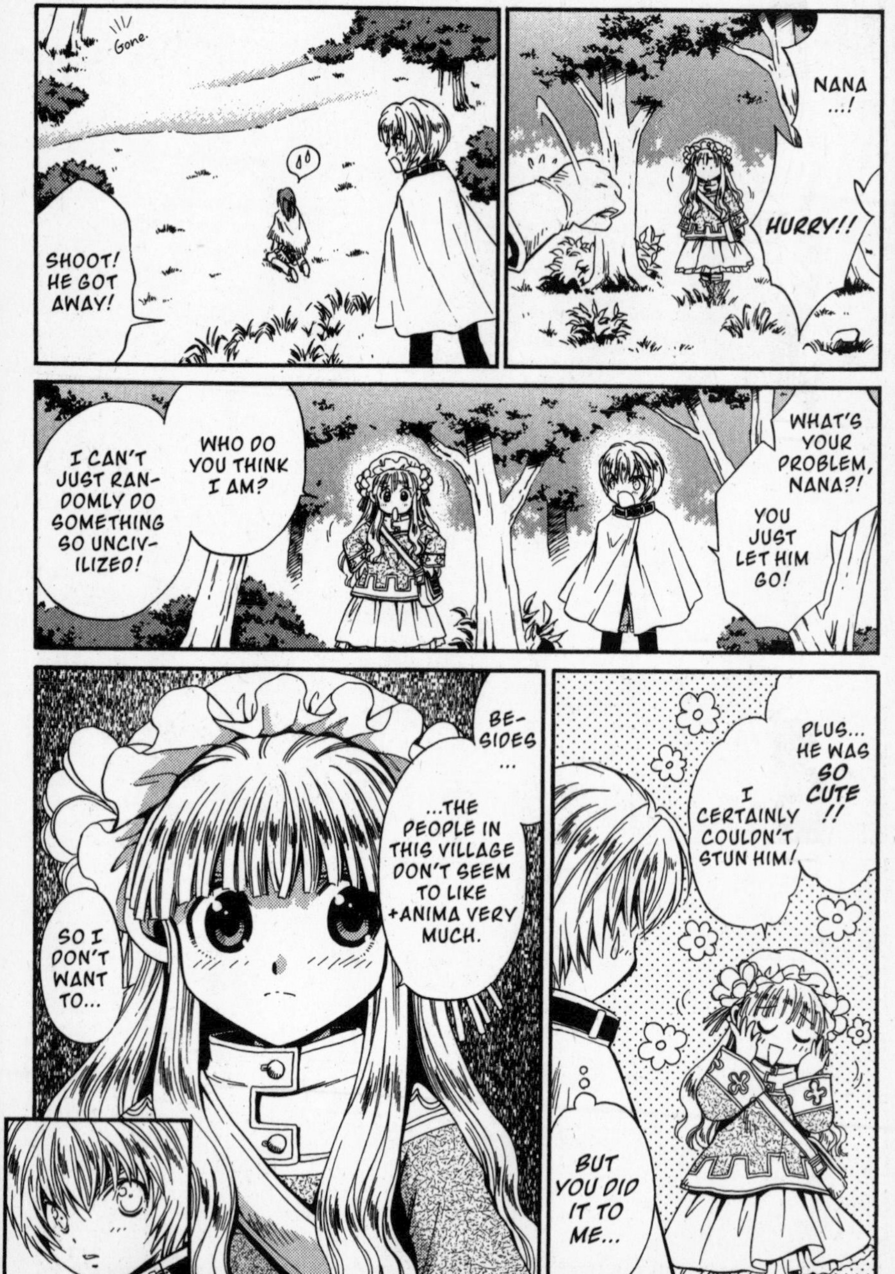
NANA ...!
HURRY!!
Gone.
SHOOT! HE GOT AWAY!
WHAT'S YOUR PROBLEM, NANA?!
YOU JUST LET HIM GO!
WHO DO YOU THINK I AM?
I CAN'T JUST RAN-DOMLY DO SOMETHING SO UNCIV-ILIZED!
PLUS... HE WAS SO CUTE!!
I CERTAINLY COULDN'T STUN HIM!
BUT YOU DID IT TO ME...
BE-SIDES ...
...THE PEOPLE IN THIS VILLAGE DON'T SEEM TO LIKE +ANIMA VERY MUCH.
SO I DON'T WANT TO...

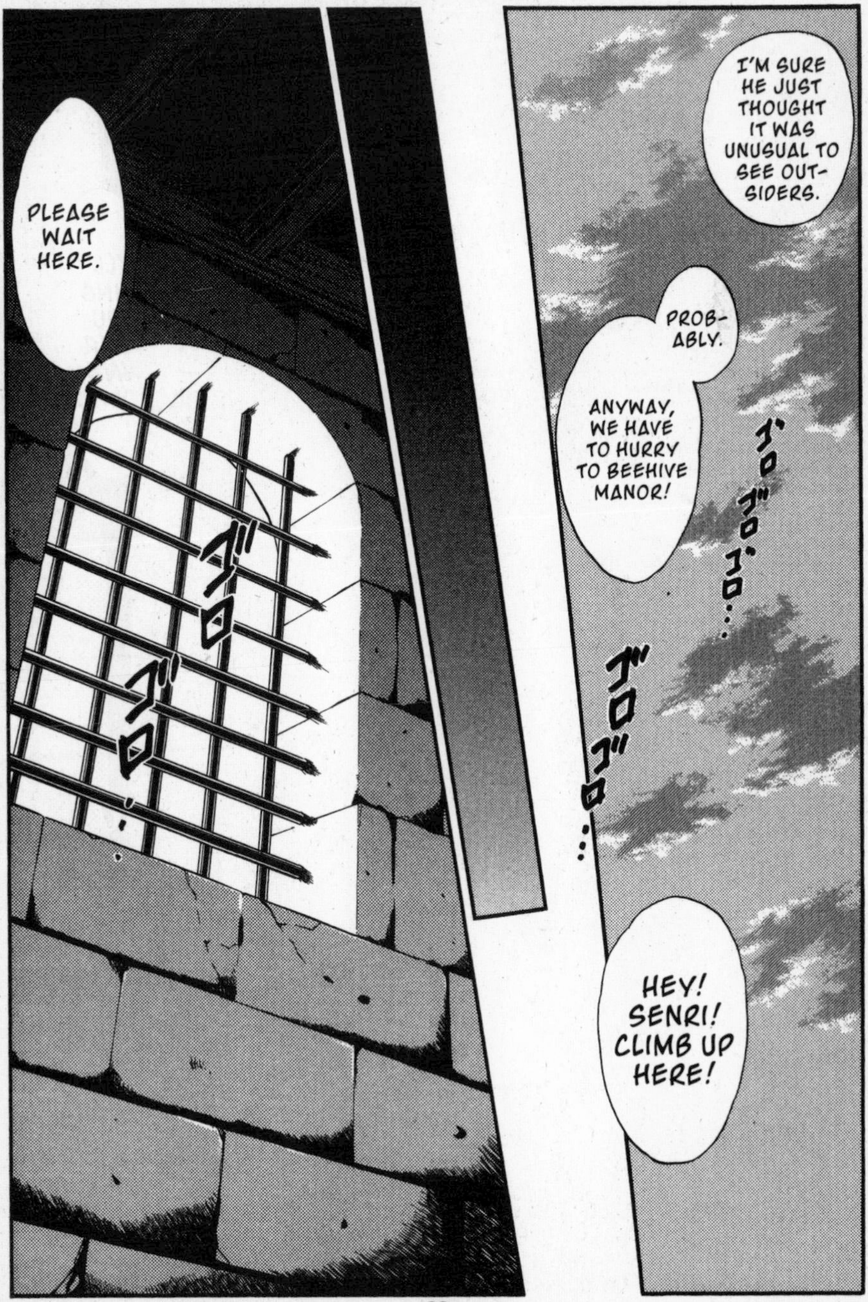
I'M SURE HE JUST THOUGHT IT WAS UNUSUAL TO SEE OUT-SIDERS.
PROB-ABLY.
ANYWAY, WE HAVE TO HURRY TO BEEHIVE MANOR!
ゴロゴロゴロ…
ゴロゴロ…
HEY! SENRI! CLIMB UP HERE!
PLEASE WAIT HERE.
ゴロゴロ…

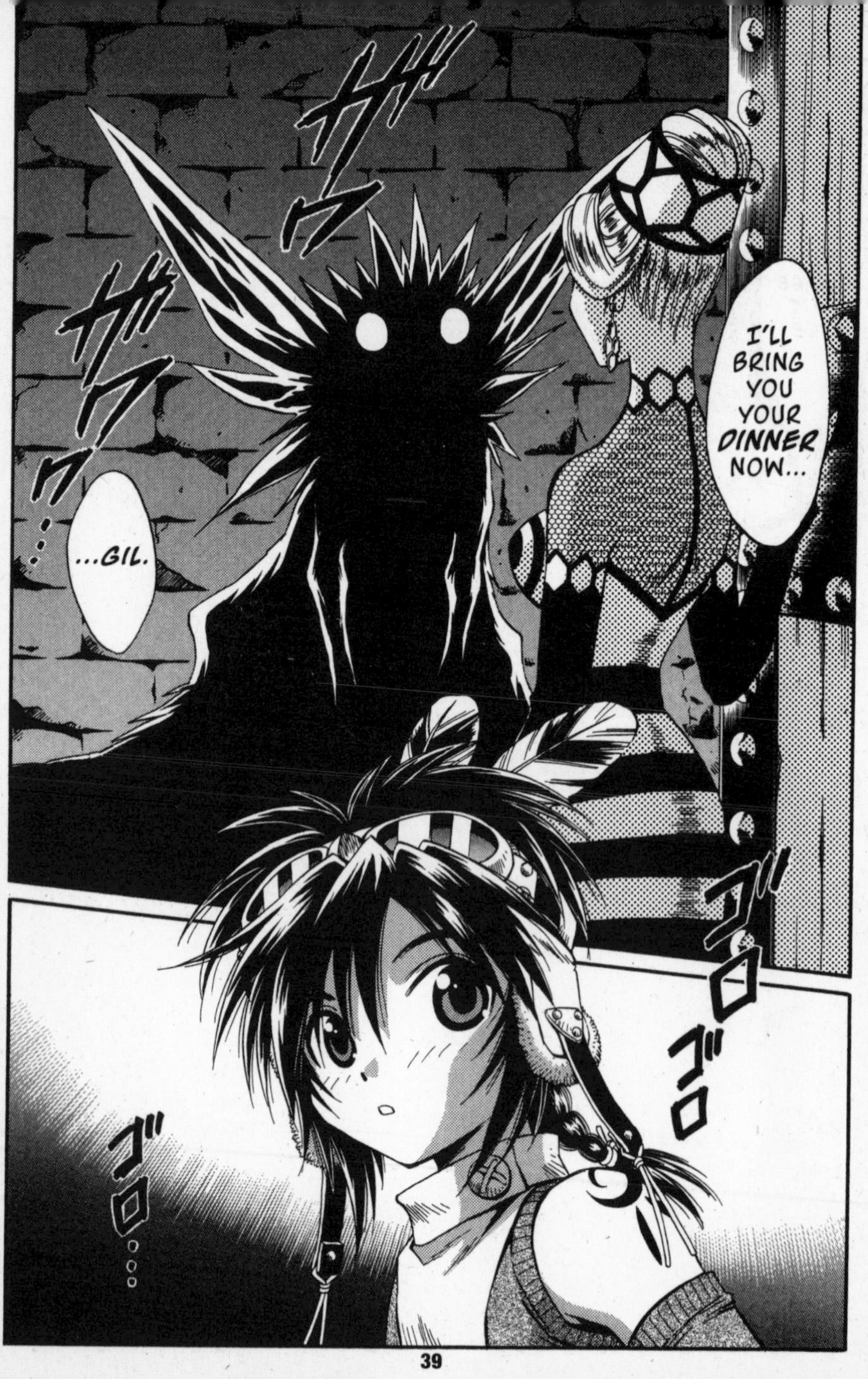
I'LL BRING YOU YOUR DINNER NOW...
...GIL.

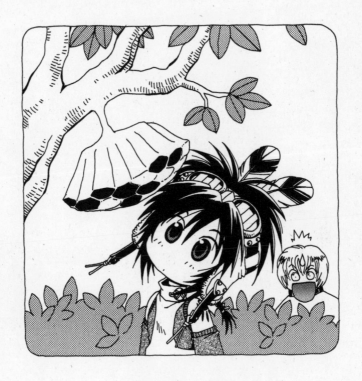

What's this?

Chapter 7
The Secret of Beehive Manor—Part 2

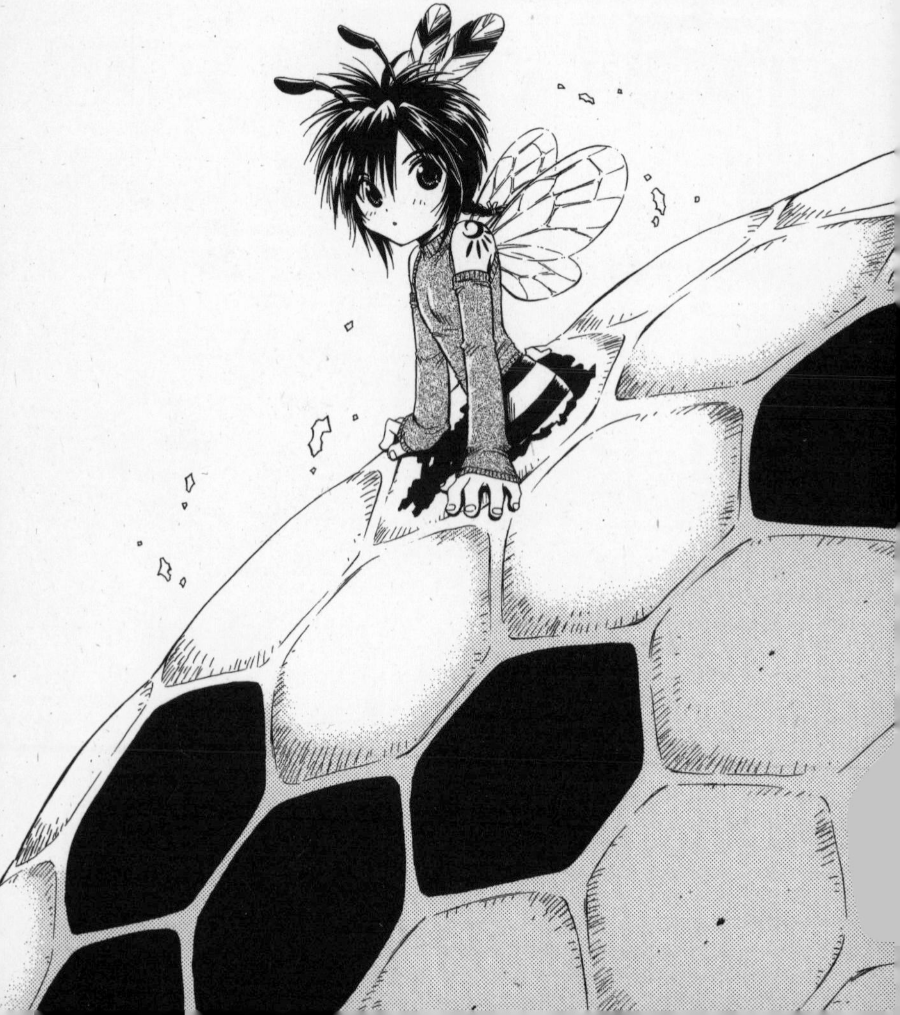

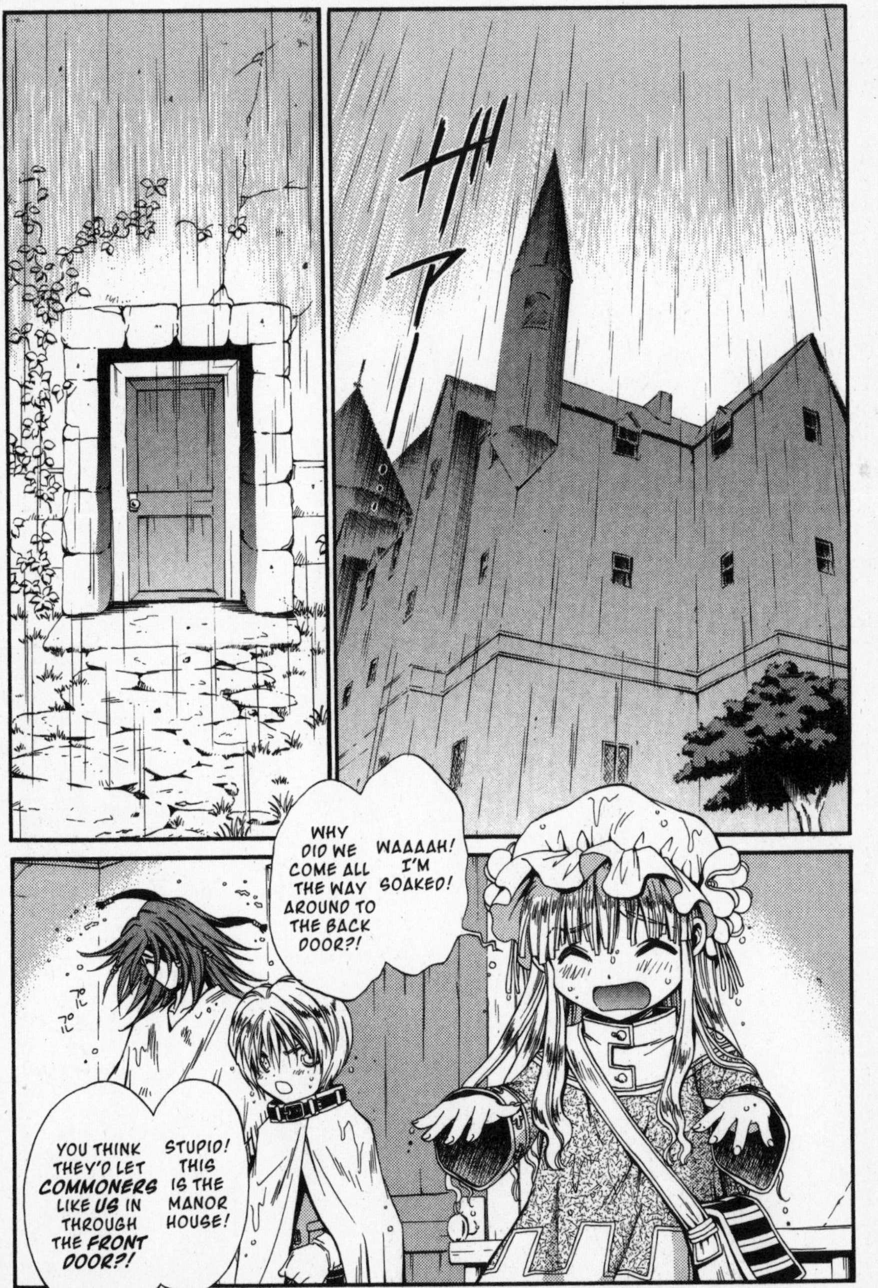
ザァー
WAAAAH! I'M SOAKED!
WHY DID WE COME ALL THE WAY AROUND TO THE BACK DOOR?!
STUPID! THIS IS THE MANOR HOUSE!
YOU THINK THEY'D LET COMMONERS LIKE US IN THROUGH THE FRONT DOOR?!

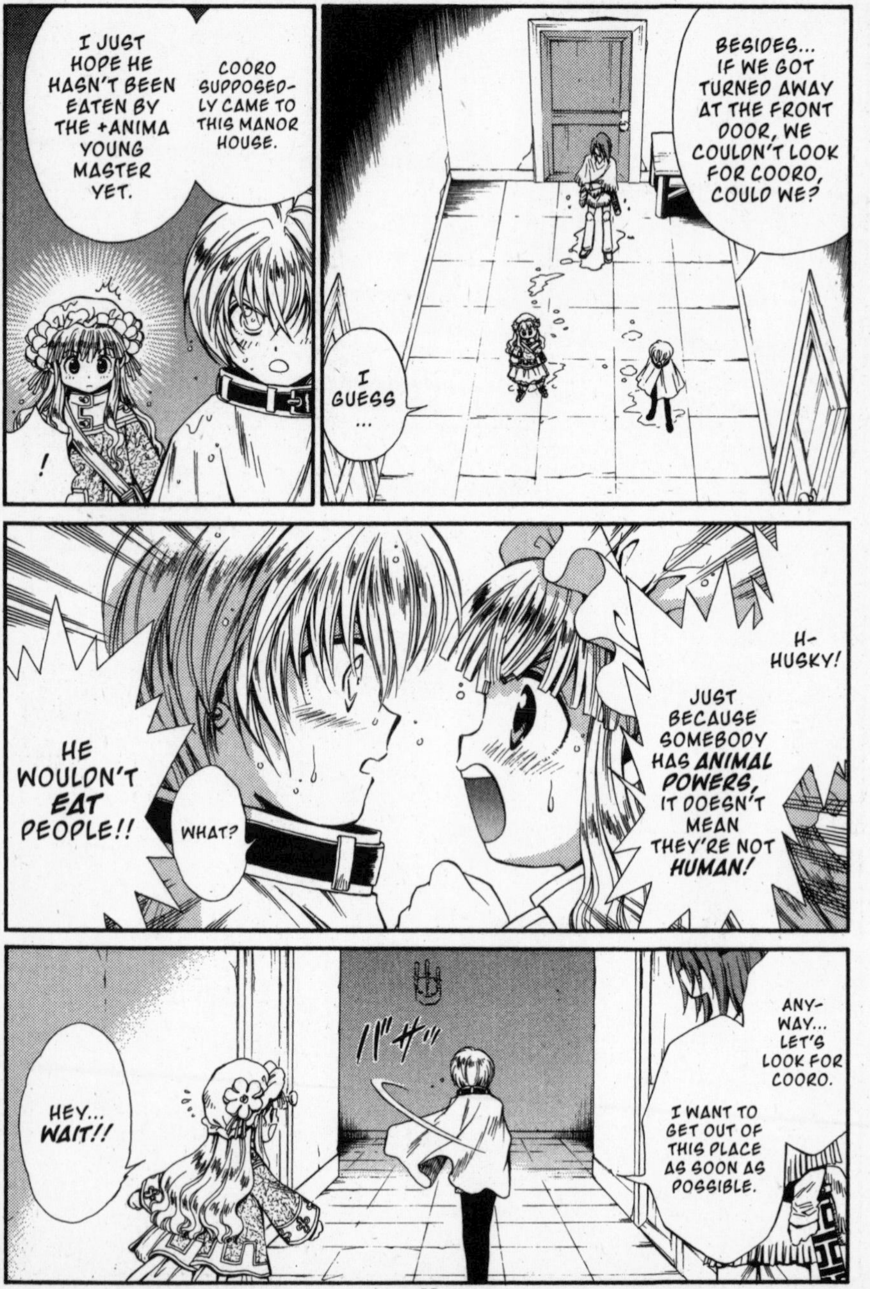
BESIDES... IF WE GOT TURNED AWAY AT THE FRONT DOOR, WE COULDN'T LOOK FOR COORO, COULD WE?
I GUESS...
COORO SUPPOSEDLY CAME TO THIS MANOR HOUSE.
I JUST HOPE HE HASN'T BEEN EATEN BY THE +ANIMA YOUNG MASTER YET.
!
H-HUSKY!
JUST BECAUSE SOMEBODY HAS ANIMAL POWERS, IT DOESN'T MEAN THEY'RE NOT HUMAN!
WHAT?
HE WOULDN'T EAT PEOPLE!!
ANYWAY... LET'S LOOK FOR COORO.
I WANT TO GET OUT OF THIS PLACE AS SOON AS POSSIBLE.
バサッ
HEY... WAIT!!

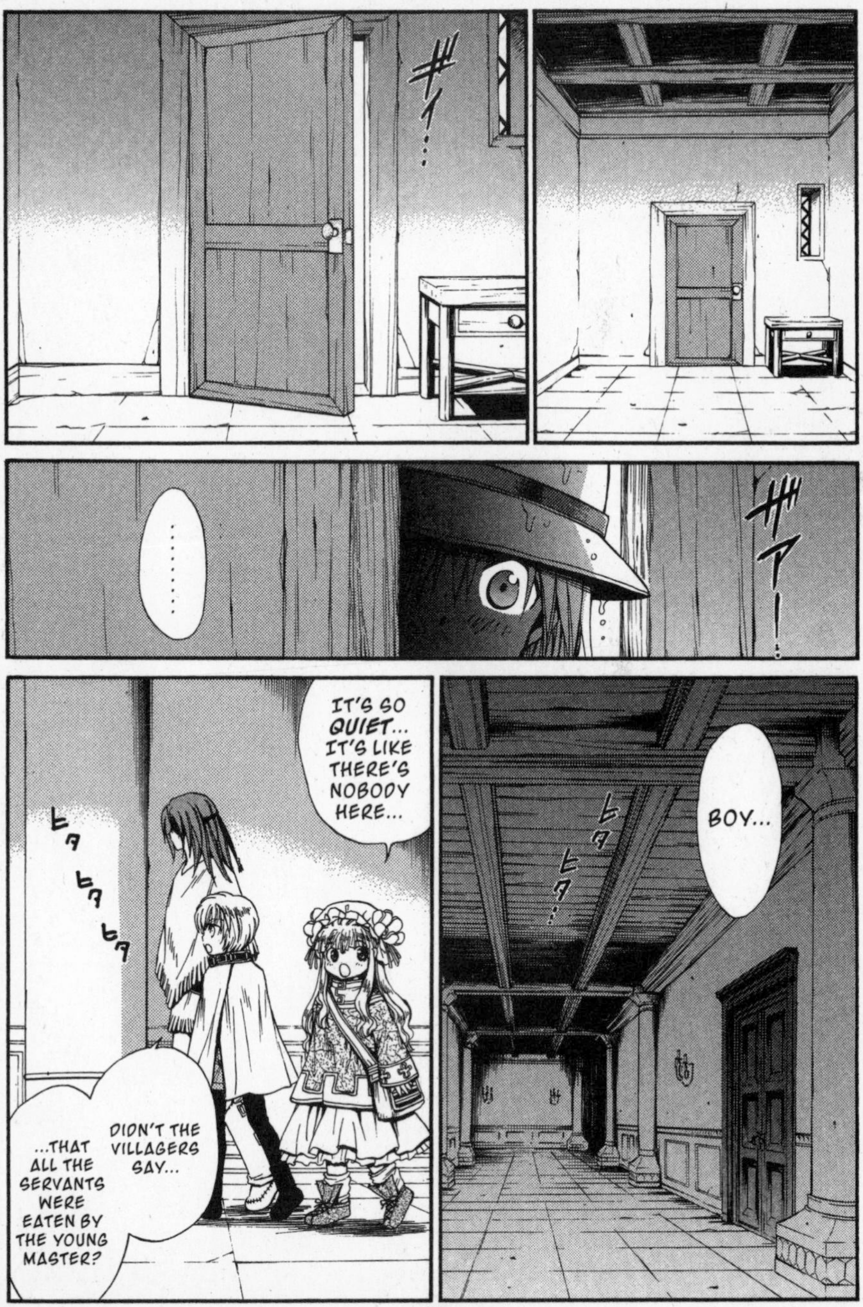
ギイ…
ザァー…!
……
BOY...
ヒタヒタ…
IT'S SO QUIET... IT'S LIKE THERE'S NOBODY HERE...
ヒタ ヒタ ヒタ
DIDN'T THE VILLAGERS SAY...
...THAT ALL THE SERVANTS WERE EATEN BY THE YOUNG MASTER?

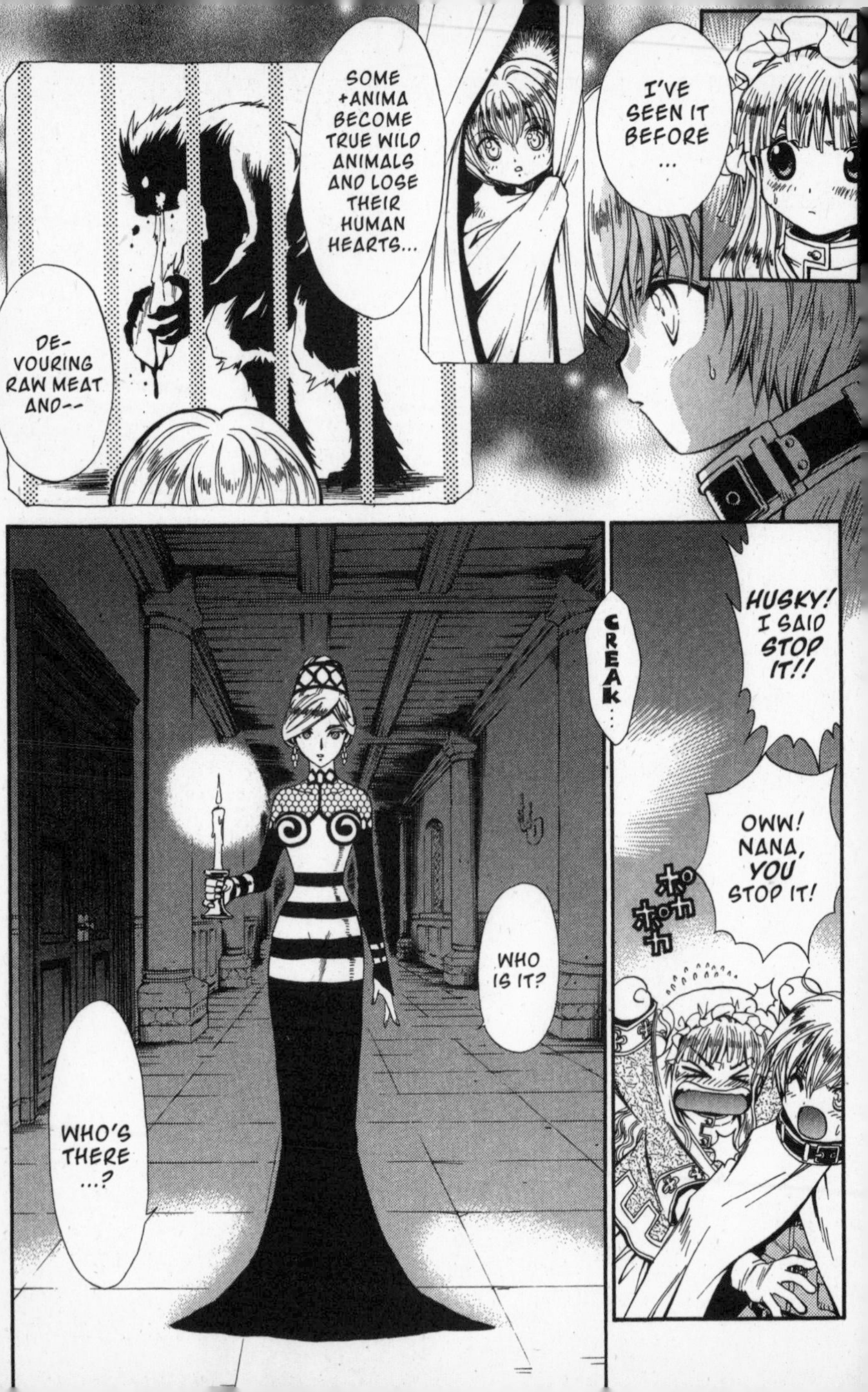
I'VE SEEN IT BEFORE ...
SOME +ANIMA BECOME TRUE WILD ANIMALS AND LOSE THEIR HUMAN HEARTS...
DE-VOURING RAW MEAT AND--
HUSKY! I SAID STOP IT!!
OWW! NANA, YOU STOP IT!
ポカ ポカ
CREAK...
WHO IS IT?
WHO'S THERE ...?

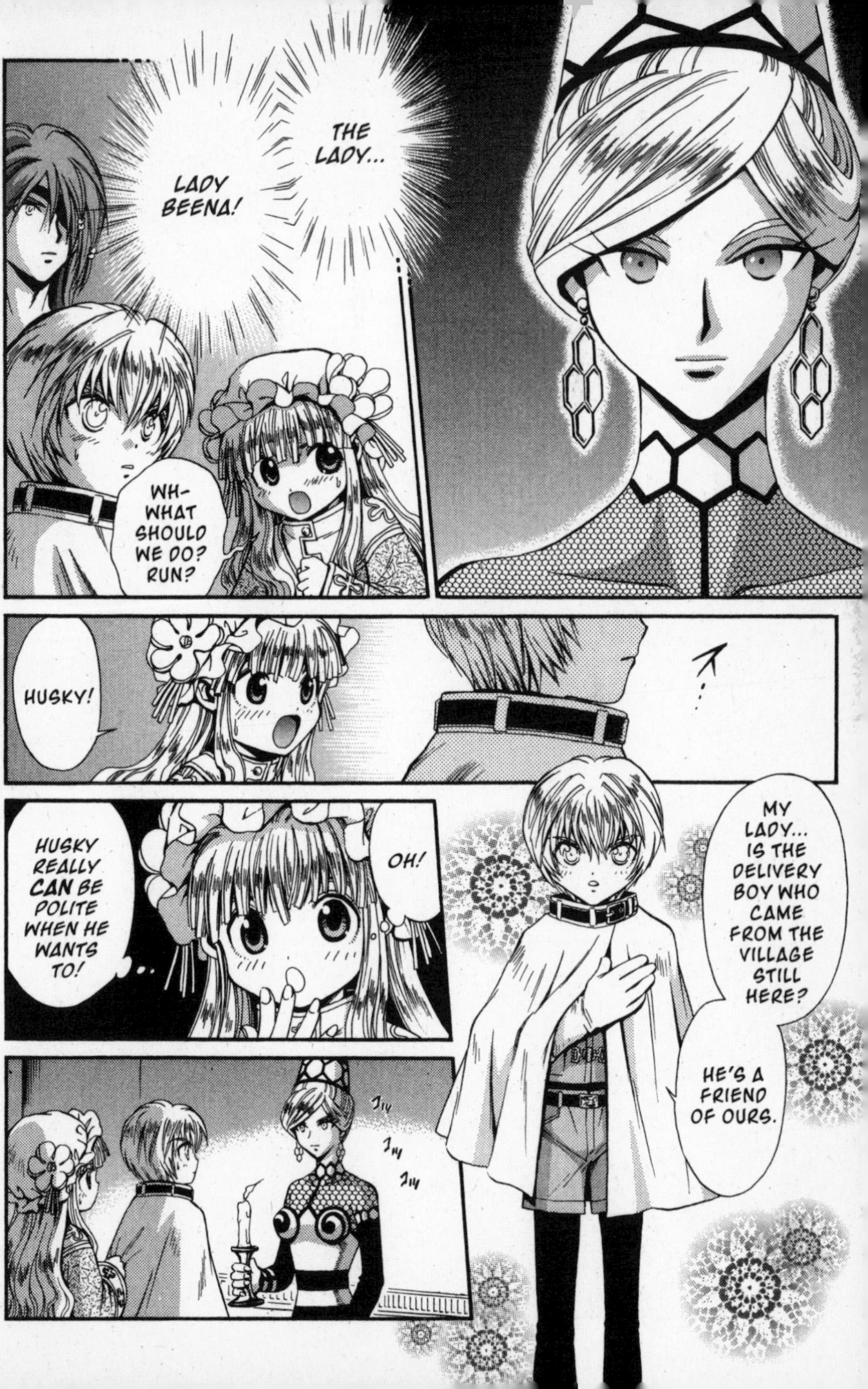
THE LADY...
LADY BEENA!
WH- WHAT SHOULD WE DO? RUN?
...
HUSKY!
MY LADY... IS THE DELIVERY BOY WHO CAME FROM THE VILLAGE STILL HERE?
HE'S A FRIEND OF OURS.
OH!
HUSKY REALLY **CAN** BE POLITE WHEN HE WANTS TO!
...

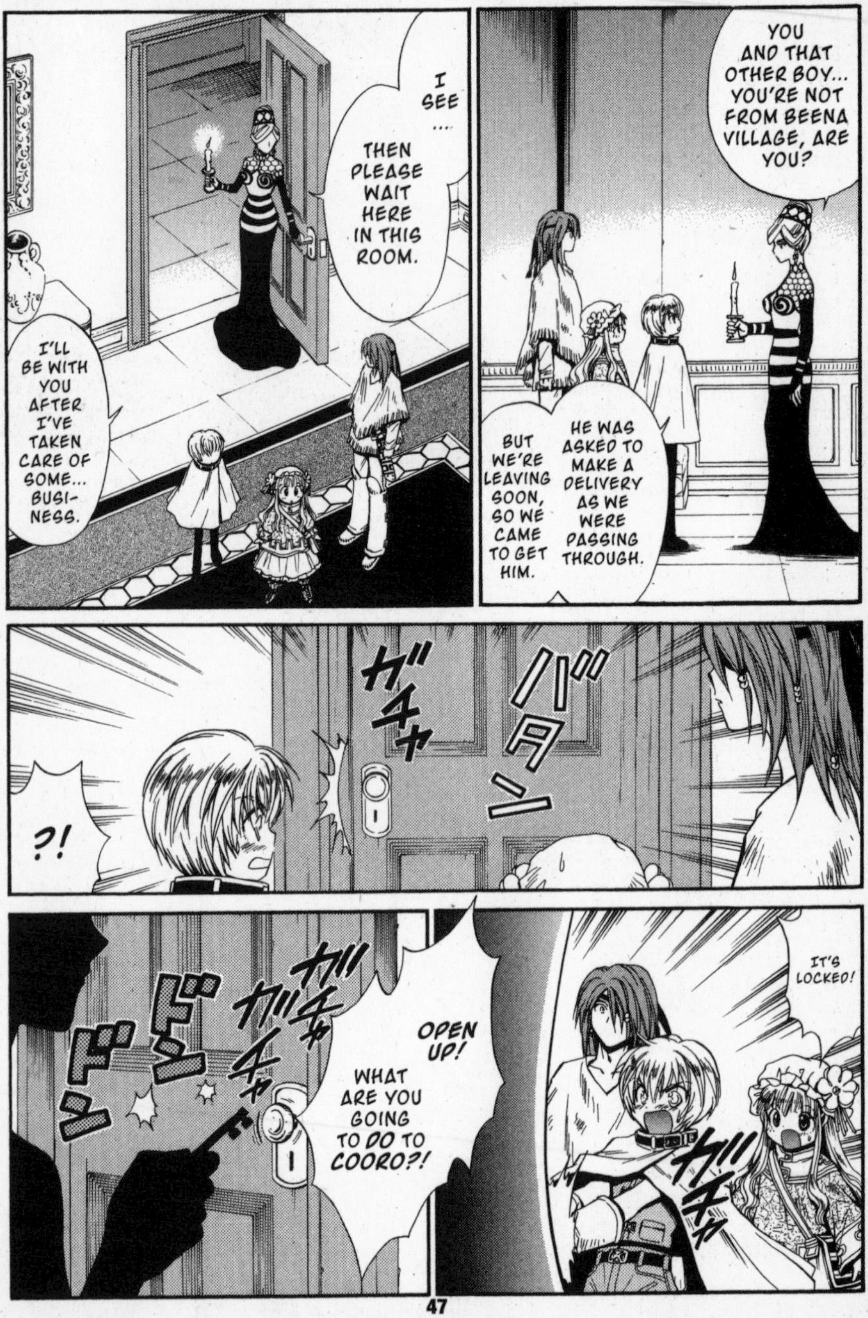
YOU AND THAT OTHER BOY... YOU'RE NOT FROM BEENA VILLAGE, ARE YOU?
HE WAS ASKED TO MAKE A DELIVERY AS WE WERE PASSING THROUGH.
BUT WE'RE LEAVING SOON, SO WE CAME TO GET HIM.
I SEE ....
THEN PLEASE WAIT HERE IN THIS ROOM.
I'LL BE WITH YOU AFTER I'VE TAKEN CARE OF SOME... BUSINESS.
バタン
ガチャ
?!
IT'S LOCKED!
ガチャ
OPEN UP!
WHAT ARE YOU GOING TO DO TO COORO?!
ガチャガチャ
ドンドン

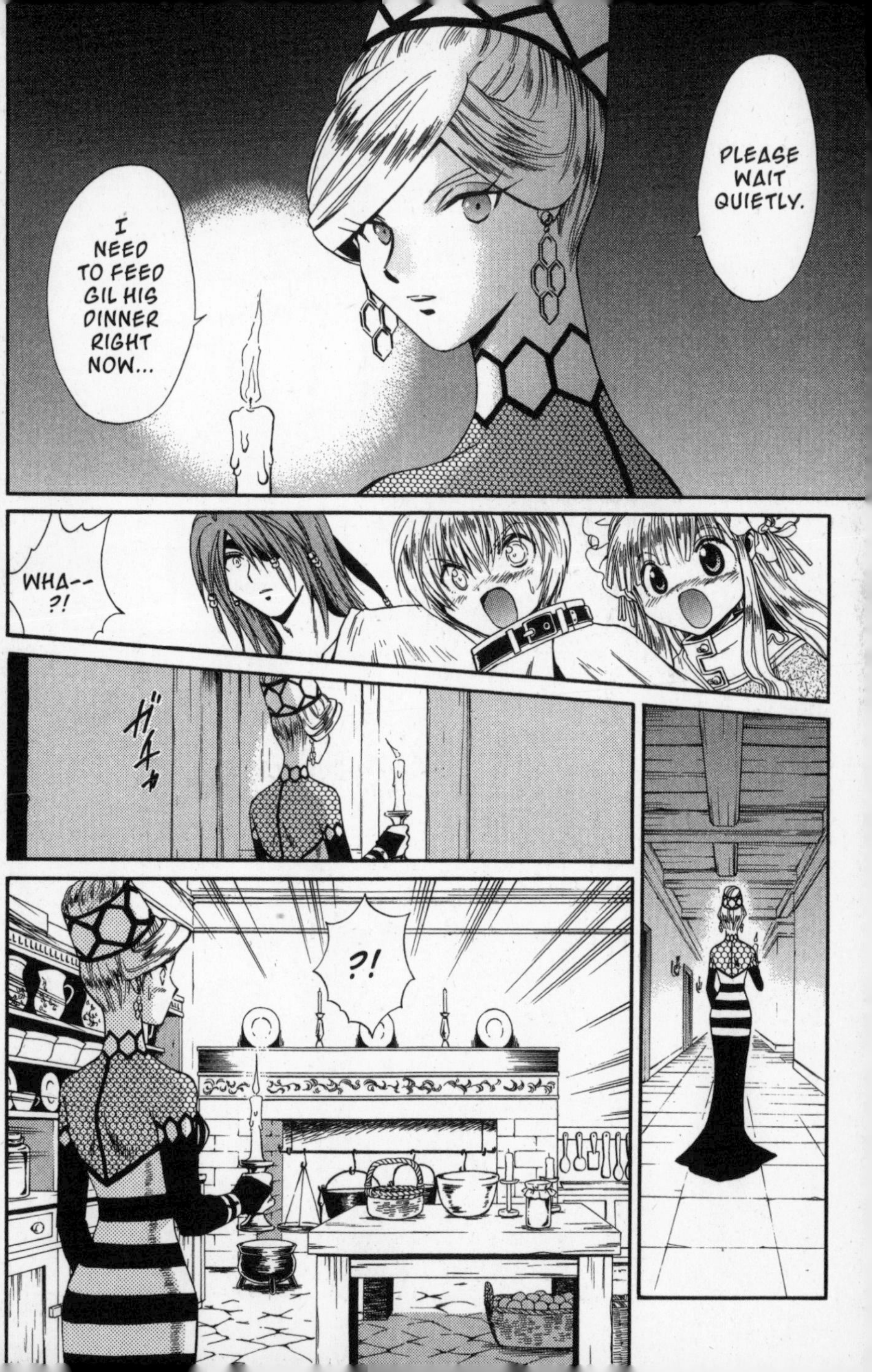
PLEASE WAIT QUIETLY.
I NEED TO FEED GIL HIS DINNER RIGHT NOW...
WHA-- ?!
ガチャ
?!

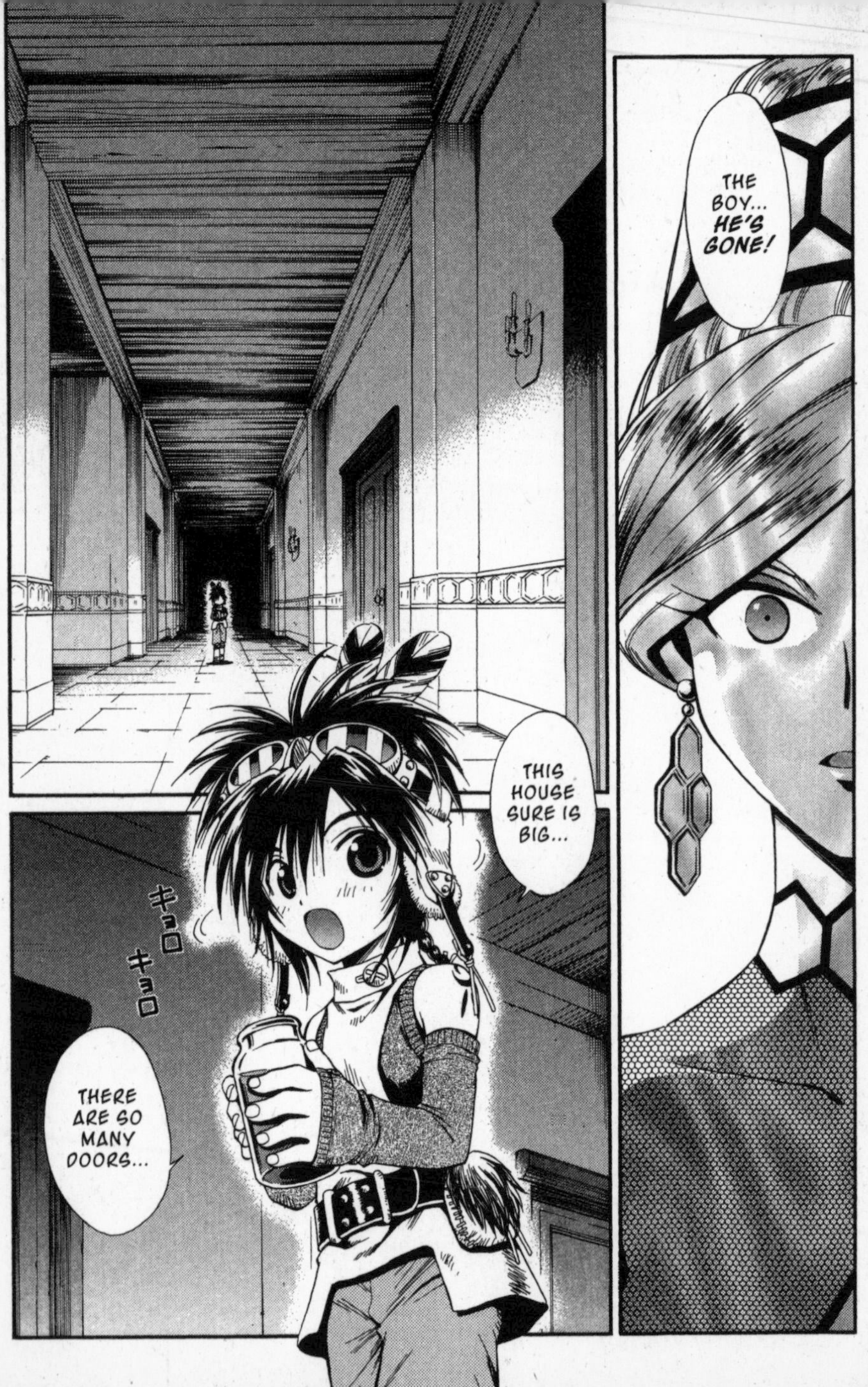
THE BOY... HE'S GONE!
THIS HOUSE SURE IS BIG...
キョロ キョロ
THERE ARE SO MANY DOORS...

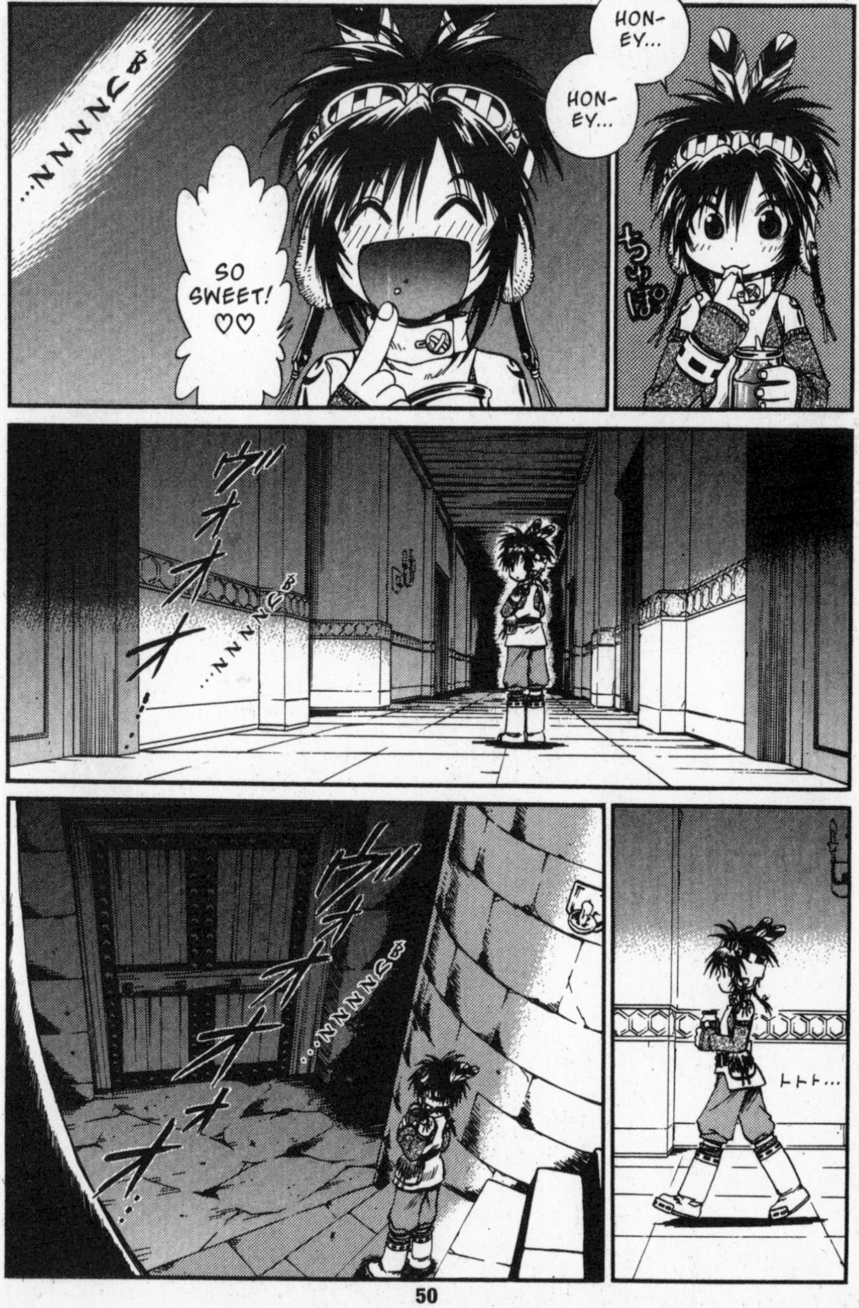
HON-
EY...
HON-
EY...
ちゅぽ
...NNNNUB
SO
SWEET!
♡♡
ヴォオオオ…!!
BUNNNN...
トトト...
ヴォオオオオオ…!
...NNNNNUB

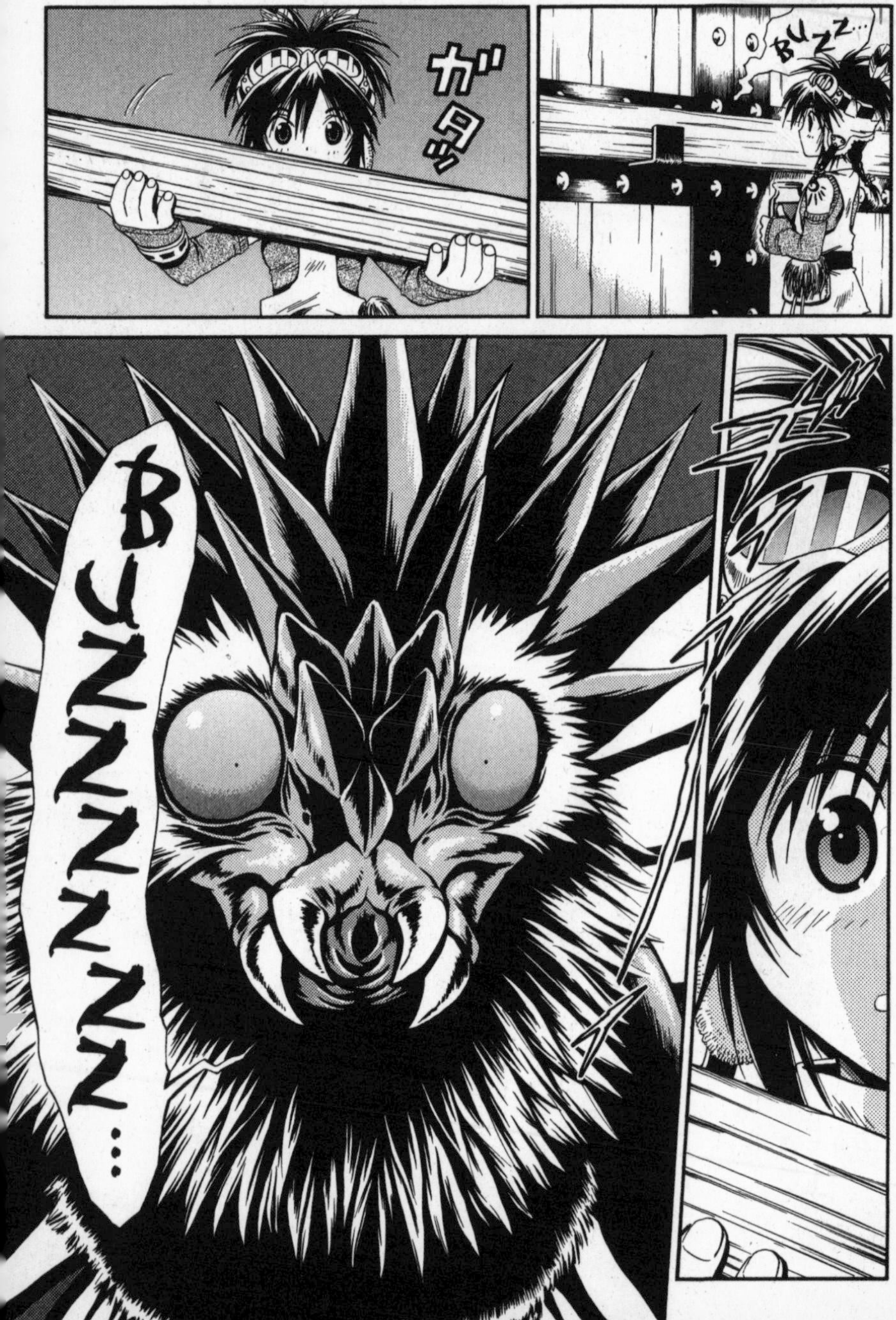
BUZZ...
ガタッ
BUZZZZZZ...

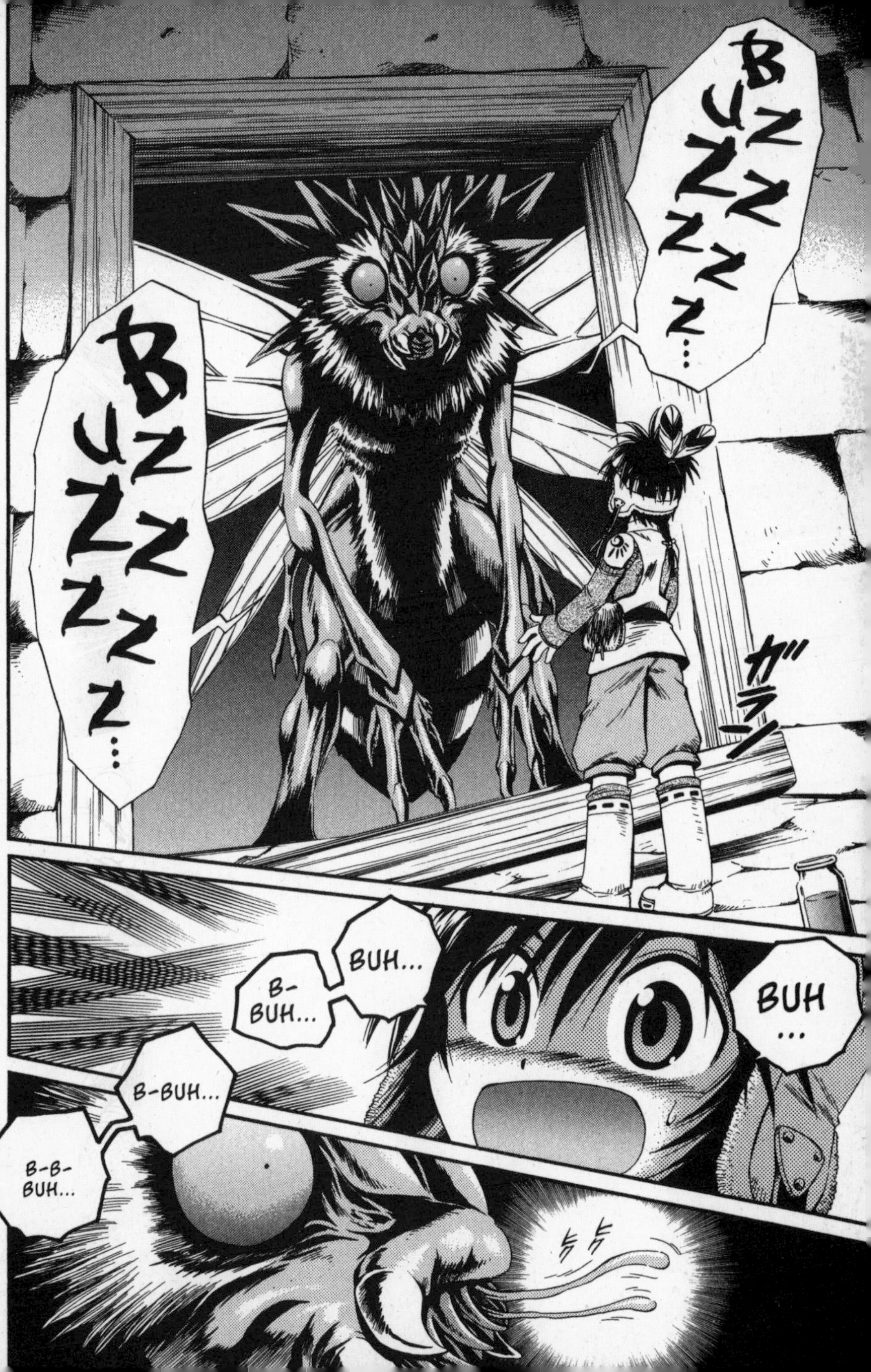
BUZZZZZZ...
BUZZZZZZ...
ガラン
BUH ...
BUH...
B-BUH...
B-BUH...
B-B-BUH...

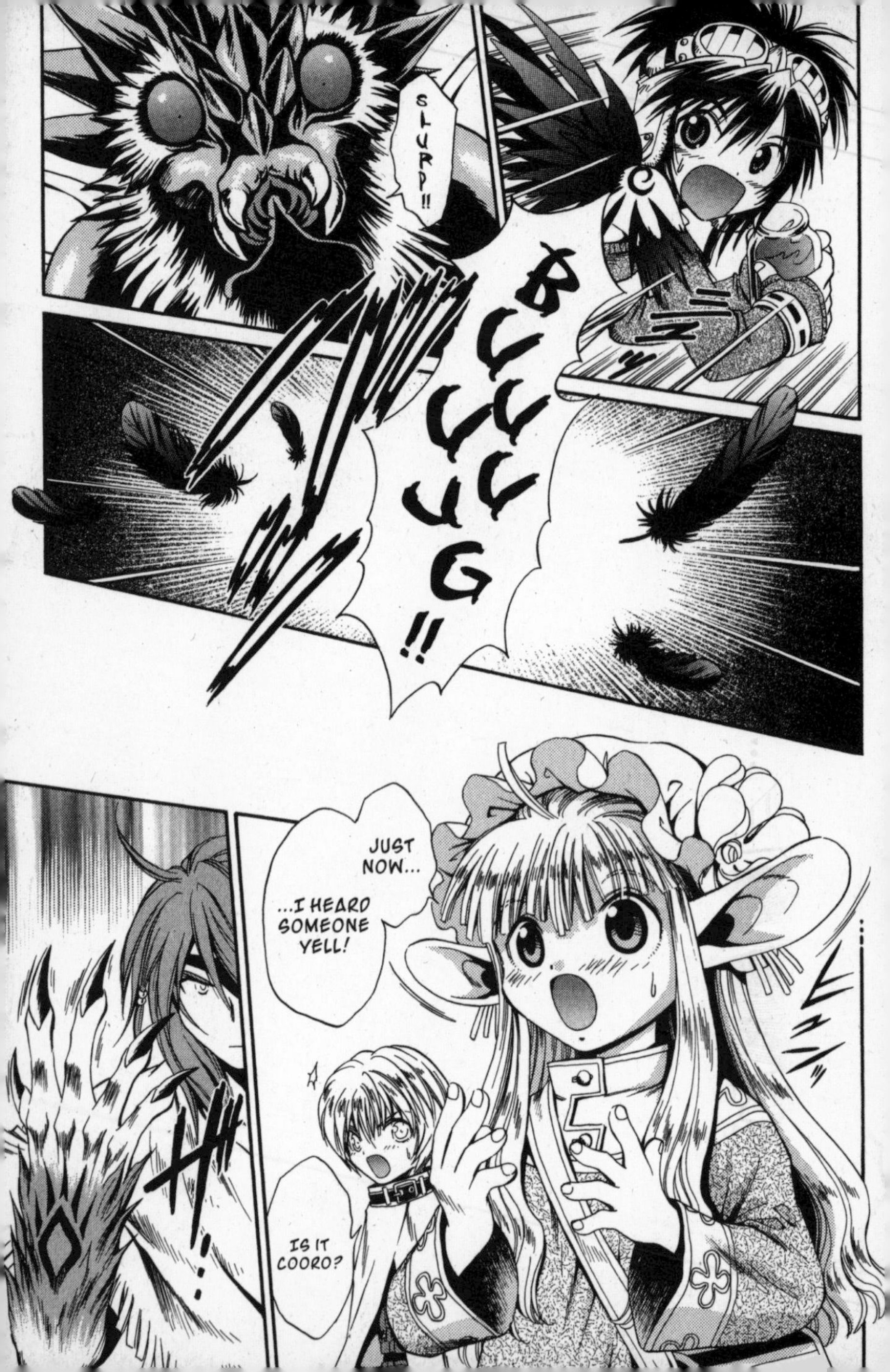
SLURP!!
BUUUUG!!
JUST NOW...
...I HEARD SOMEONE YELL!
IS IT COORO?

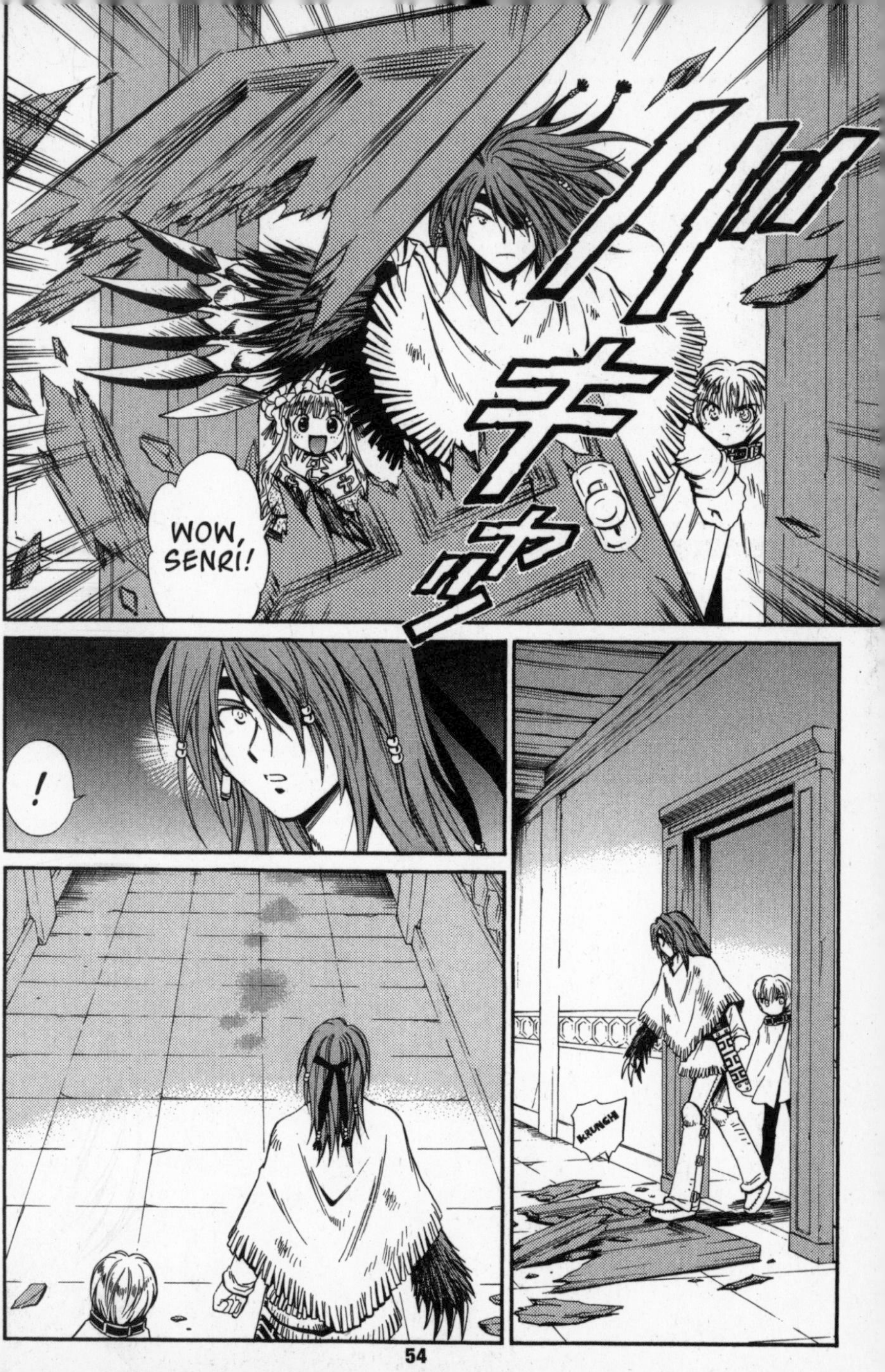
WOW, SENRI!
KRUNCH
!

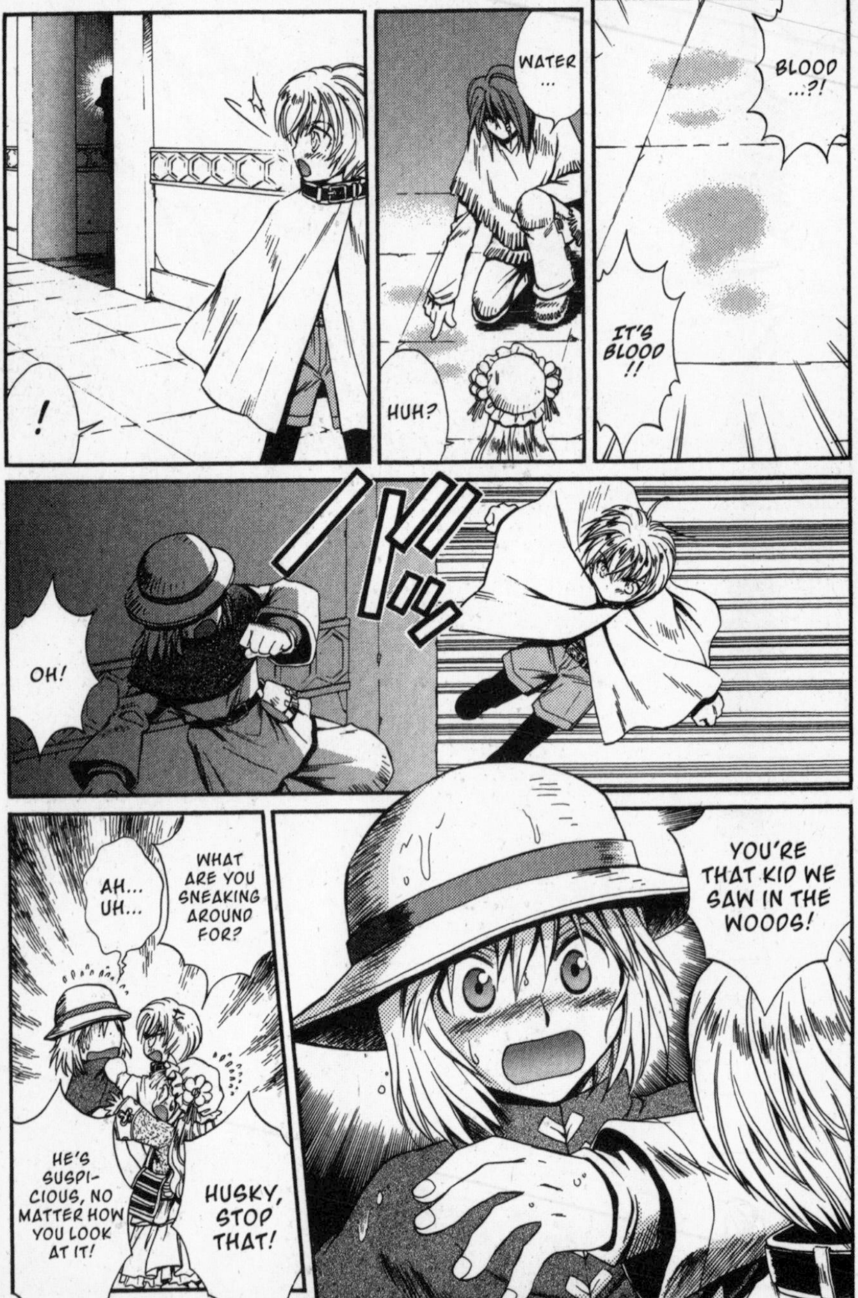

BLOOD ...?!
IT'S BLOOD !!
WATER ...
HUH?
!
OH!
YOU'RE THAT KID WE SAW IN THE WOODS!
WHAT ARE YOU SNEAKING AROUND FOR?
AH... UH...
HUSKY, STOP THAT!
HE'S SUSPICIOUS, NO MATTER HOW YOU LOOK AT IT!

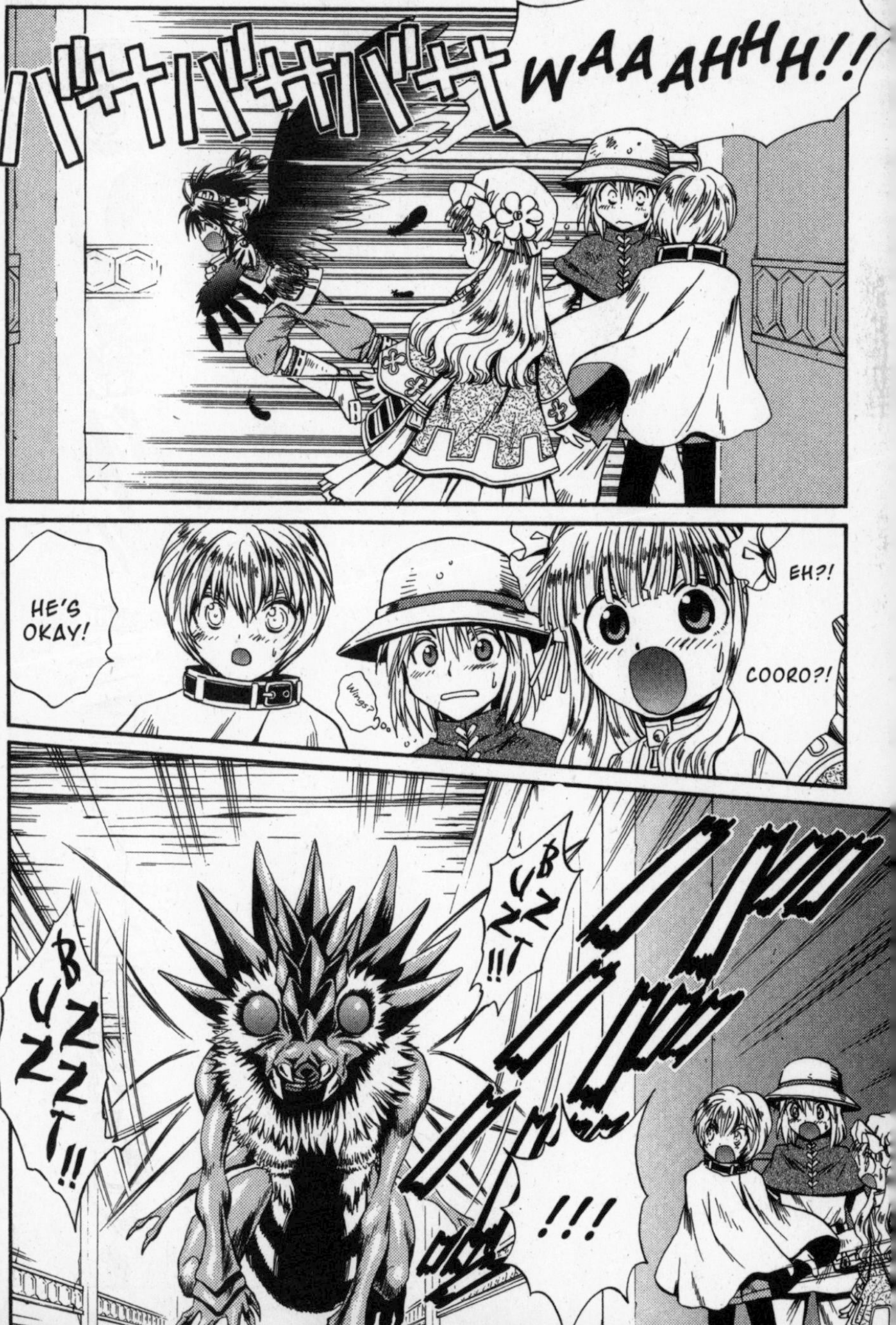
WAAAHHHH!!
バサバサバサ
EH?!
COORO?!
Wings?
HE'S OKAY!
BUZZT!!!
!!!
BUZZZT!!

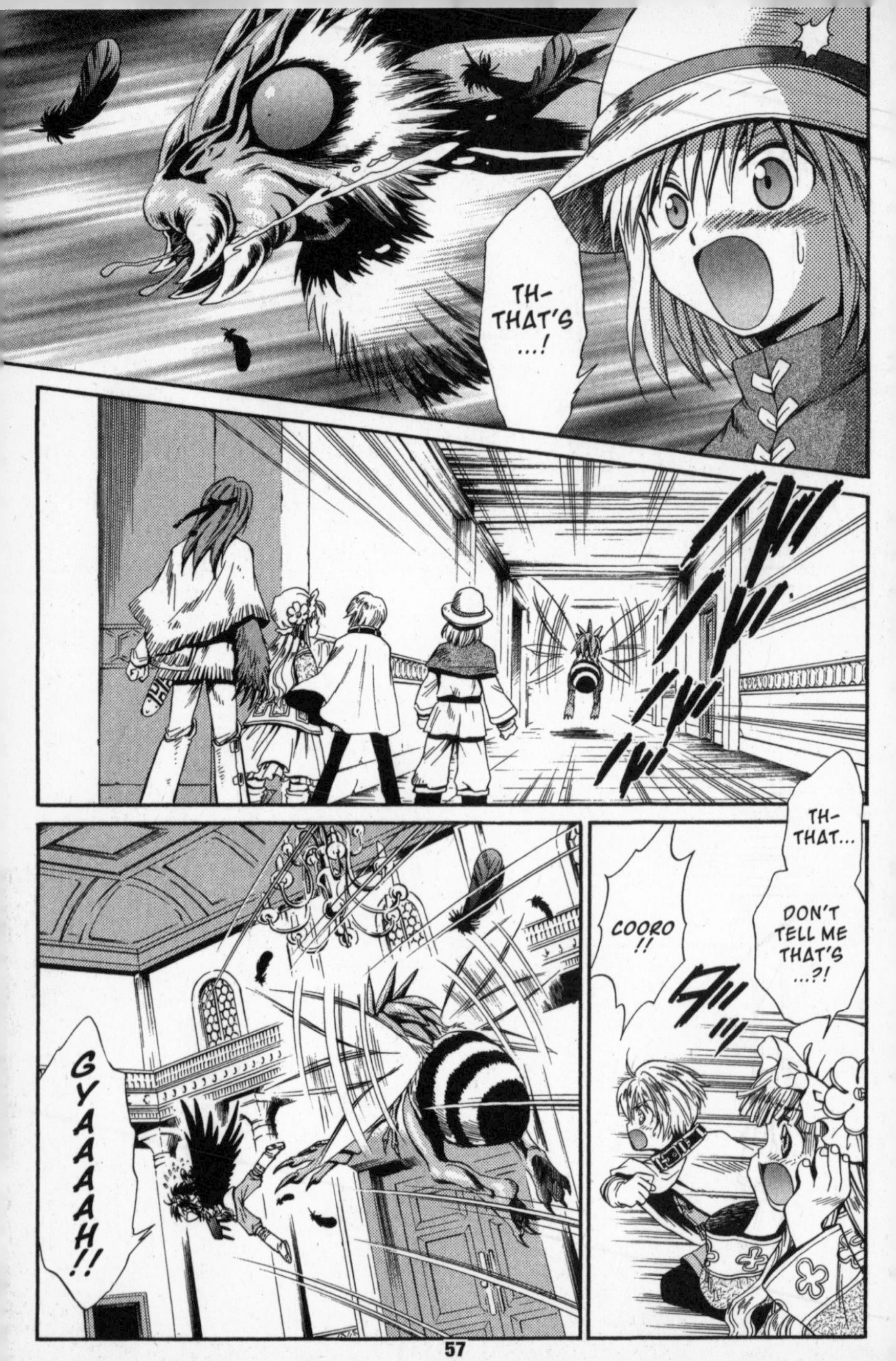
TH-THAT'S ...!
TH-THAT...
DON'T TELL ME THAT'S ...?!
COORO !!
GYAAAAAH!!

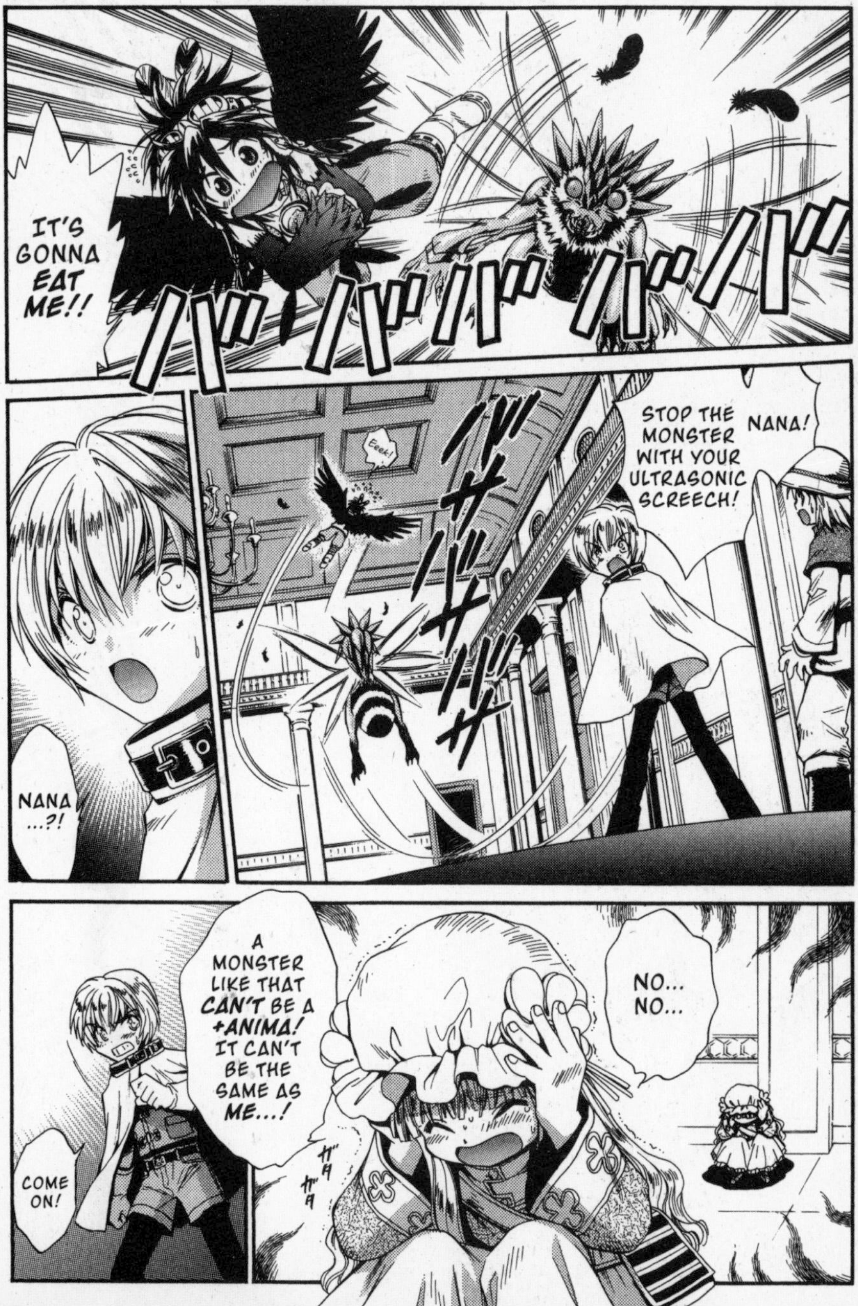
IT'S GONNA EAT ME!!
NANA!
STOP THE MONSTER WITH YOUR ULTRASONIC SCREECH!
Eeek!
NANA ...?!
NO... NO...
A MONSTER LIKE THAT CAN'T BE A +ANIMA! IT CAN'T BE THE SAME AS ME...!
COME ON!

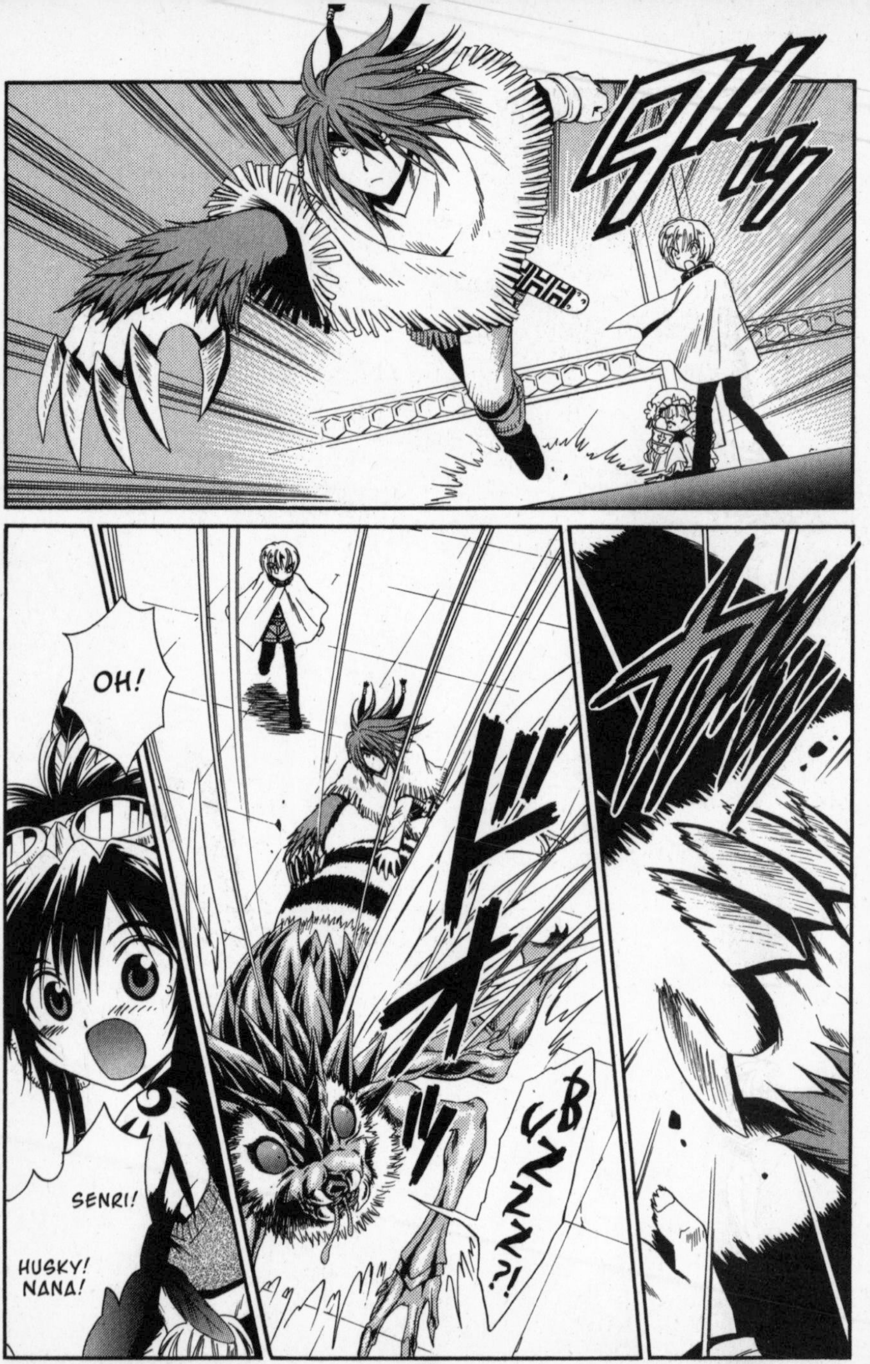
BUZZZZ?!
OH!
SENRI!
HUSKY! NANA!

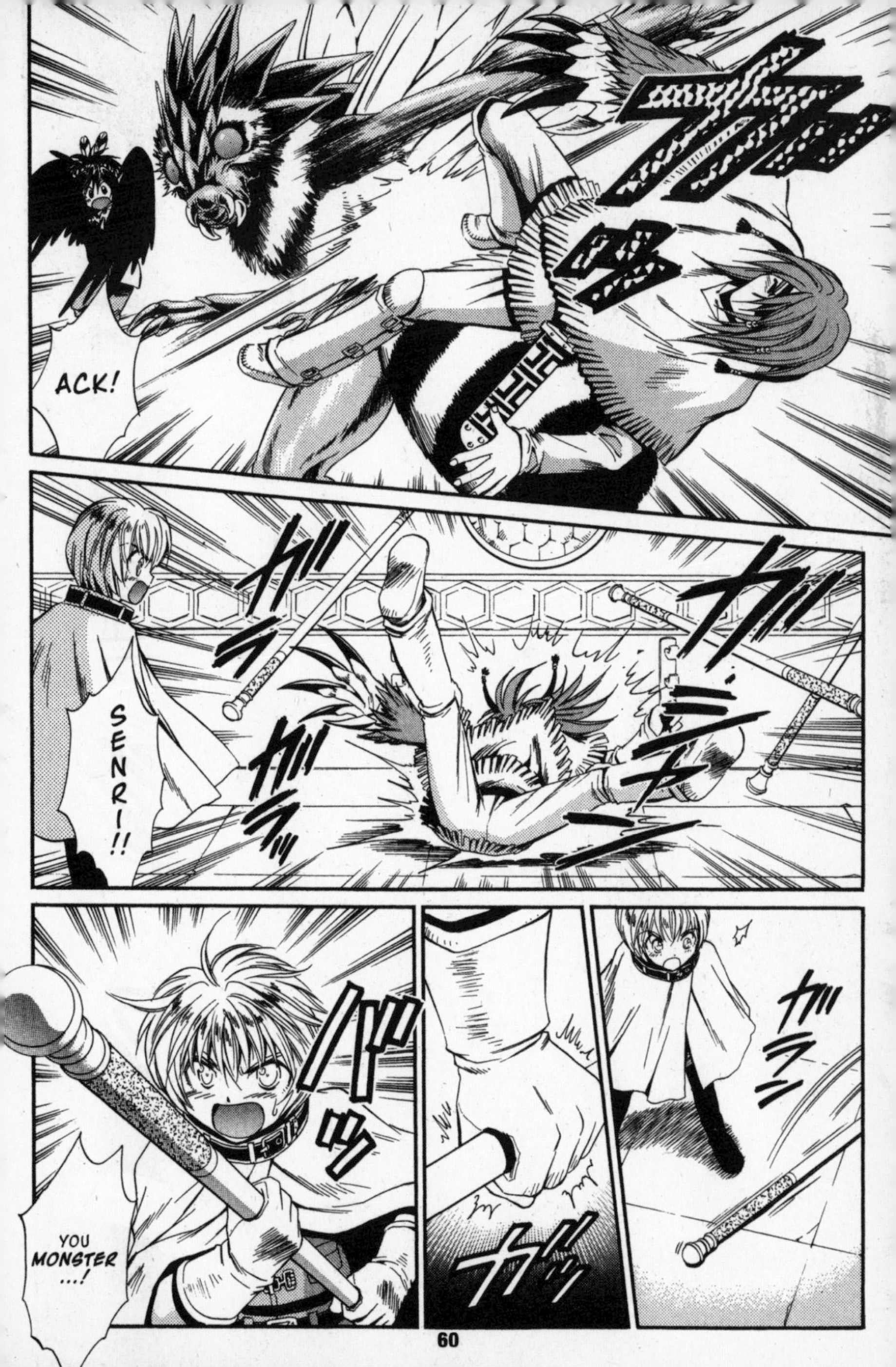
ACK!
SENRI!!
YOU MONSTER...!

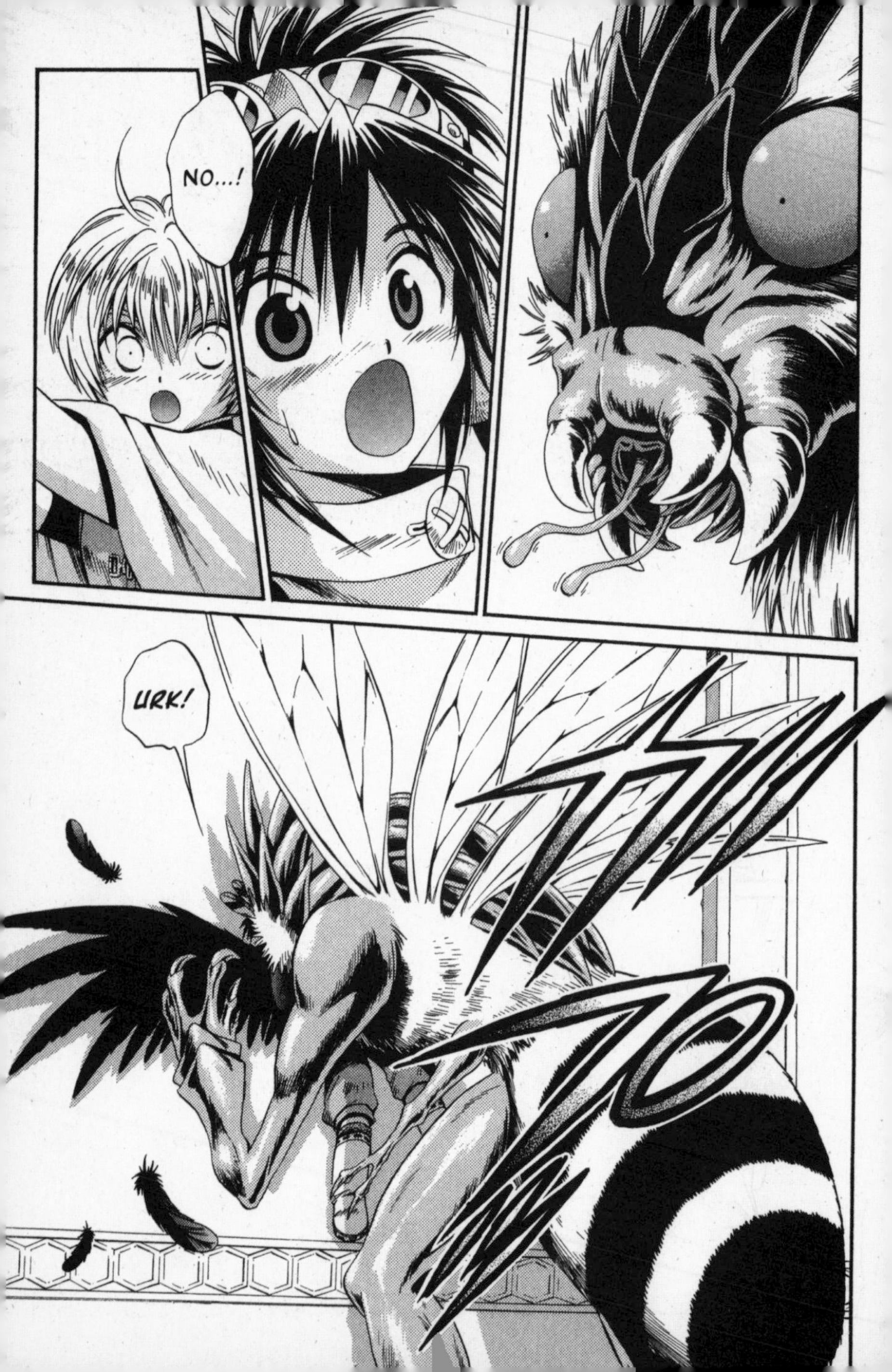
NO...!
URK!

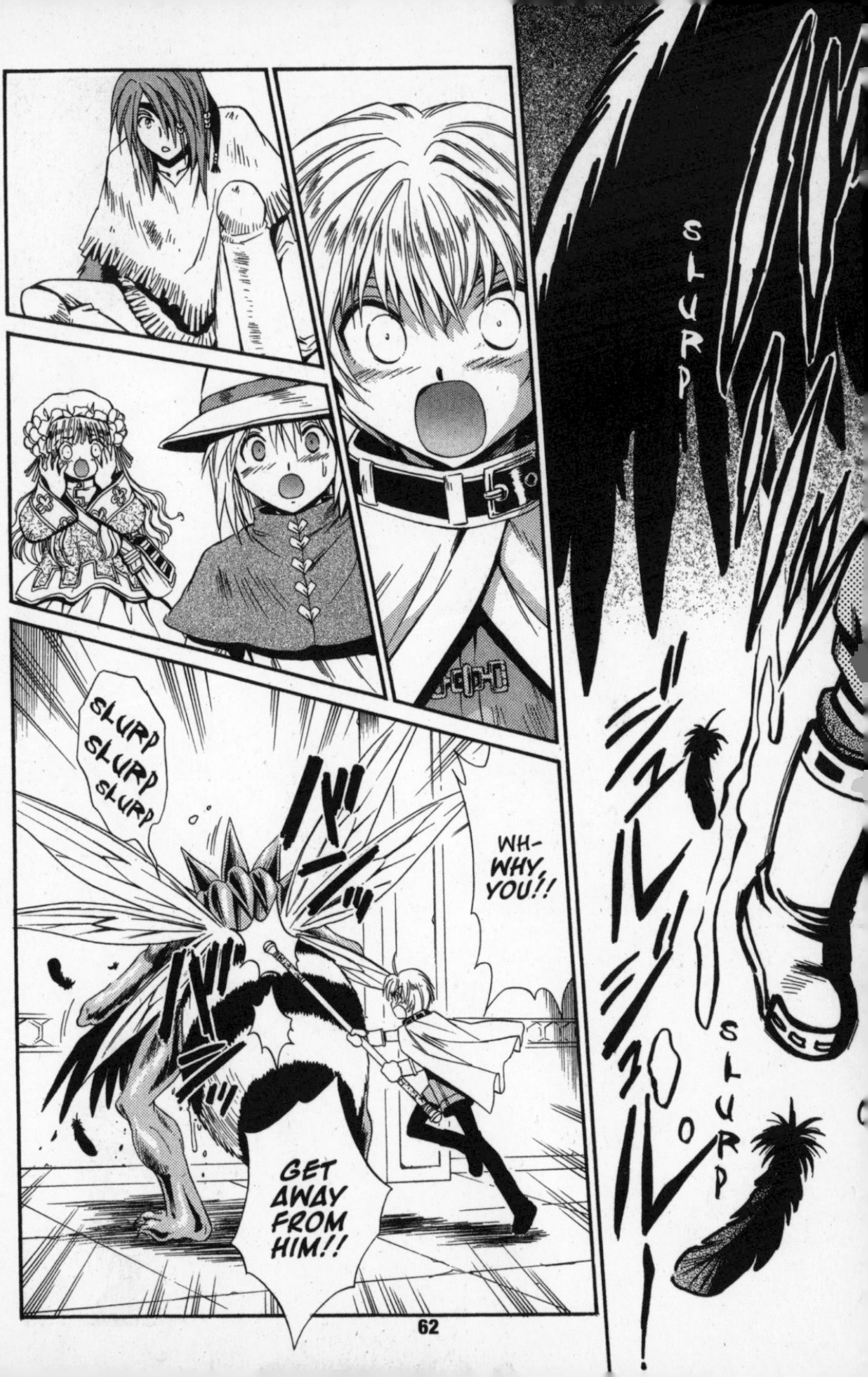
SLURP
SLURP
SLURP
SLURP
SLURP
SLURP
WH- WHY, YOU!!
GET AWAY FROM HIM!!

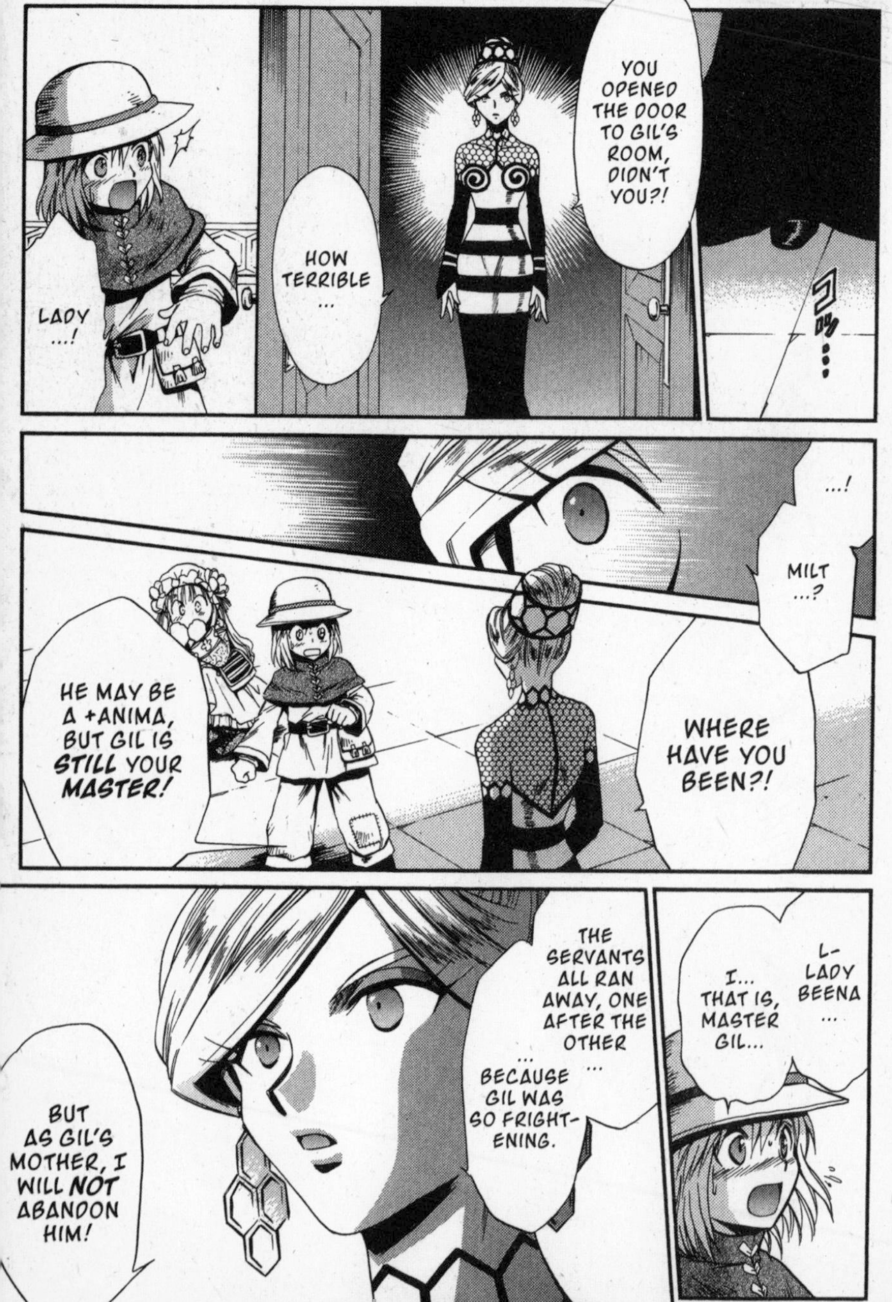
YOU OPENED THE DOOR TO GIL'S ROOM, DIDN'T YOU?!
HOW TERRIBLE ...
LADY ...!
...!
MILT ...?
WHERE HAVE YOU BEEN?!
HE MAY BE A +ANIMA, BUT GIL IS STILL YOUR MASTER!
L-LADY BEENA ...
I... THAT IS, MASTER GIL...
THE SERVANTS ALL RAN AWAY, ONE AFTER THE OTHER ...
... BECAUSE GIL WAS SO FRIGHT-ENING.
BUT AS GIL'S MOTHER, I WILL NOT ABANDON HIM!

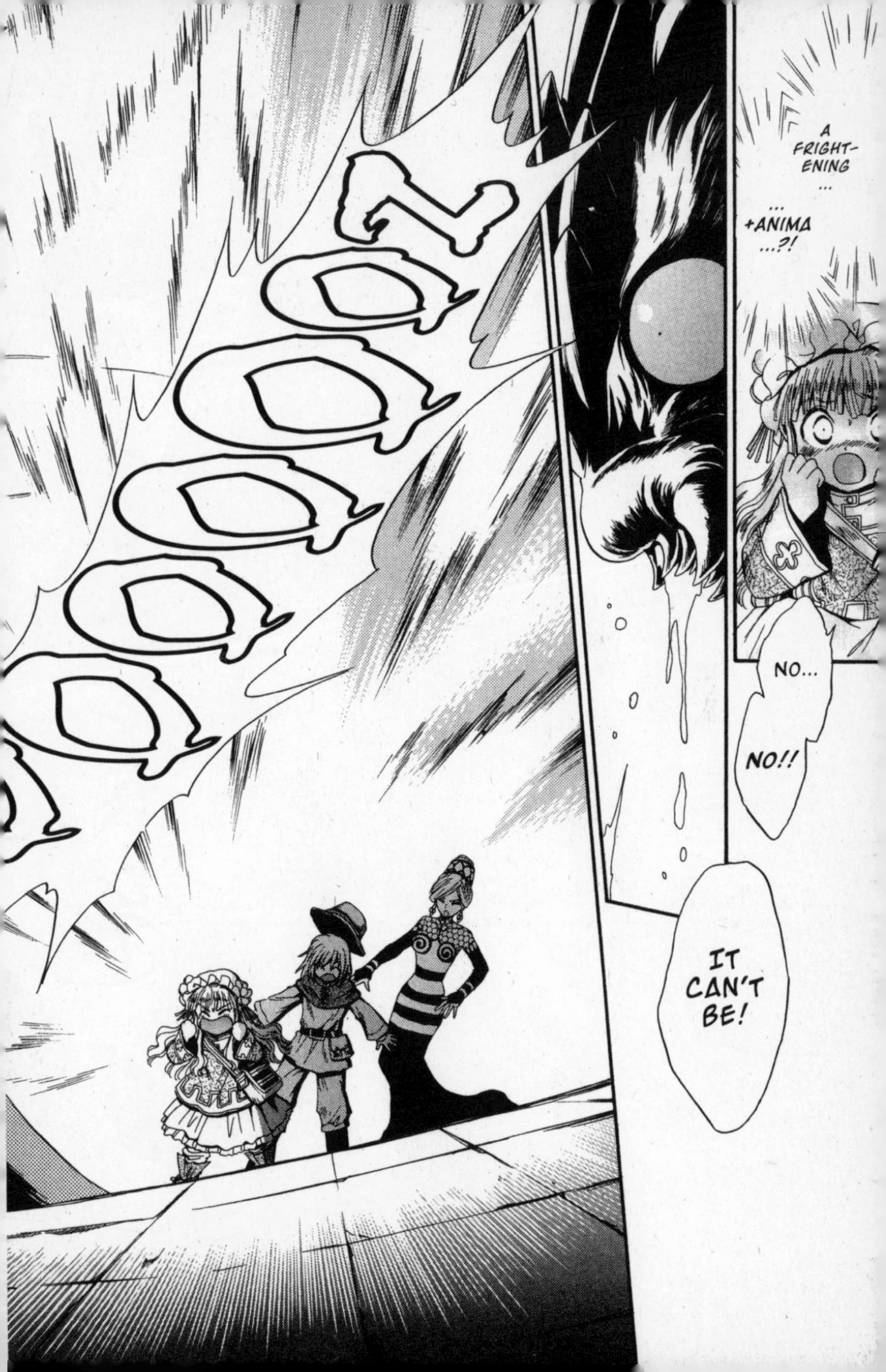
A FRIGHT-ENING ...
... +ANIMA ...?!
NO...
NO!!
IT CAN'T BE!

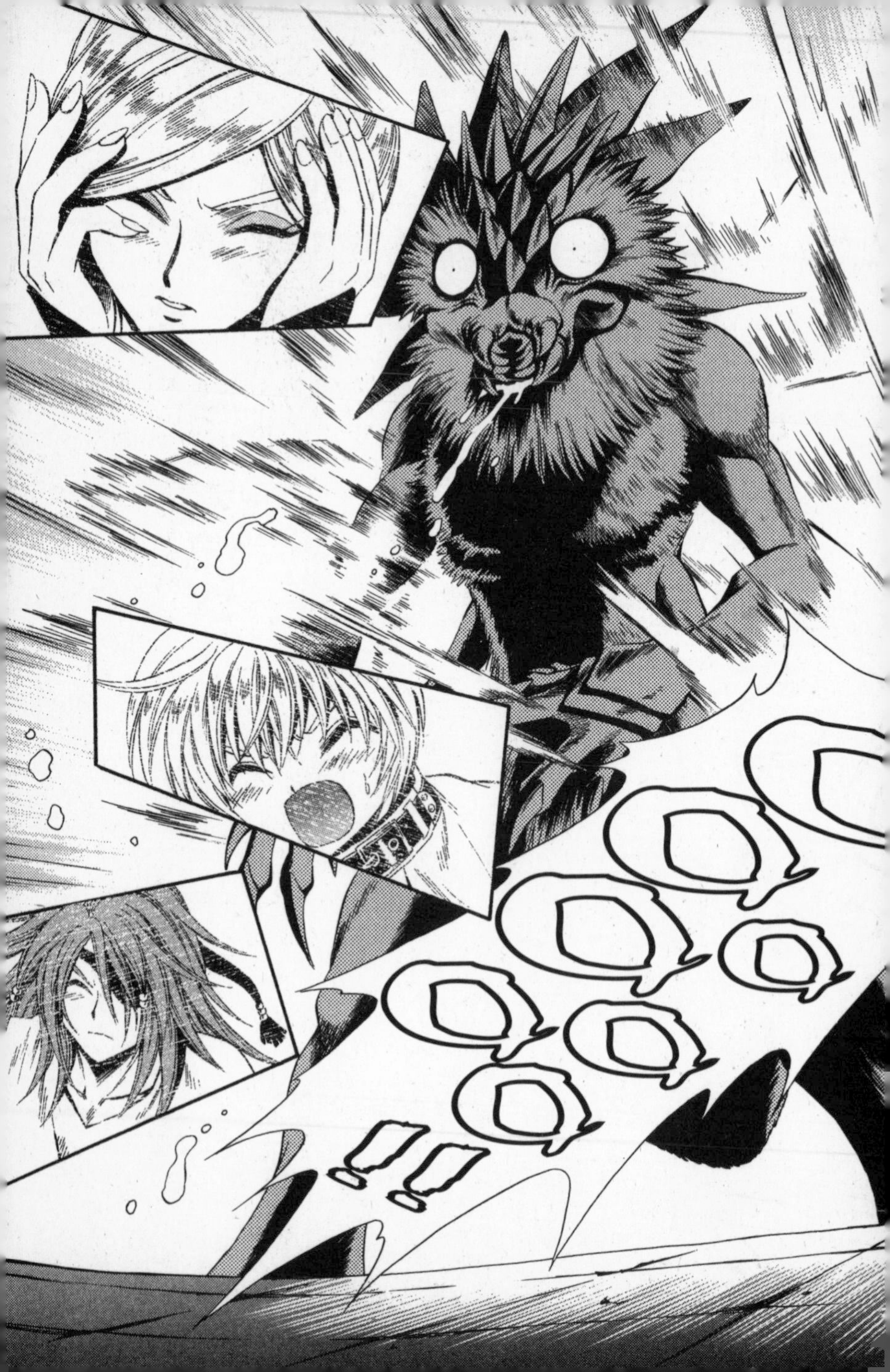
OOOOOOO!!

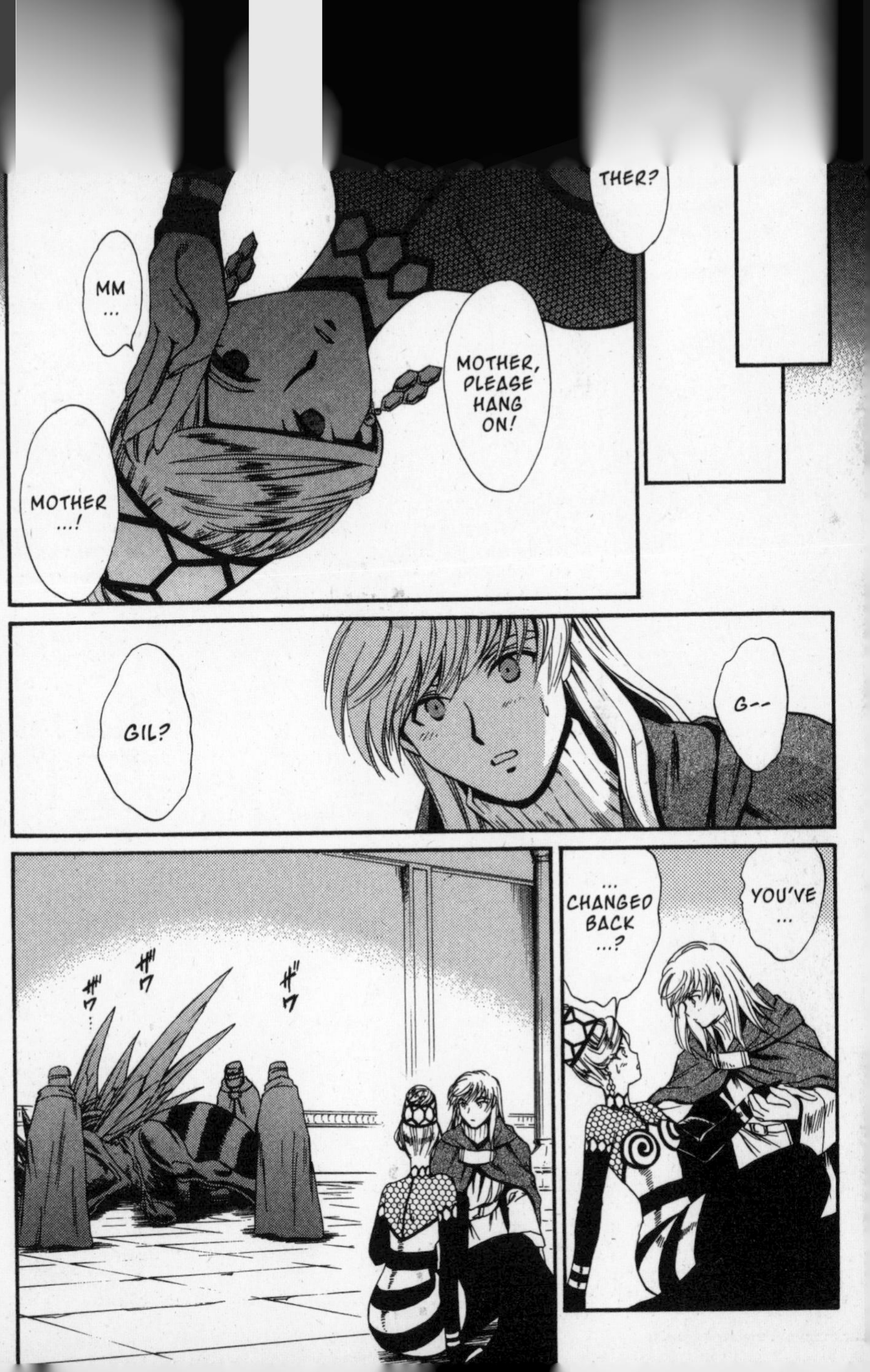
THER?
MOTHER, PLEASE HANG ON!
MM ...
MOTHER ...!
G--
GIL?
YOU'VE ...
... CHANGED BACK ...?
ザワ
ザワ
ザワ ...

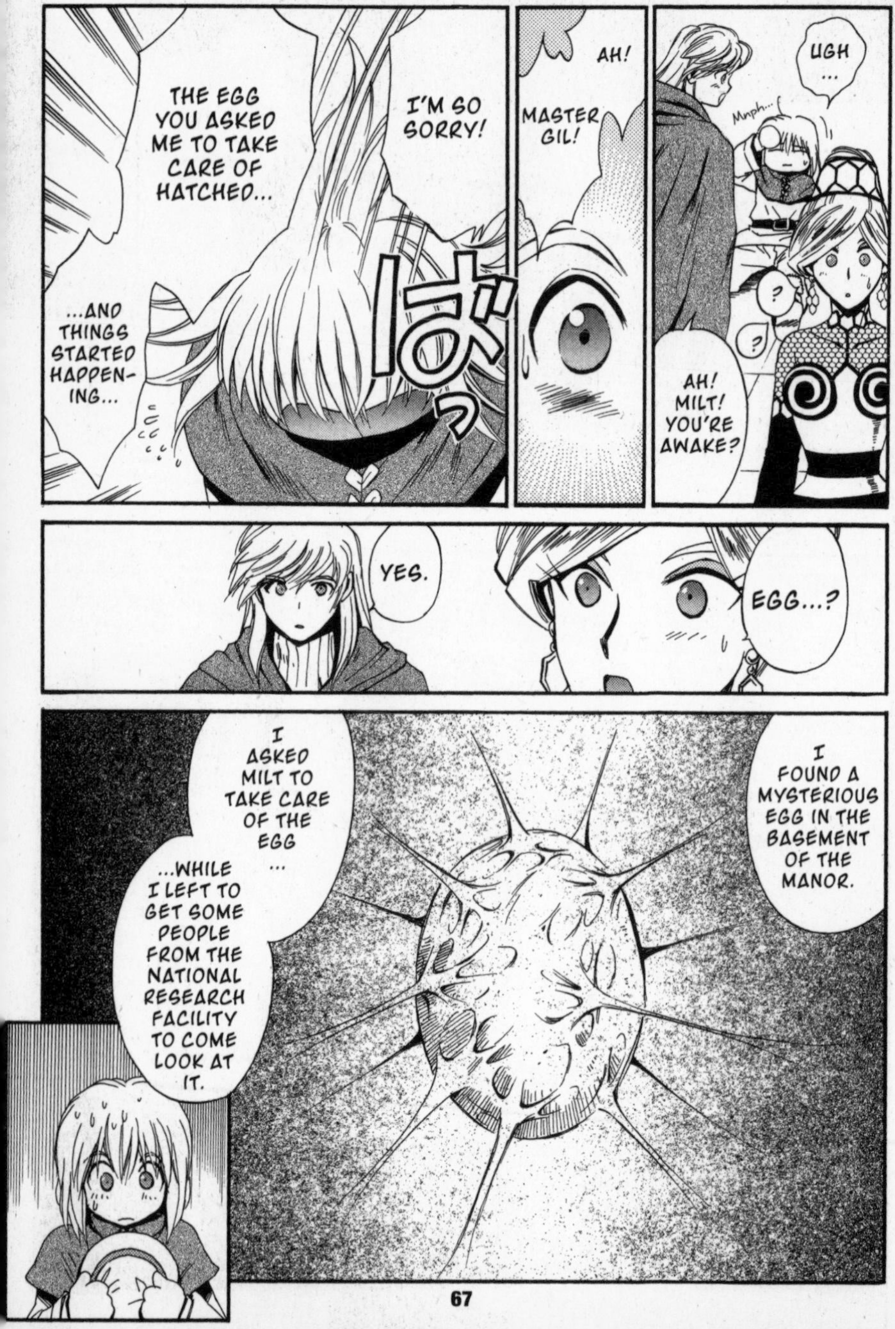
UGH ...
Mnph...
?
?
AH! MILT! YOU'RE AWAKE?
AH!
MASTER GIL!
ばっ
I'M SO SORRY!
THE EGG YOU ASKED ME TO TAKE CARE OF HATCHED...
...AND THINGS STARTED HAPPEN-ING...
EGG...?
YES.
I FOUND A MYSTERIOUS EGG IN THE BASEMENT OF THE MANOR.
I ASKED MILT TO TAKE CARE OF THE EGG ...
...WHILE I LEFT TO GET SOME PEOPLE FROM THE NATIONAL RESEARCH FACILITY TO COME LOOK AT IT.

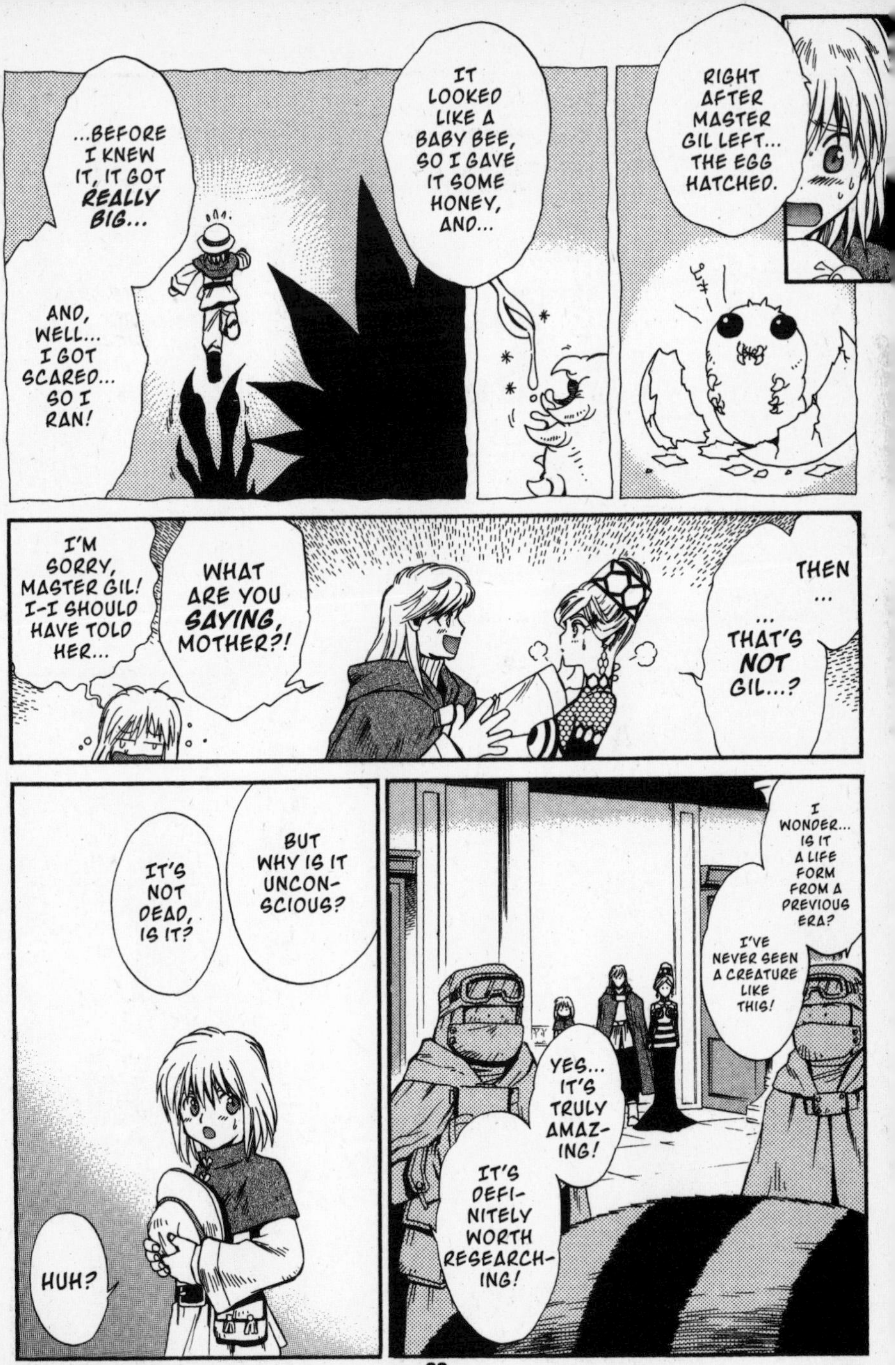
RIGHT AFTER MASTER GIL LEFT... THE EGG HATCHED.
IT LOOKED LIKE A BABY BEE, SO I GAVE IT SOME HONEY, AND...
...BEFORE I KNEW IT, IT GOT REALLY BIG...
AND, WELL... I GOT SCARED... SO I RAN!
THEN ...
... THAT'S NOT GIL...?
WHAT ARE YOU SAYING, MOTHER?!
I'M SORRY, MASTER GIL! I-I SHOULD HAVE TOLD HER...
I WONDER... IS IT A LIFE FORM FROM A PREVIOUS ERA?
I'VE NEVER SEEN A CREATURE LIKE THIS!
YES... IT'S TRULY AMAZ-ING!
IT'S DEFI-NITELY WORTH RESEARCH-ING!
BUT WHY IS IT UNCON-SCIOUS?
IT'S NOT DEAD, IS IT?
HUH?

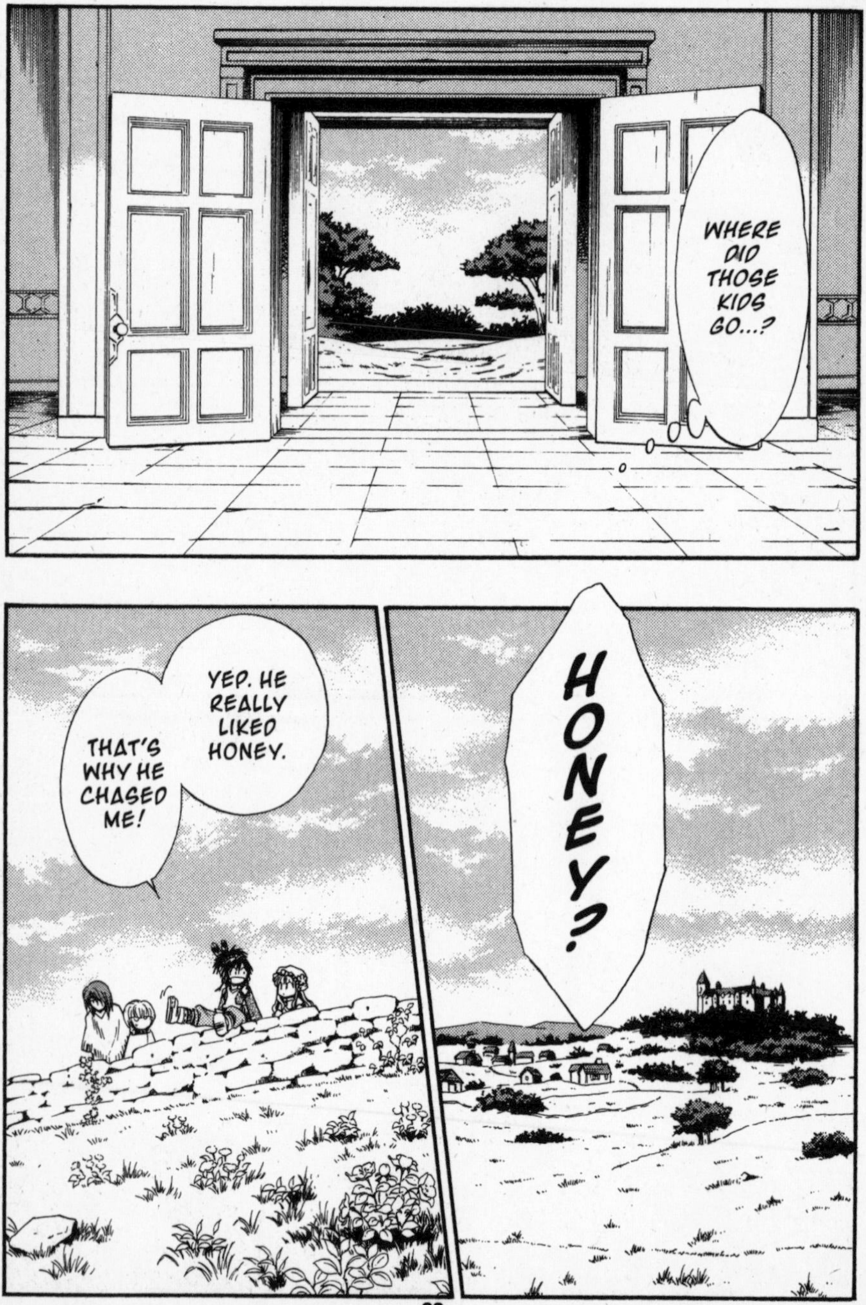
WHERE DID THOSE KIDS GO...?
HONEY?
YEP. HE REALLY LIKED HONEY.
THAT'S WHY HE CHASED ME!

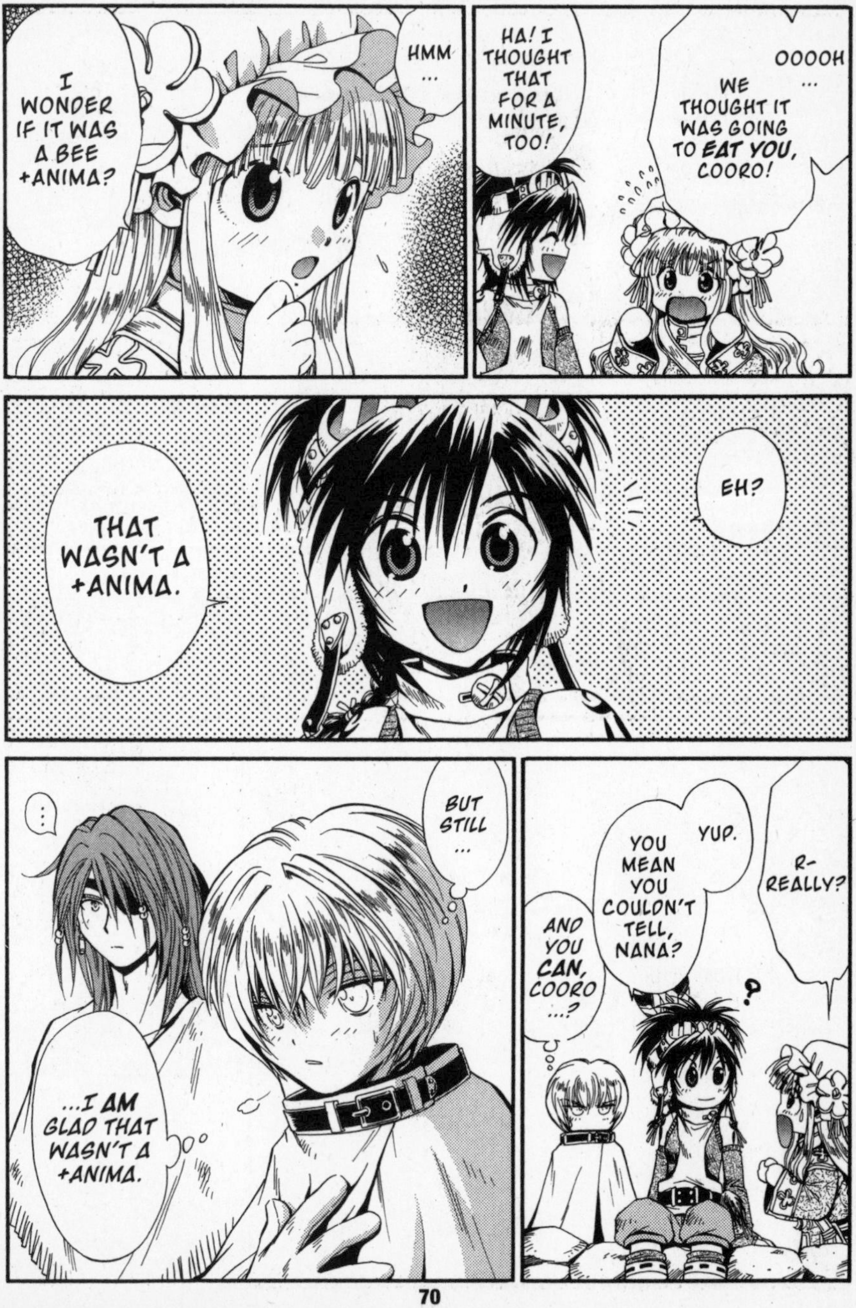
OOOOH ... WE THOUGHT IT WAS GOING TO **EAT YOU**, COORO!
HA! I THOUGHT THAT FOR A MINUTE, TOO!
HMM ...
I WONDER IF IT WAS A BEE +ANIMA?
EH?
THAT WASN'T A +ANIMA.
R-REALLY?
YUP.
YOU MEAN YOU COULDN'T TELL, NANA?
AND YOU **CAN**, COORO ...?
BUT STILL ...
...
...**I AM** GLAD THAT WASN'T A +ANIMA.

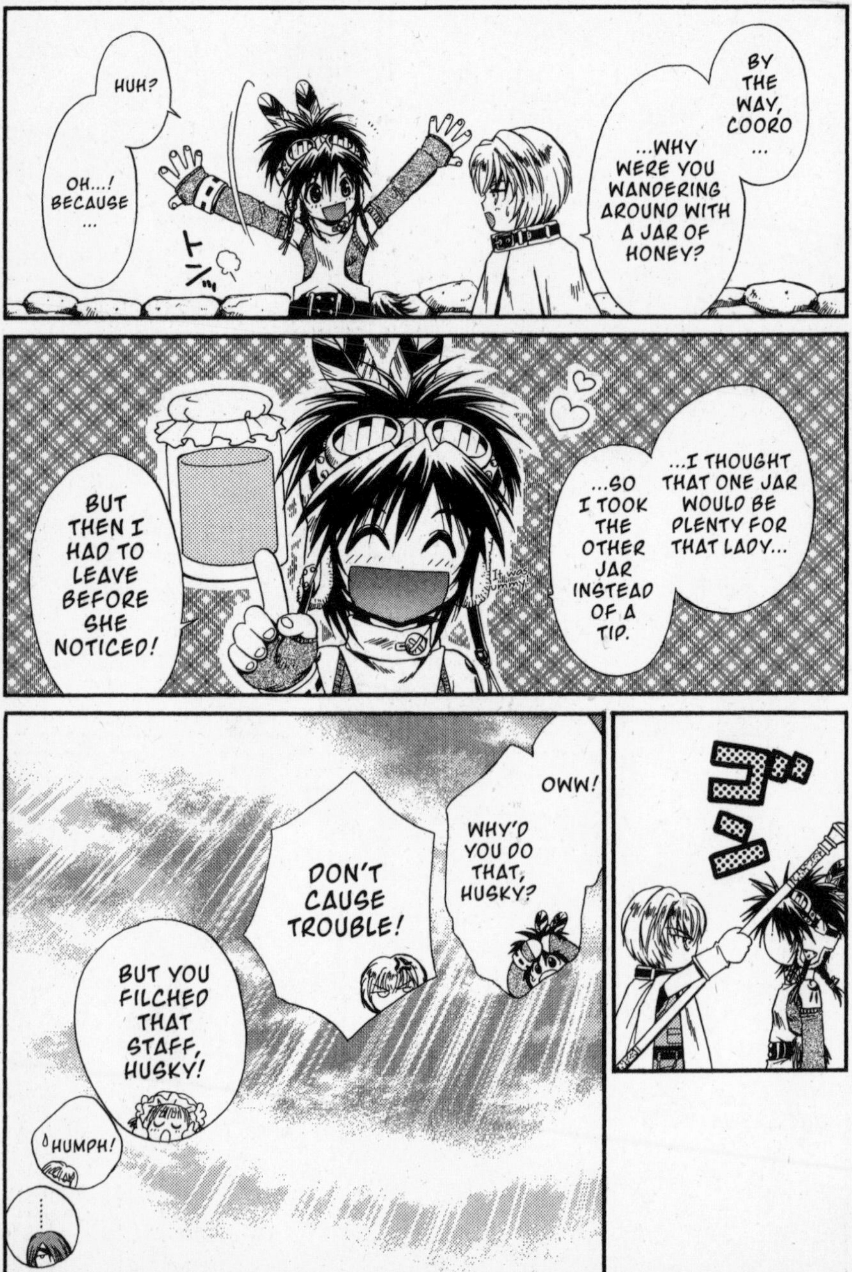

BY THE WAY, COORO ...
...WHY WERE YOU WANDERING AROUND WITH A JAR OF HONEY?
HUH?
OH...! BECAUSE ...
...I THOUGHT THAT ONE JAR WOULD BE PLENTY FOR THAT LADY...
...SO I TOOK THE OTHER JAR INSTEAD OF A TIP.
It was yummy!
BUT THEN I HAD TO LEAVE BEFORE SHE NOTICED!
OWW!
WHY'D YOU DO THAT, HUSKY?
DON'T CAUSE TROUBLE!
BUT YOU FILCHED THAT STAFF, HUSKY!
HUMPH!
...

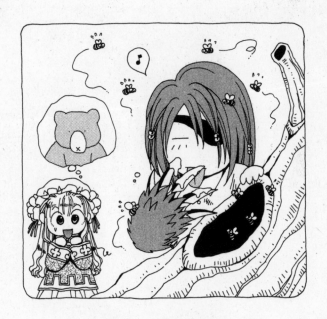

Favorite dish!

Chapter 8
Desert Rose

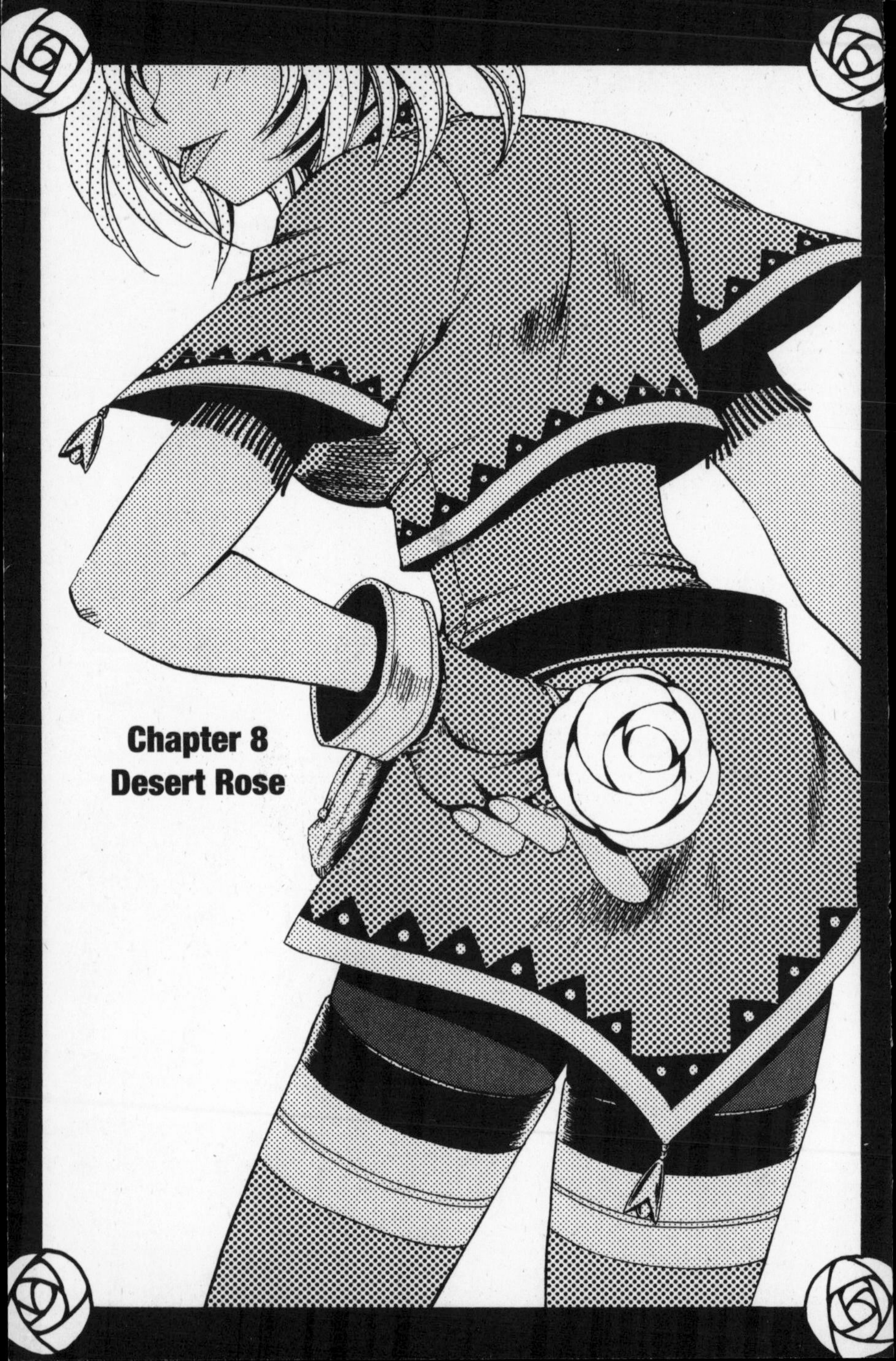

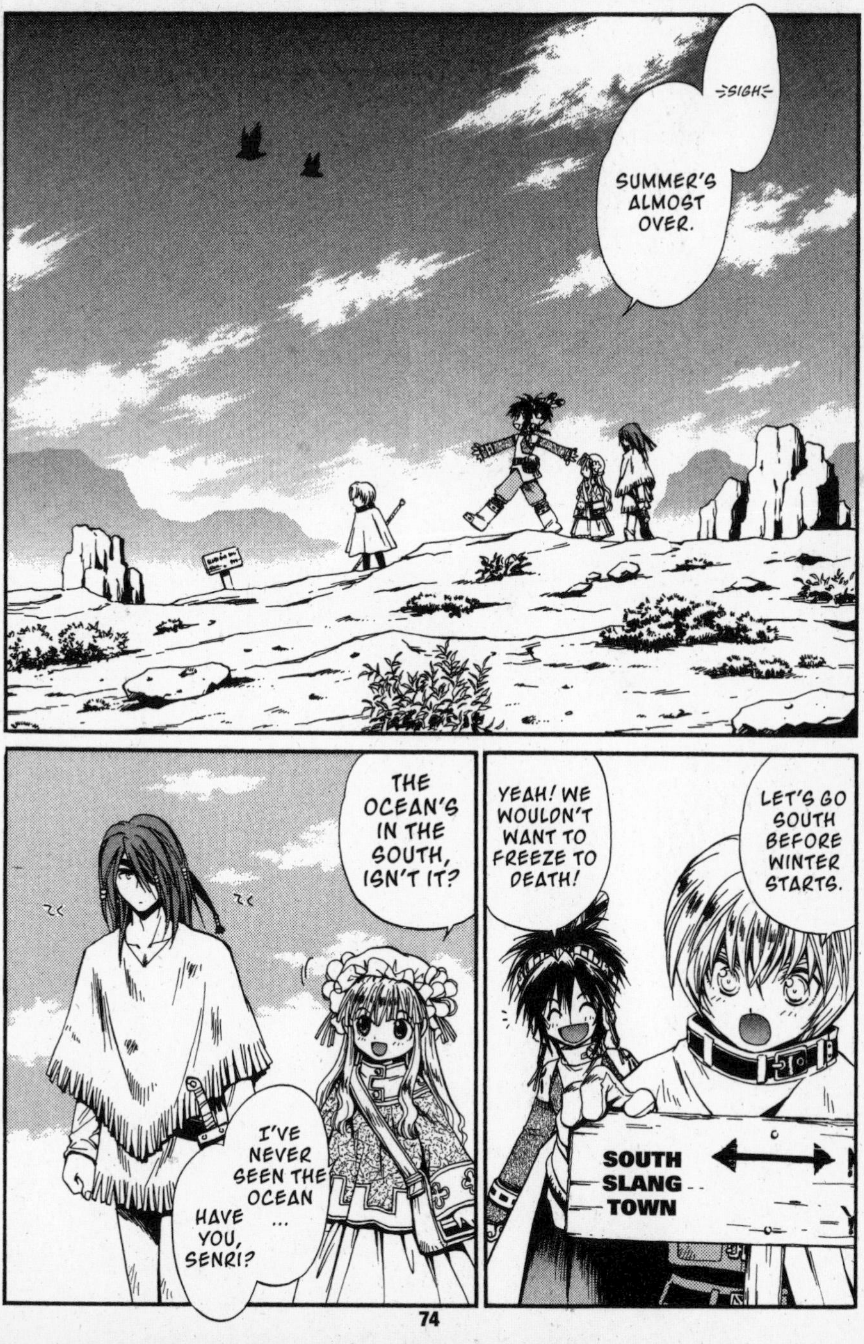

=SIGH=
SUMMER'S ALMOST OVER.
LET'S GO SOUTH BEFORE WINTER STARTS.
YEAH! WE WOULDN'T WANT TO FREEZE TO DEATH!
SOUTH SLANG TOWN
THE OCEAN'S IN THE SOUTH, ISN'T IT?
I'VE NEVER SEEN THE OCEAN ...
HAVE YOU, SENRI?

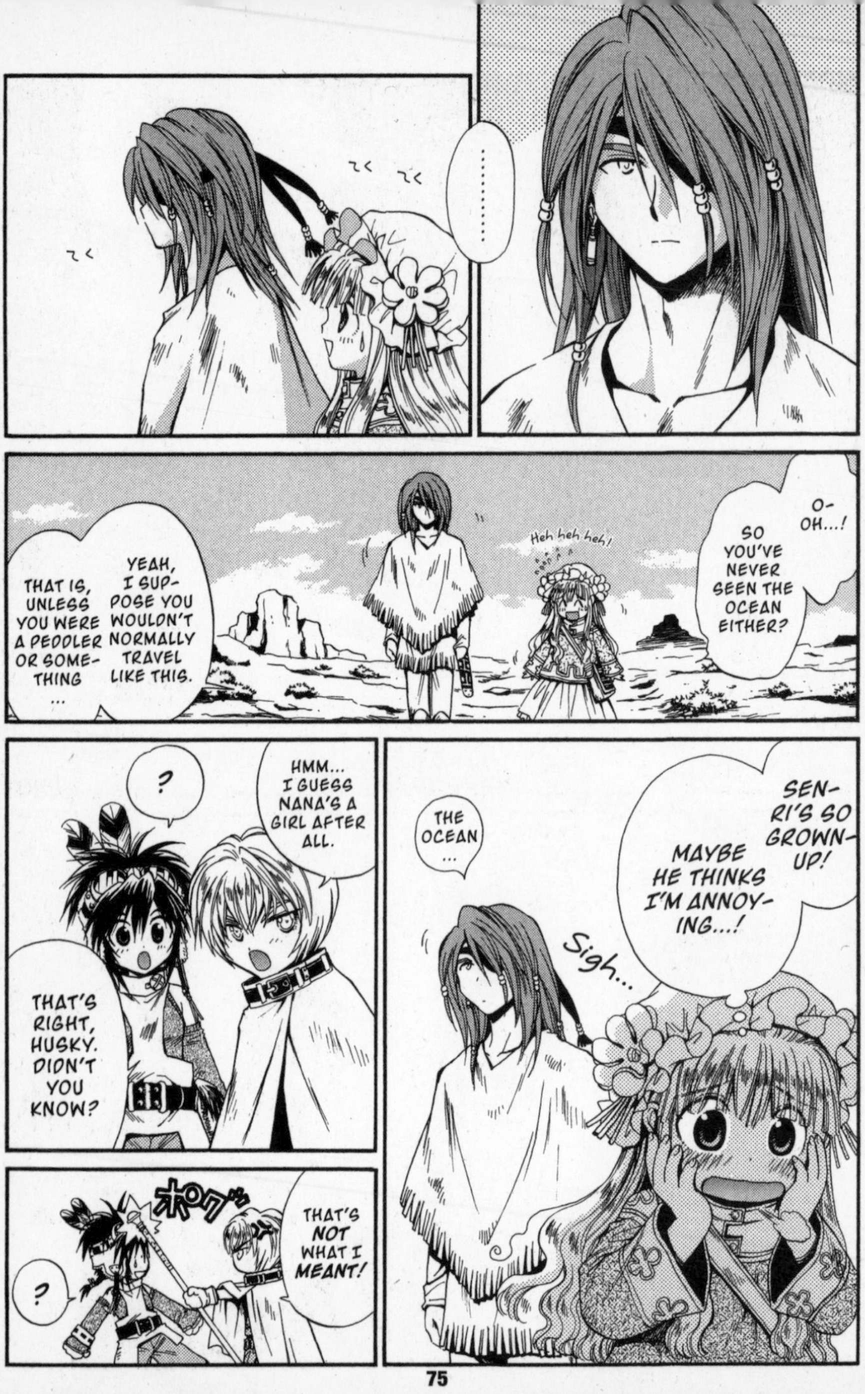

......
てく
てく
てく
O-OH...!
SO YOU'VE NEVER SEEN THE OCEAN EITHER?
Heh heh heh!
YEAH, I SUP-POSE YOU WOULDN'T NORMALLY TRAVEL LIKE THIS.
THAT IS, UNLESS YOU WERE A PEDDLER OR SOME-THING ...
SEN-RI'S SO GROWN-UP!
MAYBE HE THINKS I'M ANNOY-ING...!
Sigh...
THE OCEAN ...
HMM... I GUESS NANA'S A GIRL AFTER ALL.
?
THAT'S RIGHT, HUSKY. DIDN'T YOU KNOW?
THAT'S *NOT* WHAT I *MEANT*!
?

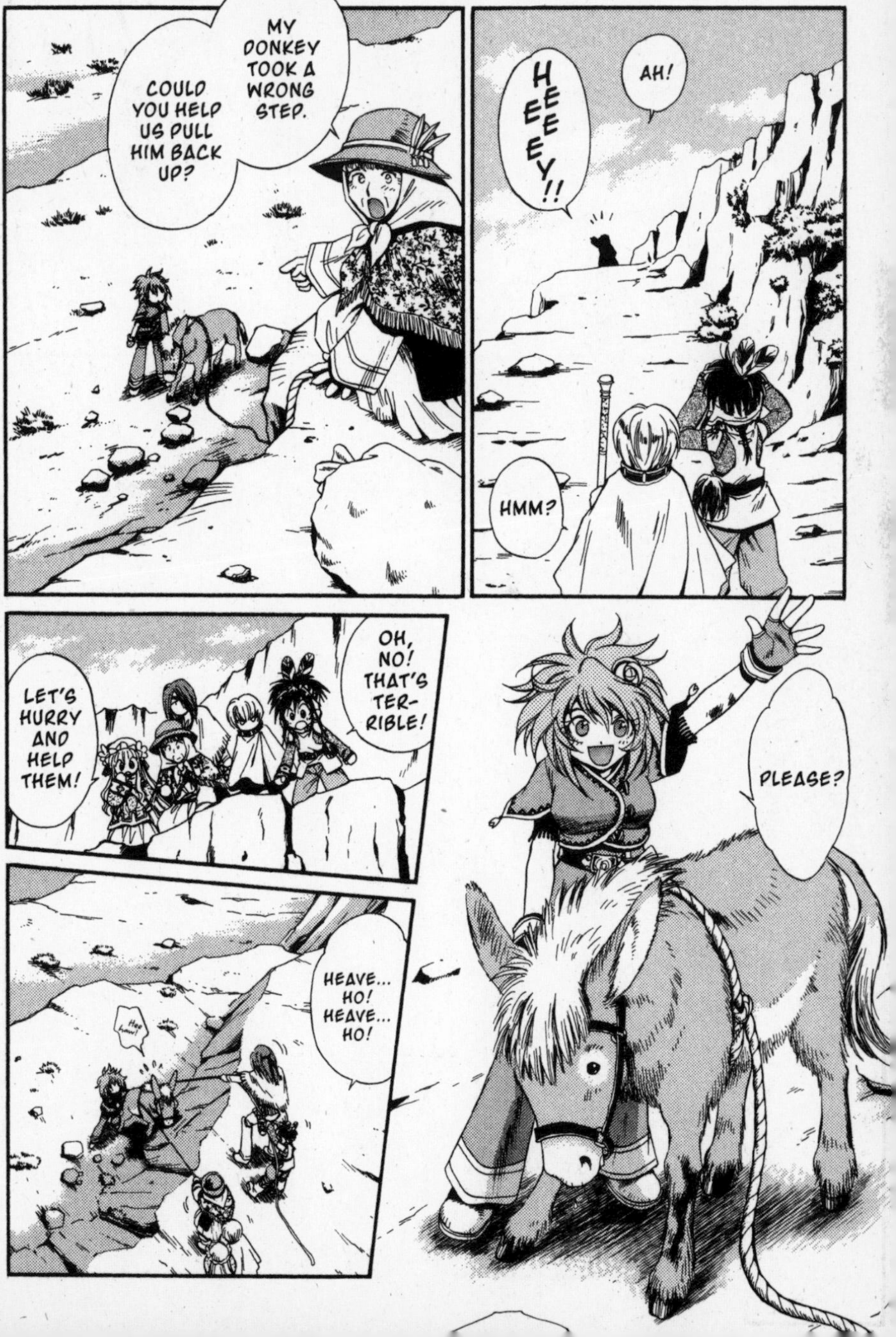
AH!
HEEEEY!!
HMM?
MY DONKEY TOOK A WRONG STEP.
COULD YOU HELP US PULL HIM BACK UP?
PLEASE?
OH, NO! THAT'S TER-RIBLE!
LET'S HURRY AND HELP THEM!
HEAVE... HO! HEAVE... HO!
Hee haw!

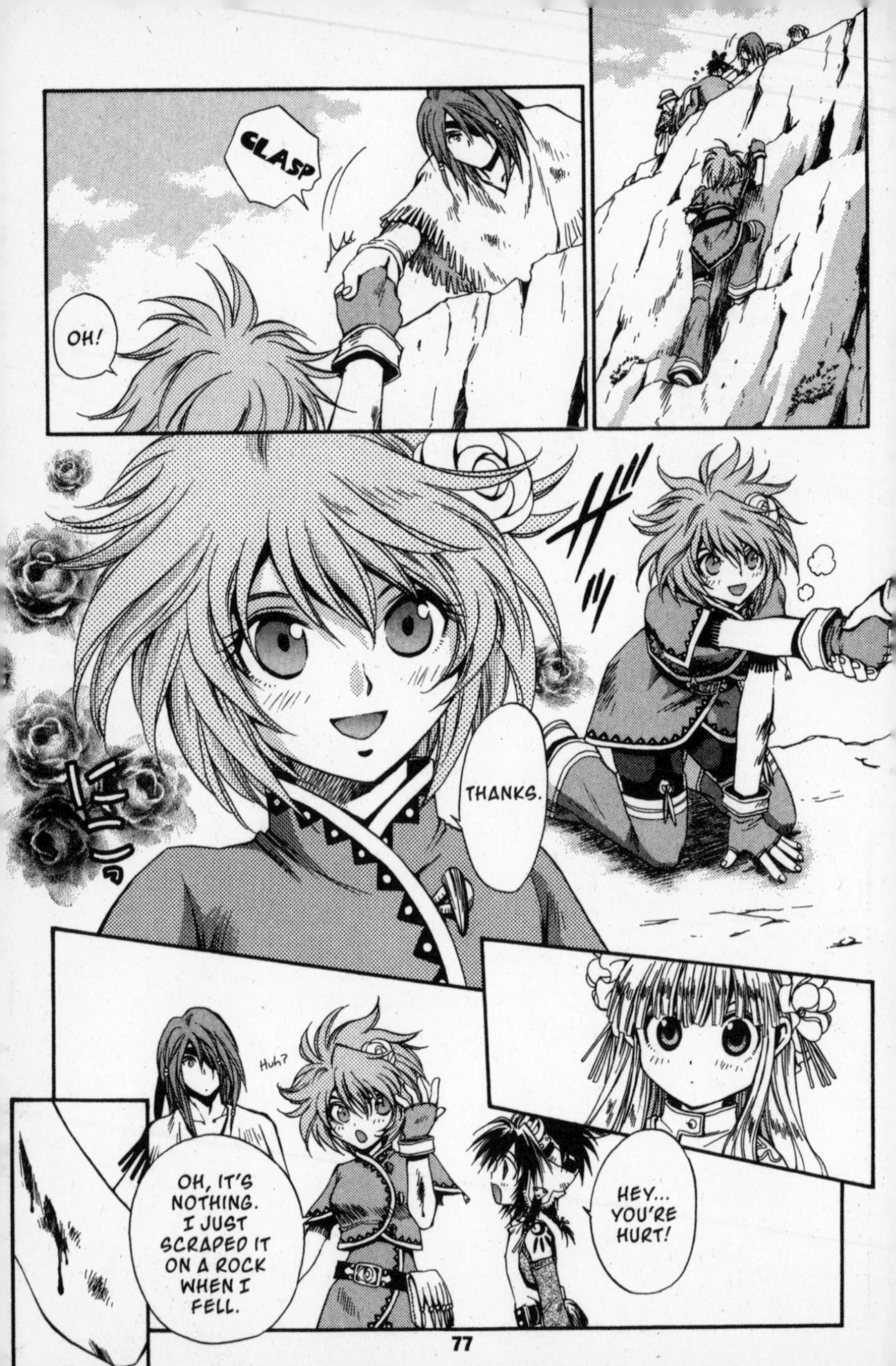
CLASP
OH!
THANKS.
HEY... YOU'RE HURT!
Huh?
OH, IT'S NOTHING. I JUST SCRAPED IT ON A ROCK WHEN I FELL.

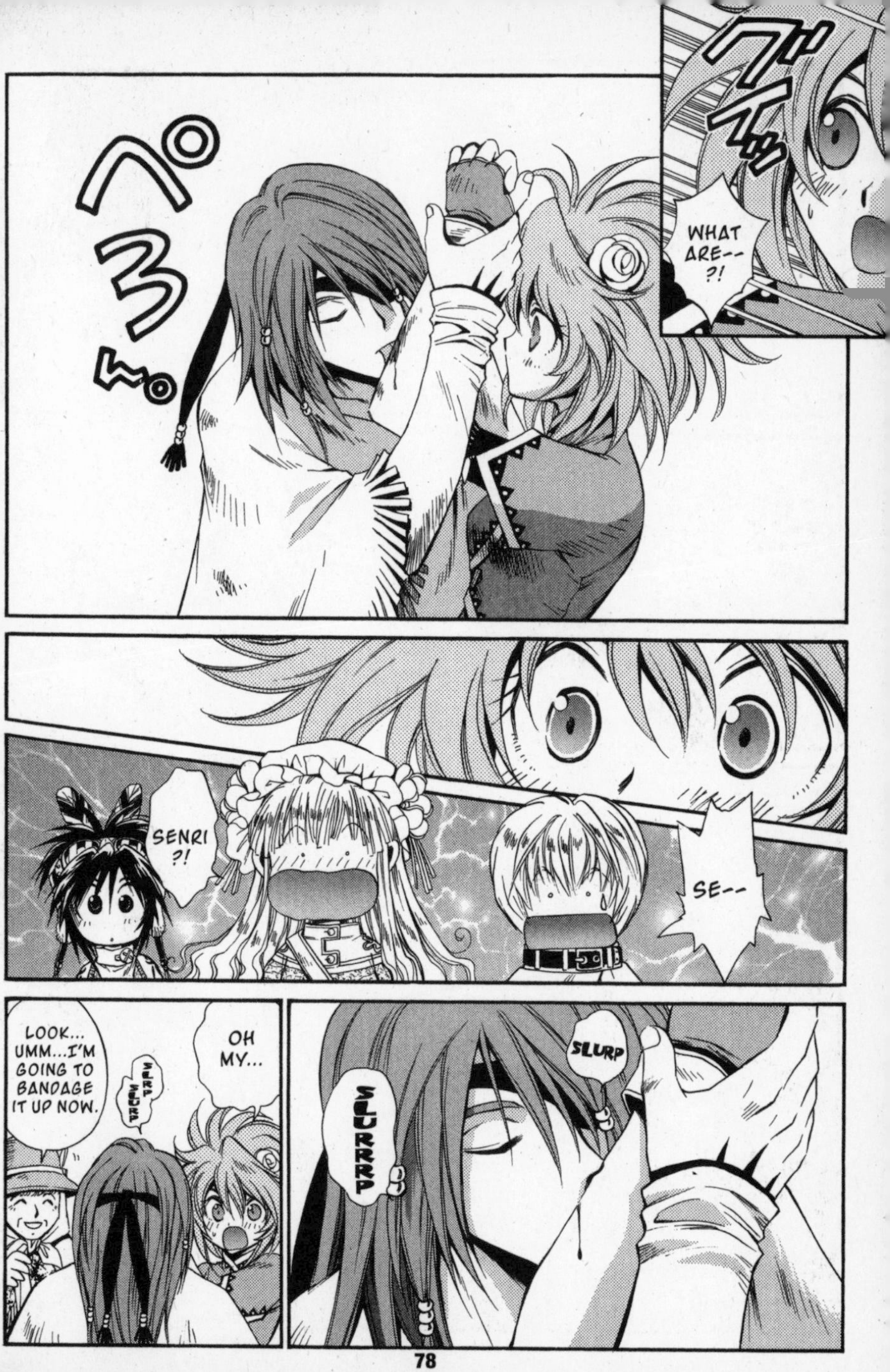

グイッ
WHAT ARE--?!
ぺろ
SE--
SENRI?!
SLURP
SLURRRP
OH MY...
SLURP SLURP
LOOK... UMM...I'M GOING TO BANDAGE IT UP NOW.

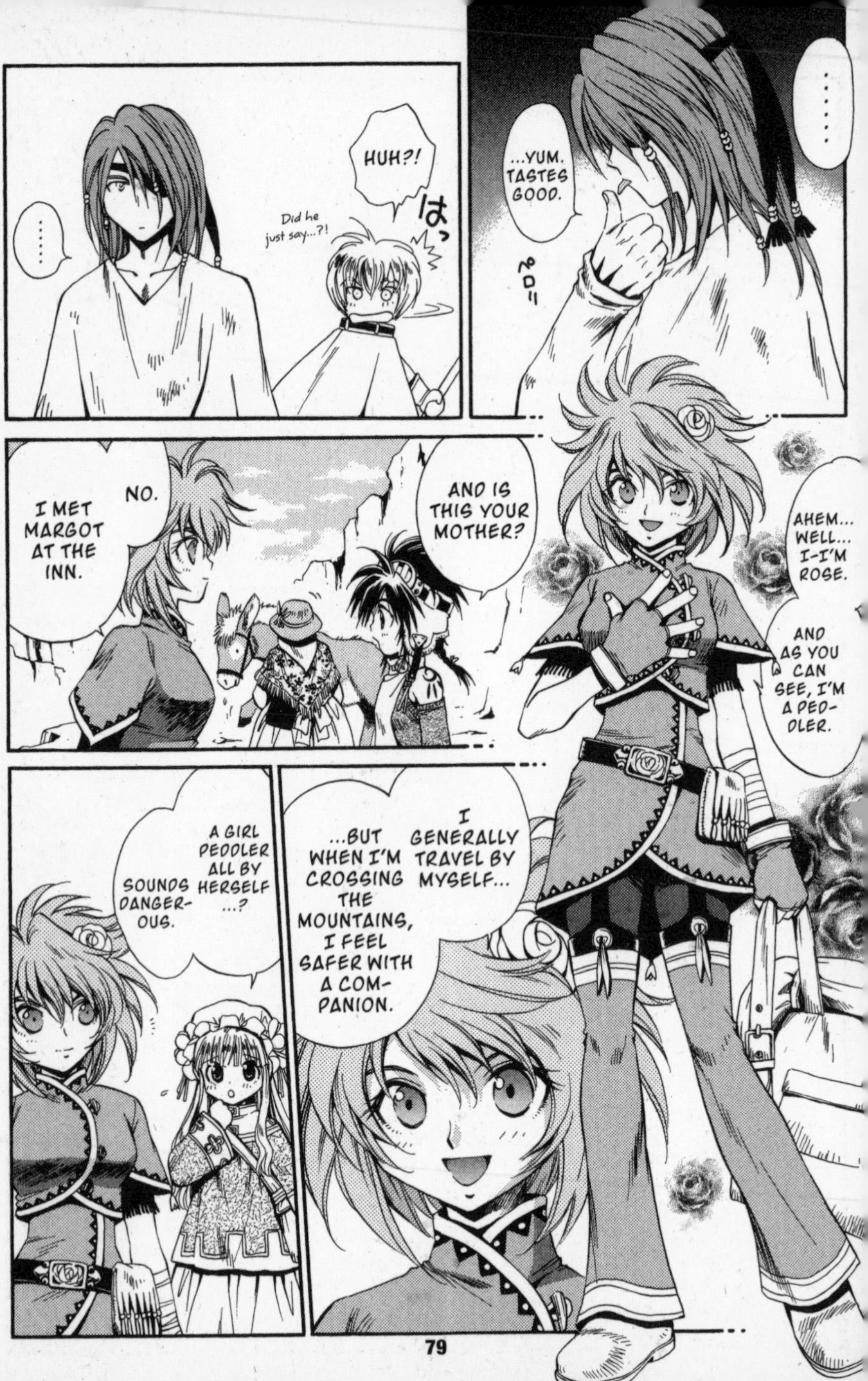
......
...YUM. TASTES GOOD.
ペロー
HUH?!
Did he just say...?!
はっ
......
AHEM... WELL... I-I'M ROSE.
AND AS YOU CAN SEE, I'M A PEDDLER.
AND IS THIS YOUR MOTHER?
NO.
I MET MARGOT AT THE INN.
I GENERALLY TRAVEL BY MYSELF...
...BUT WHEN I'M CROSSING THE MOUNTAINS, I FEEL SAFER WITH A COMPANION.
A GIRL PEDDLER ALL BY HERSELF ...?
SOUNDS DANGEROUS.

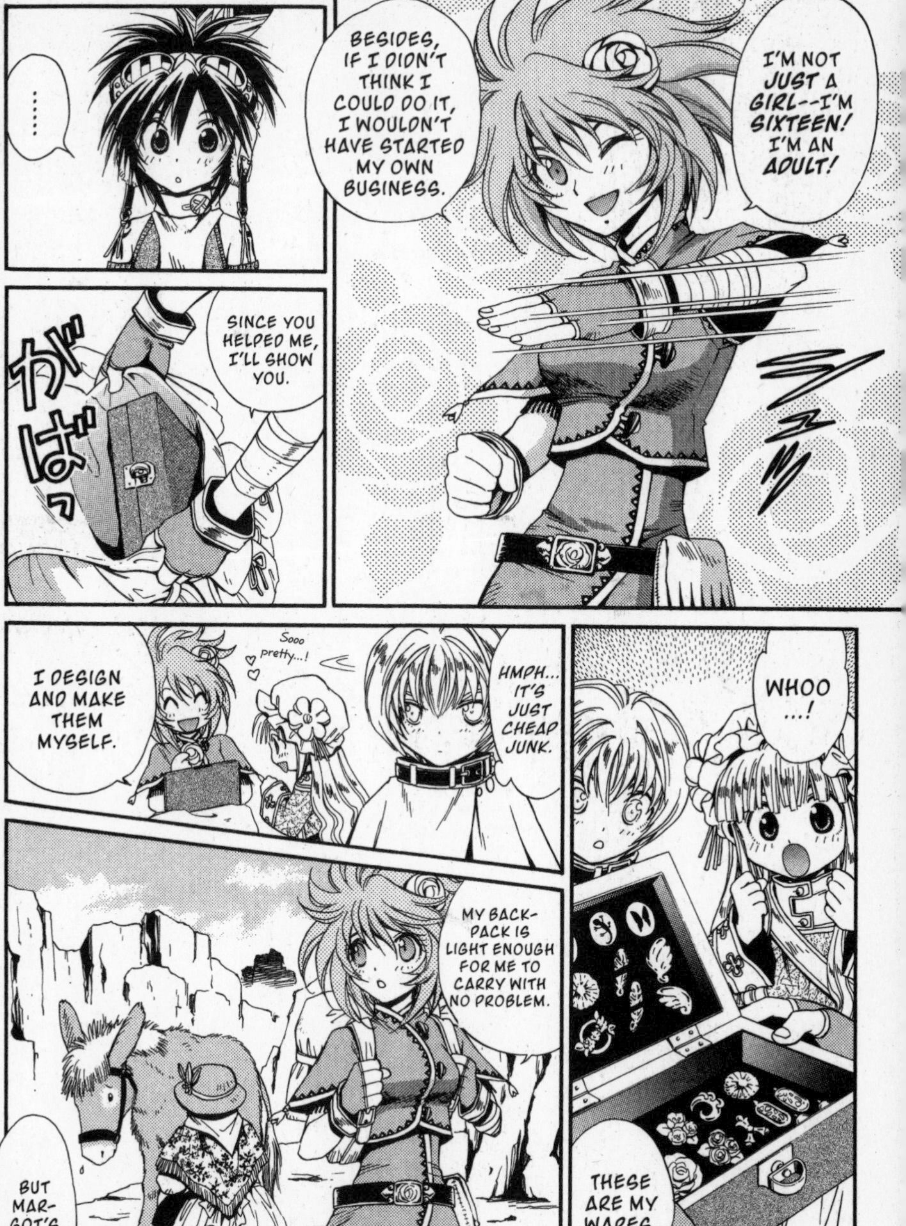
I'M NOT JUST A GIRL--I'M SIXTEEN! I'M AN ADULT!
BESIDES, IF I DIDN'T THINK I COULD DO IT, I WOULDN'T HAVE STARTED MY OWN BUSINESS.
......
SINCE YOU HELPED ME, I'LL SHOW YOU.
わ゛ばっ
WHOO ...!
THESE ARE MY WARES.
HMPH... IT'S JUST CHEAP JUNK.
Sooo pretty...!
I DESIGN AND MAKE THEM MYSELF.
MY BACK-PACK IS LIGHT ENOUGH FOR ME TO CARRY WITH NO PROBLEM.
BUT MAR-GOT'S BAGS...

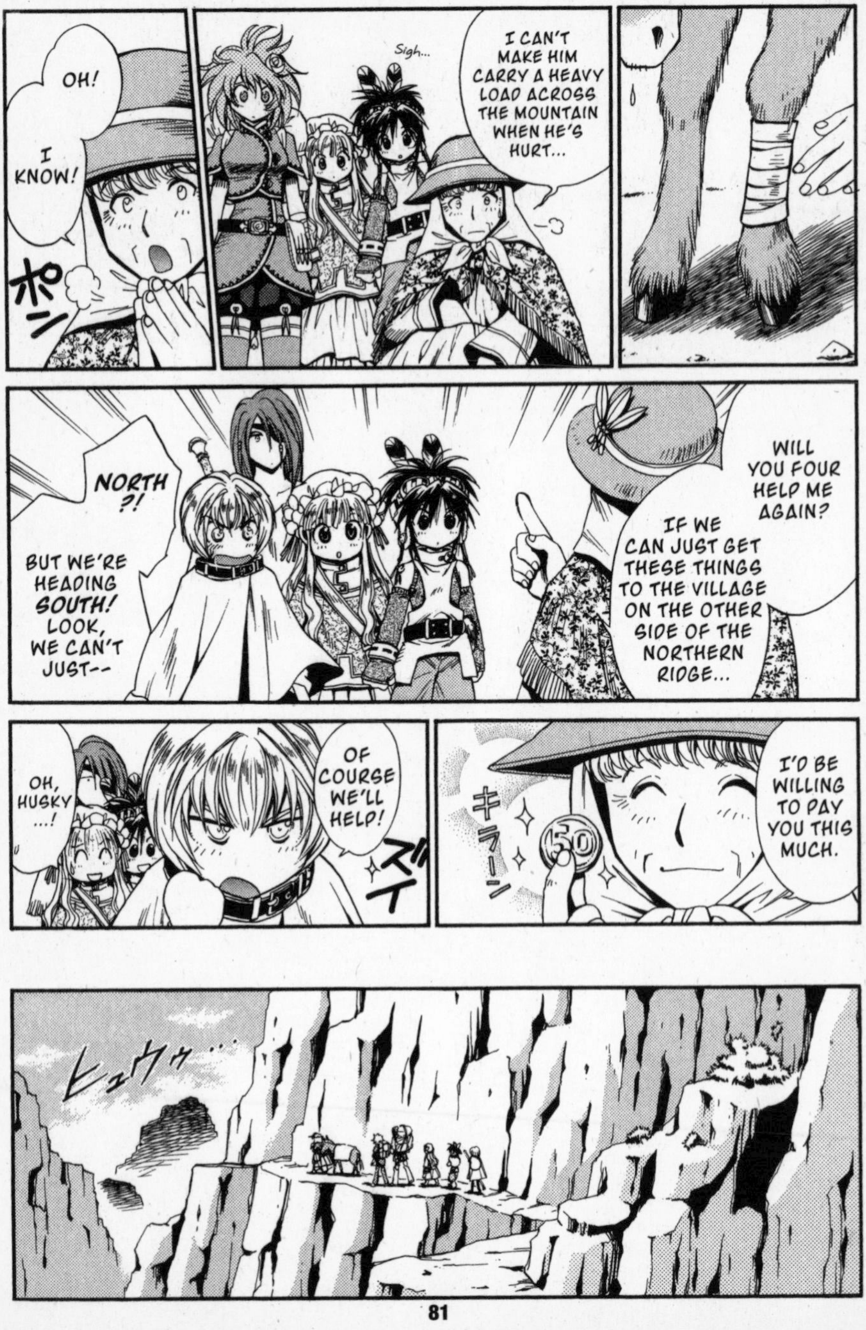
I CAN'T MAKE HIM CARRY A HEAVY LOAD ACROSS THE MOUNTAIN WHEN HE'S HURT...
Sigh...
OH!
I KNOW!
ポン
WILL YOU FOUR HELP ME AGAIN?
IF WE CAN JUST GET THESE THINGS TO THE VILLAGE ON THE OTHER SIDE OF THE NORTHERN RIDGE...
NORTH?!
BUT WE'RE HEADING SOUTH! LOOK, WE CAN'T JUST--
I'D BE WILLING TO PAY YOU THIS MUCH.
キラーン
50
OF COURSE WE'LL HELP!
ズイ
OH, HUSKY ...!
ヒュウゥ・・・

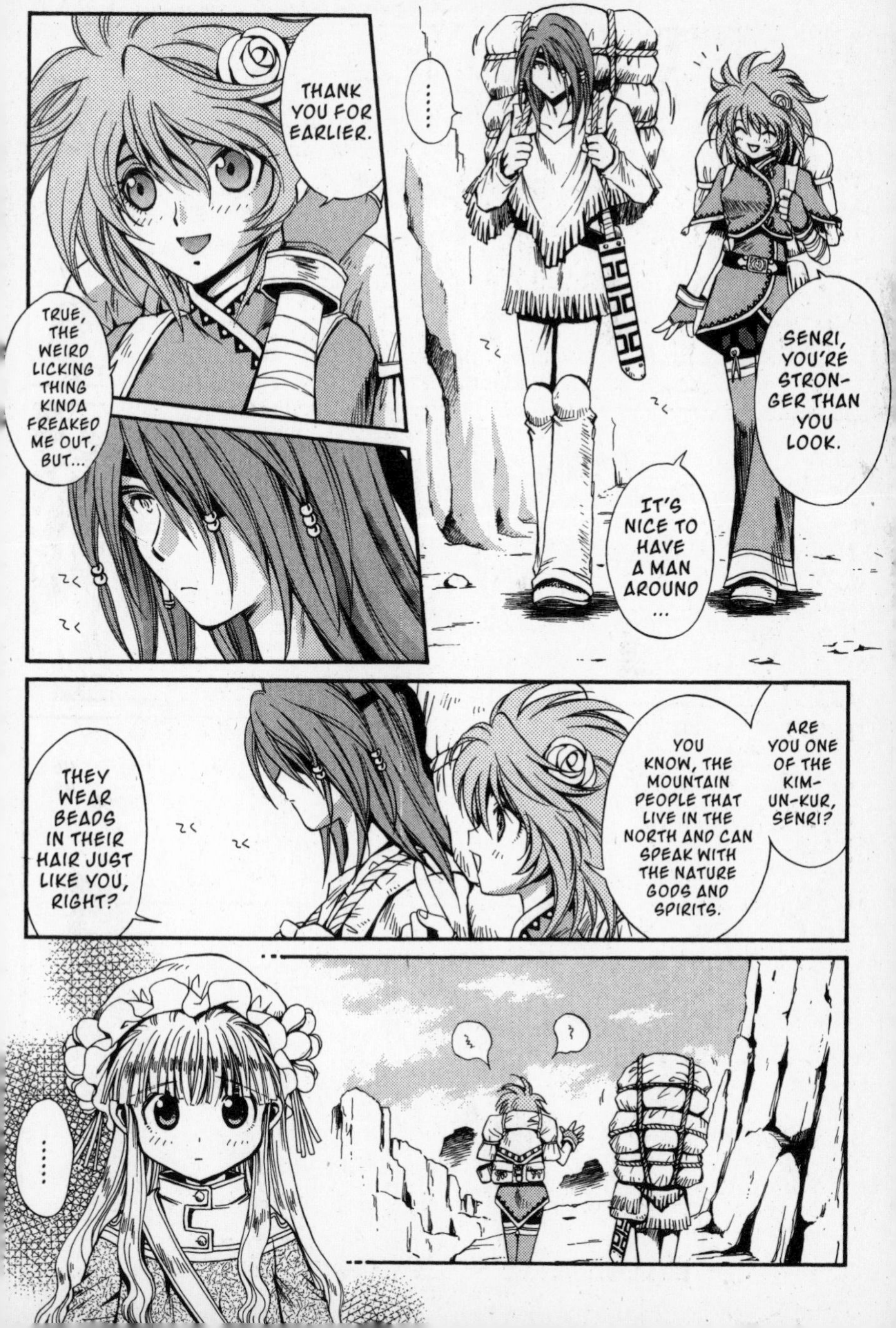
......
SENRI, YOU'RE STRONGER THAN YOU LOOK.
IT'S NICE TO HAVE A MAN AROUND...
THANK YOU FOR EARLIER.
TRUE, THE WEIRD LICKING THING KINDA FREAKED ME OUT, BUT...
ARE YOU ONE OF THE KIM-UN-KUR, SENRI?
YOU KNOW, THE MOUNTAIN PEOPLE THAT LIVE IN THE NORTH AND CAN SPEAK WITH THE NATURE GODS AND SPIRITS.
THEY WEAR BEADS IN THEIR HAIR JUST LIKE YOU, RIGHT?
?
?
......

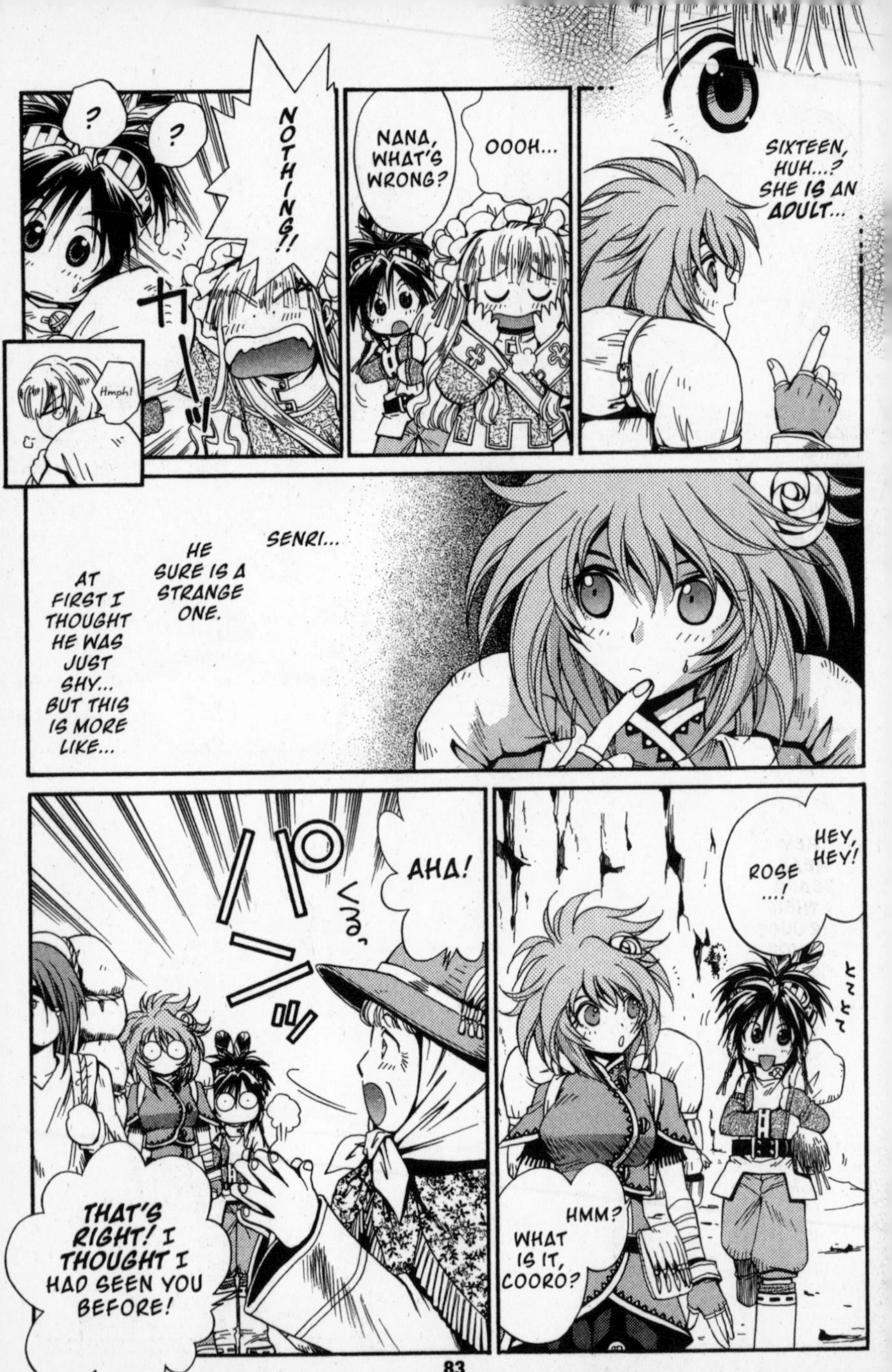
SIXTEEN, HUH...? SHE IS AN ADULT...
OOOH...
NANA, WHAT'S WRONG?
NOTHING!!
?
?
Hmph!
SENRI...
HE SURE IS A STRANGE ONE.
AT FIRST I THOUGHT HE WAS JUST SHY... BUT THIS IS MORE LIKE...
HEY, HEY!
ROSE ...!
HMM? WHAT IS IT, COORO?
AHA!
THAT'S RIGHT! I THOUGHT I HAD SEEN YOU BEFORE!

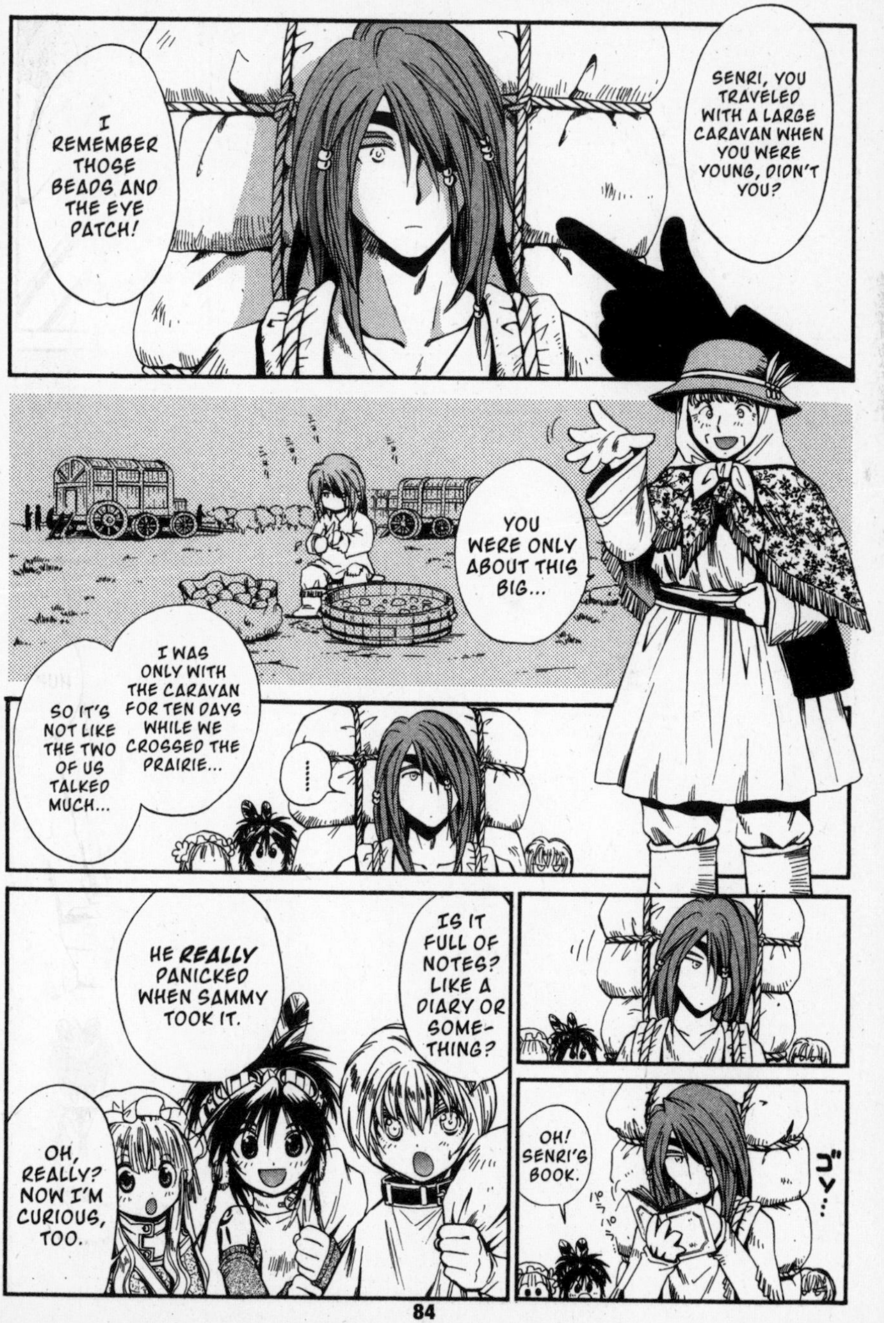
SENRI, YOU TRAVELED WITH A LARGE CARAVAN WHEN YOU WERE YOUNG, DIDN'T YOU?
I REMEMBER THOSE BEADS AND THE EYE PATCH!
YOU WERE ONLY ABOUT THIS BIG...
......
I WAS ONLY WITH THE CARAVAN FOR TEN DAYS WHILE WE CROSSED THE PRAIRIE...
SO IT'S NOT LIKE THE TWO OF US TALKED MUCH...
ゴソ…
OH! SENRI'S BOOK.
IS IT FULL OF NOTES? LIKE A DIARY OR SOME-THING?
HE *REALLY* PANICKED WHEN SAMMY TOOK IT.
OH, REALLY? NOW I'M CURIOUS, TOO.

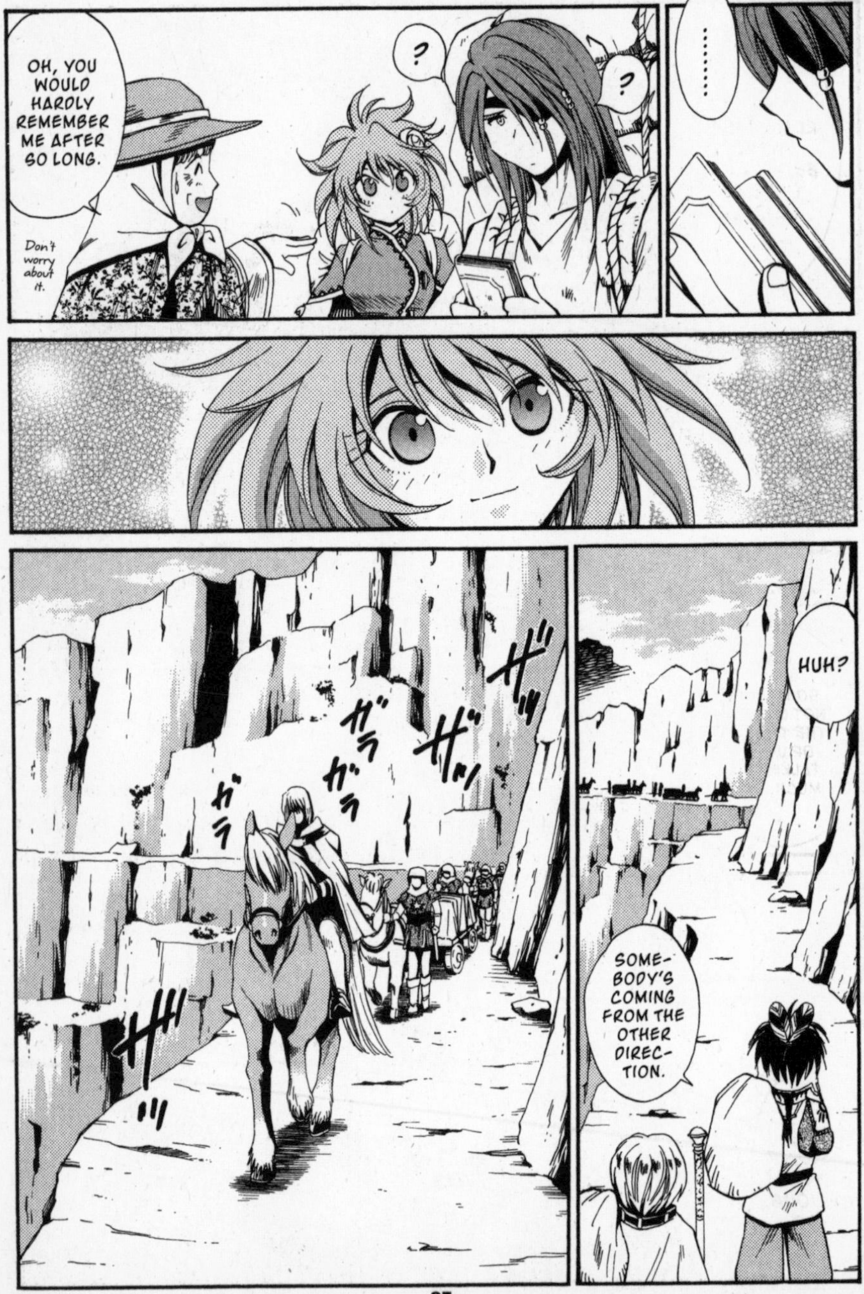

......
?
?
OH, YOU WOULD HARDLY REMEMBER ME AFTER SO LONG.
Don't worry about it.
HUH?
SOME-BODY'S COMING FROM THE OTHER DIREC-TION.
ザッ
ガラ
ガラ
ガラ
ザッ
ザッ

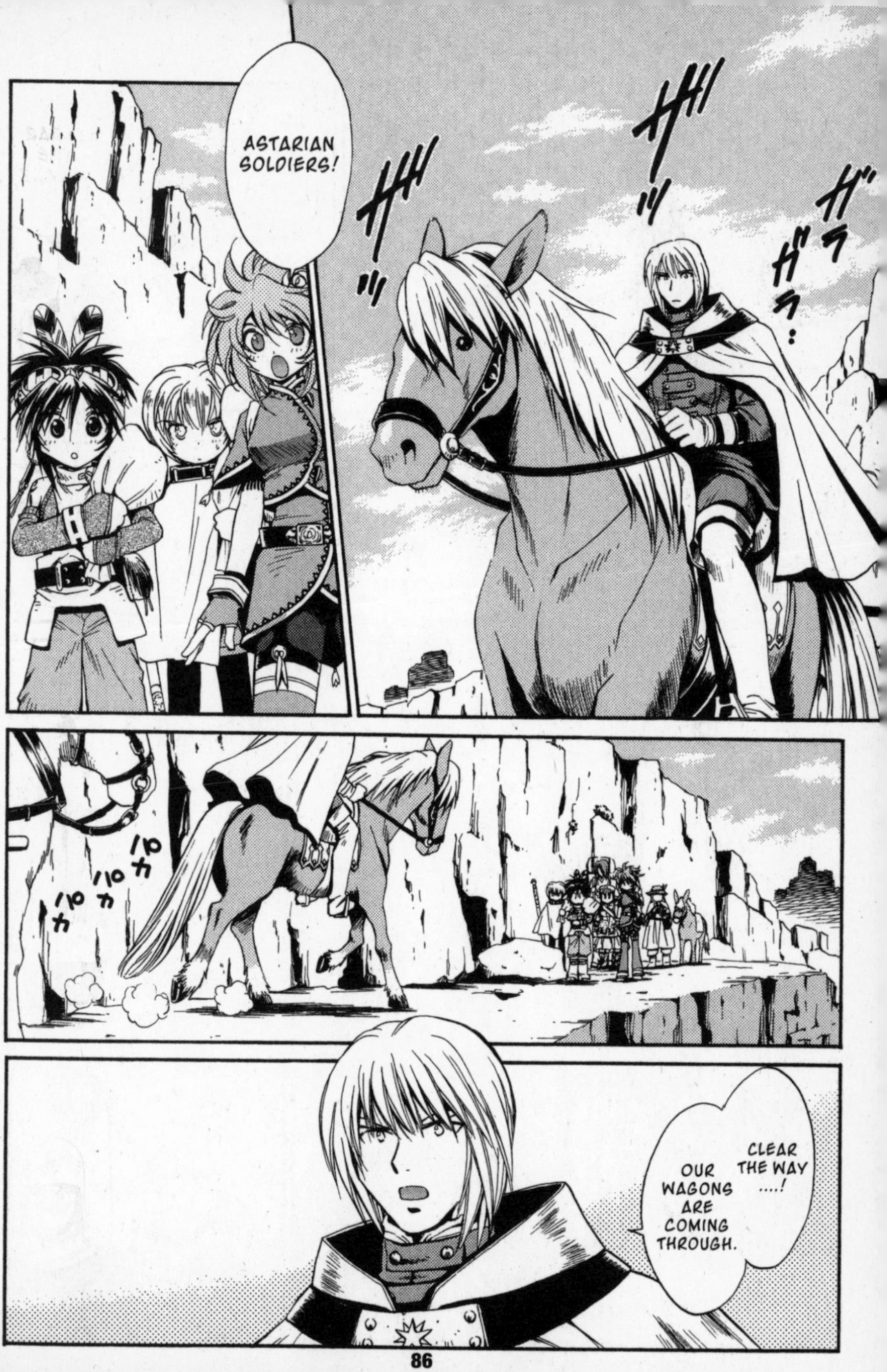
ガラガラ
ASTARIAN SOLDIERS!
パカパカパカ
CLEAR THE WAY ....!
OUR WAGONS ARE COMING THROUGH.

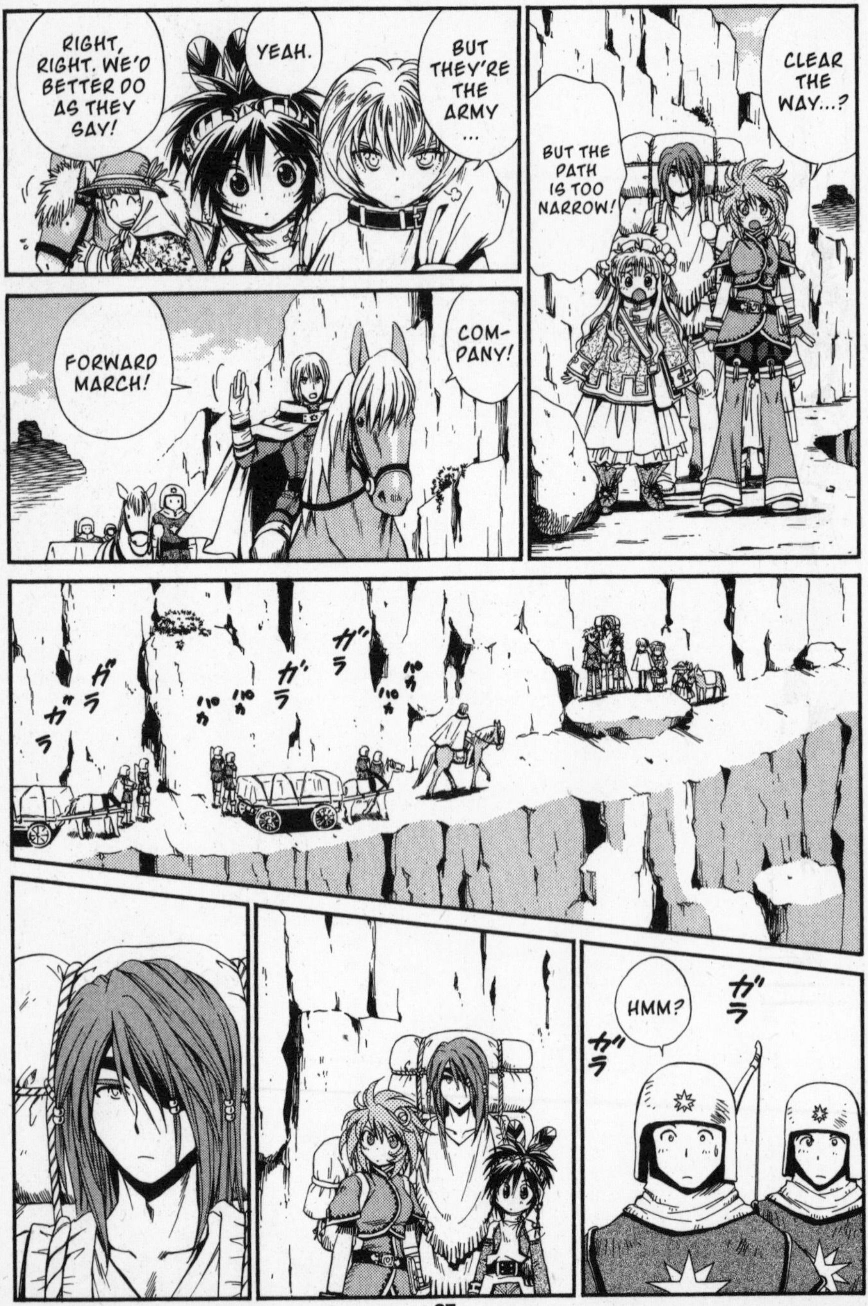
CLEAR THE WAY...?
BUT THE PATH IS TOO NARROW!
BUT THEY'RE THE ARMY ...
YEAH.
RIGHT, RIGHT. WE'D BETTER DO AS THEY SAY!
COM-PANY!
FORWARD MARCH!
ガラ
パカ パカ
ガラ
パカ パカ
ガラ
ガラ
HMM?
ガラ
ガラ

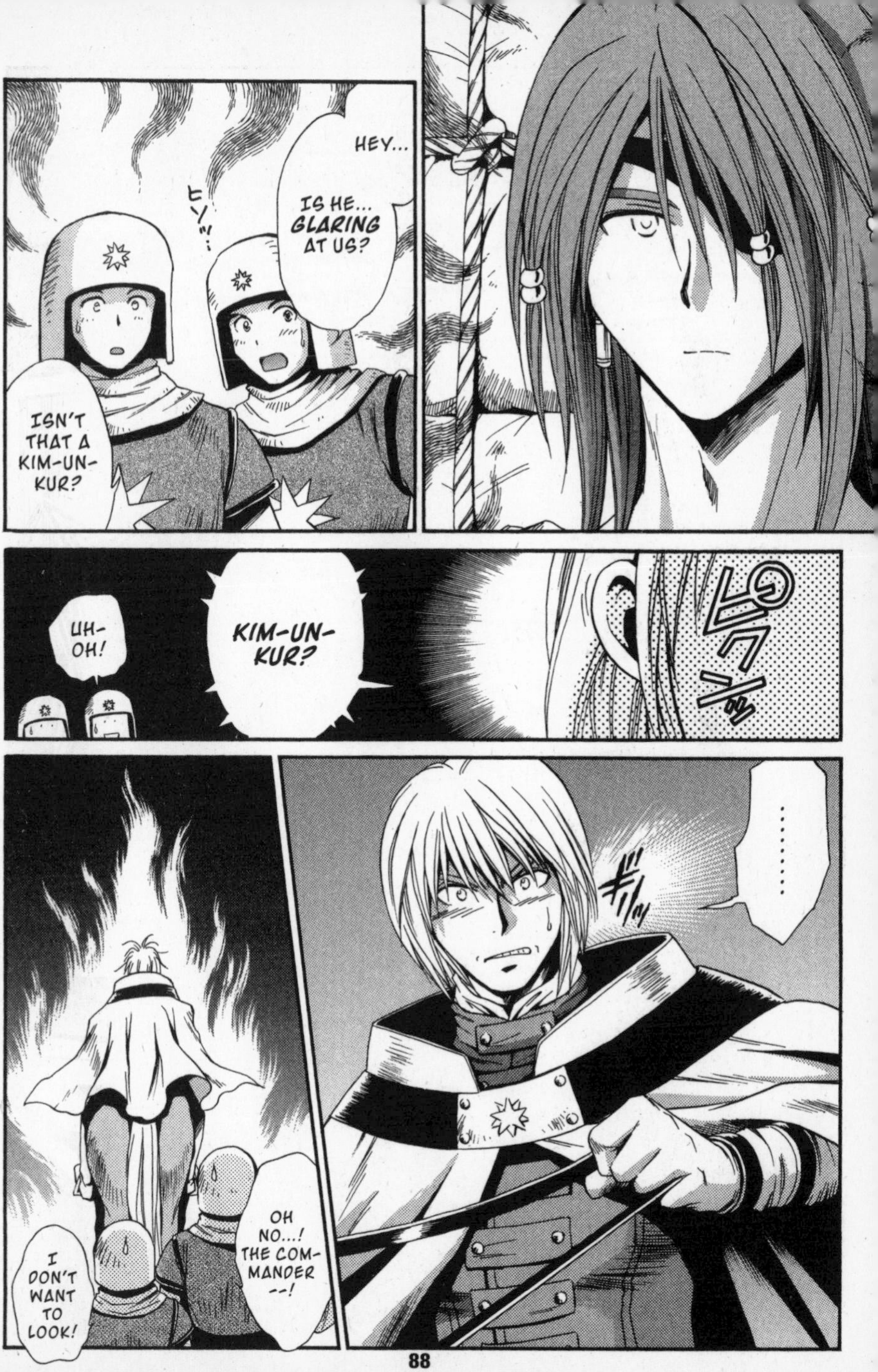
HEY...
IS HE... GLARING AT US?
ISN'T THAT A KIM-UN-KUR?
KIM-UN-KUR?
UH-OH!
......
OH NO...! THE COMMANDER --!
I DON'T WANT TO LOOK!

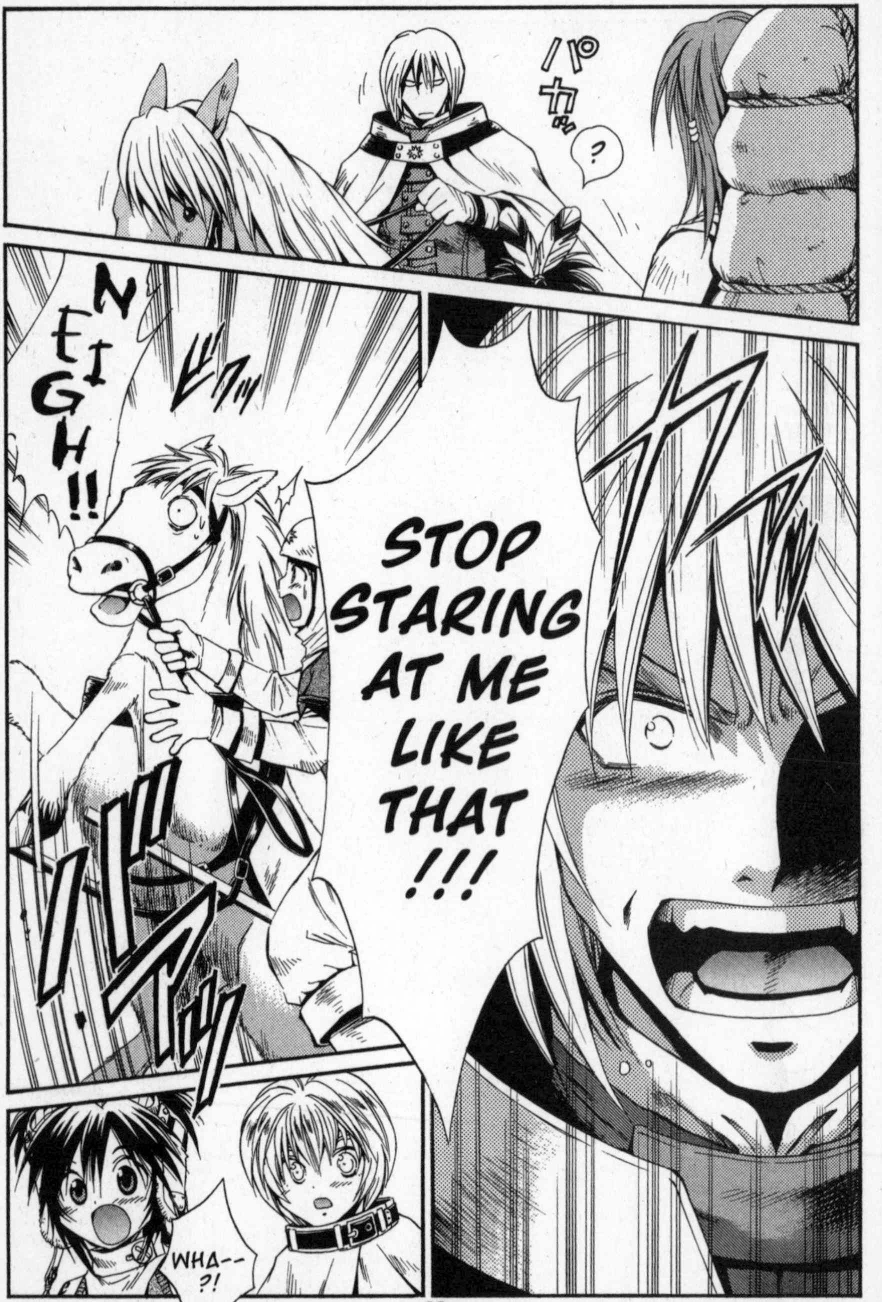

パカッ
?
STOP STARING AT ME LIKE THAT!!!
NEIGH!!
ビクッ
WHA-- ?!

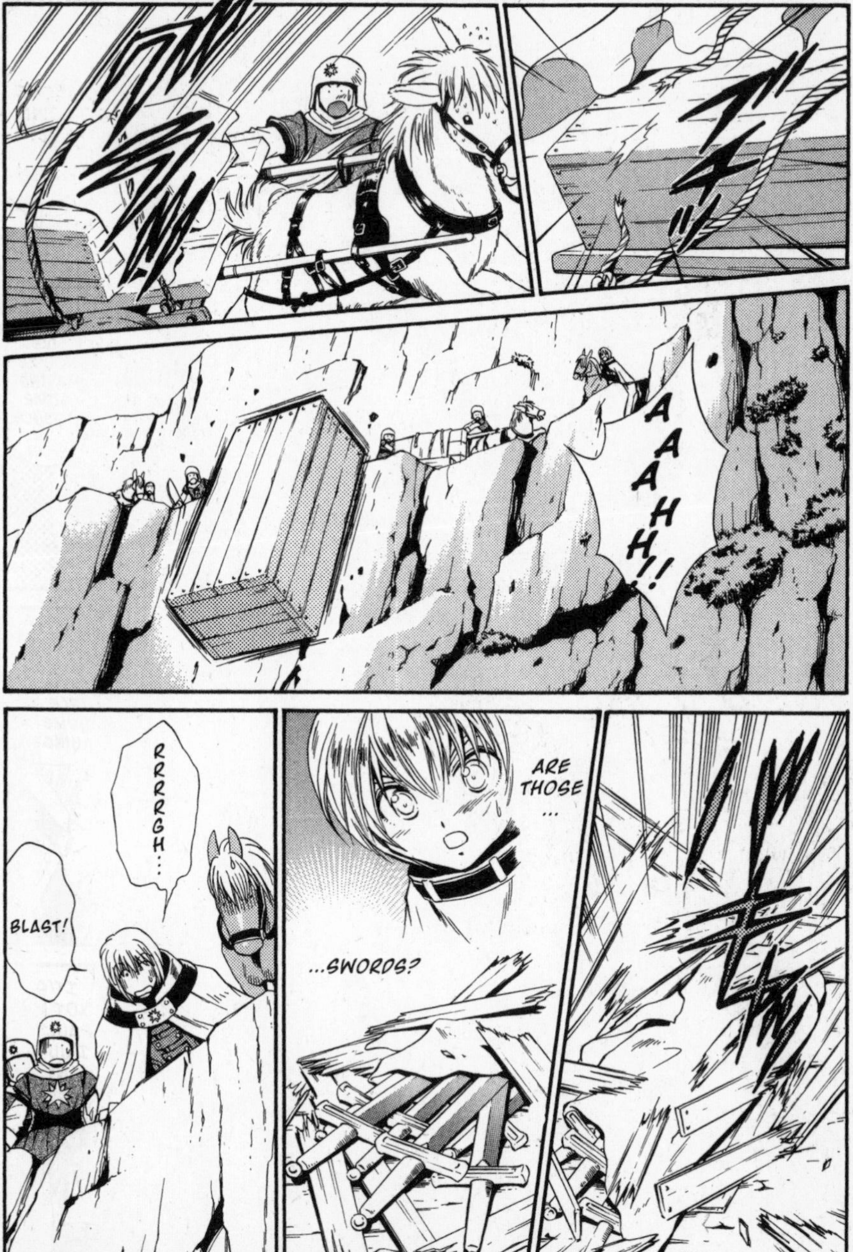
AAAAHH!!
ARE THOSE ...
...SWORDS?
RRRRGH...
BLAST!

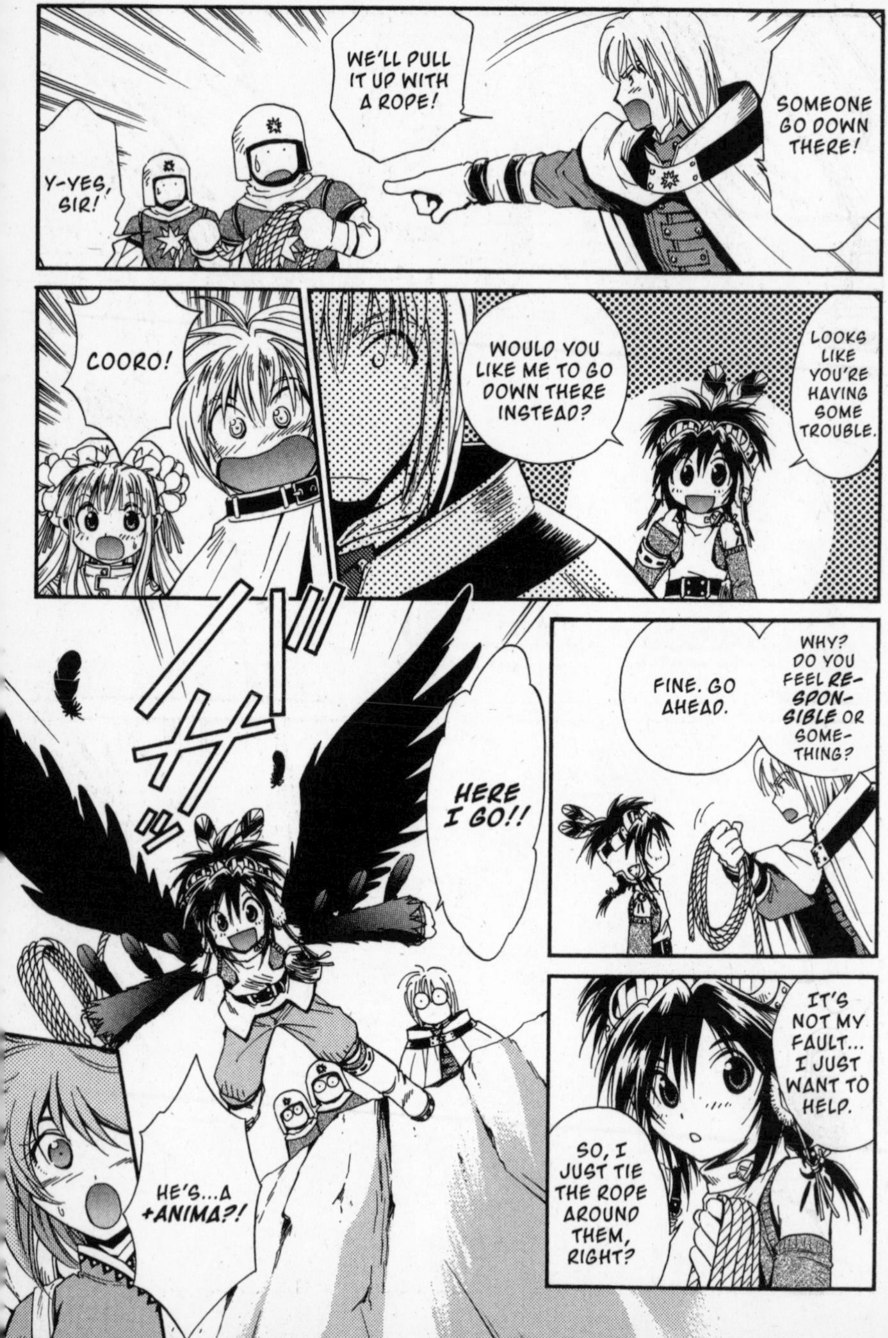
SOMEONE GO DOWN THERE!
WE'LL PULL IT UP WITH A ROPE!
Y-YES, SIR!
LOOKS LIKE YOU'RE HAVING SOME TROUBLE.
WOULD YOU LIKE ME TO GO DOWN THERE INSTEAD?
COORO!
WHY? DO YOU FEEL **RE-SPON-SIBLE** OR SOME-THING?
FINE. GO AHEAD.
IT'S NOT MY FAULT... I JUST WANT TO HELP.
SO, I JUST TIE THE ROPE AROUND THEM, RIGHT?
HERE I GO!!
HE'S...A +ANIMA?!

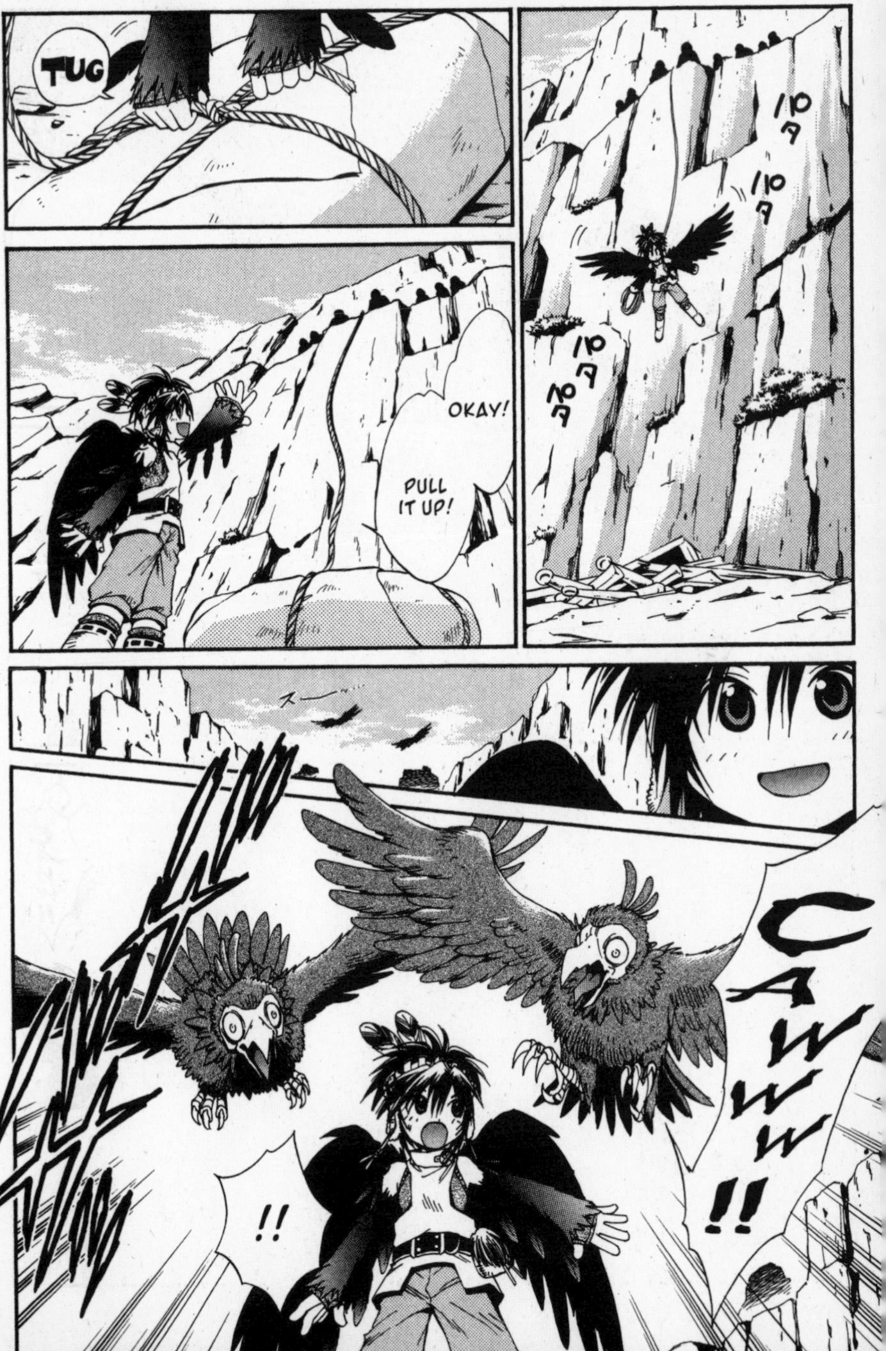
パタ
パタ
パタ
パタ
TUG
OKAY!
PULL IT UP!
スー
CAWWWW!!
!!

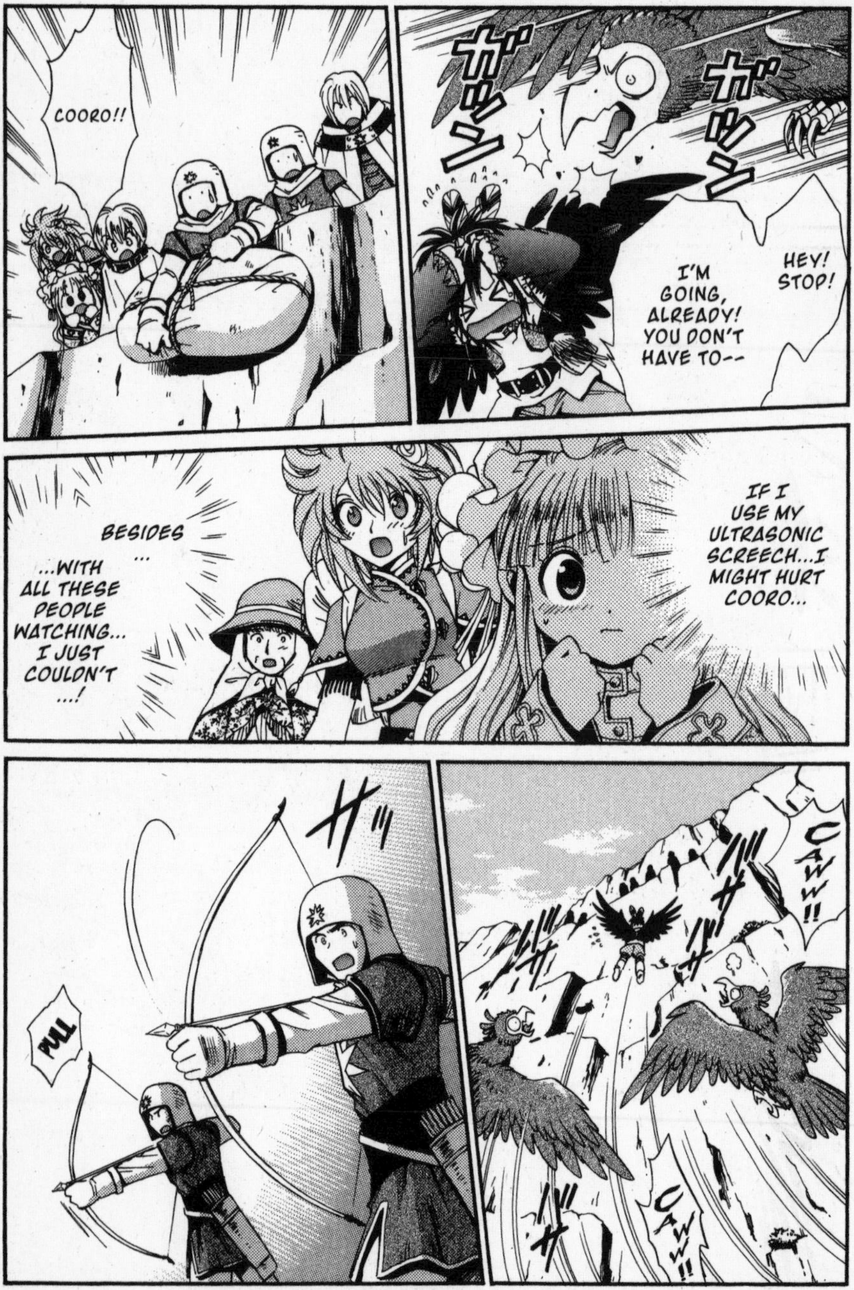
HEY! STOP!
I'M GOING, ALREADY! YOU DON'T HAVE TO--
COORO!!
IF I USE MY ULTRASONIC SCREECH...I MIGHT HURT COORO...
BESIDES ...
...WITH ALL THESE PEOPLE WATCHING... I JUST COULDN'T ...!
CAWW!!
CAWW!!
PULL

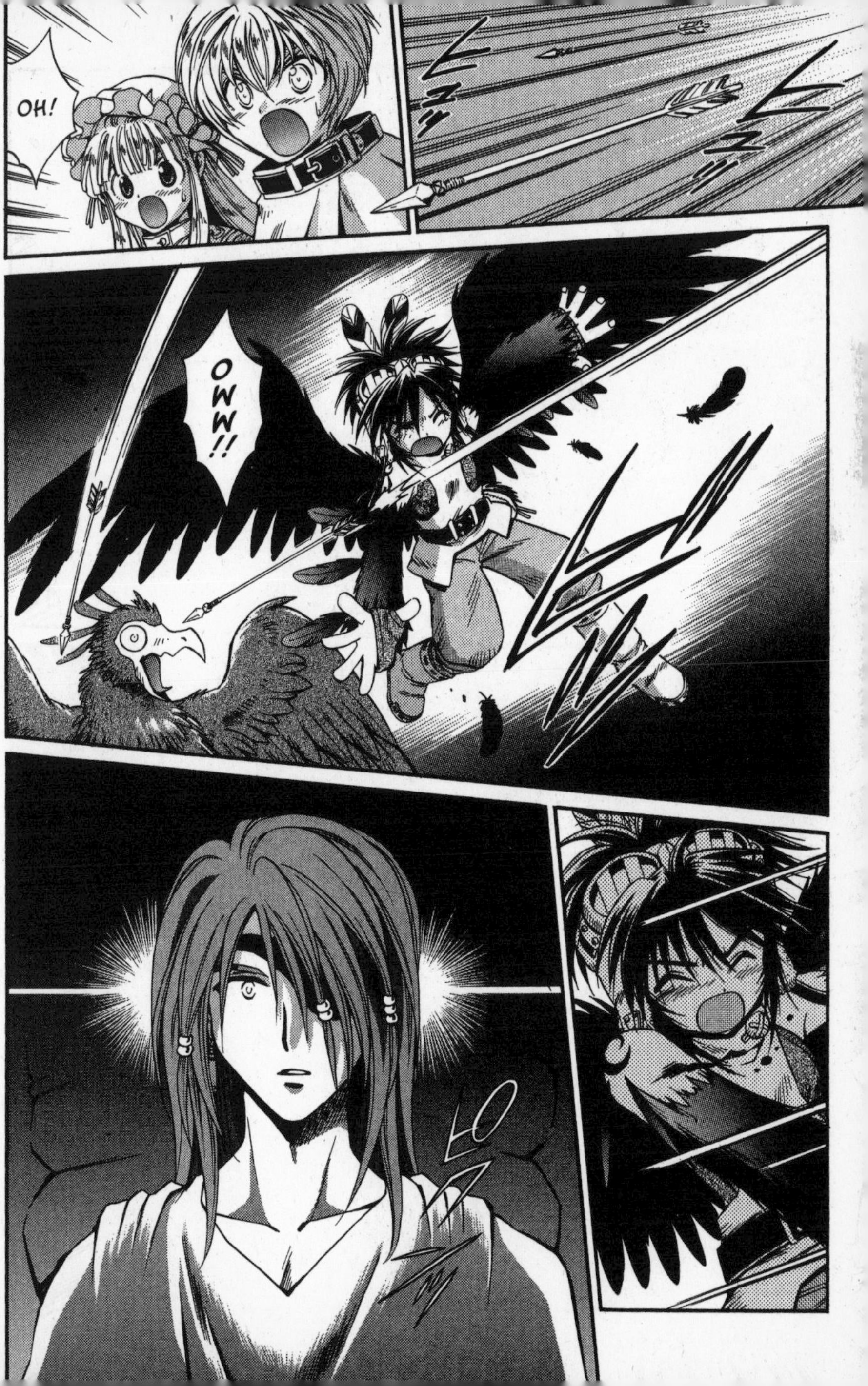
OH!
OWW!!

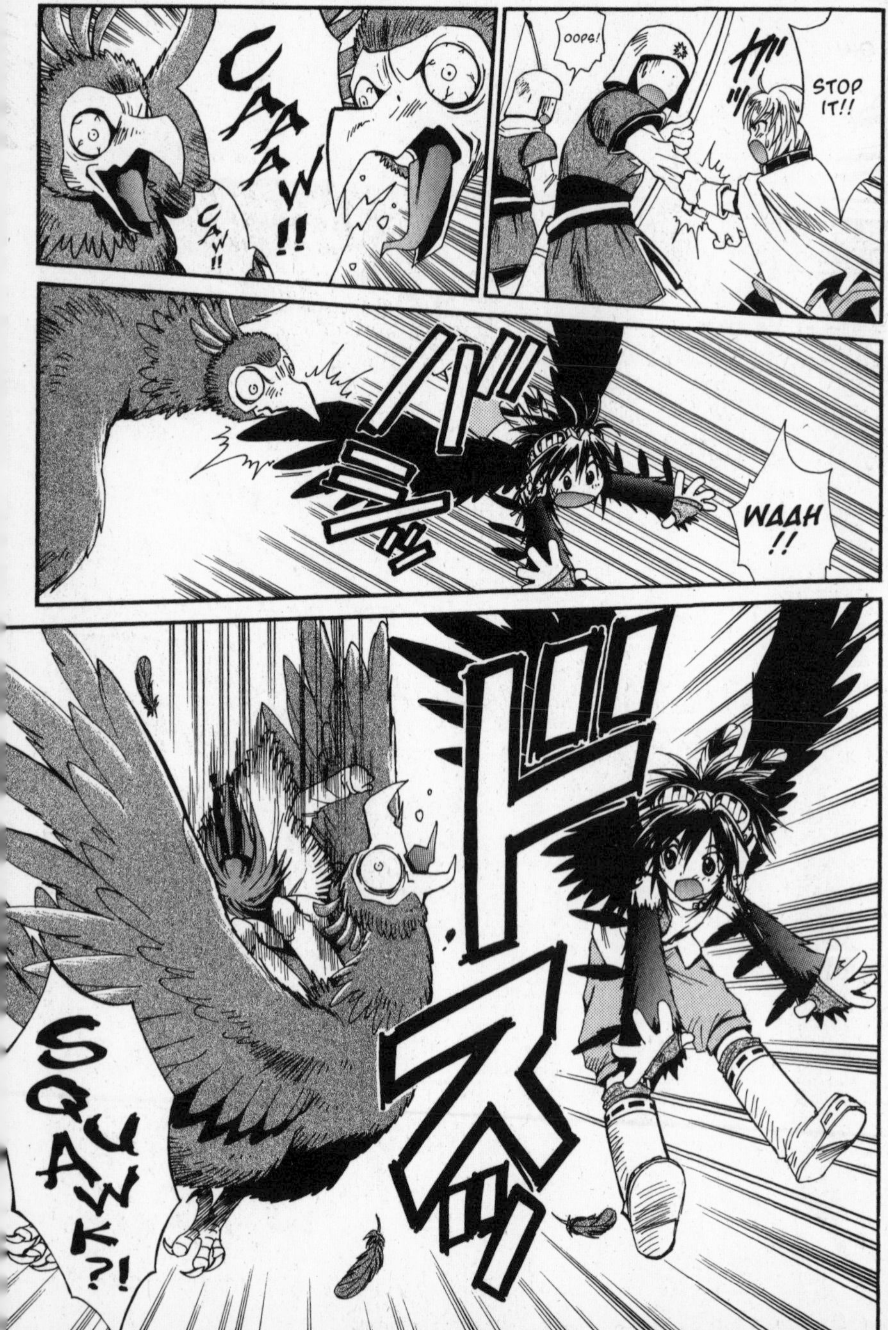
OOPS!
STOP IT!!
CAAAW!!
CAW!!
WAAH!!
SQUAWK?!

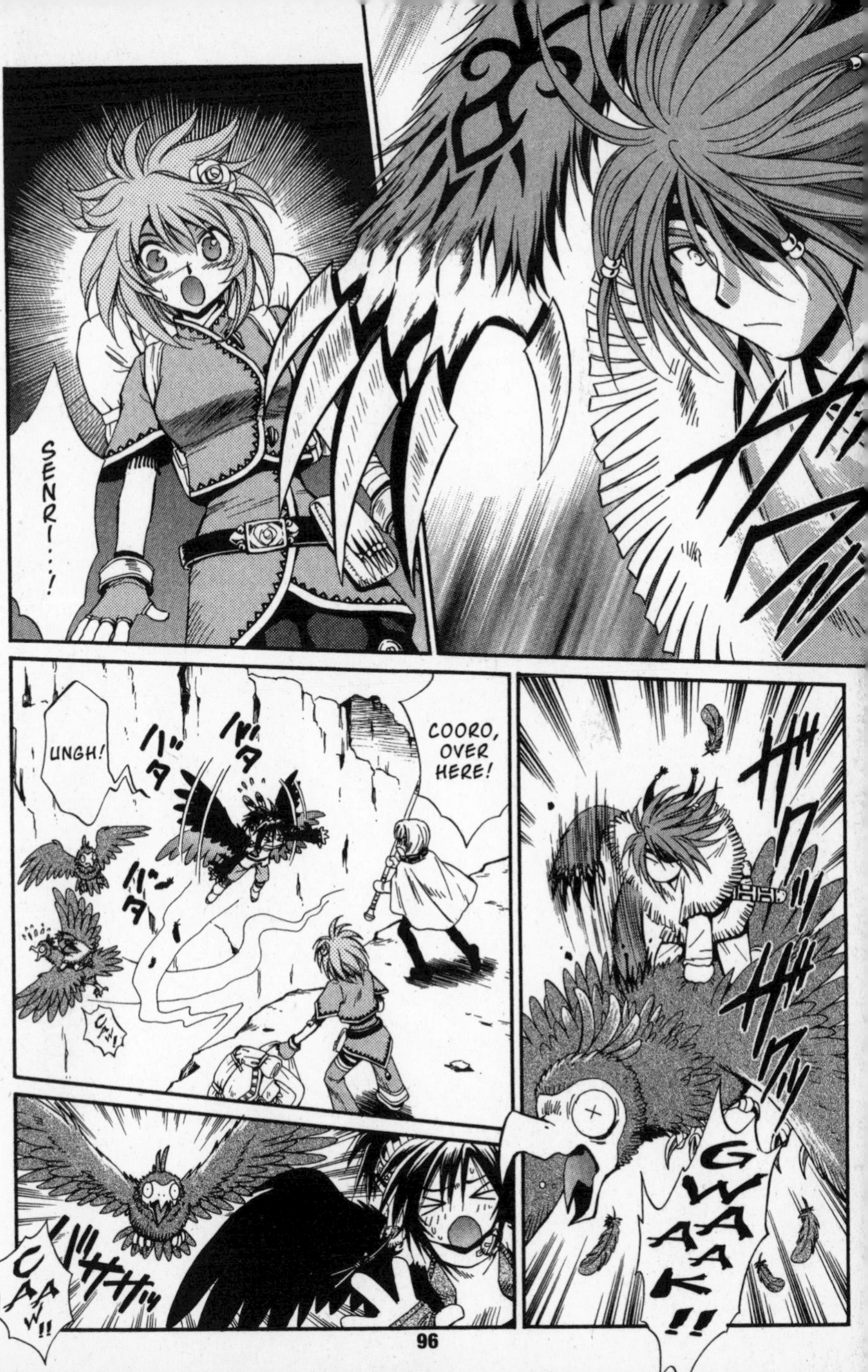
SENRI...!
GWAAAK!!
UNGH!
COORO, OVER HERE!
CAAW!!

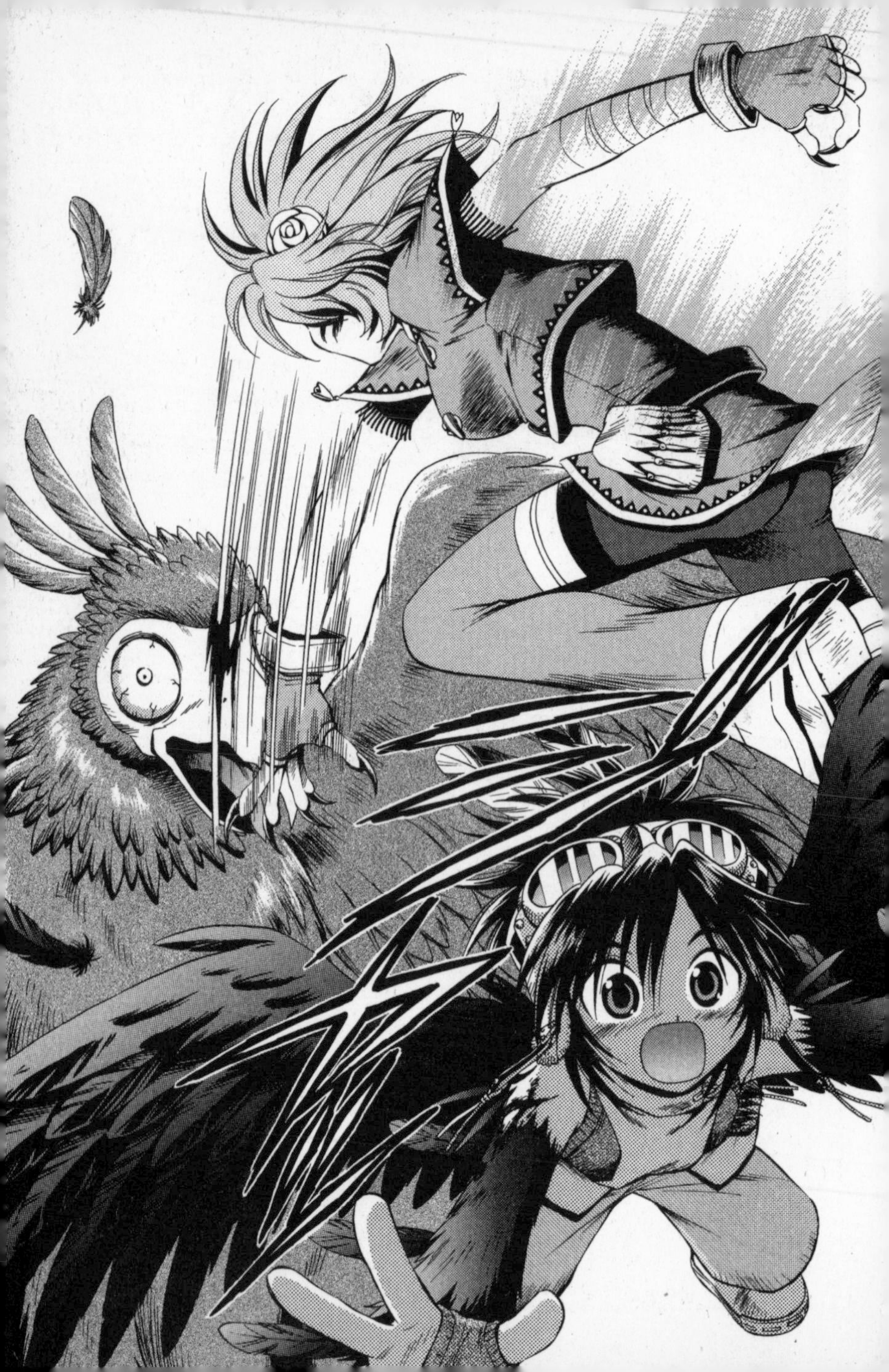

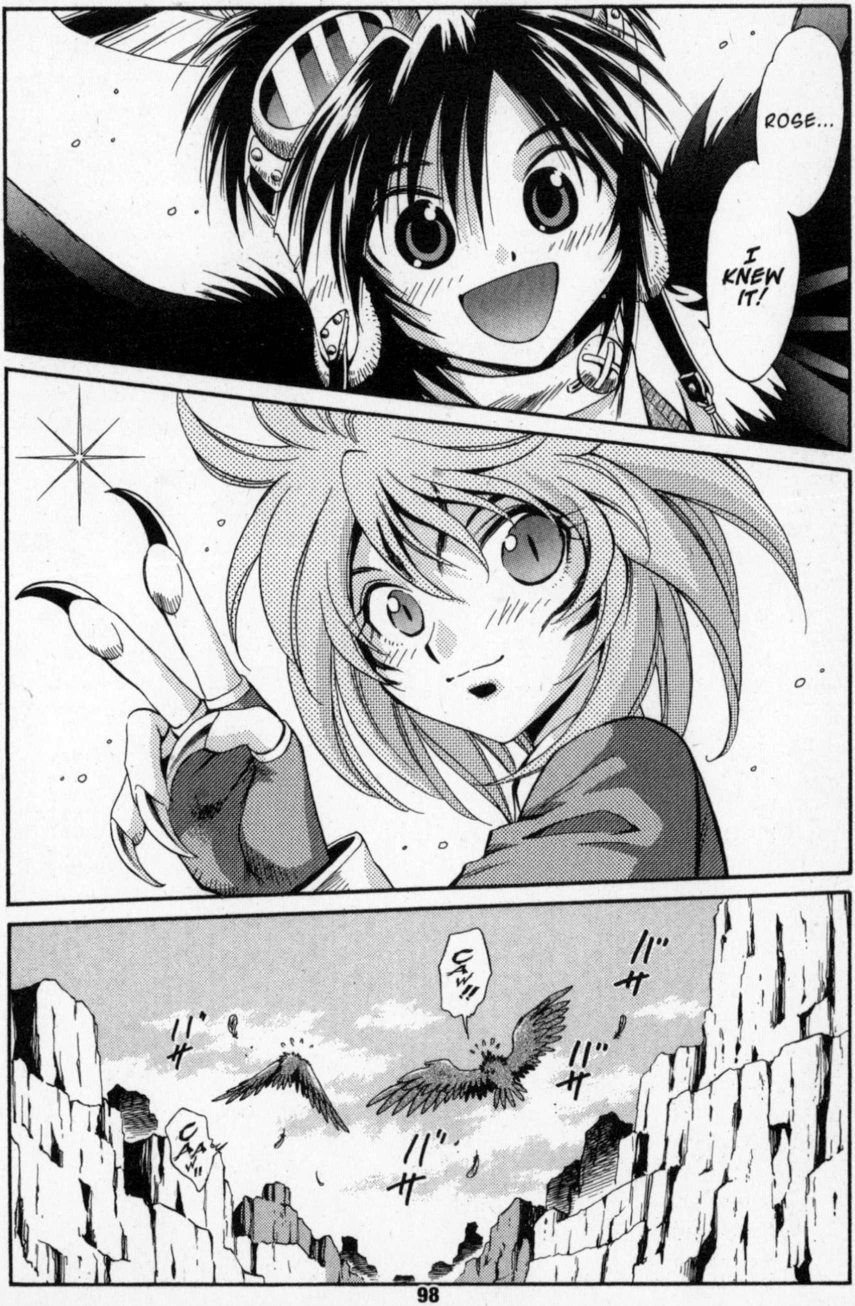
ROSE...
I KNEW IT!
バサ
CAW!!
バサ
バサ
CAW!!
バサ

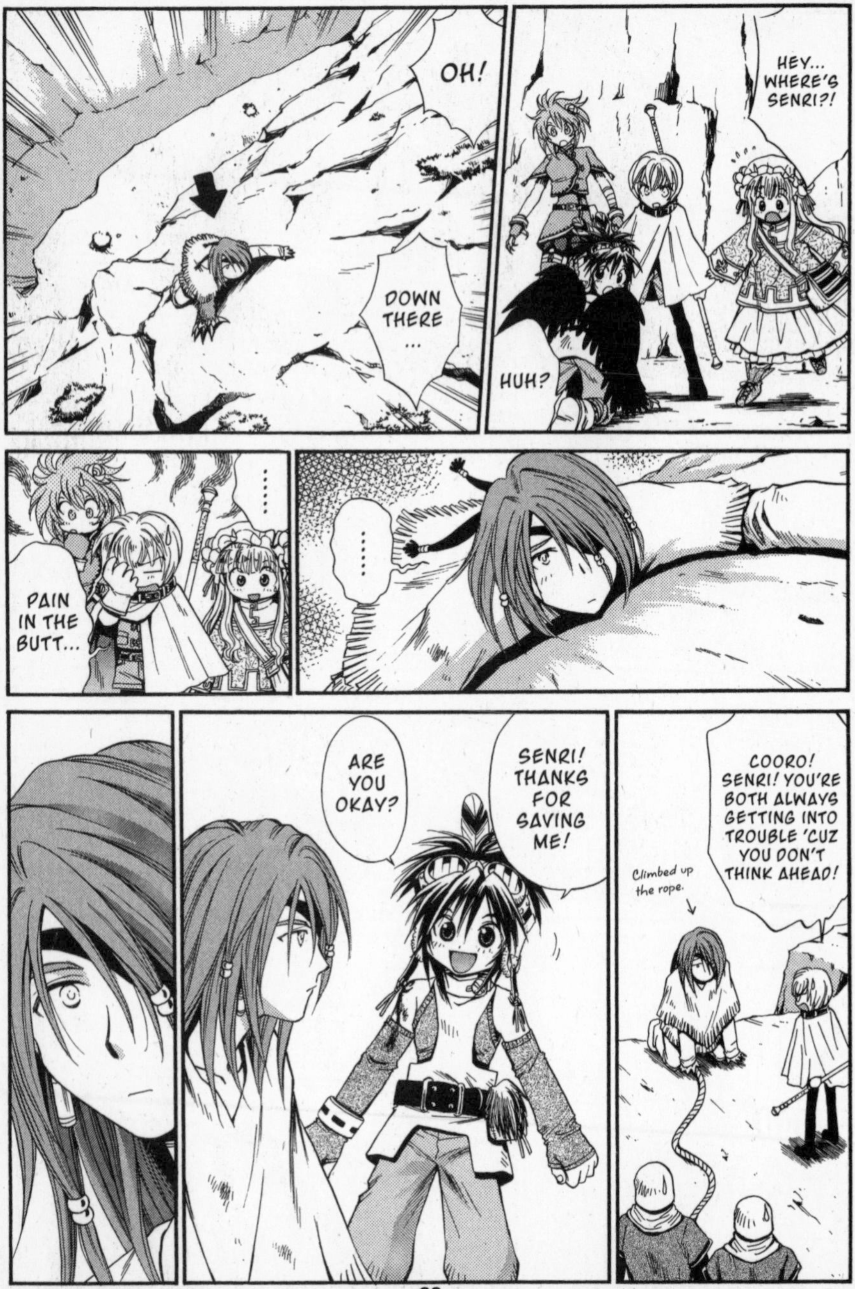
HEY... WHERE'S SENRI?!
HUH?
OH!
DOWN THERE ...
......
......
PAIN IN THE BUTT...
COORO! SENRI! YOU'RE BOTH ALWAYS GETTING INTO TROUBLE 'CUZ YOU DON'T THINK AHEAD!
Climbed up the rope.
SENRI! THANKS FOR SAVING ME!
ARE YOU OKAY?

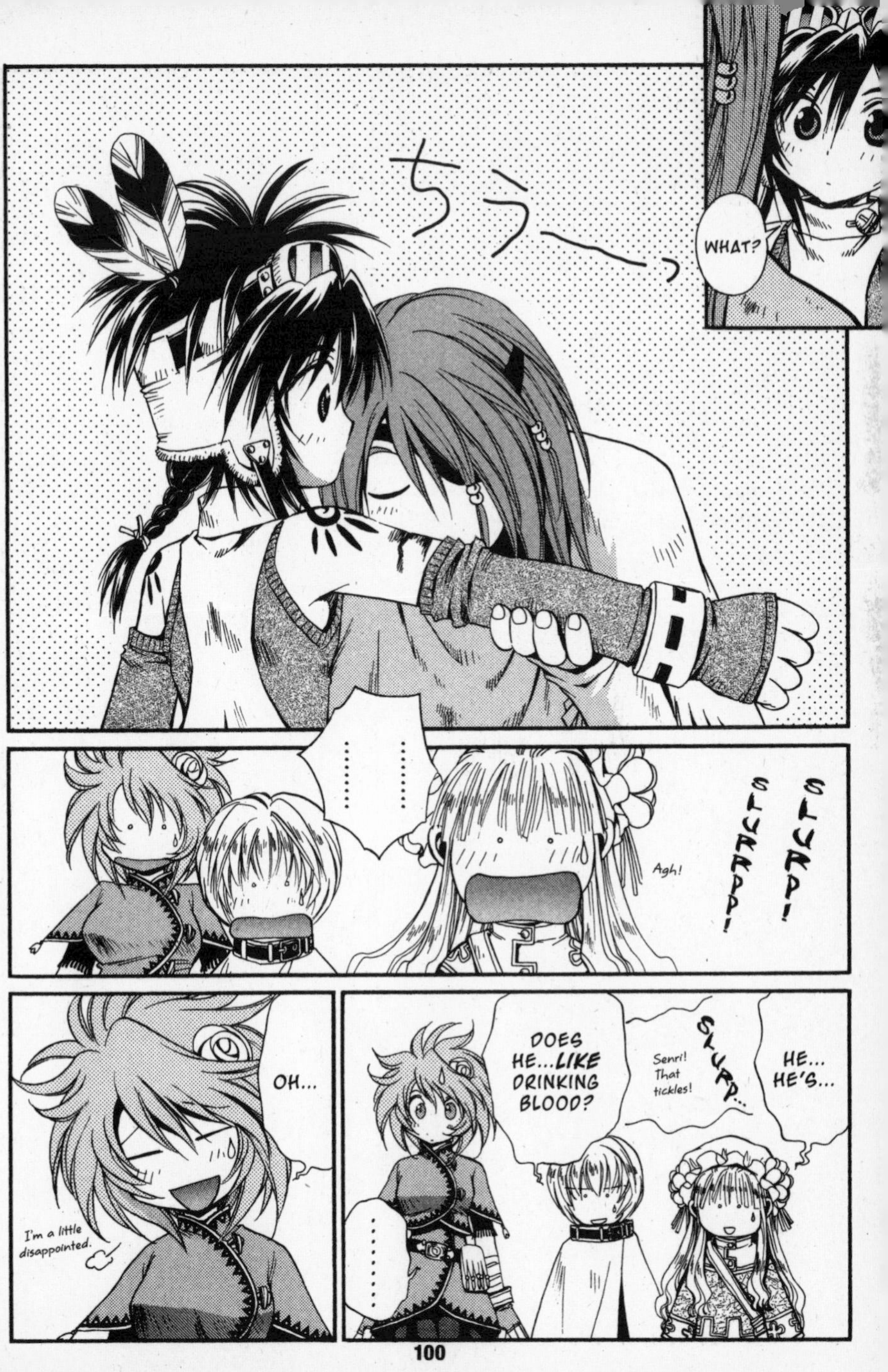

WHAT?
ちう～～っ
SLURP!
SLURRP!
Agh!
......
HE... HE'S...
SLURP...
Senri! That tickles!
DOES HE...LIKE DRINKING BLOOD?
...
OH...
I'm a little disappointed.

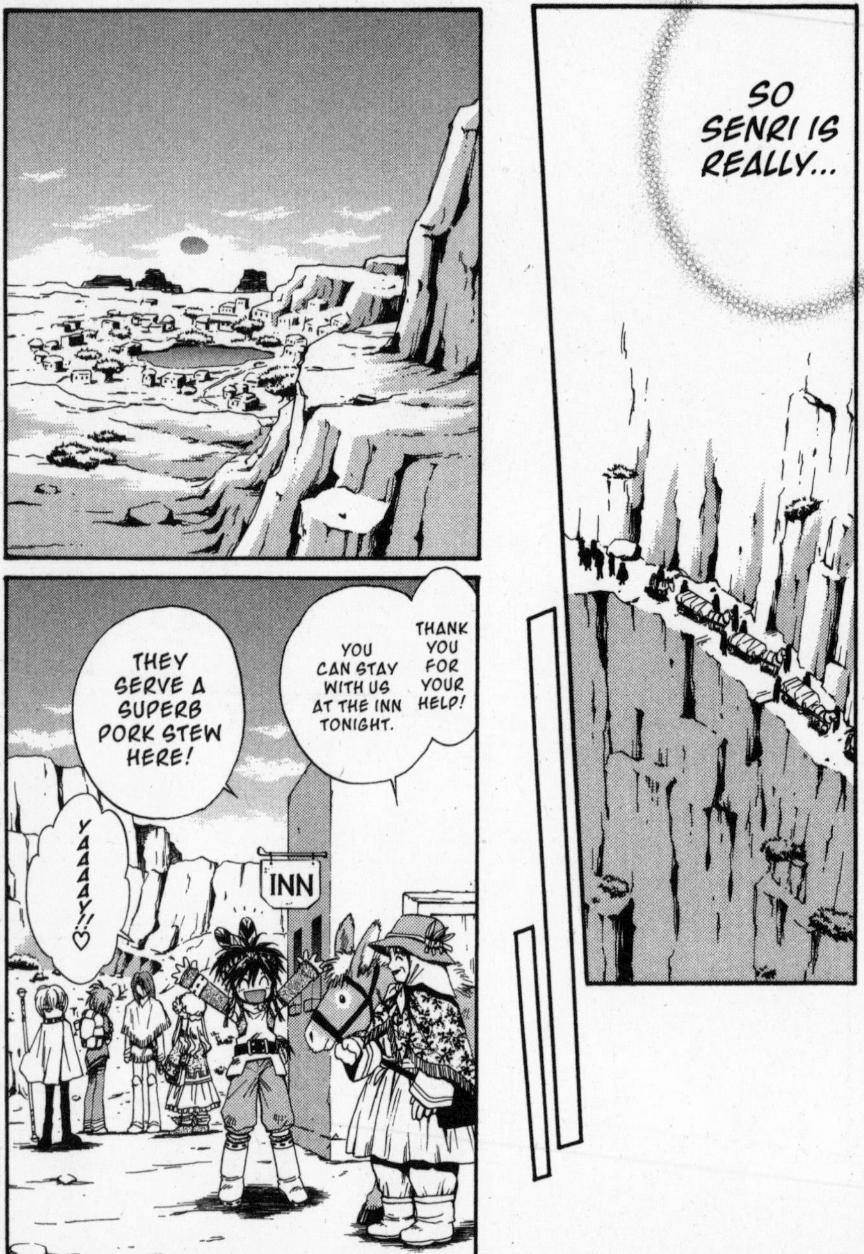
SO SENRI IS REALLY...
THANK YOU FOR YOUR HELP!
YOU CAN STAY WITH US AT THE INN TONIGHT.
THEY SERVE A SUPERB PORK STEW HERE!
INN
YAAAAAY!!♡

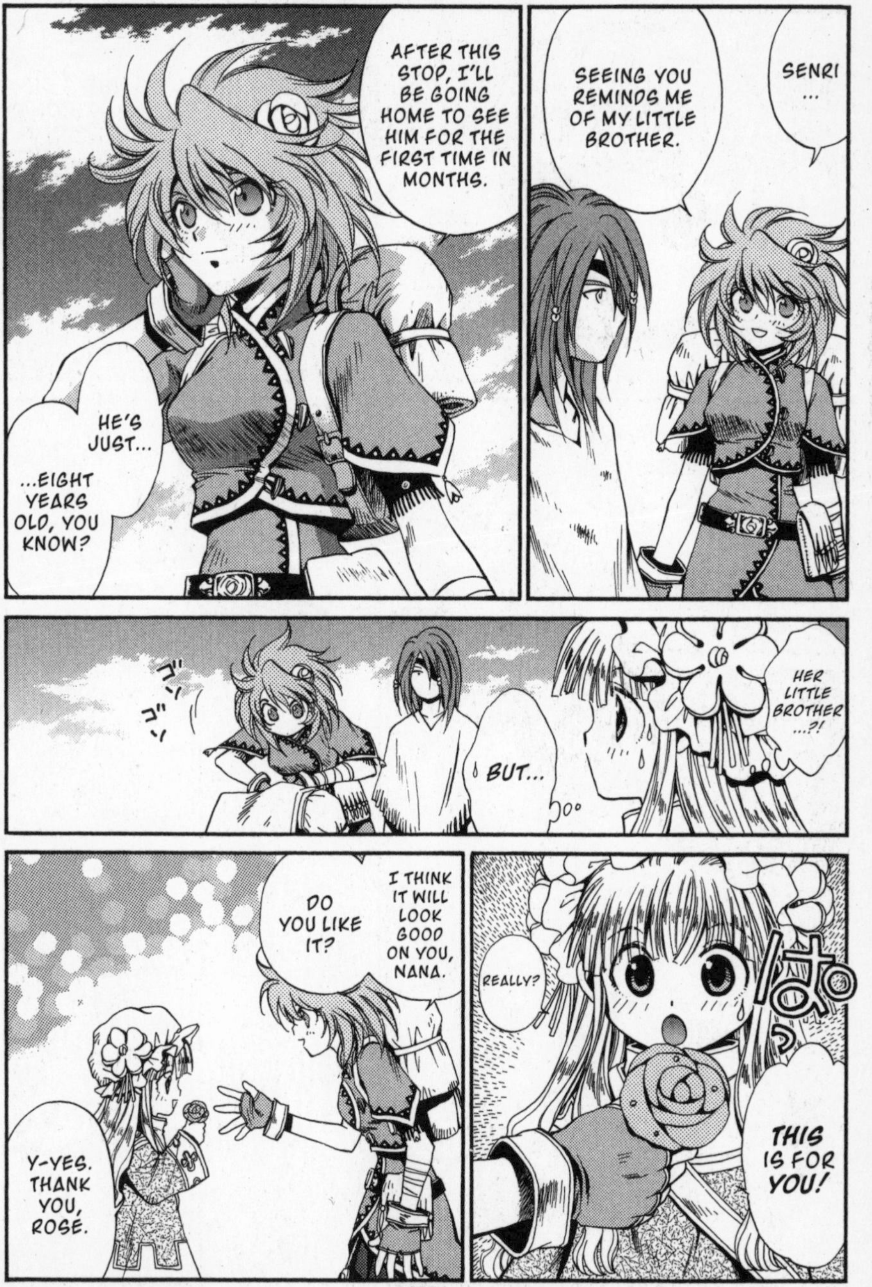
SENRI ...
SEEING YOU REMINDS ME OF MY LITTLE BROTHER.
AFTER THIS STOP, I'LL BE GOING HOME TO SEE HIM FOR THE FIRST TIME IN MONTHS.
HE'S JUST...
...EIGHT YEARS OLD, YOU KNOW?
HER LITTLE BROTHER ...?!
BUT...
ゴソゴソ
はっ
REALLY?
THIS IS FOR YOU!
I THINK IT WILL LOOK GOOD ON YOU, NANA.
DO YOU LIKE IT?
Y-YES. THANK YOU, ROSE.

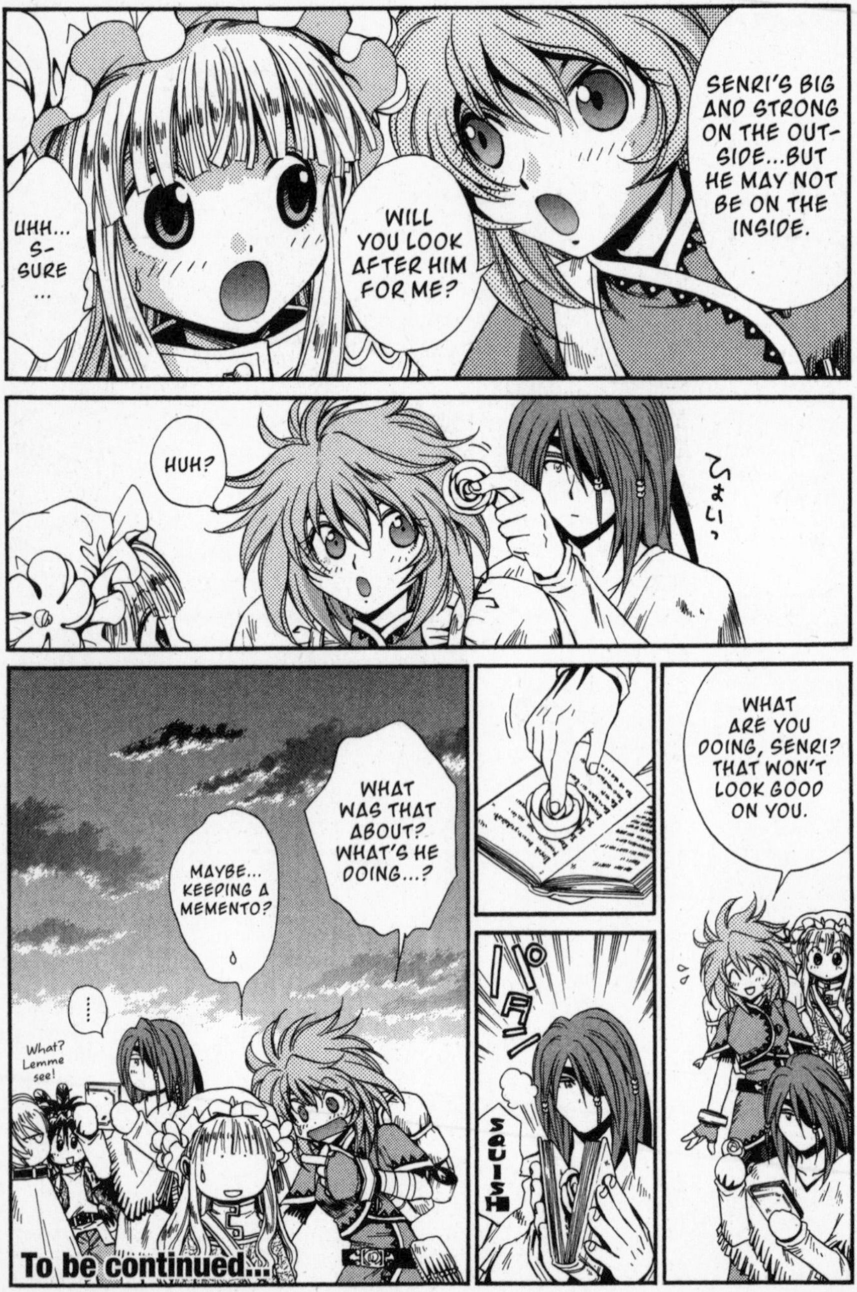
SENRI'S BIG AND STRONG ON THE OUT-SIDE...BUT HE MAY NOT BE ON THE INSIDE.
WILL YOU LOOK AFTER HIM FOR ME?
UHH... S-SURE ...
ひょいっ
HUH?
WHAT ARE YOU DOING, SENRI? THAT WON'T LOOK GOOD ON YOU.
パタン
SQUISH
WHAT WAS THAT ABOUT? WHAT'S HE DOING...?
MAYBE... KEEPING A MEMENTO?
......
What? Lemme see!
To be continued...

About Parallel 1–3

The three chapters starting on the next page are special episodes that I drew as a short series before *+Anima* was serialized! There are subtle differences in the character designs of Cooro and the others. I'd love it if you would read (and enjoy) these chapters! Just consider it a parallel world that shows what could have been...

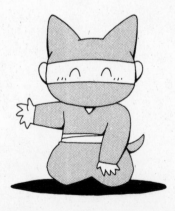

Parallel 1
Dancing on the Purple Rocks

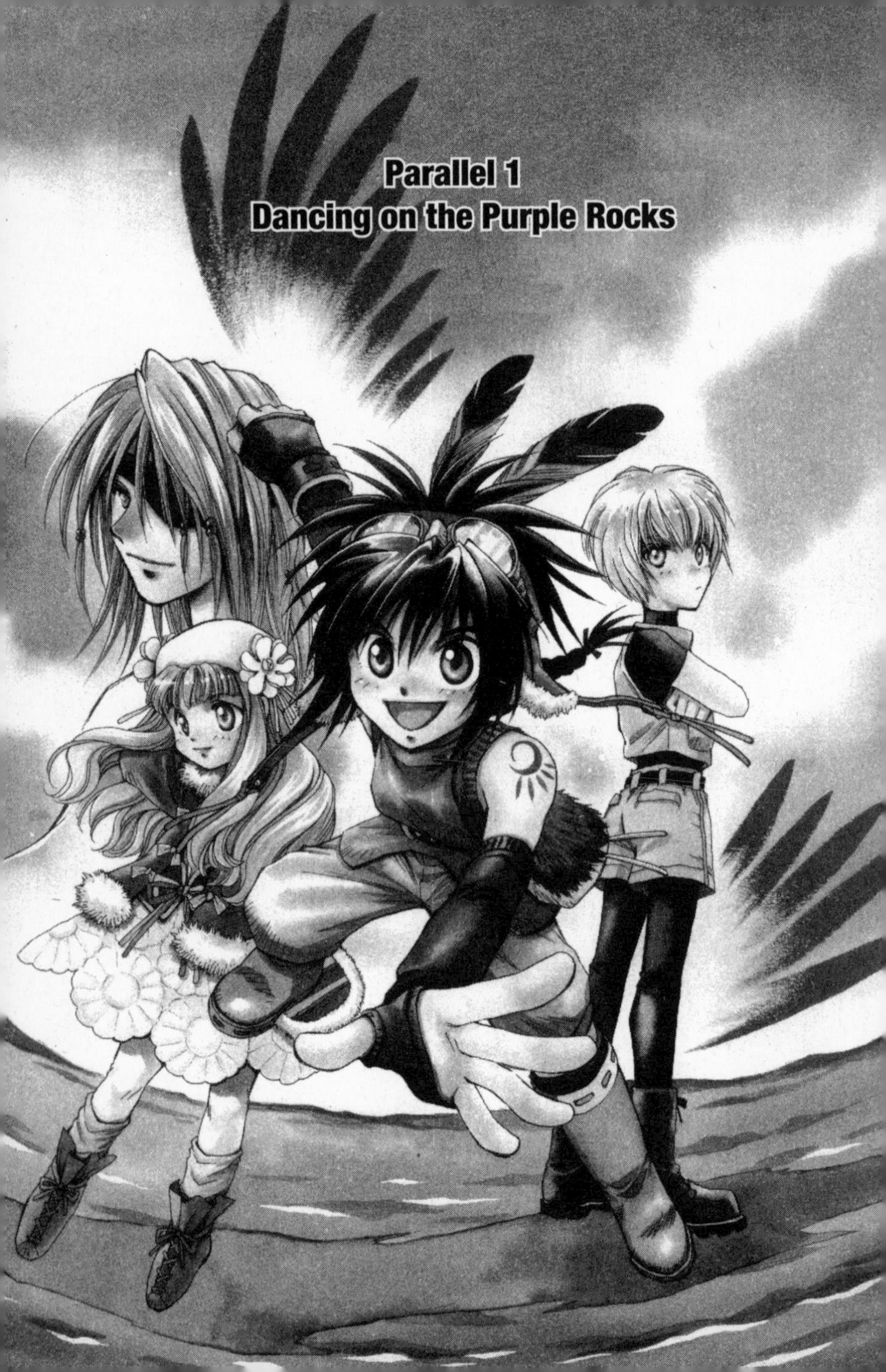

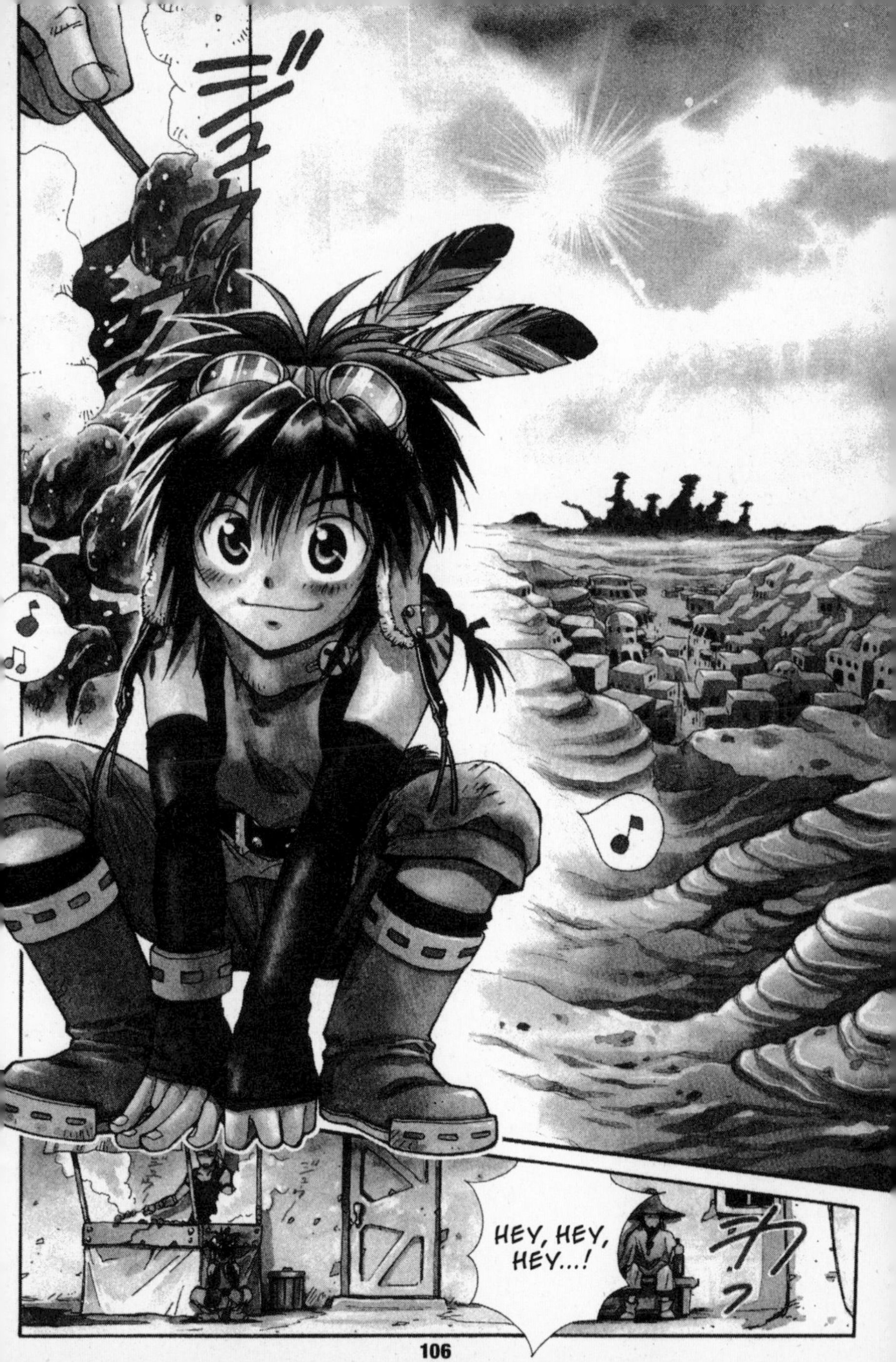
HEY, HEY, HEY...!

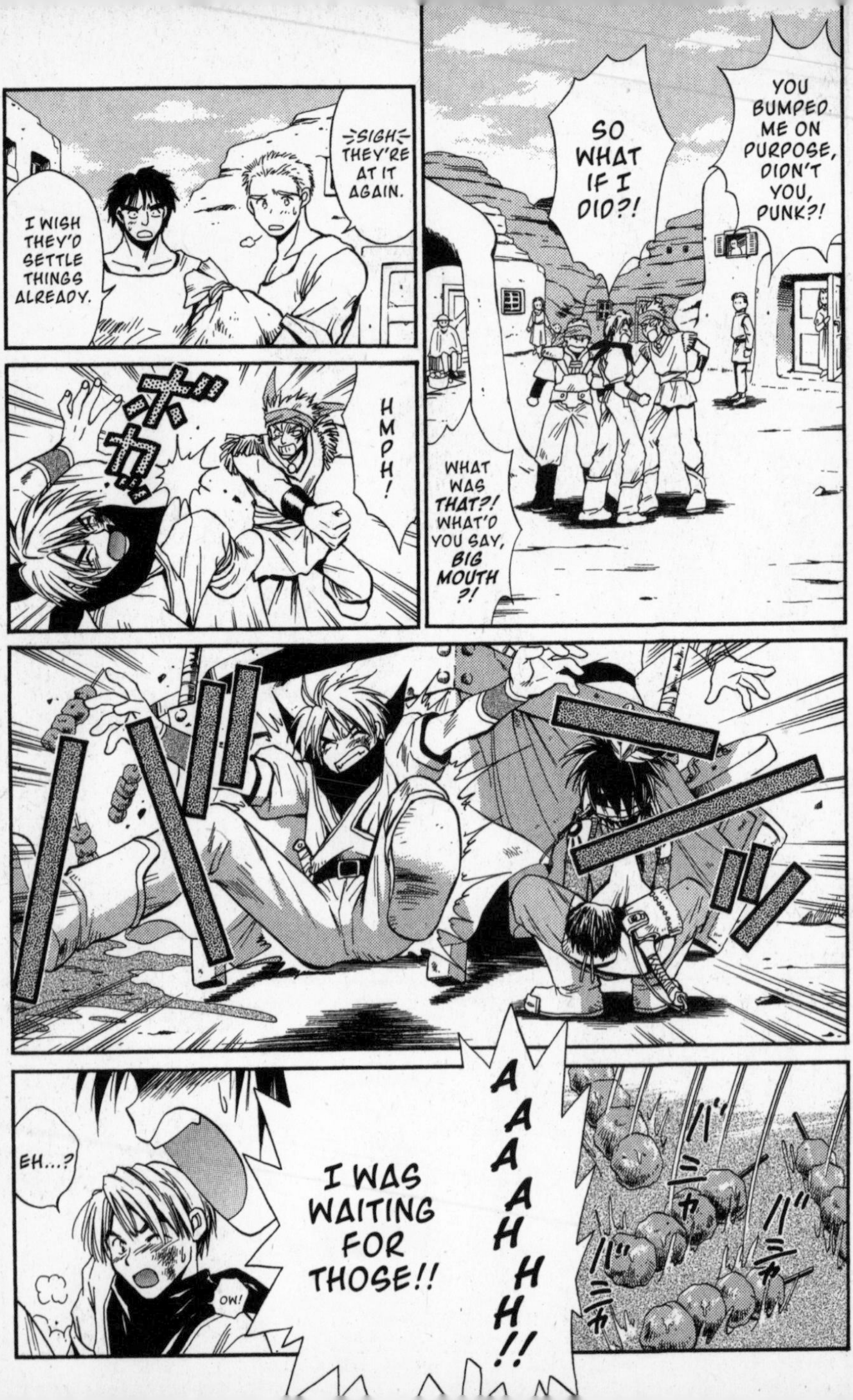
YOU BUMPED ME ON PURPOSE, DIDN'T YOU, PUNK?!
SO WHAT IF I DID?!
WHAT WAS THAT?! WHAT'D YOU SAY, BIG MOUTH?!
≈SIGH≈ THEY'RE AT IT AGAIN.
I WISH THEY'D SETTLE THINGS ALREADY.
HMPH!
AAAAHHHH!!
I WAS WAITING FOR THOSE!!
EH...?
OW!

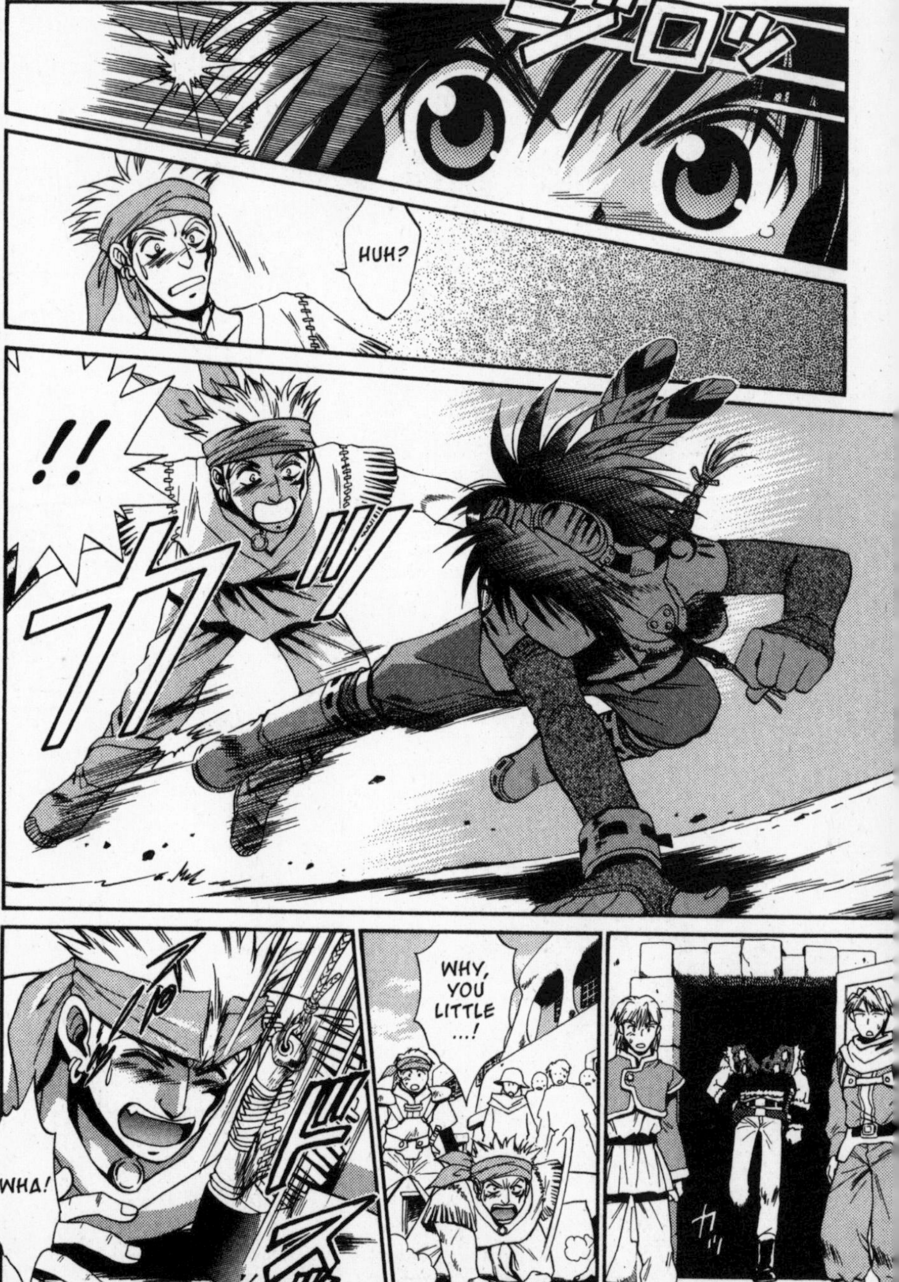
ジロッ
HUH?
!!
WHY, YOU LITTLE ...!
WHA!

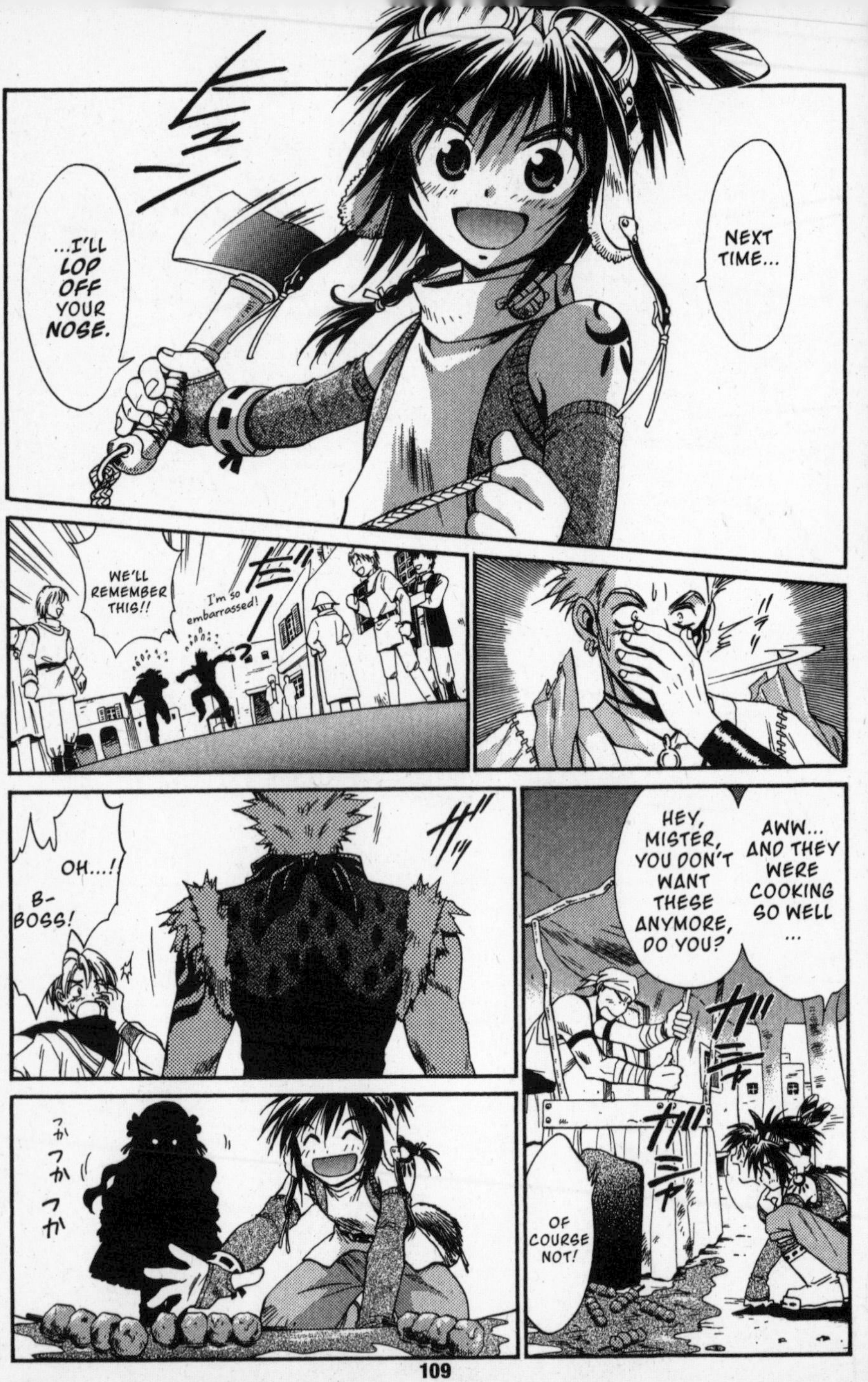
NEXT TIME...
...I'LL LOP OFF YOUR NOSE.
I'm so embarrassed!
WE'LL REMEMBER THIS!!
AWW... AND THEY WERE COOKING SO WELL ...
HEY, MISTER, YOU DON'T WANT THESE ANYMORE, DO YOU?
OF COURSE NOT!
OH...!
B-BOSS!
つかつかつか

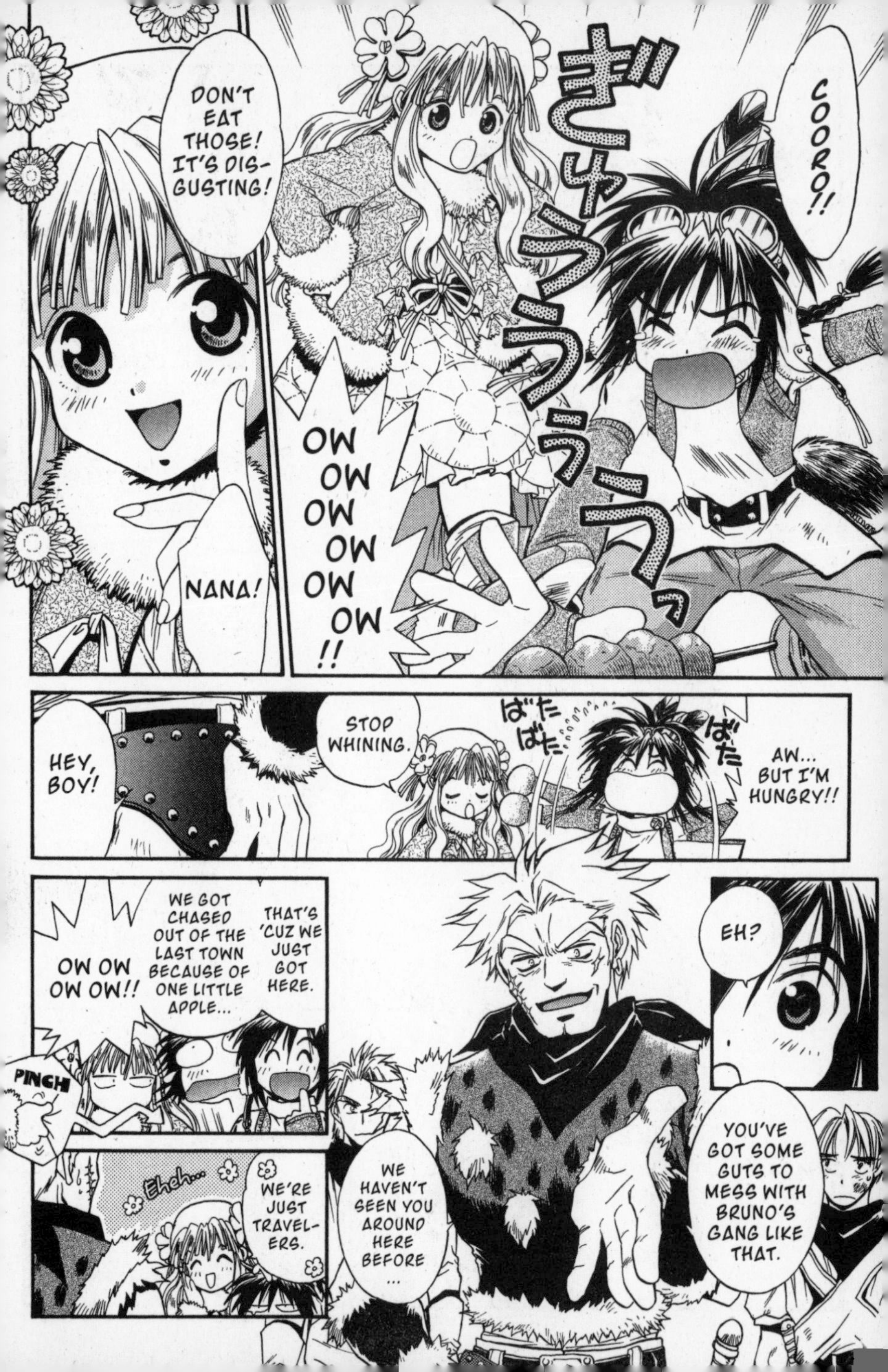
COORO!!
ぎゅううぅ～っ
OW OW OW OW OW OW OW!!
DON'T EAT THOSE! IT'S DIS-GUSTING!
NANA!
AW... BUT I'M HUNGRY!!
ばたばた ばた
STOP WHINING.
HEY, BOY!
EH?
YOU'VE GOT SOME GUTS TO MESS WITH BRUNO'S GANG LIKE THAT.
WE HAVEN'T SEEN YOU AROUND HERE BEFORE...
THAT'S 'CUZ WE JUST GOT HERE.
WE GOT CHASED OUT OF THE LAST TOWN BECAUSE OF ONE LITTLE APPLE...
OW OW OW OW!!
PINCH
WE'RE JUST TRAVEL-ERS.
Eheh...

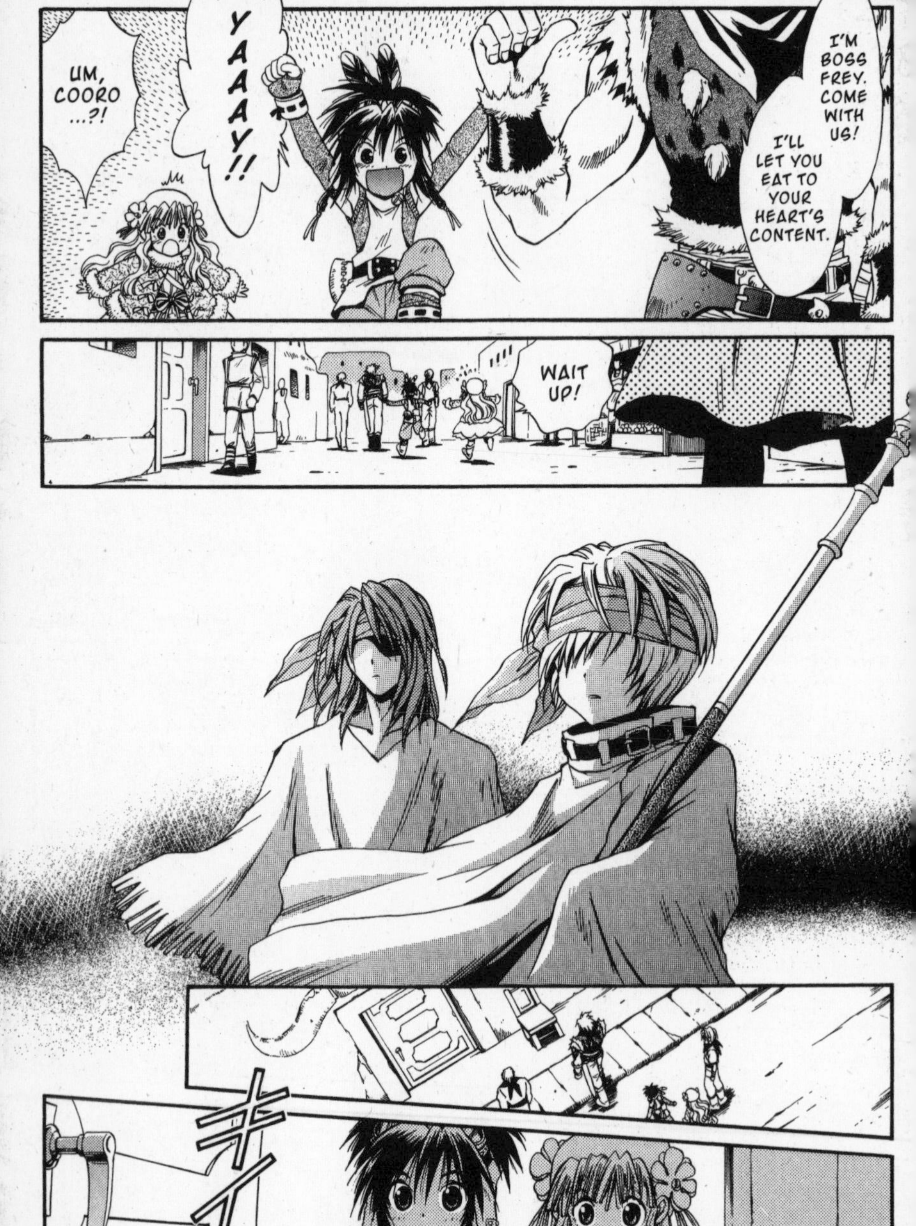
I'M BOSS FREY. COME WITH US!
I'LL LET YOU EAT TO YOUR HEART'S CONTENT.
YAAAY!!
UM, COORO ...?!
WAIT UP!
キイ

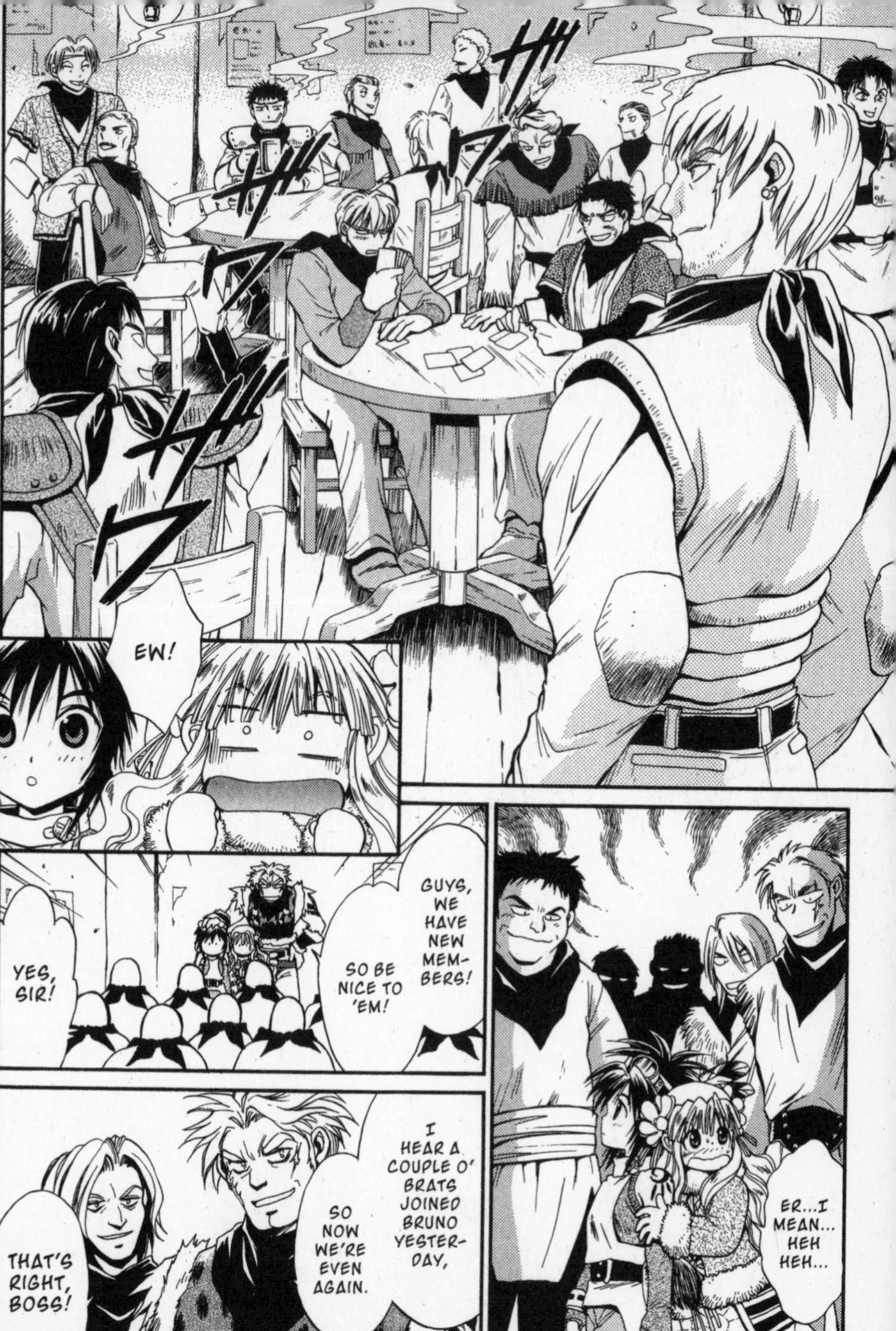
EW!
ER...I MEAN... HEH HEH...
GUYS, WE HAVE NEW MEM-BERS!
SO BE NICE TO 'EM!
YES, SIR!
I HEAR A COUPLE O' BRATS JOINED BRUNO YESTER-DAY,
SO NOW WE'RE EVEN AGAIN.
THAT'S RIGHT, BOSS!

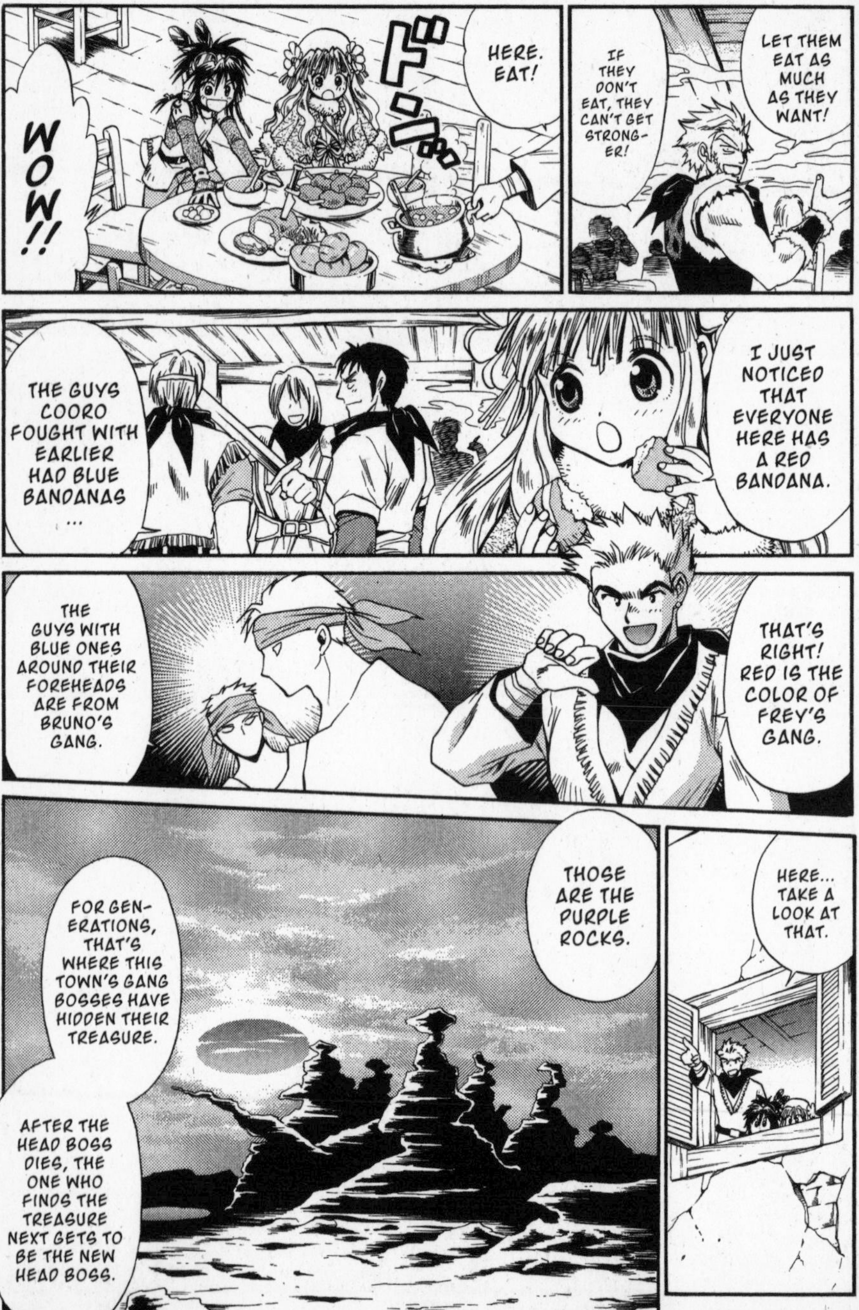
LET THEM EAT AS MUCH AS THEY WANT!
IF THEY DON'T EAT, THEY CAN'T GET STRONG-ER!
HERE. EAT!
WOW!!
I JUST NOTICED THAT EVERYONE HERE HAS A RED BANDANA.
THE GUYS COORO FOUGHT WITH EARLIER HAD BLUE BANDANAS ...
THAT'S RIGHT! RED IS THE COLOR OF FREY'S GANG.
THE GUYS WITH BLUE ONES AROUND THEIR FOREHEADS ARE FROM BRUNO'S GANG.
HERE... TAKE A LOOK AT THAT.
THOSE ARE THE PURPLE ROCKS.
FOR GEN-ERATIONS, THAT'S WHERE THIS TOWN'S GANG BOSSES HAVE HIDDEN THEIR TREASURE.
AFTER THE HEAD BOSS DIES, THE ONE WHO FINDS THE TREASURE NEXT GETS TO BE THE NEW HEAD BOSS.

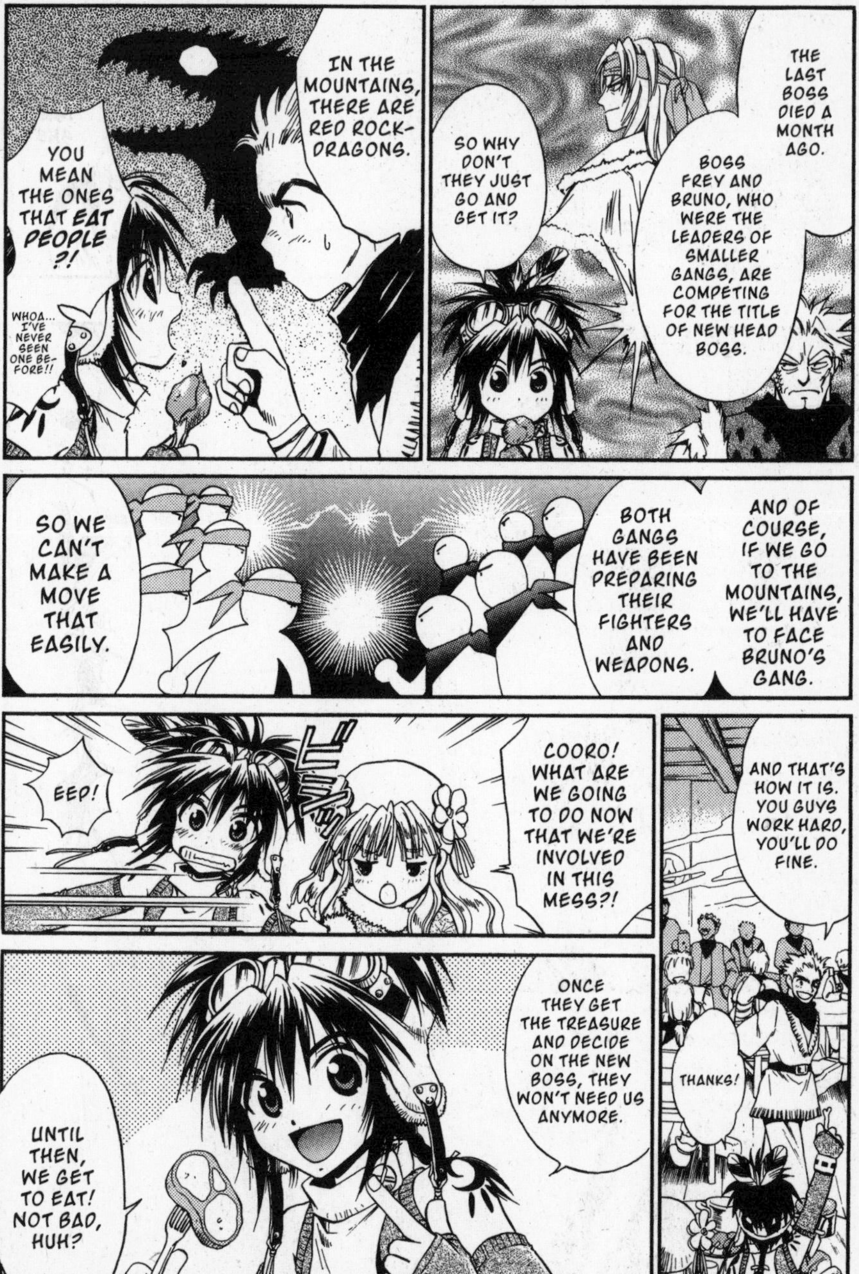
THE LAST BOSS DIED A MONTH AGO.
BOSS FREY AND BRUNO, WHO WERE THE LEADERS OF SMALLER GANGS, ARE COMPETING FOR THE TITLE OF NEW HEAD BOSS.
SO WHY DON'T THEY JUST GO AND GET IT?
IN THE MOUNTAINS, THERE ARE RED ROCK-DRAGONS.
YOU MEAN THE ONES THAT *EAT PEOPLE*?!
WHOA... I'VE NEVER SEEN ONE BEFORE!!
AND OF COURSE, IF WE GO TO THE MOUNTAINS, WE'LL HAVE TO FACE BRUNO'S GANG.
BOTH GANGS HAVE BEEN PREPARING THEIR FIGHTERS AND WEAPONS.
SO WE CAN'T MAKE A MOVE THAT EASILY.
AND THAT'S HOW IT IS. YOU GUYS WORK HARD, YOU'LL DO FINE.
THANKS!
COORO! WHAT ARE WE GOING TO DO NOW THAT WE'RE INVOLVED IN THIS MESS?!
EEP!
ONCE THEY GET THE TREASURE AND DECIDE ON THE NEW BOSS, THEY WON'T NEED US ANYMORE.
UNTIL THEN, WE GET TO EAT! NOT BAD, HUH?

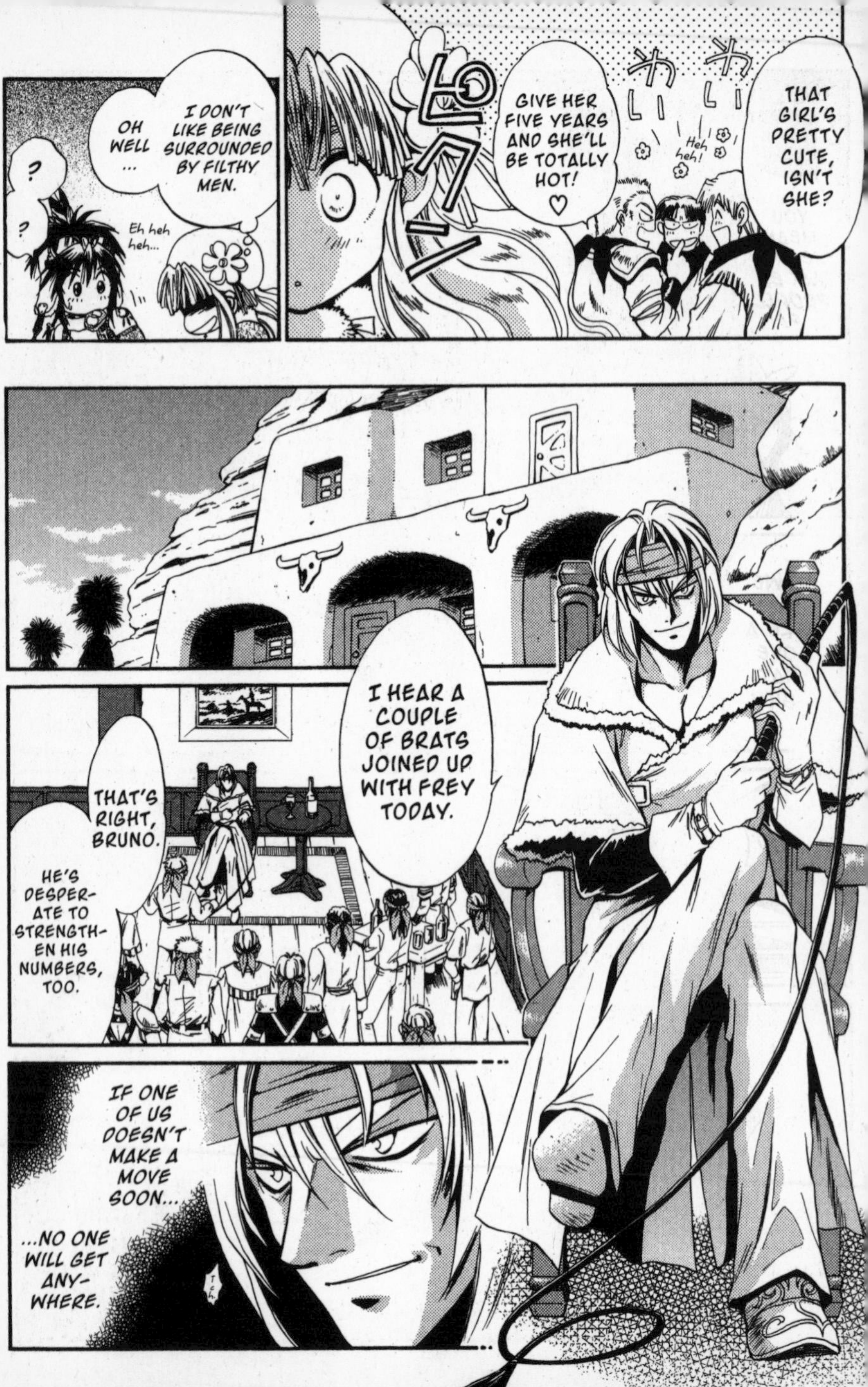
THAT GIRL'S PRETTY CUTE, ISN'T SHE?
Heh heh!
GIVE HER FIVE YEARS AND SHE'LL BE TOTALLY HOT! ♡
I DON'T LIKE BEING SURROUNDED BY FILTHY MEN.
OH WELL ...
Eh heh heh...
?
?
I HEAR A COUPLE OF BRATS JOINED UP WITH FREY TODAY.
THAT'S RIGHT, BRUNO.
HE'S DESPERATE TO STRENGTHEN HIS NUMBERS, TOO.
IF ONE OF US DOESN'T MAKE A MOVE SOON...
...NO ONE WILL GET ANYWHERE.
Tch

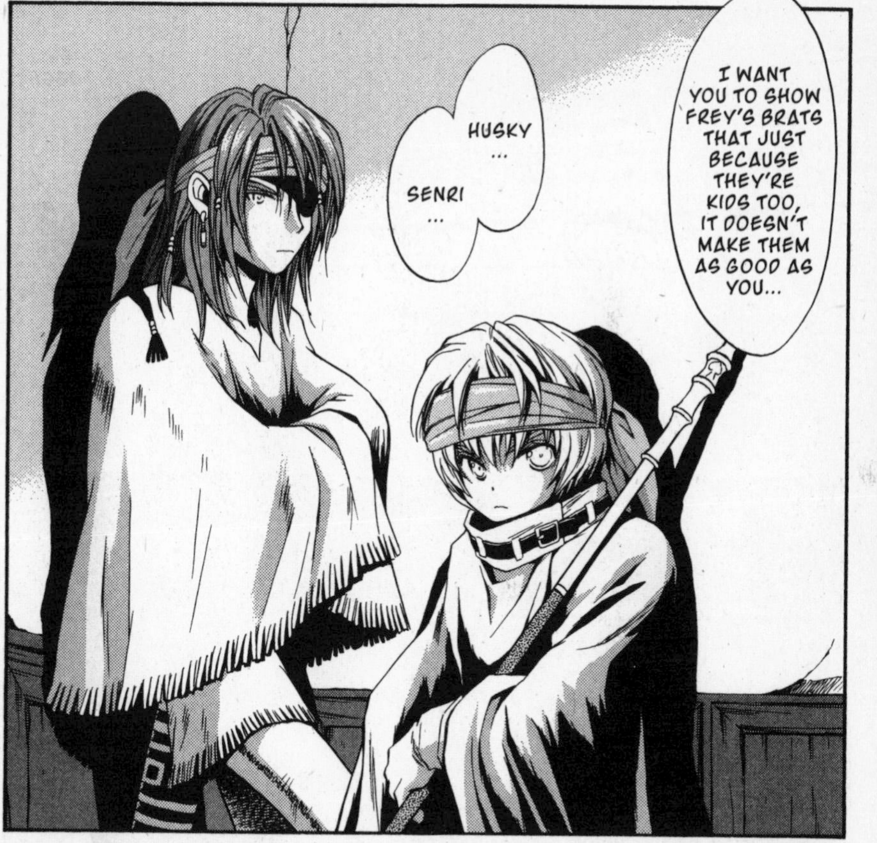
I WANT YOU TO SHOW FREY'S BRATS THAT JUST BECAUSE THEY'RE KIDS TOO, IT DOESN'T MAKE THEM AS GOOD AS YOU...
HUSKY ... SENRI ...
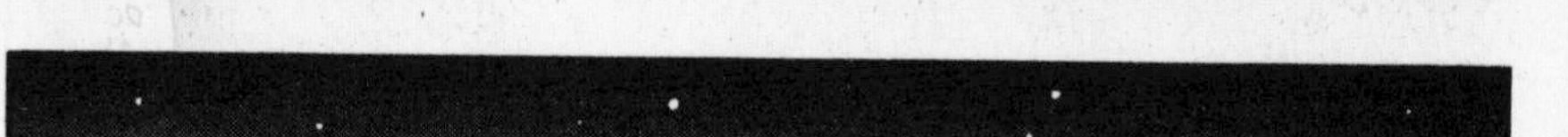
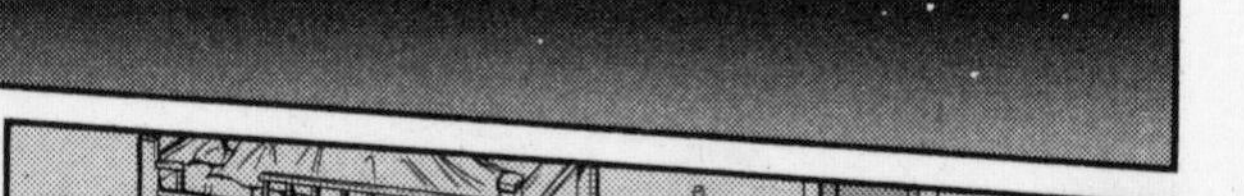
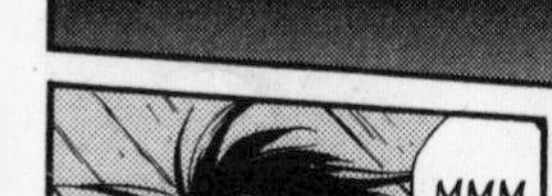
MMM ...
PASS THE... GRAVY ...

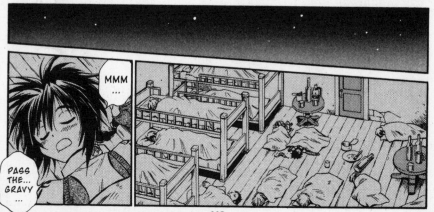

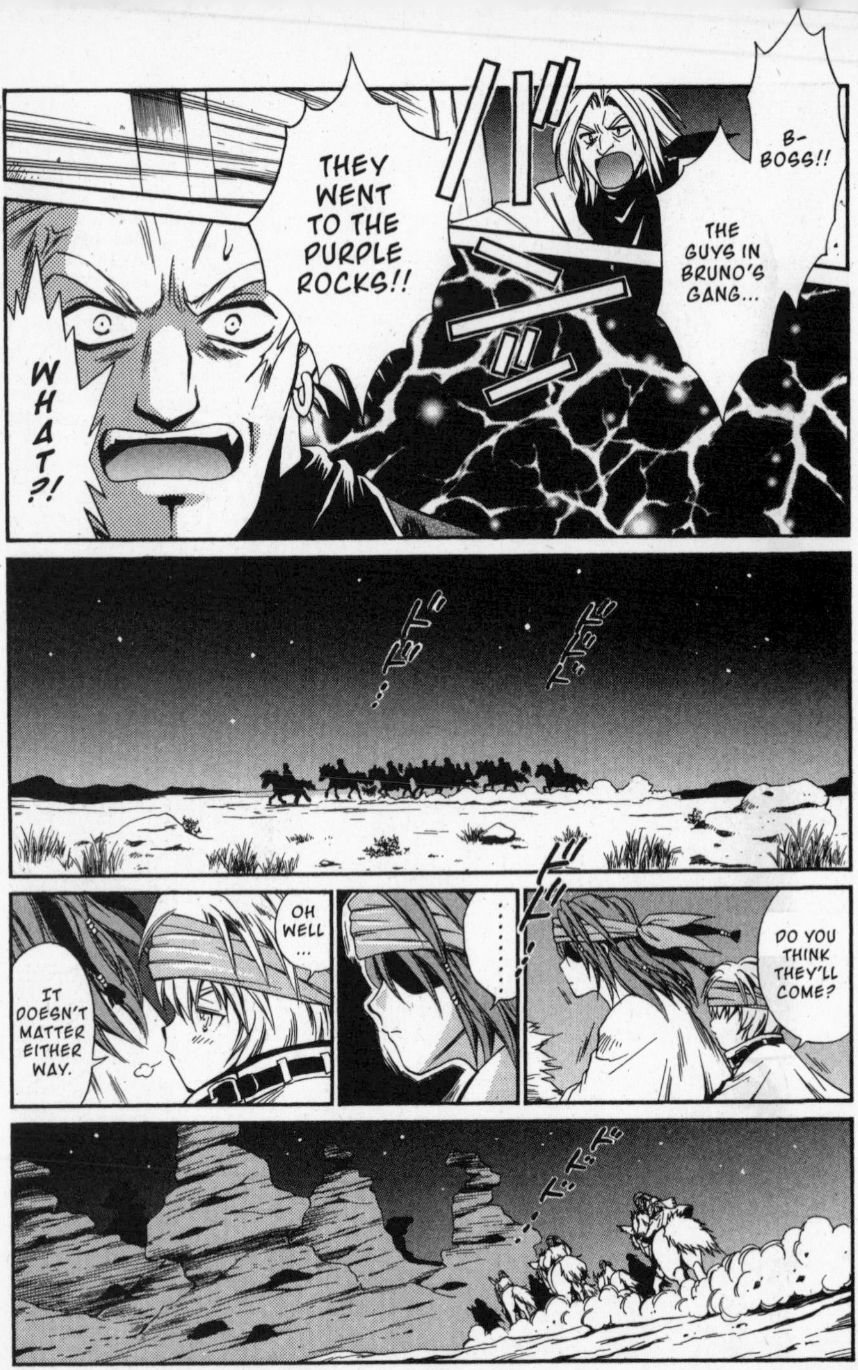
B-BOSS!!
THE GUYS IN BRUNO'S GANG...
THEY WENT TO THE PURPLE ROCKS!!
WHAT?!
DO YOU THINK THEY'LL COME?
......
OH WELL ...
IT DOESN'T MATTER EITHER WAY.

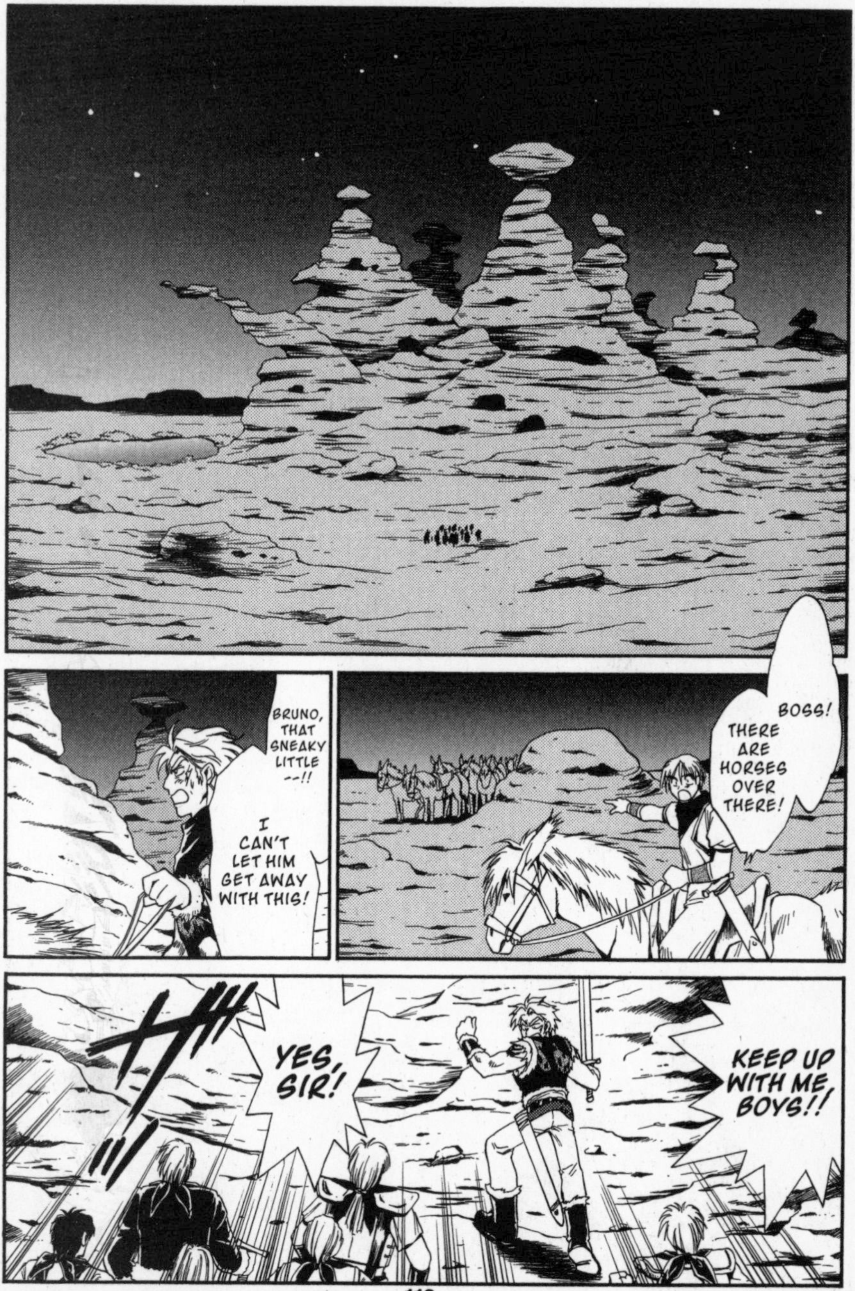
BOSS! THERE ARE HORSES OVER THERE!
BRUNO, THAT SNEAKY LITTLE --!!
I CAN'T LET HIM GET AWAY WITH THIS!
KEEP UP WITH ME, BOYS!!
YES, SIR!

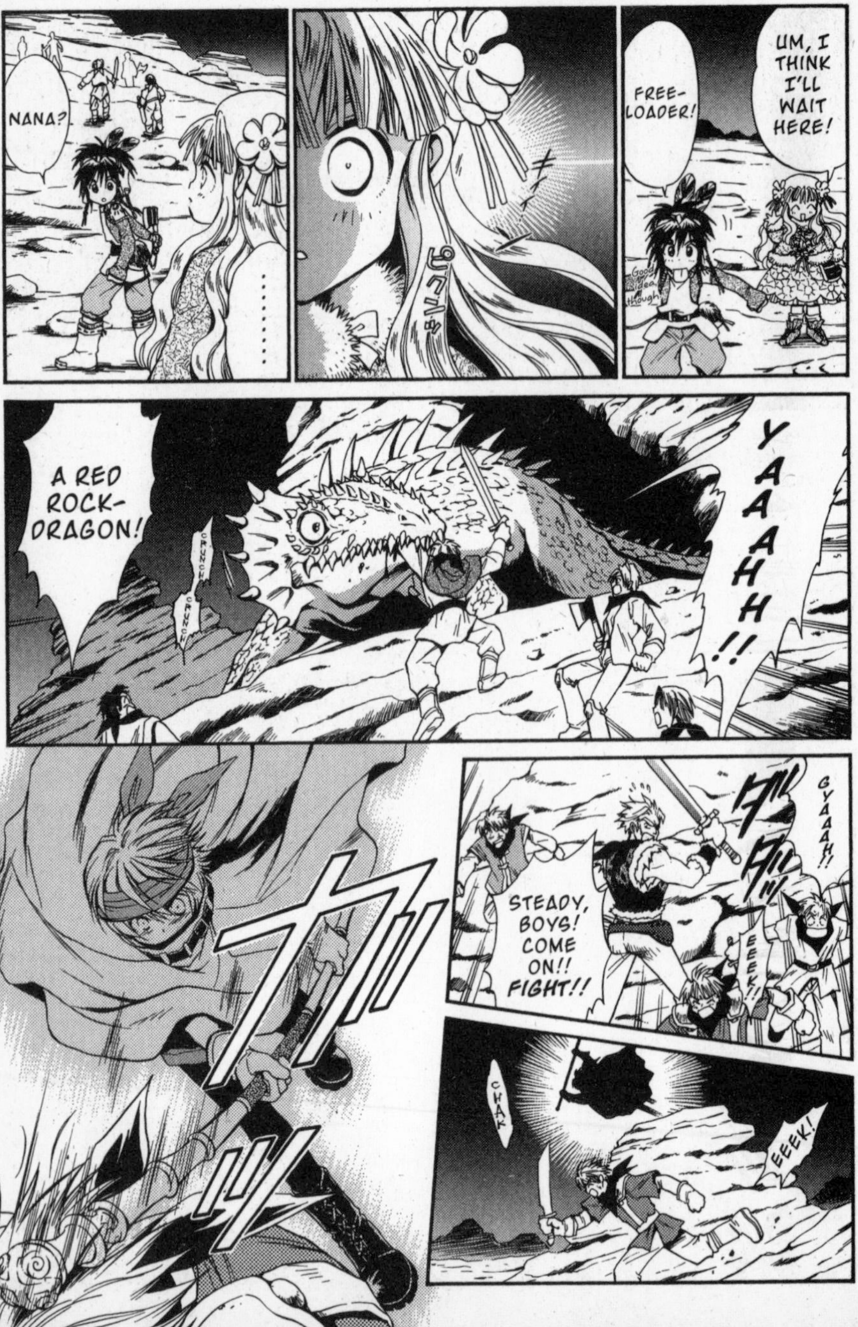
UM, I THINK I'LL WAIT HERE!
FREE-LOADER!
Good idea, though
NANA?
......
YAAAAHH!!
A RED ROCK-DRAGON!
CRUNCH
CRUNCH
GYAAAH!!
STEADY, BOYS! COME ON!! FIGHT!!
EEEK!!
EEEK!
CHAK

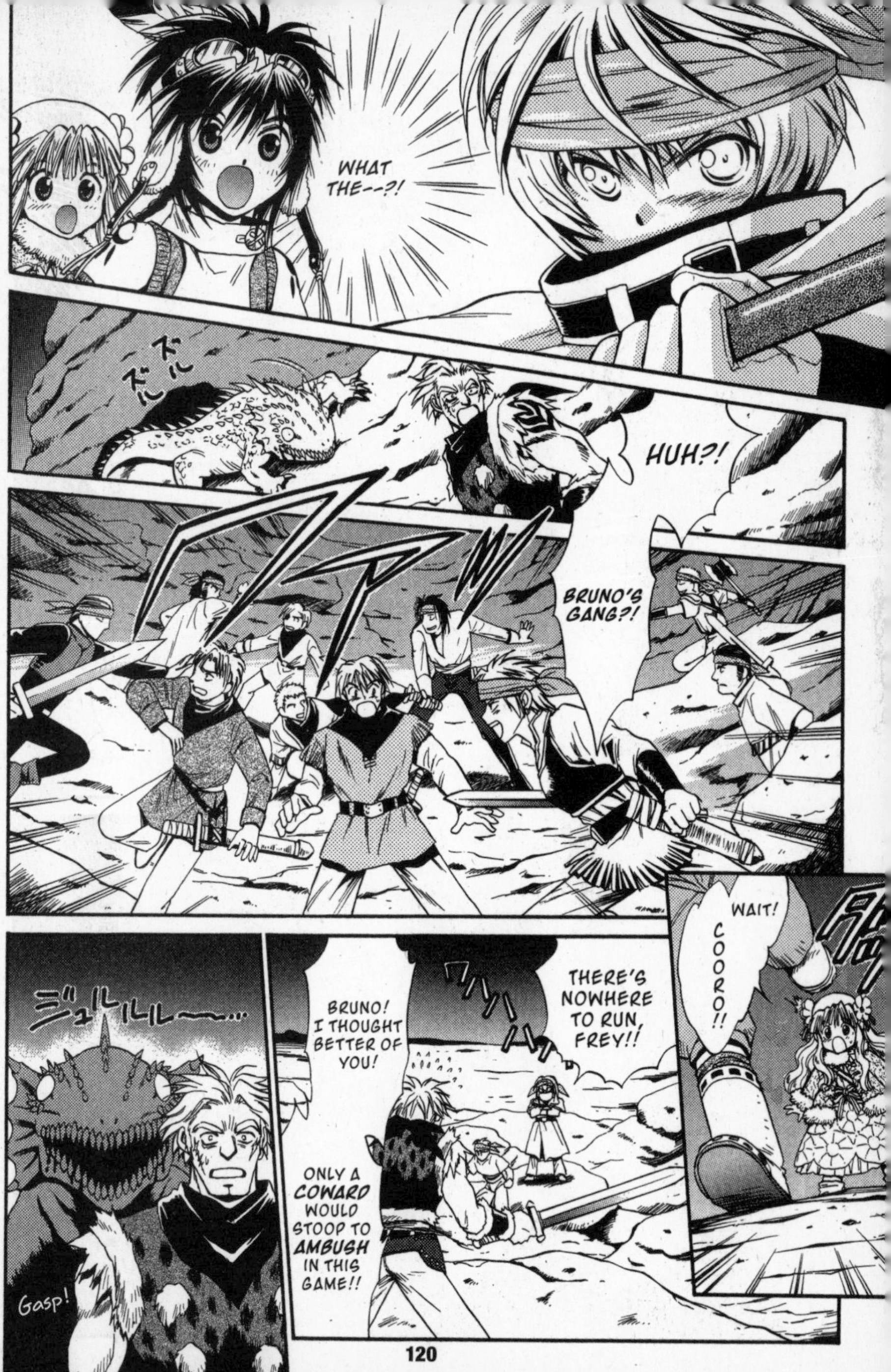
WHAT THE--?!
HUH?!
BRUNO'S GANG?!
WAIT! COORO!!
THERE'S NOWHERE TO RUN, FREY!!
BRUNO! I THOUGHT BETTER OF YOU!
ONLY A COWARD WOULD STOOP TO AMBUSH IN THIS GAME!!
Gasp!

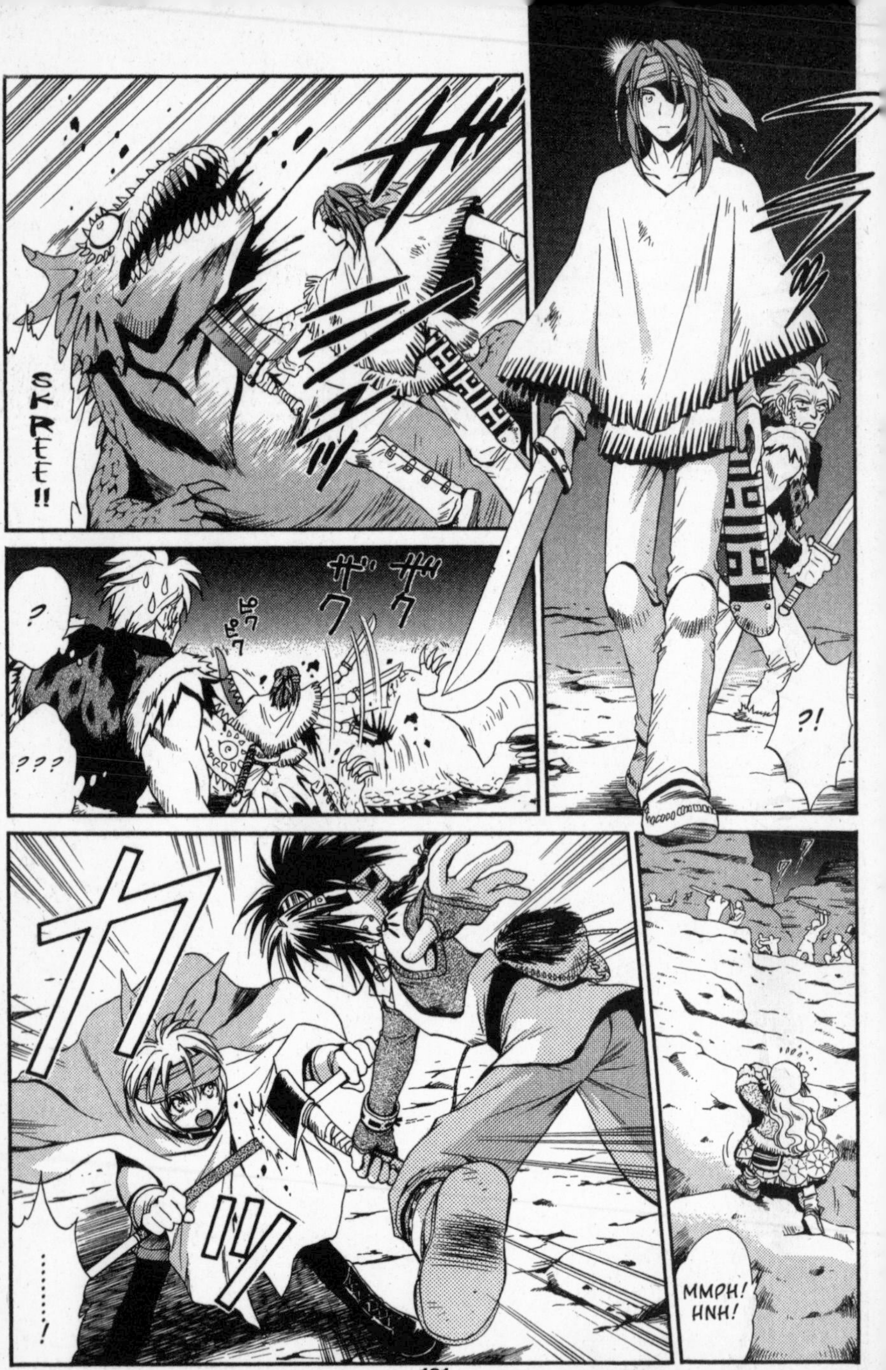
?!
SKREEE!!
ザク ザク
ピク ピク
?
???
MMPH! HNH!
......!

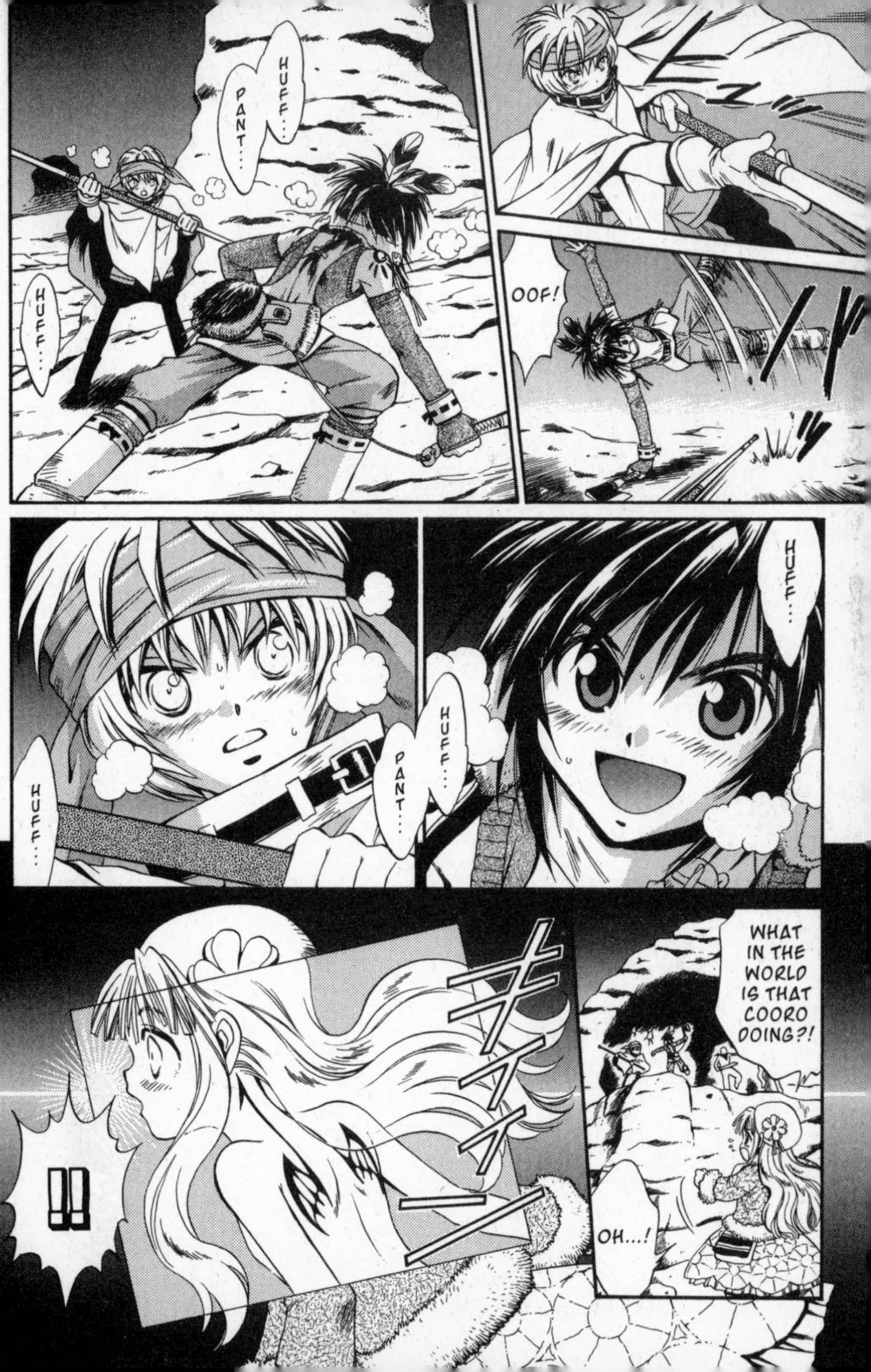
OOF!
HUFF... PANT...
HUFF...
HUFF...
HUFF... PANT...
HUFF...
WHAT IN THE WORLD IS THAT COORO DOING?!
OH...!
!!

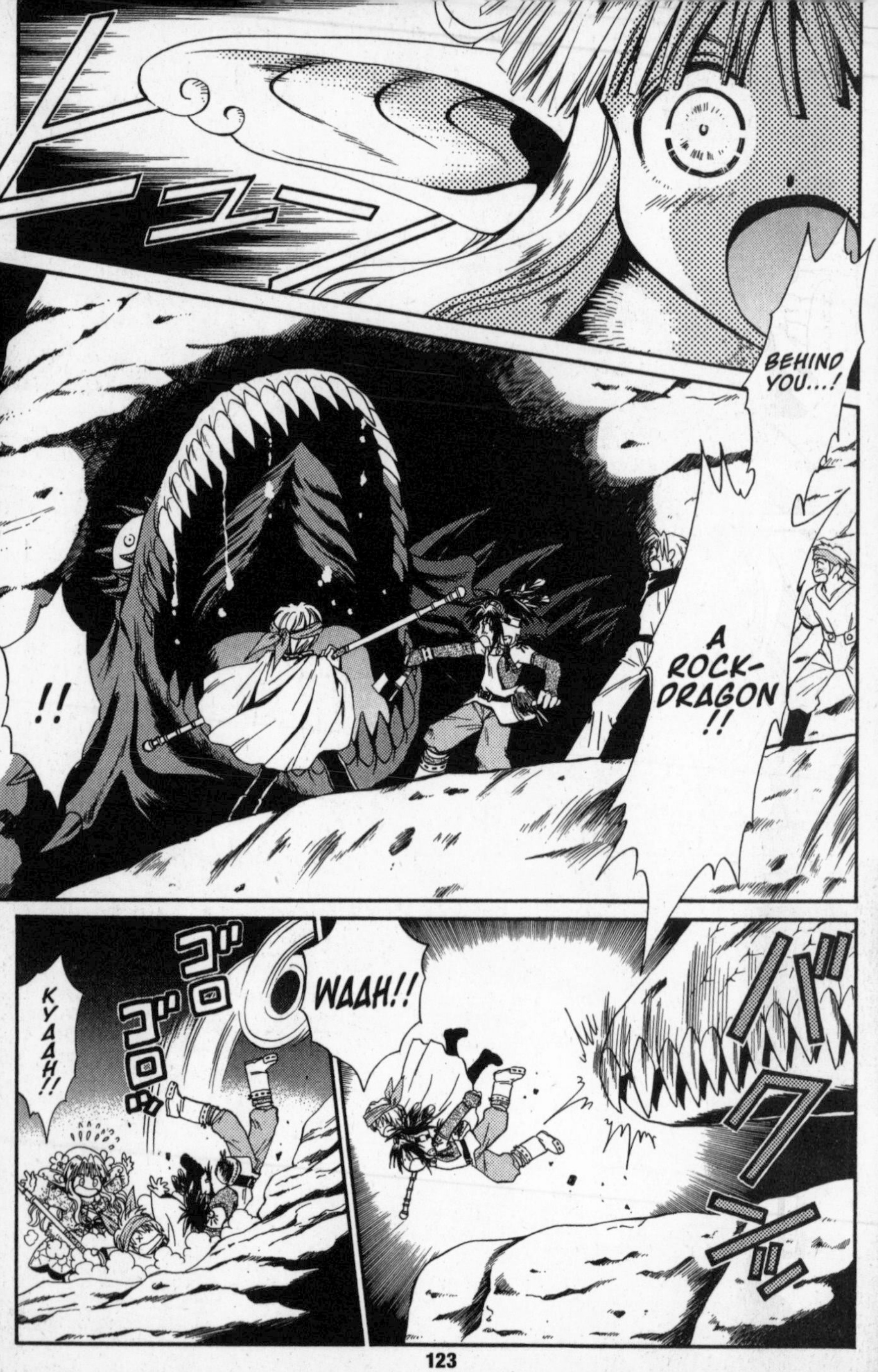
BEHIND YOU...!
A ROCK-DRAGON!!
!!
WAAH!!
KYAAH!!

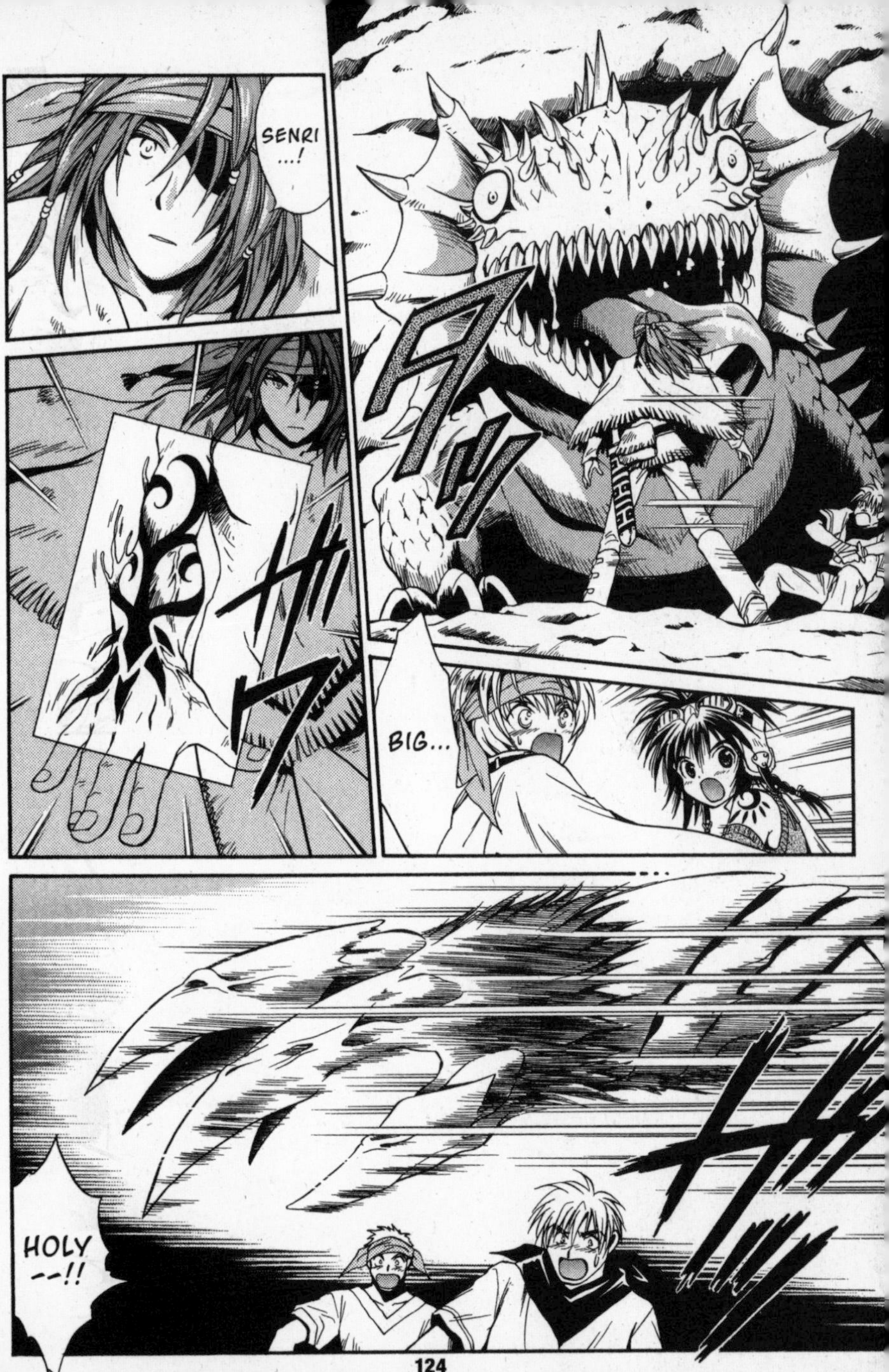

SENRI ...!
BIG...
HOLY --!!

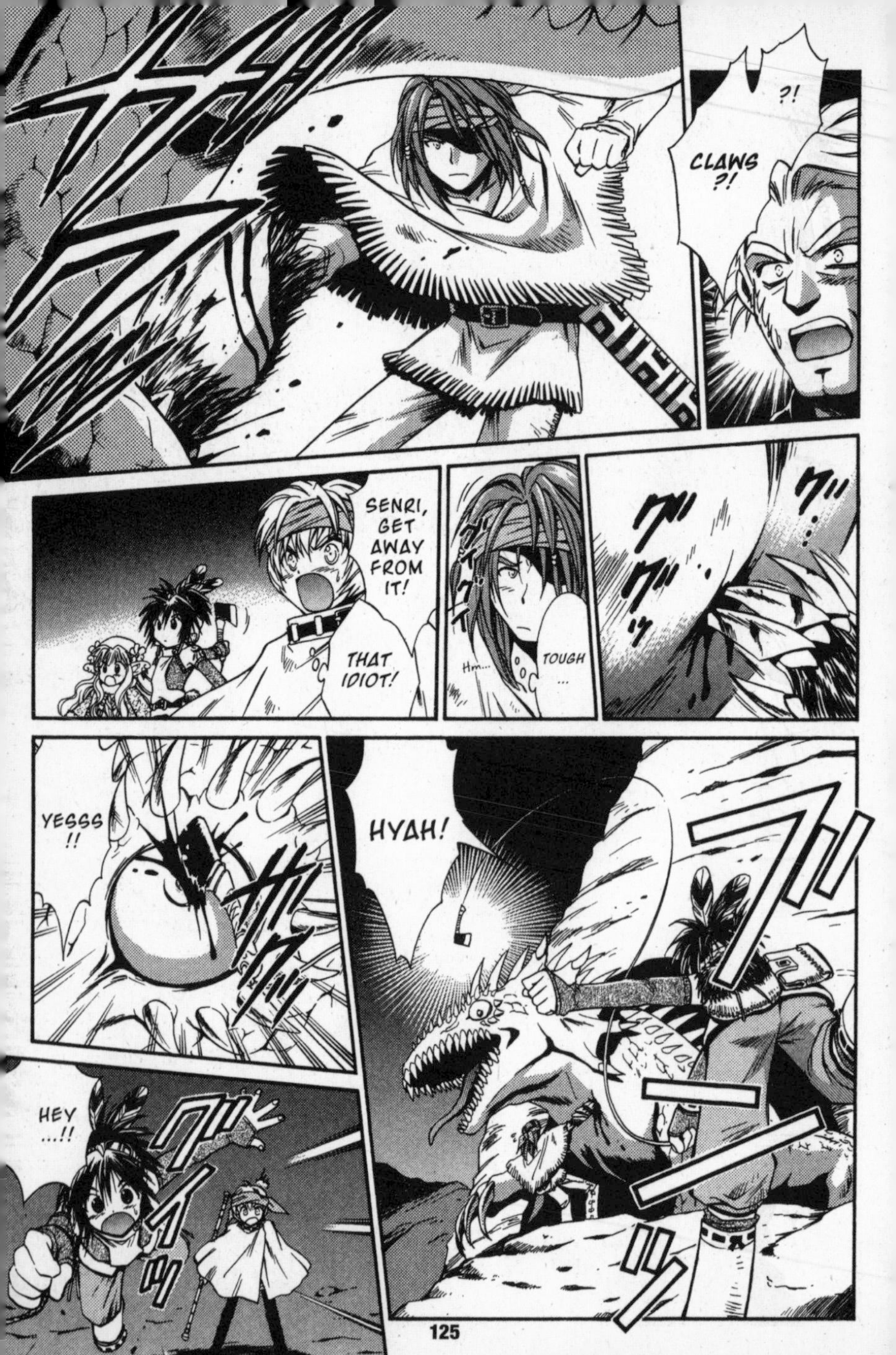
?!
CLAWS ?!
Hm...
TOUGH ...
SENRI, GET AWAY FROM IT!
THAT IDIOT!
HYAH!
YESSS !!
HEY ...!!

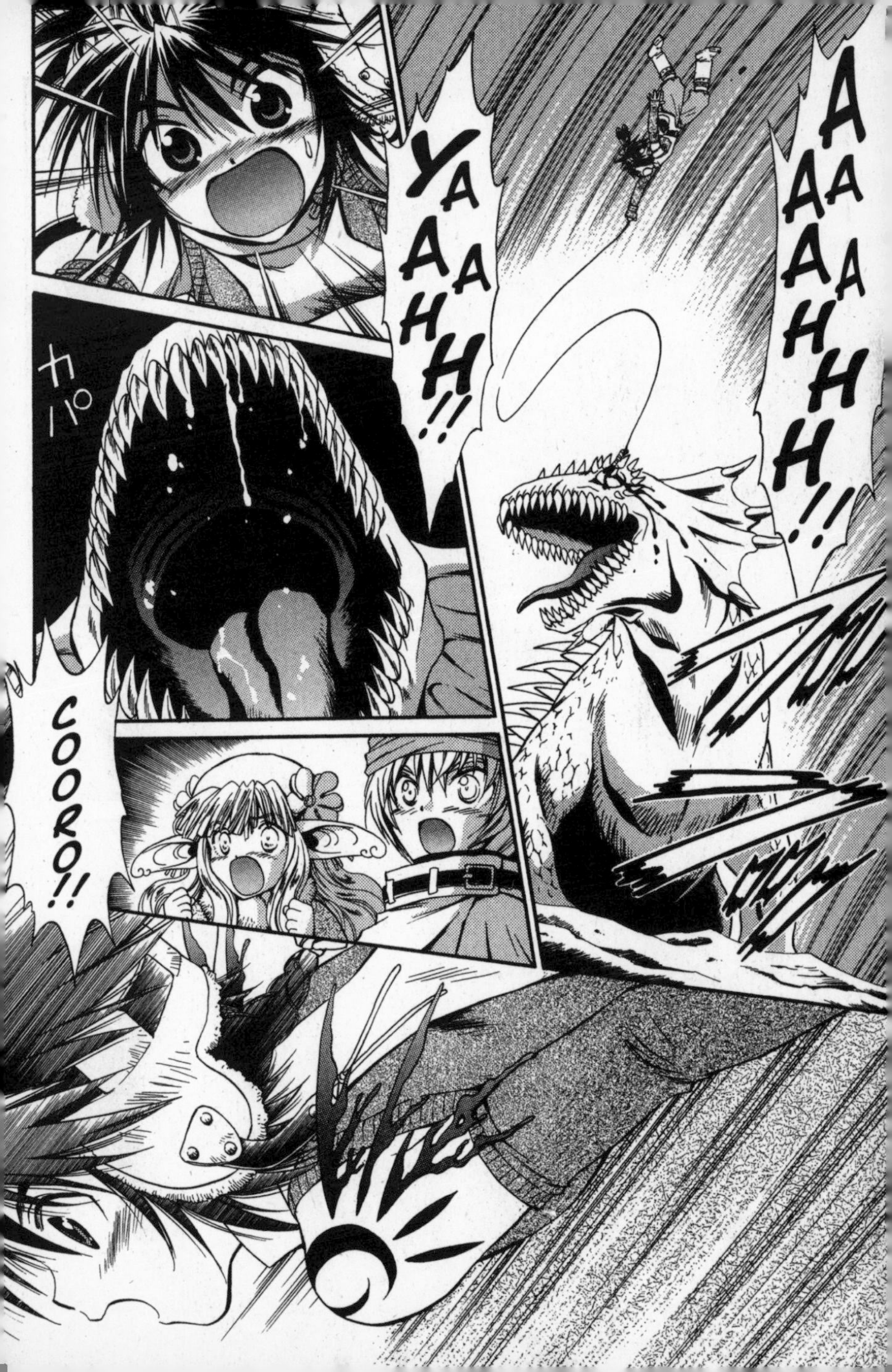
AAAAAAAHHHH!!
YAAAHH!!
カパ
COOORO!!

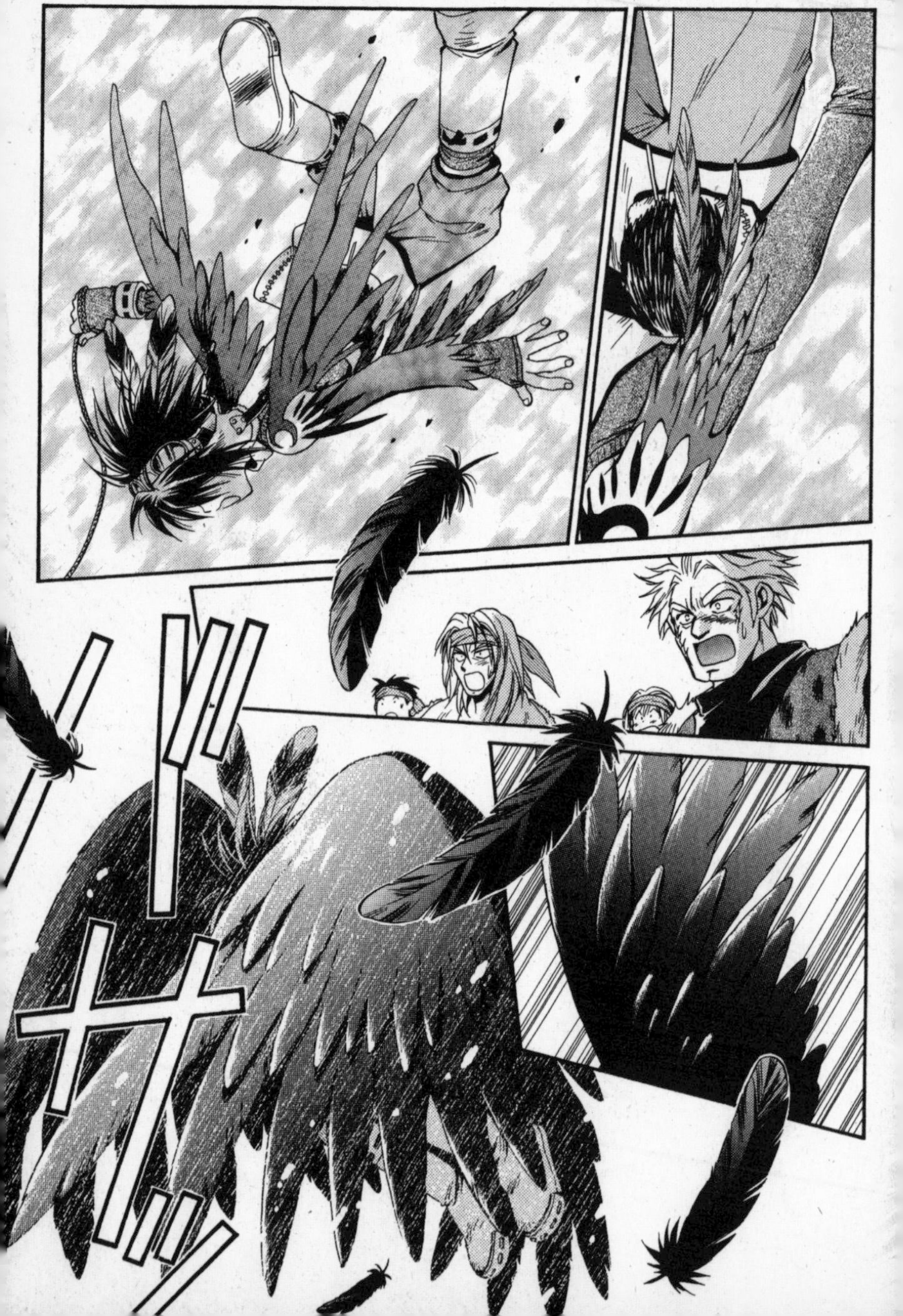
ドサッ

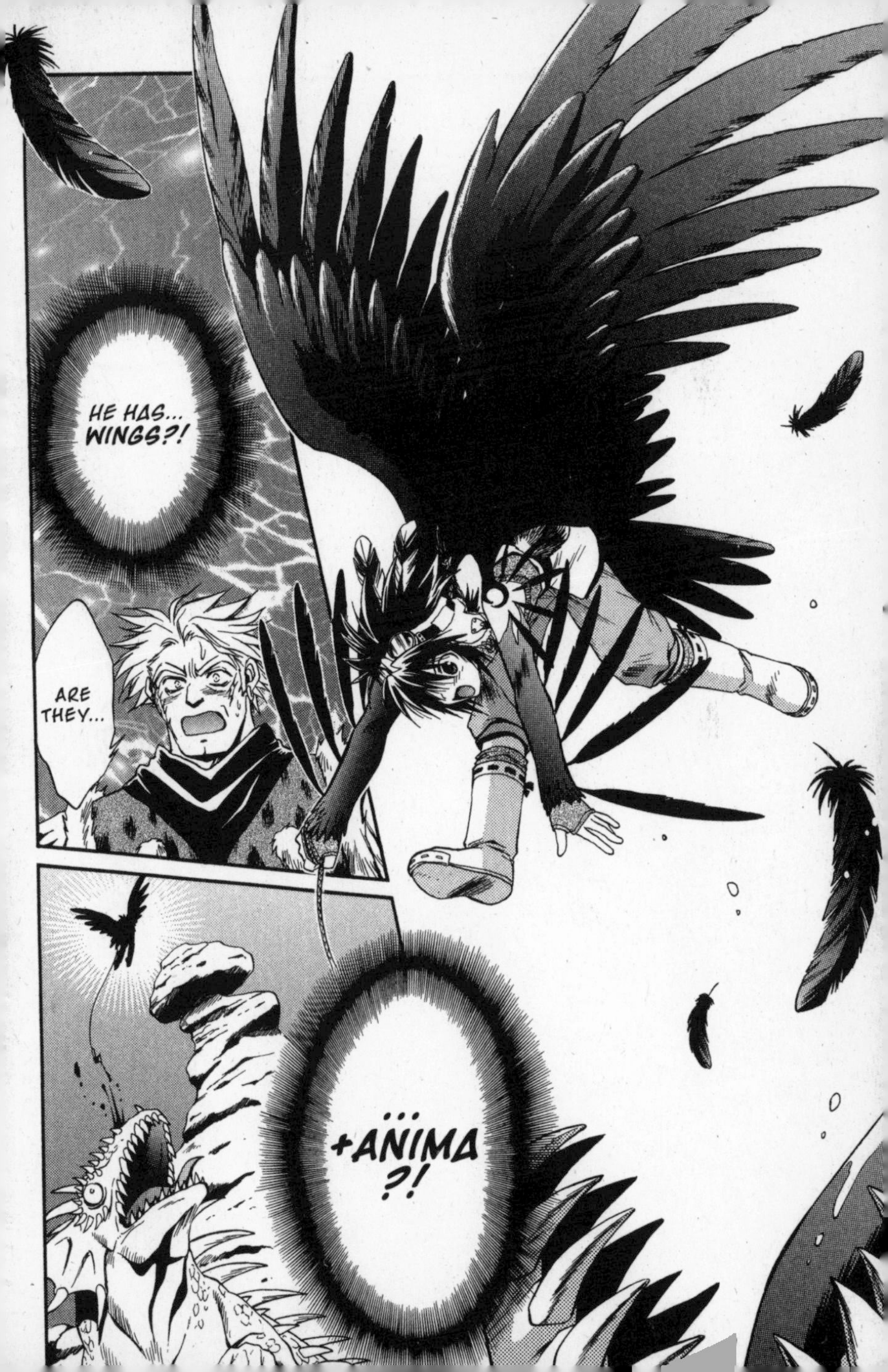
HE HAS... WINGS?!
ARE THEY...
...+ANIMA ?!

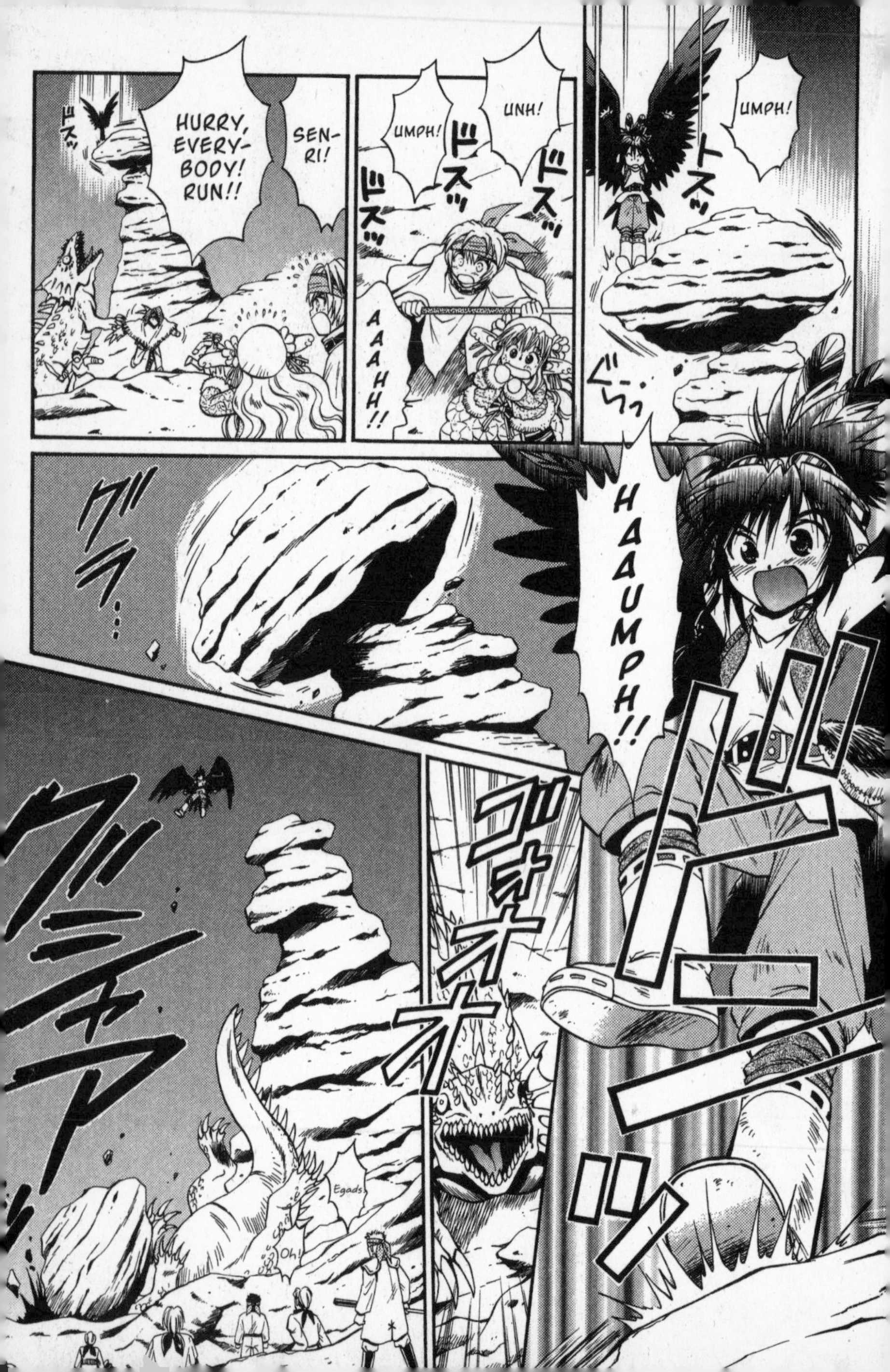
UMPH!
トスッ
ぐらっ
UNH!
UMPH!
ドスッ
ドスッ
ドスッ
AAAHH!!
SEN-RI!
HURRY, EVERY-BODY! RUN!!
ドスッ
HAAUMPH!!
ドン
グラ…
ゴォオオ
Egads.
Oh!
グシャア…

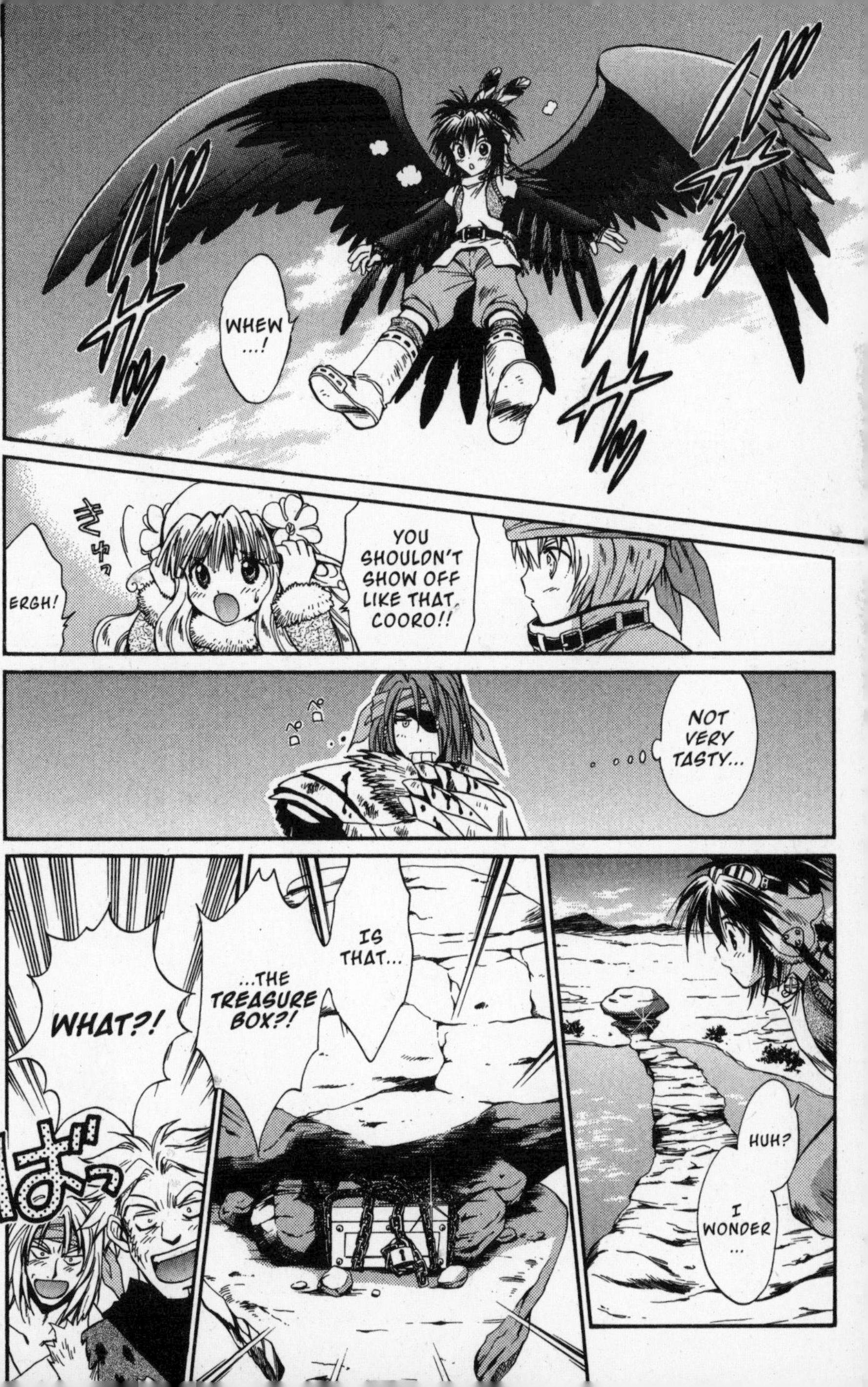
WHEW ...!
YOU SHOULDN'T SHOW OFF LIKE THAT, COORO!!
ERGH!
NOT VERY TASTY...
HUH?
I WONDER ...
IS THAT...
...THE TREASURE BOX?!
WHAT?!
ばっ

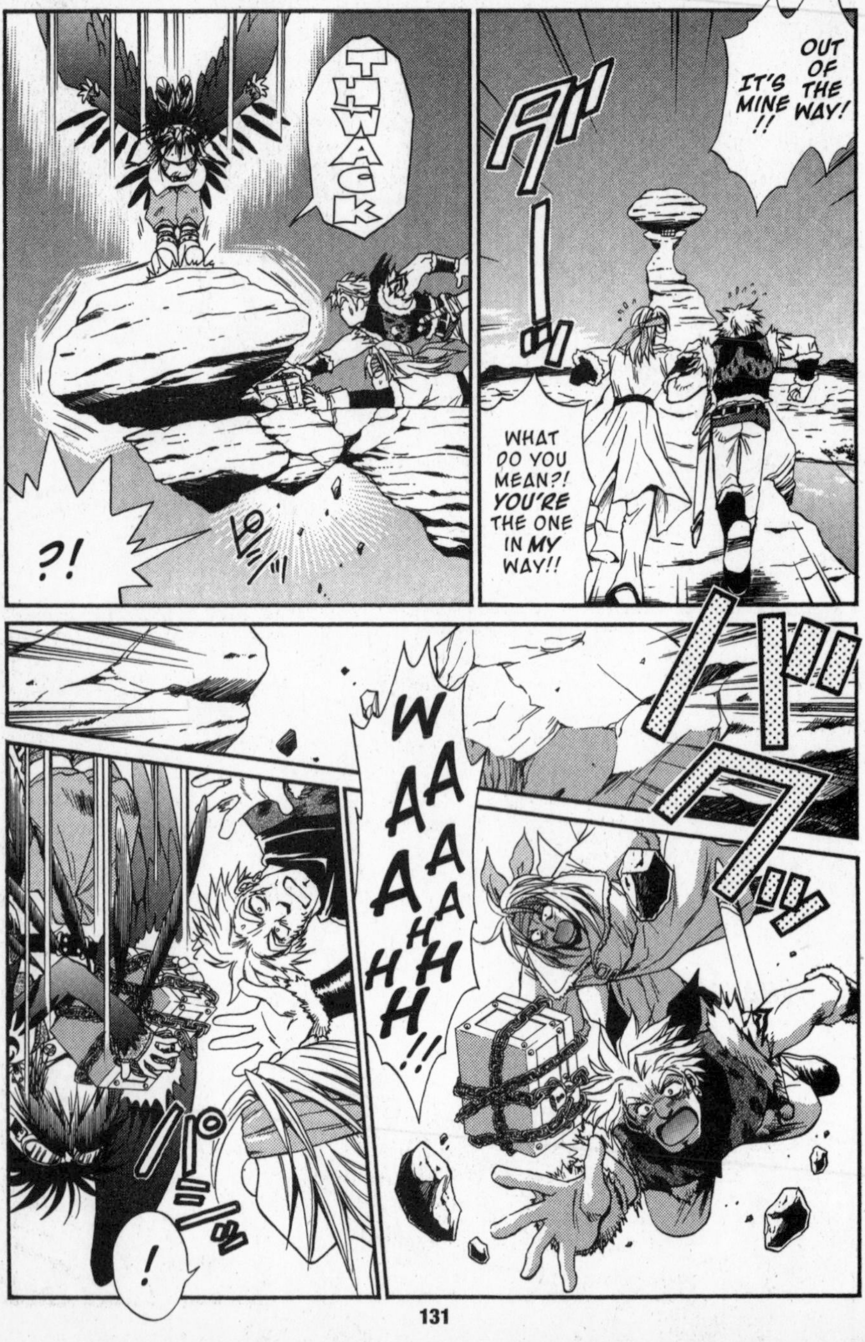
OUT OF THE WAY!
IT'S MINE!!
WHAT DO YOU MEAN?! YOU'RE THE ONE IN MY WAY!!
THWACK
?!
WAAAAAAHHHHH!!
!

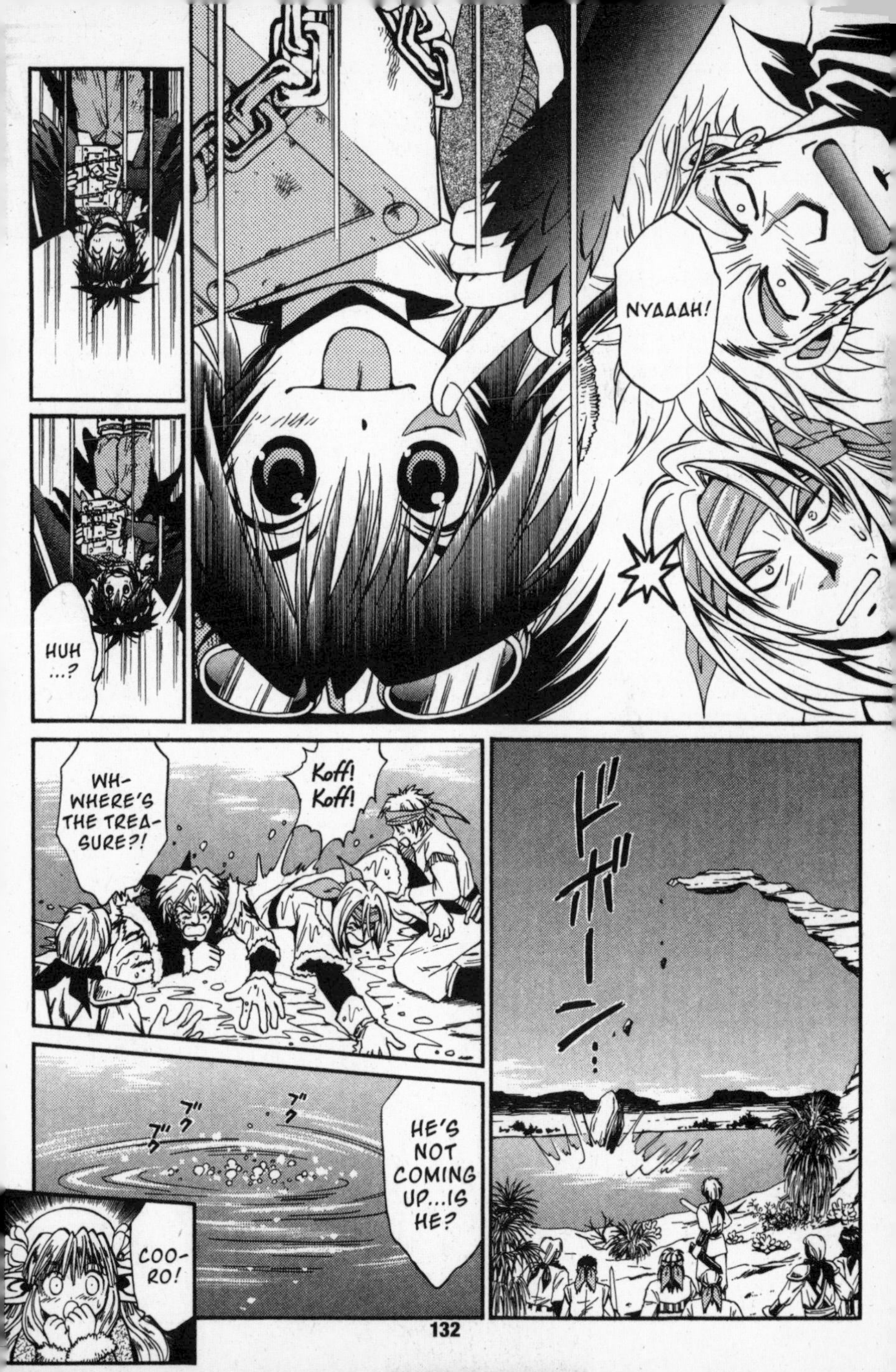
NYAAAH!
HUH ...?
ドボーン…
Koff! Koff!
WH-WHERE'S THE TREASURE?!
HE'S NOT COMING UP...IS HE?
ブク ブク ブク
COO-RO!

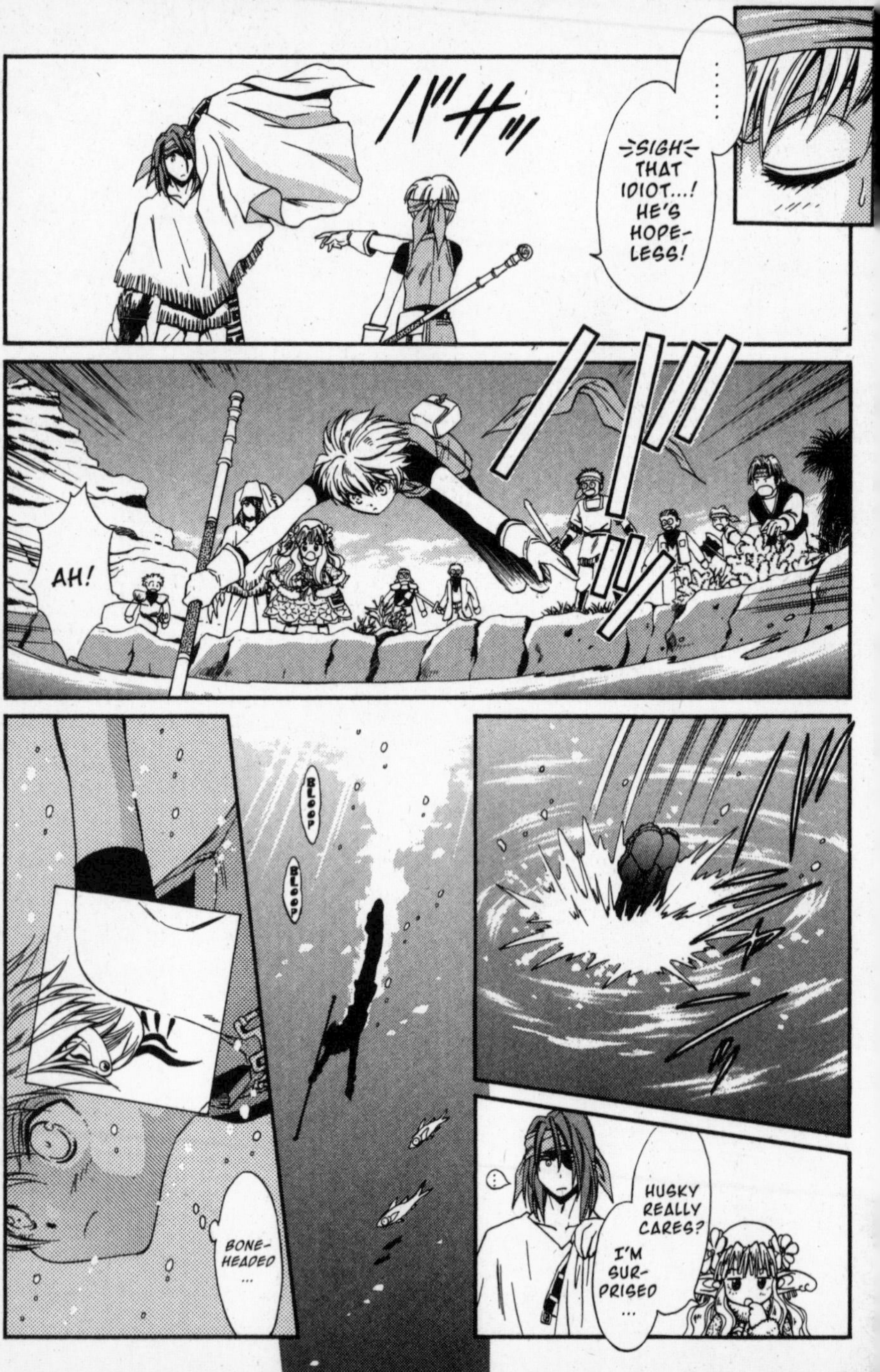
......
=SIGH= THAT IDIOT....! HE'S HOPE-LESS!
バサッ
AH!
...
HUSKY REALLY CARES? I'M SUR-PRISED ...
BLOOP
BLOOP
BONE-HEADED ...

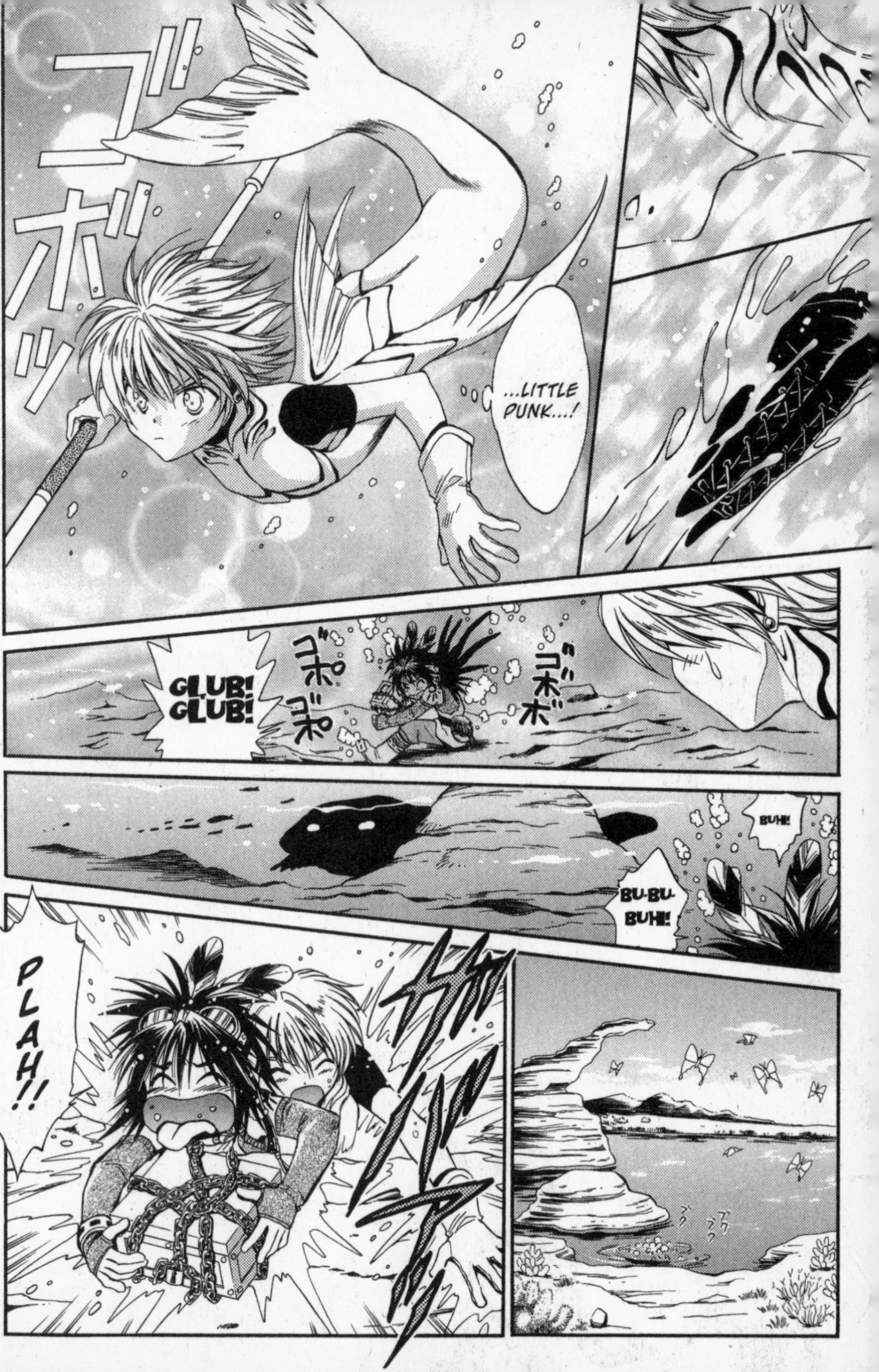
ゴボッ
...LITTLE PUNK...!
ゴボボ
ゴポゴポ
GLUB! GLUB!
BUH!
BU-BU-BUH!
PLAH!!

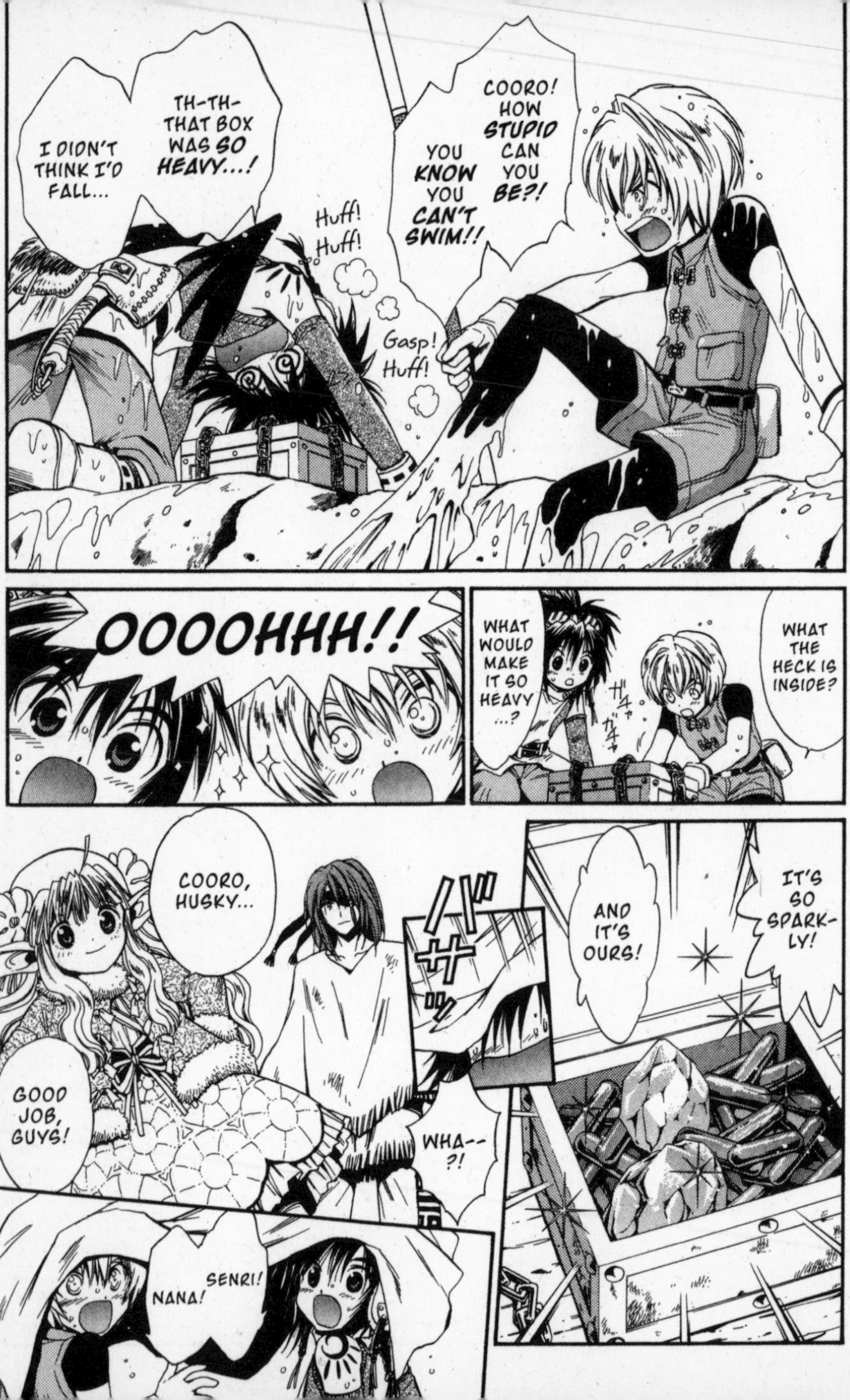
COORO! HOW STUPID CAN YOU BE?!
YOU KNOW YOU CAN'T SWIM!!
Gasp! Huff!
Huff! Huff!
TH-TH-THAT BOX WAS SO HEAVY...!
I DIDN'T THINK I'D FALL...
WHAT THE HECK IS INSIDE?
WHAT WOULD MAKE IT SO HEAVY...?
OOOOHHH!!
IT'S SO SPARKLY!
AND IT'S OURS!
COORO, HUSKY...
GOOD JOB, GUYS!
WHA--?!
SENRI!
NANA!

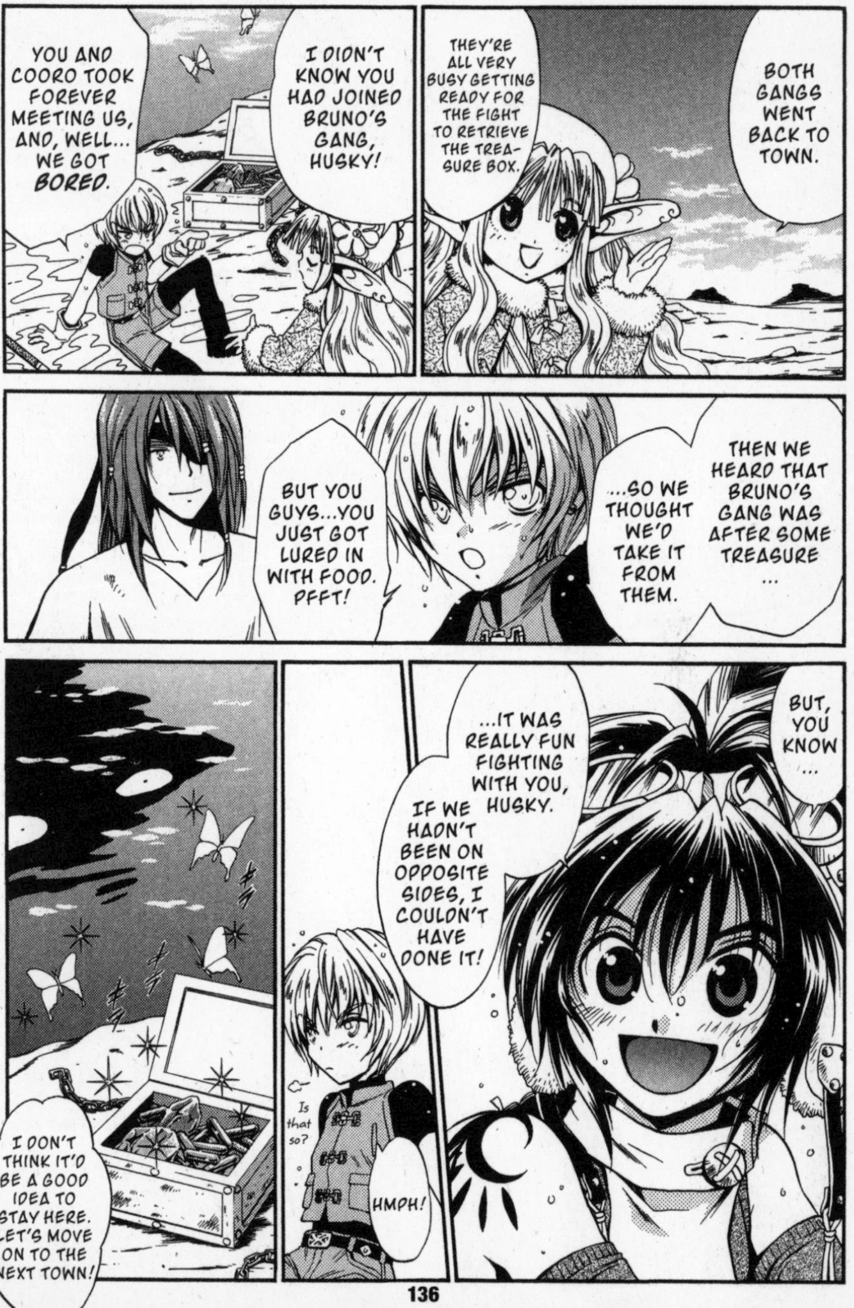

BOTH GANGS WENT BACK TO TOWN.
THEY'RE ALL VERY BUSY GETTING READY FOR THE FIGHT TO RETRIEVE THE TREASURE BOX.
I DIDN'T KNOW YOU HAD JOINED BRUNO'S GANG, HUSKY!
YOU AND COORO TOOK FOREVER MEETING US, AND, WELL... WE GOT *BORED*.
THEN WE HEARD THAT BRUNO'S GANG WAS AFTER SOME TREASURE...
...SO WE THOUGHT WE'D TAKE IT FROM THEM.
BUT YOU GUYS...YOU JUST GOT LURED IN WITH FOOD. PFFT!
BUT, YOU KNOW...
...IT WAS REALLY FUN FIGHTING WITH YOU, HUSKY.
IF WE HADN'T BEEN ON OPPOSITE SIDES, I COULDN'T HAVE DONE IT!
Is that so?
HMPH!
I DON'T THINK IT'D BE A GOOD IDEA TO STAY HERE. LET'S MOVE ON TO THE NEXT TOWN!

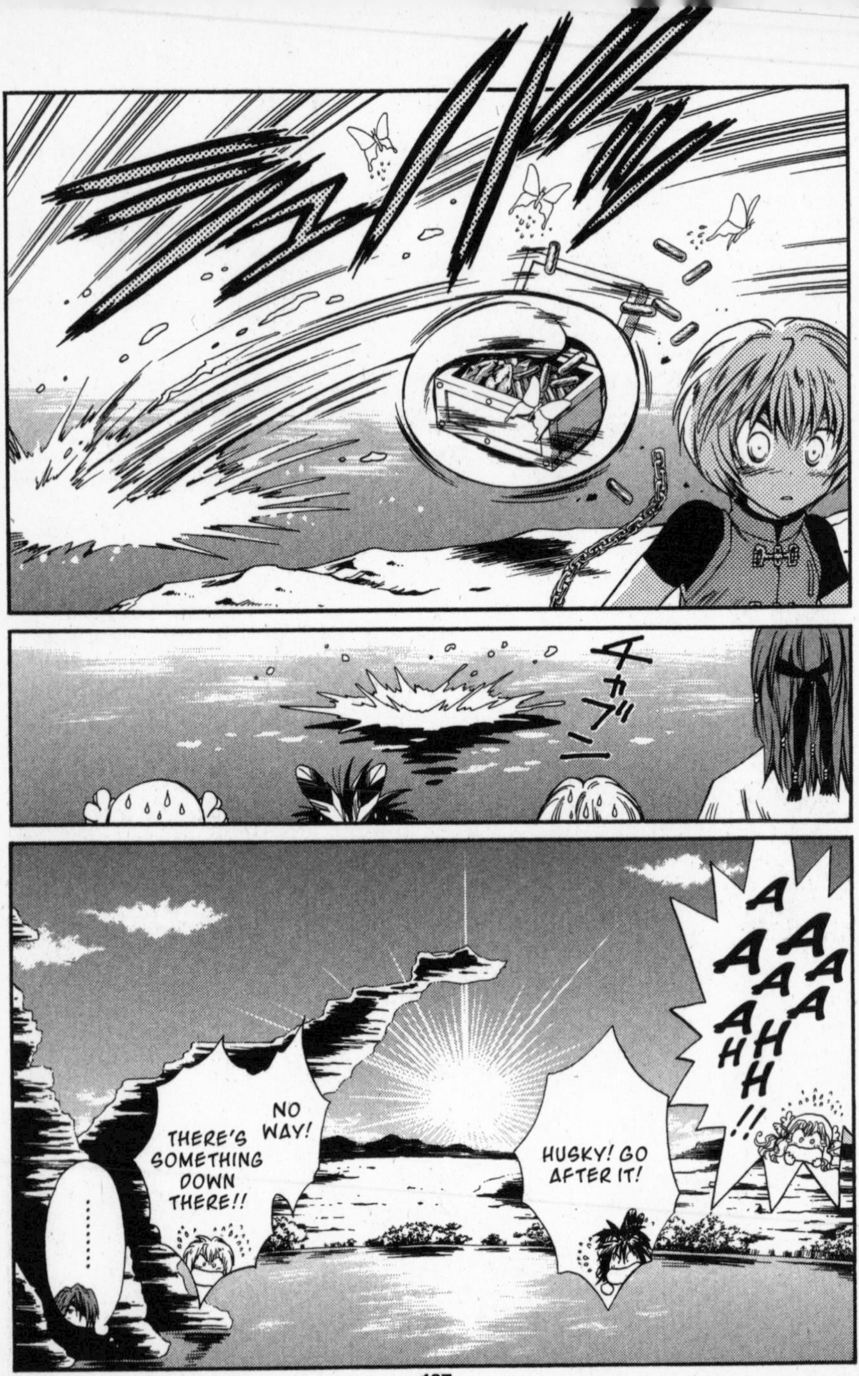
AAAAAAAAAAHHHH!!
HUSKY! GO AFTER IT!
NO WAY!
THERE'S SOMETHING DOWN THERE!!
......

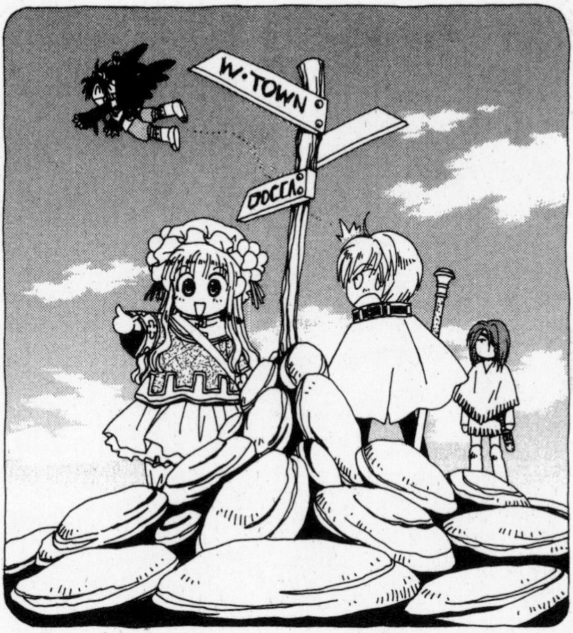
W·TOWN
DOCCA

Where do you go?

Parallel 2
Dreaming in the Ocean

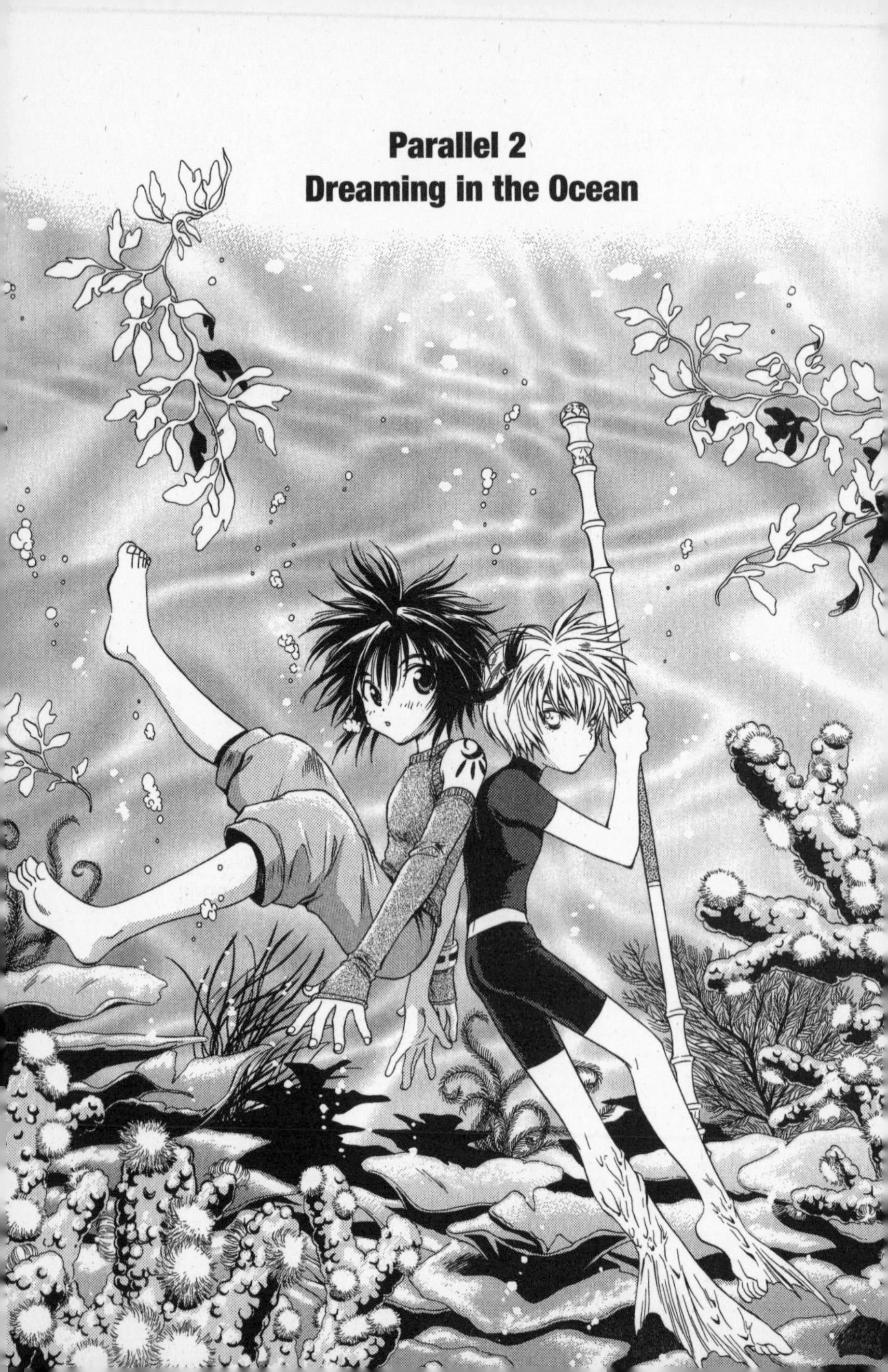

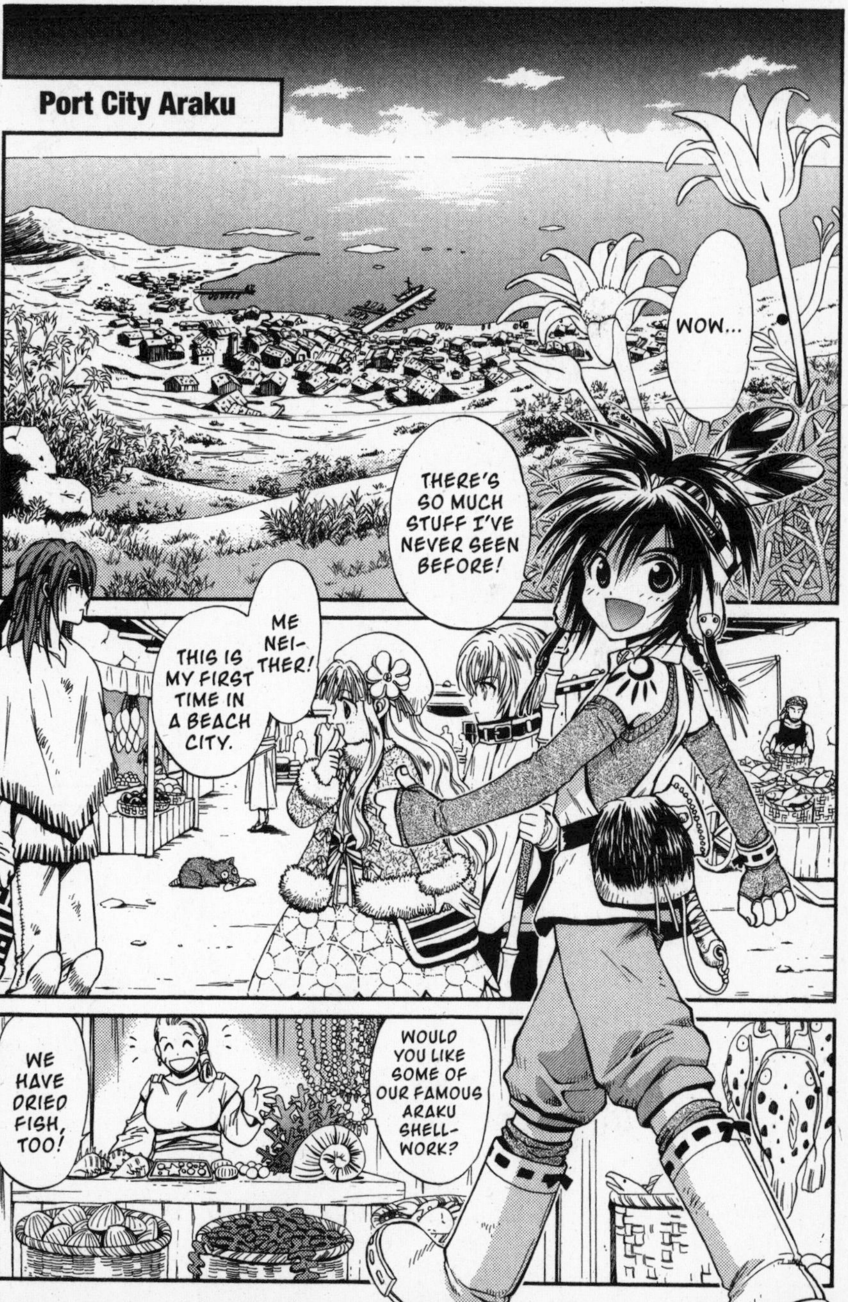
Port City Araku
WOW...
THERE'S SO MUCH STUFF I'VE NEVER SEEN BEFORE!
ME NEI-THER!
THIS IS MY FIRST TIME IN A BEACH CITY.
WOULD YOU LIKE SOME OF OUR FAMOUS ARAKU SHELL-WORK?
WE HAVE DRIED FISH, TOO!

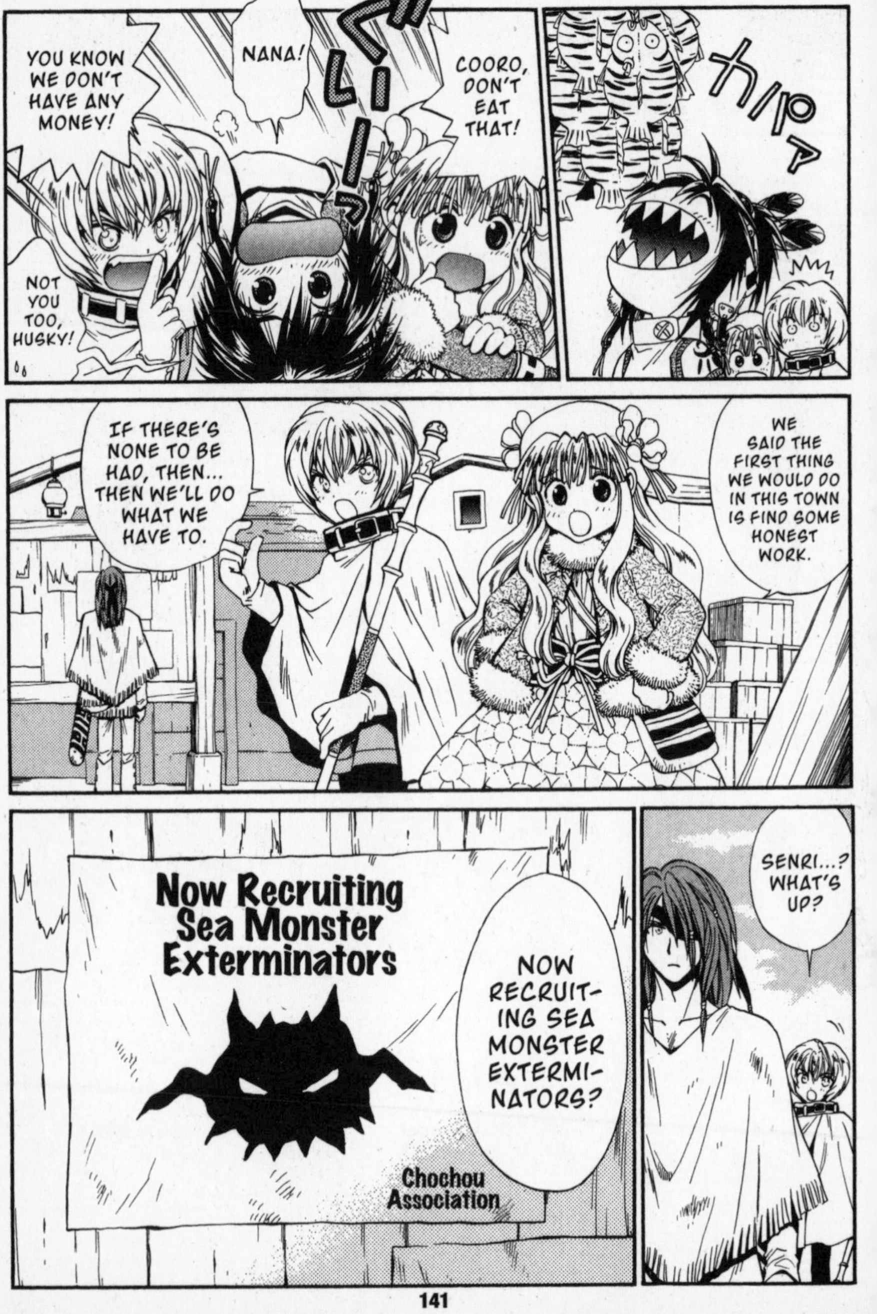
カパァ
COORO, DON'T EAT THAT!
ぐいーっ
NANA!
YOU KNOW WE DON'T HAVE ANY MONEY!
NOT YOU TOO, HUSKY!
WE SAID THE FIRST THING WE WOULD DO IN THIS TOWN IS FIND SOME HONEST WORK.
IF THERE'S NONE TO BE HAD, THEN... THEN WE'LL DO WHAT WE HAVE TO.
SENRI...? WHAT'S UP?
NOW RECRUIT-ING SEA MONSTER EXTERMI-NATORS?
Now Recruiting Sea Monster Exterminators
Chochou Association

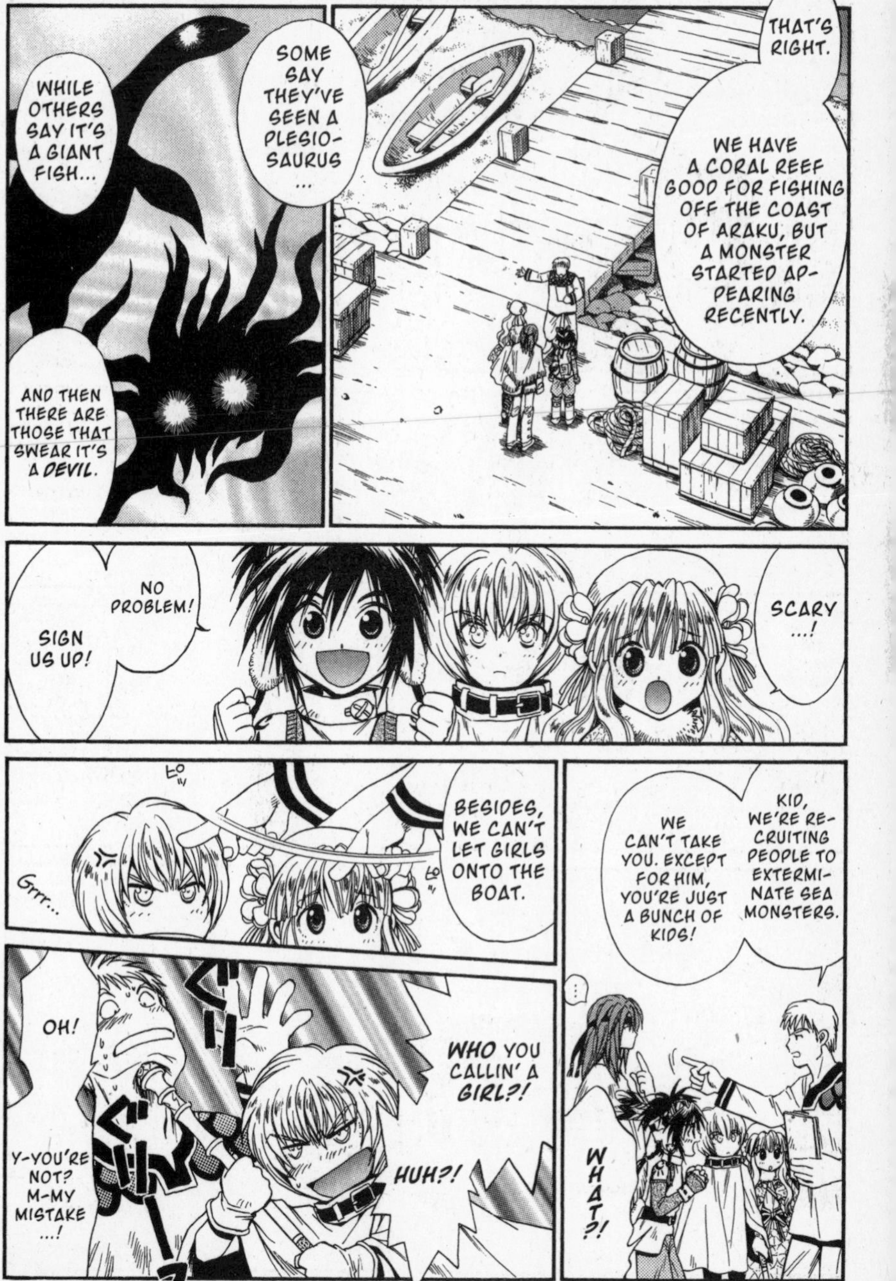

THAT'S RIGHT.
WE HAVE A CORAL REEF GOOD FOR FISHING OFF THE COAST OF ARAKU, BUT A MONSTER STARTED APPEARING RECENTLY.
SOME SAY THEY'VE SEEN A PLESIOSAURUS ...
WHILE OTHERS SAY IT'S A GIANT FISH...
AND THEN THERE ARE THOSE THAT SWEAR IT'S A *DEVIL*.
SCARY ...!
NO PROBLEM!
SIGN US UP!
KID, WE'RE RECRUITING PEOPLE TO EXTERMINATE SEA MONSTERS.
WE CAN'T TAKE YOU. EXCEPT FOR HIM, YOU'RE JUST A BUNCH OF KIDS!
...
WHAT?!
BESIDES, WE CAN'T LET GIRLS ONTO THE BOAT.
Grrr...
WHO YOU CALLIN' A *GIRL?!*
HUH?!
OH!
Y-YOU'RE NOT? M-MY MISTAKE ...!

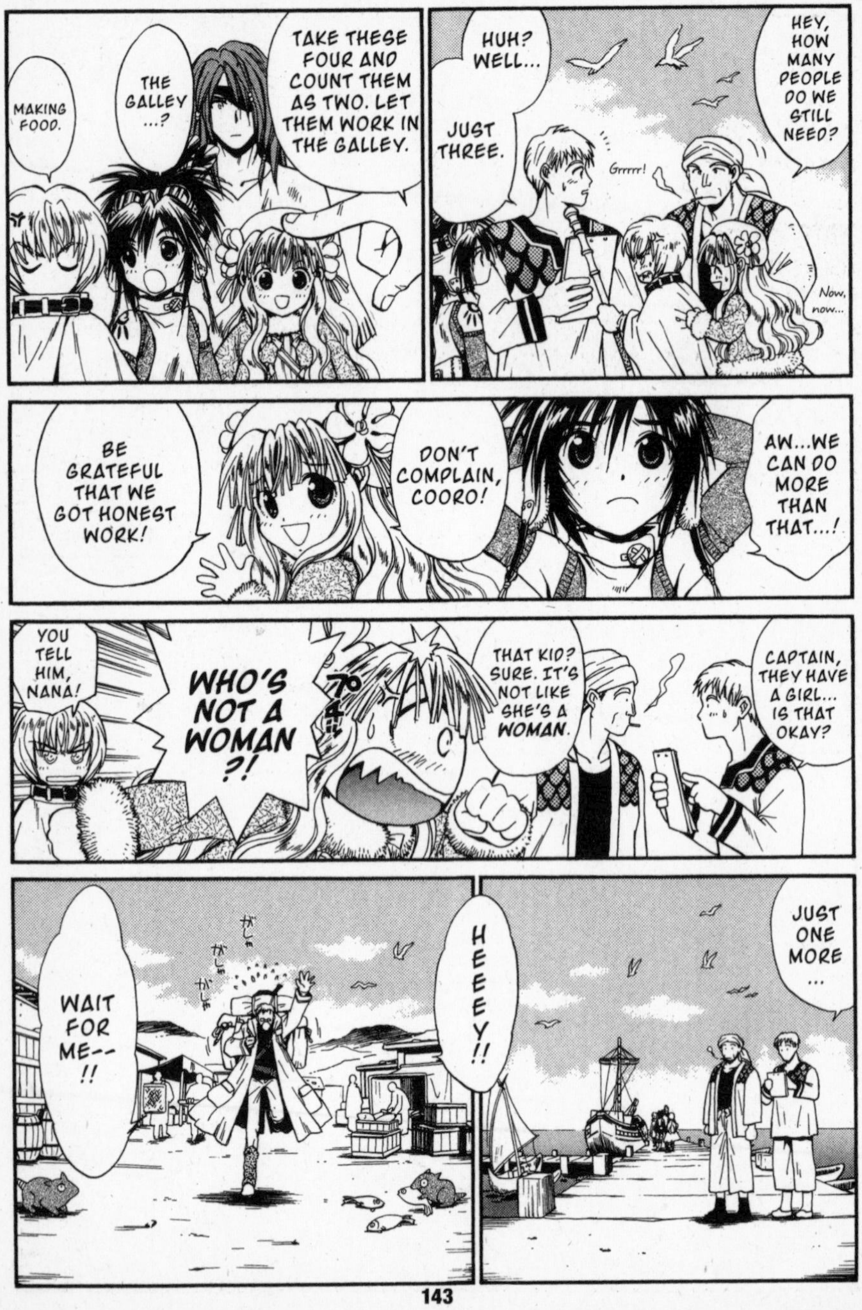
HEY, HOW MANY PEOPLE DO WE STILL NEED?
Grrrrr!
HUH? WELL...
JUST THREE.
Now, now...
TAKE THESE FOUR AND COUNT THEM AS TWO. LET THEM WORK IN THE GALLEY.
THE GALLEY ...?
MAKING FOOD.
AW...WE CAN DO MORE THAN THAT...!
DON'T COMPLAIN, COORO!
BE GRATEFUL THAT WE GOT HONEST WORK!
CAPTAIN, THEY HAVE A GIRL... IS THAT OKAY?
THAT KID? SURE. IT'S NOT LIKE SHE'S A WOMAN.
WHO'S NOT A WOMAN ?!
YOU TELL HIM, NANA!
JUST ONE MORE ...
HEEEEY!!
WAIT FOR ME-- !!

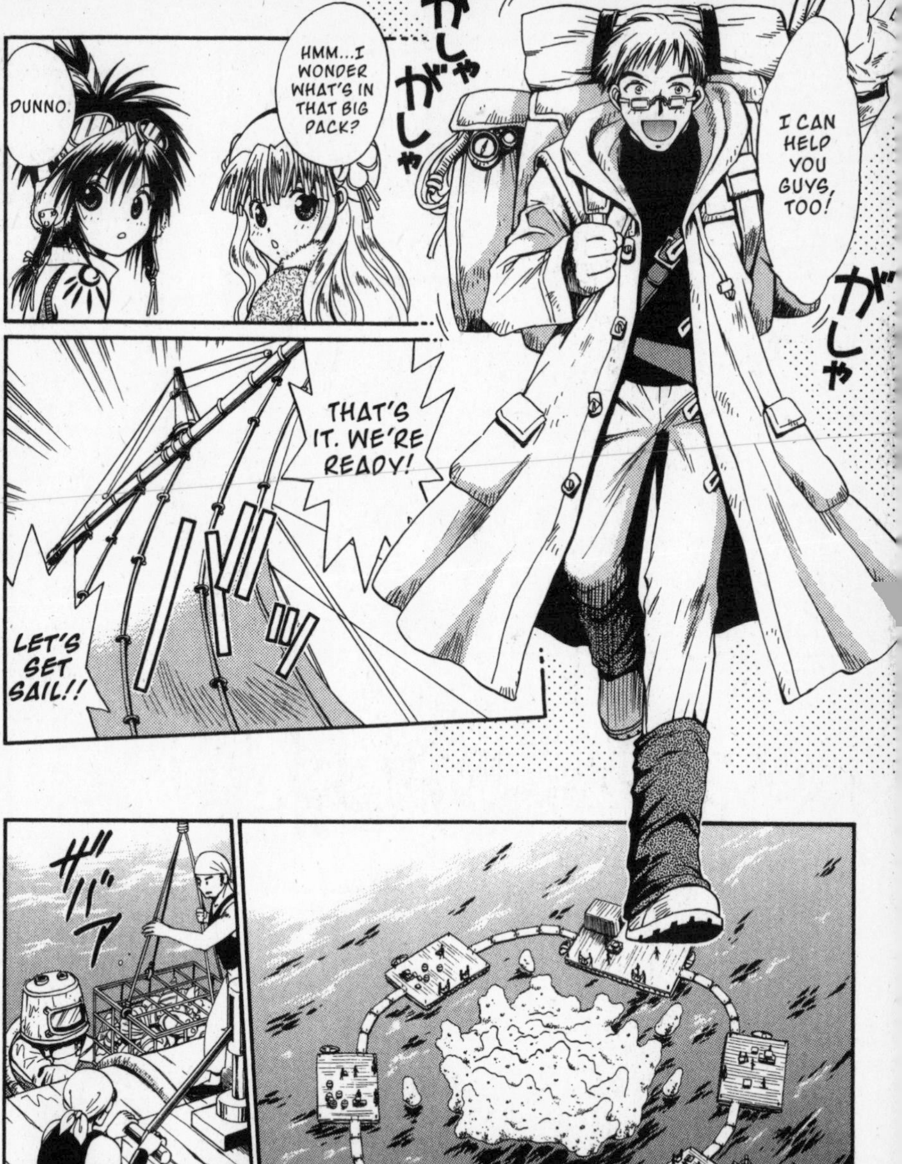
がしゃがしゃ
I CAN HELP YOU GUYS, TOO!
がしゃ
HMM...I WONDER WHAT'S IN THAT BIG PACK?
DUNNO.
THAT'S IT. WE'RE READY!
LET'S SET SAIL!!
ザバア

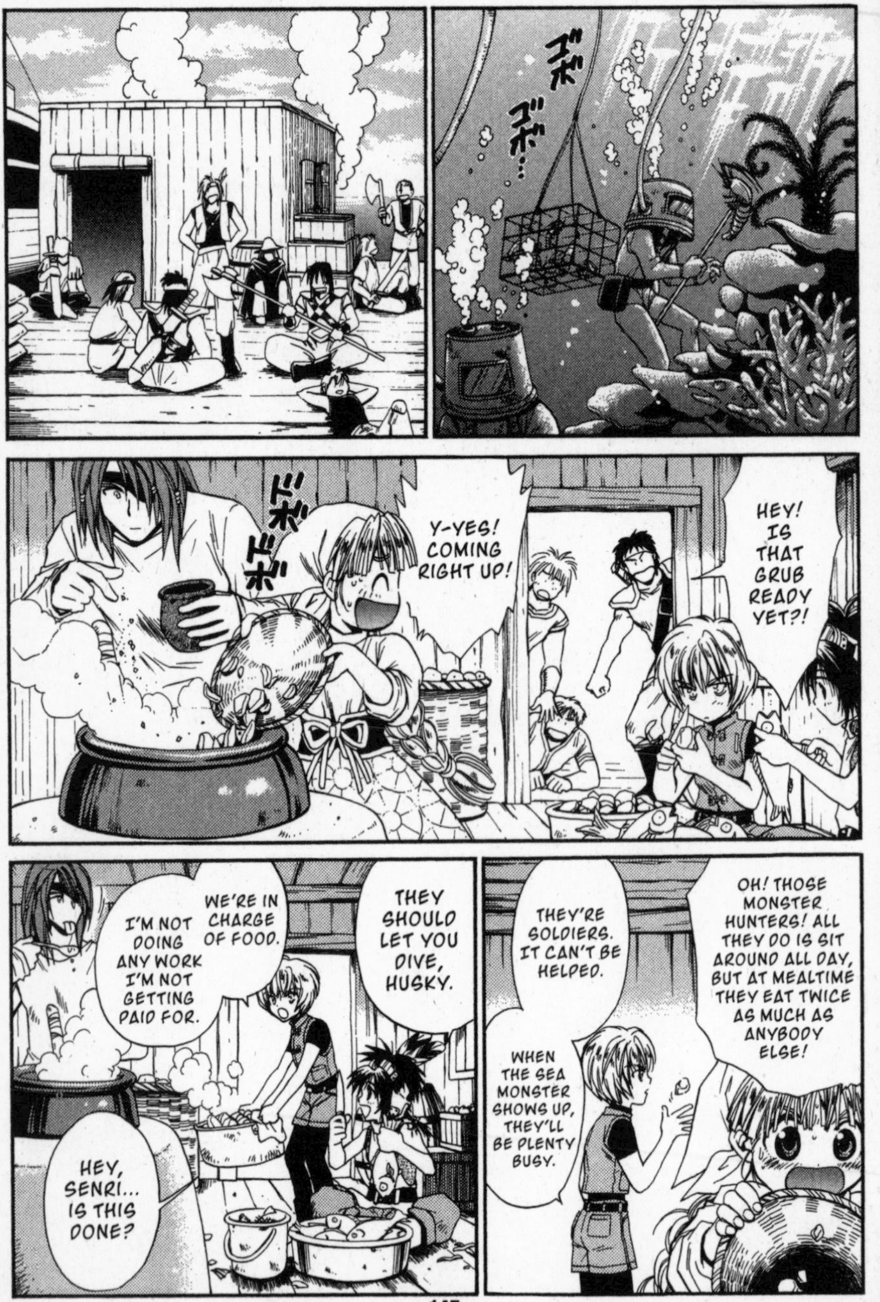
ゴボ
ゴボ…
HEY! IS THAT GRUB READY YET?!
Y-YES! COMING RIGHT UP!
ドボ
ドボ
OH! THOSE MONSTER HUNTERS! ALL THEY DO IS SIT AROUND ALL DAY, BUT AT MEALTIME THEY EAT TWICE AS MUCH AS ANYBODY ELSE!
THEY'RE SOLDIERS. IT CAN'T BE HELPED.
WHEN THE SEA MONSTER SHOWS UP, THEY'LL BE PLENTY BUSY.
THEY SHOULD LET YOU DIVE, HUSKY.
WE'RE IN CHARGE OF FOOD.
I'M NOT DOING ANY WORK I'M NOT GETTING PAID FOR.
HEY, SENRI... IS THIS DONE?

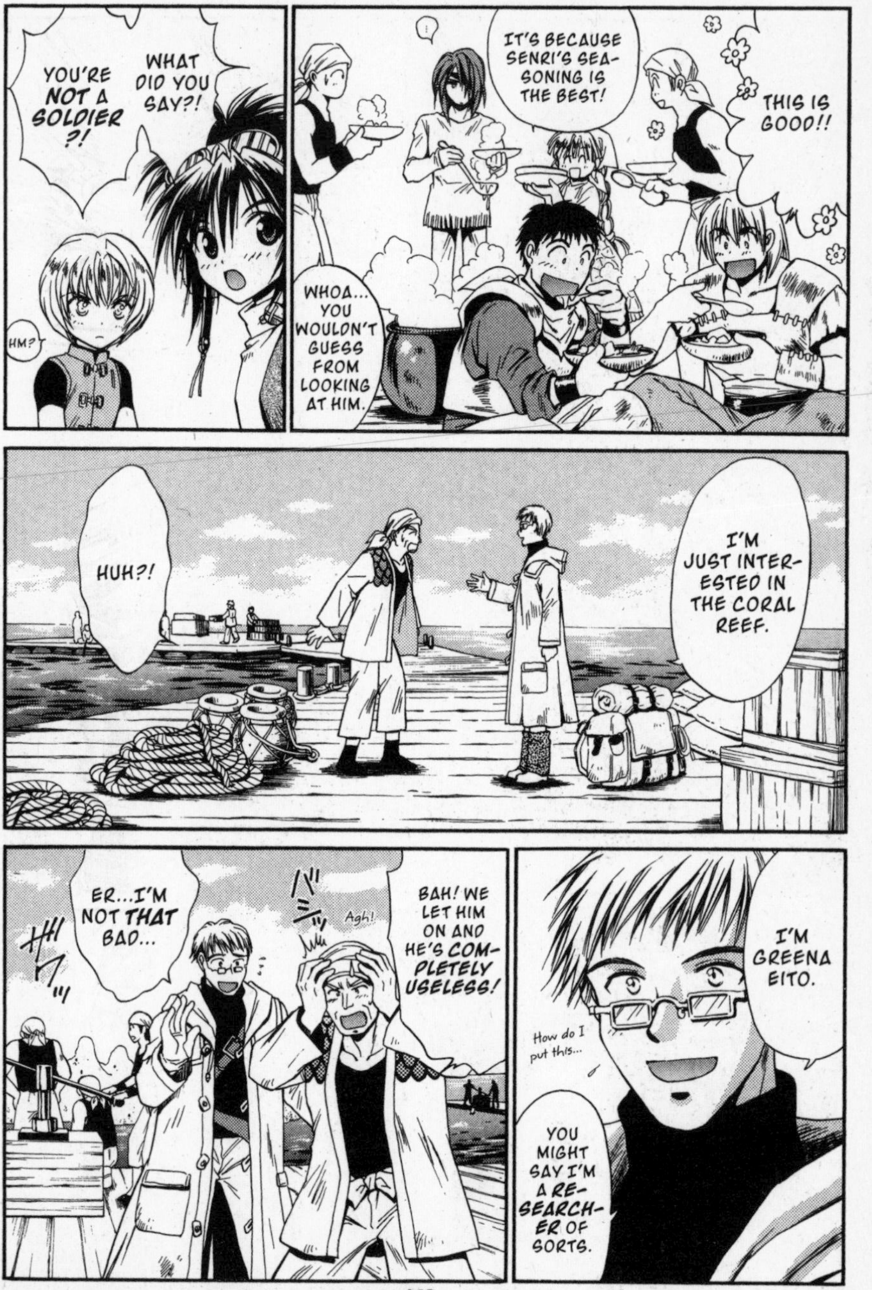
THIS IS GOOD!!
IT'S BECAUSE SENRI'S SEA-SONING IS THE BEST!
...
WHOA... YOU WOULDN'T GUESS FROM LOOKING AT HIM.
WHAT DID YOU SAY?!
YOU'RE NOT A SOLDIER ?!
HM?
I'M JUST INTER-ESTED IN THE CORAL REEF.
HUH?!
I'M GREENA EITO.
How do I put this...
YOU MIGHT SAY I'M A RE-SEARCH-ER OF SORTS.
BAH! WE LET HIM ON AND HE'S COM-PLETELY USELESS!
Agh!
ER...I'M NOT THAT BAD...

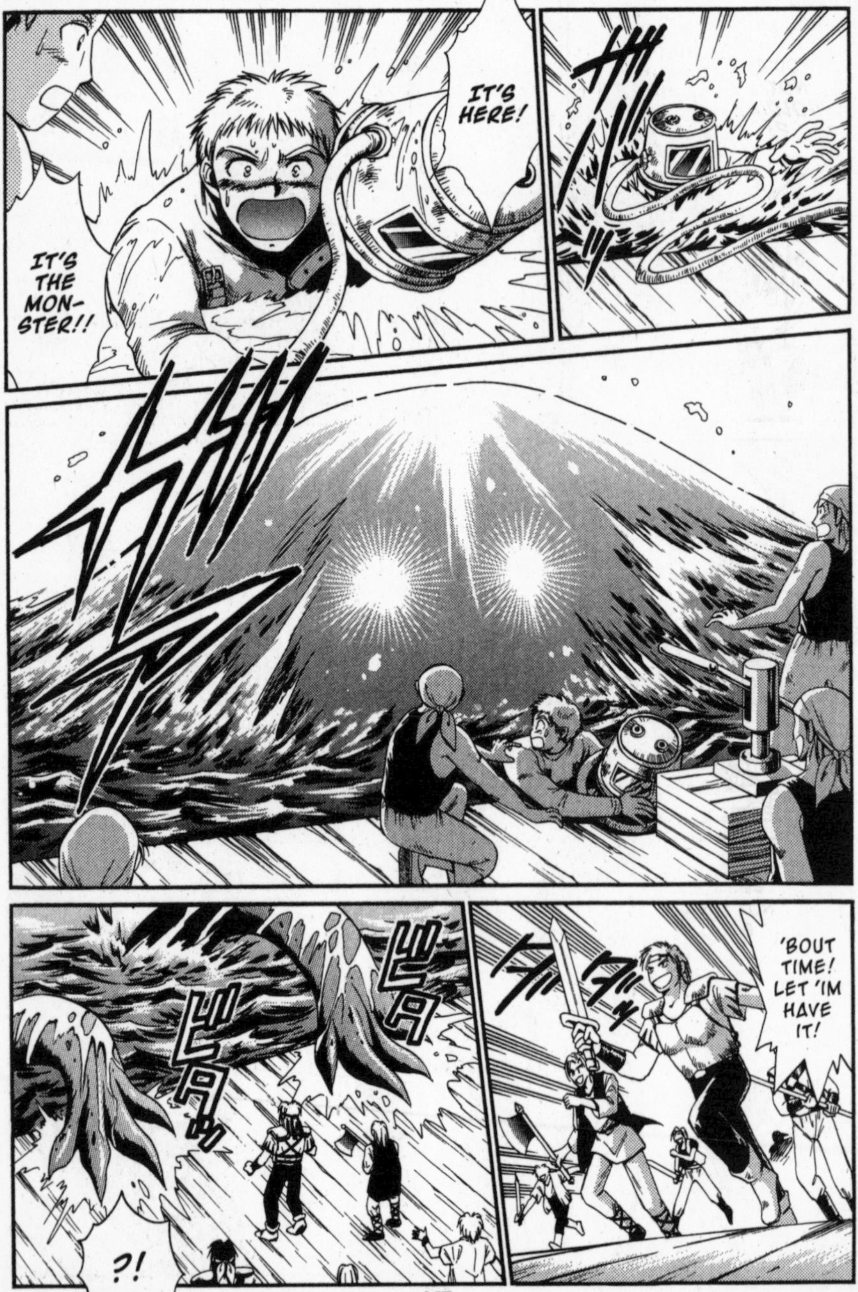
IT'S HERE!
IT'S THE MON-STER!!
'BOUT TIME! LET 'IM HAVE IT!
?!

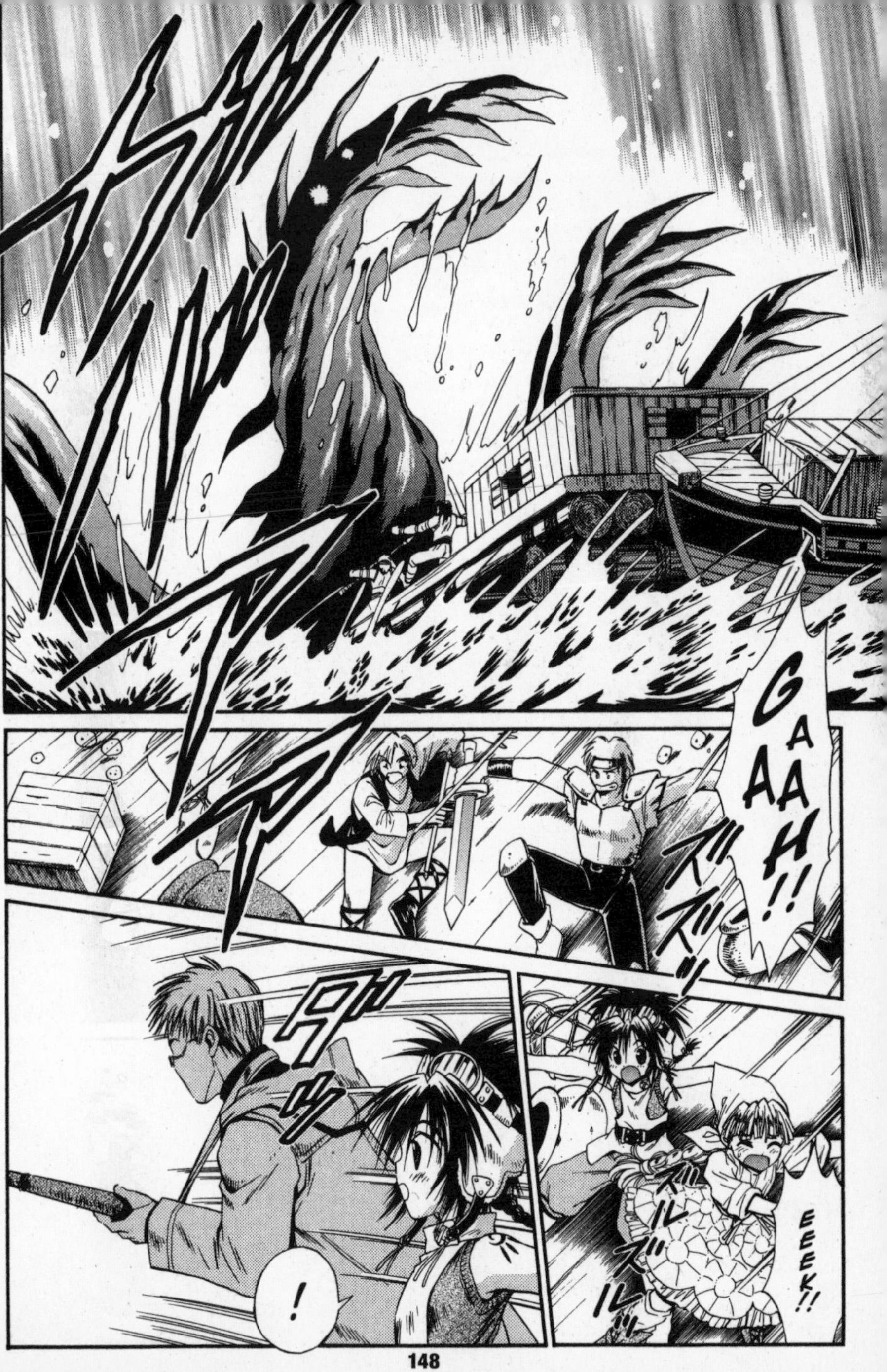
GAAAH!!
EEEK!!
!

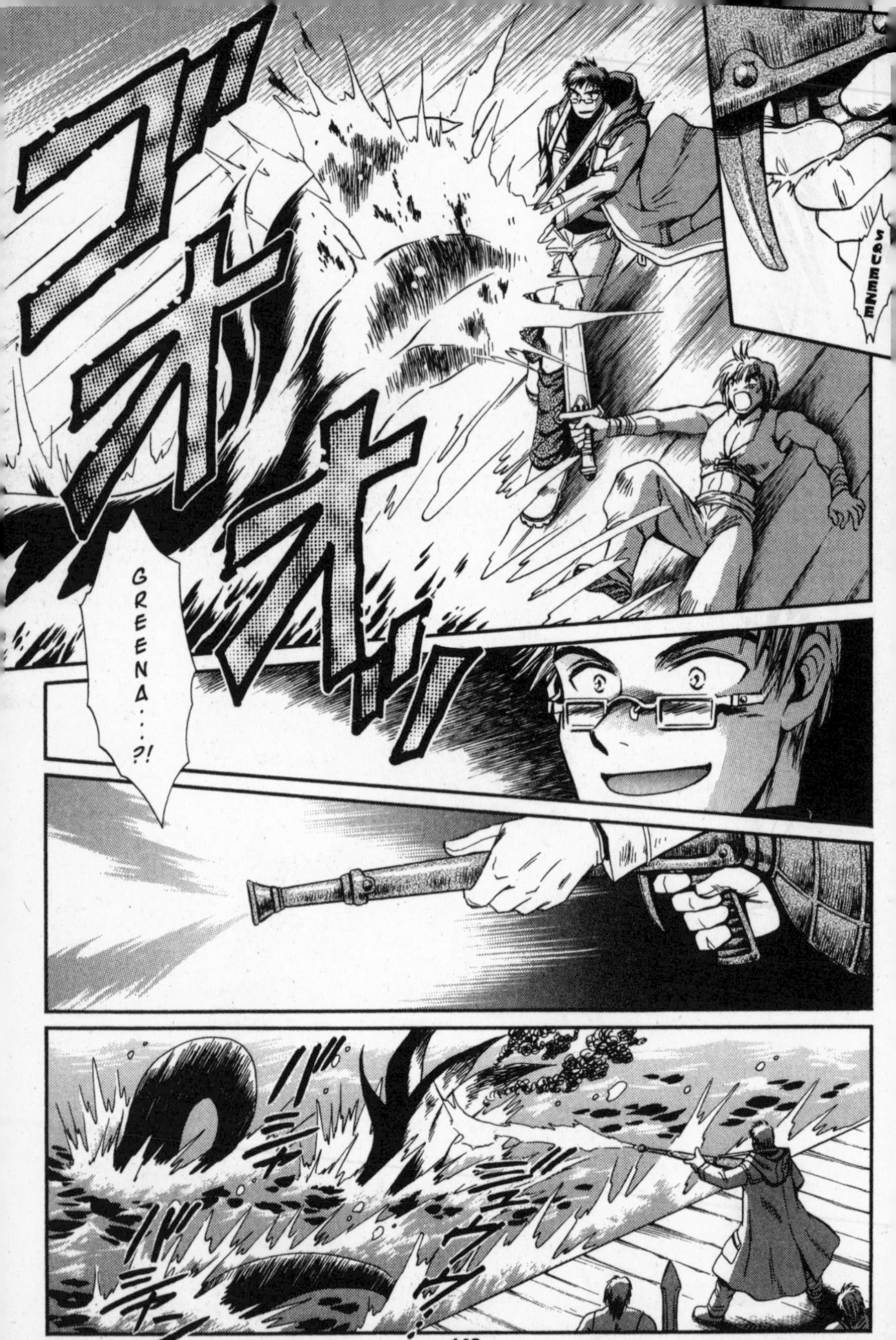
SQUEEZE
GREENA...?!

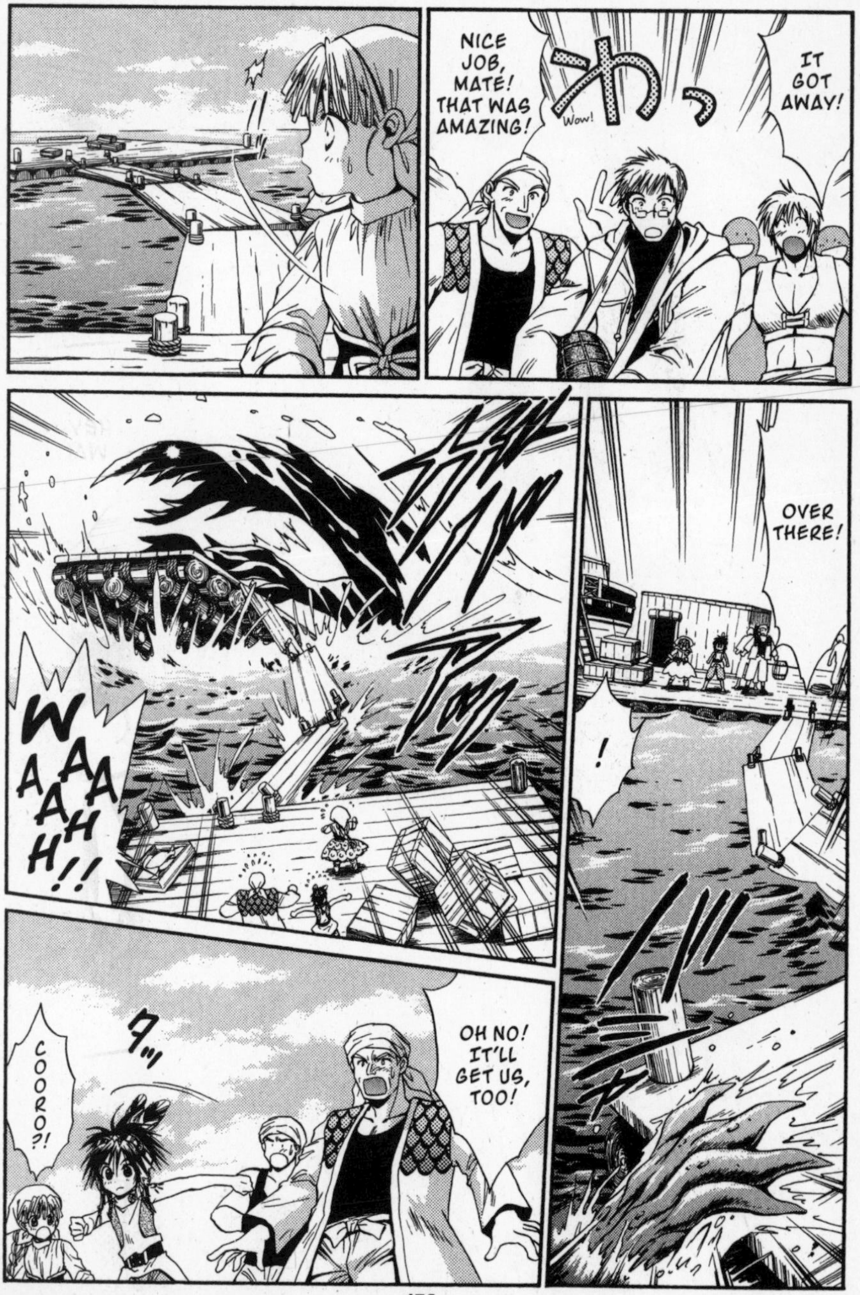

IT GOT AWAY!
わっ
Wow!
NICE JOB, MATE! THAT WAS AMAZING!
OVER THERE!
!
WAAAAHH!!
OH NO! IT'LL GET US, TOO!
タッ
COORO?!

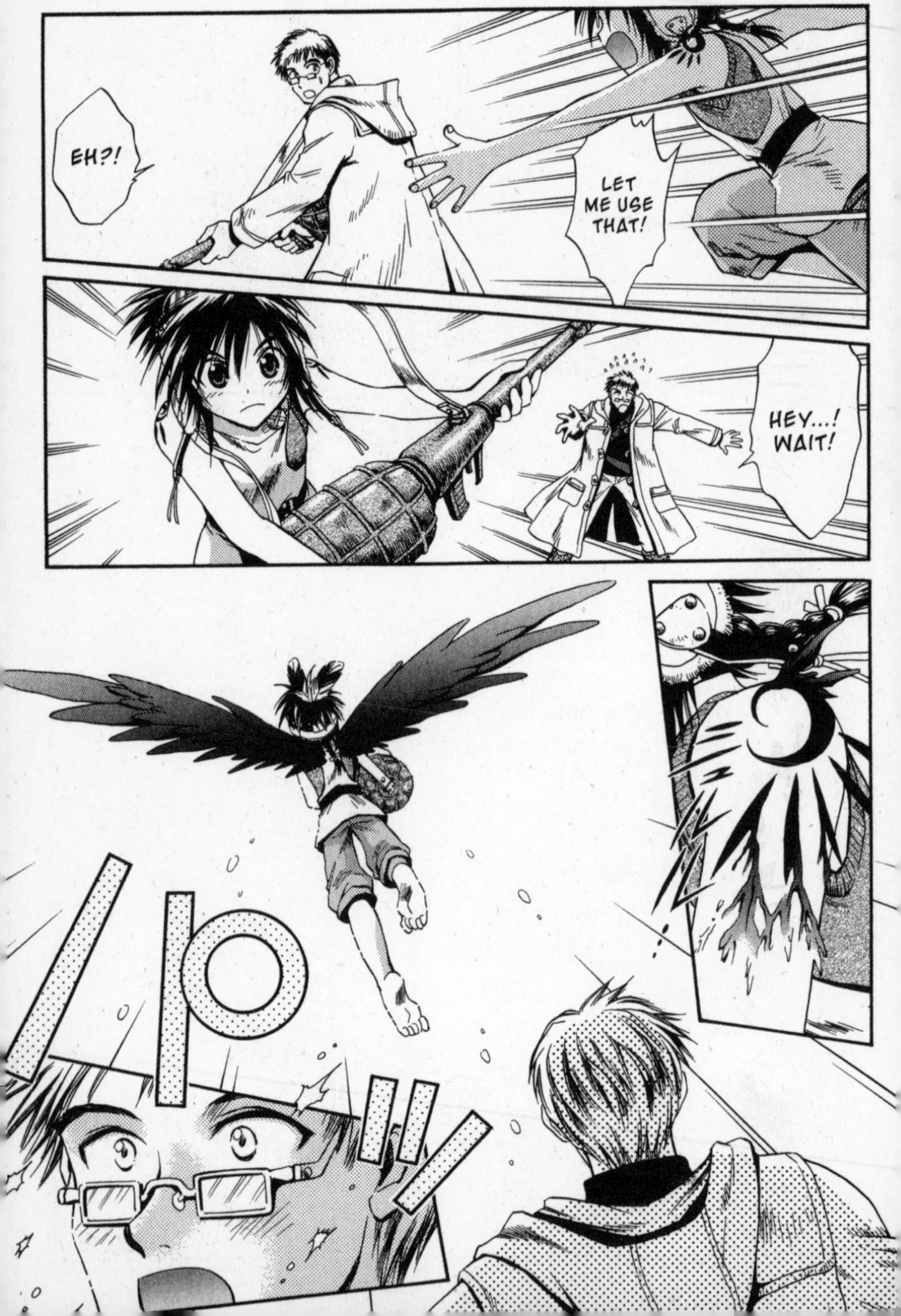
LET ME USE THAT!
EH?!
HEY...! WAIT!

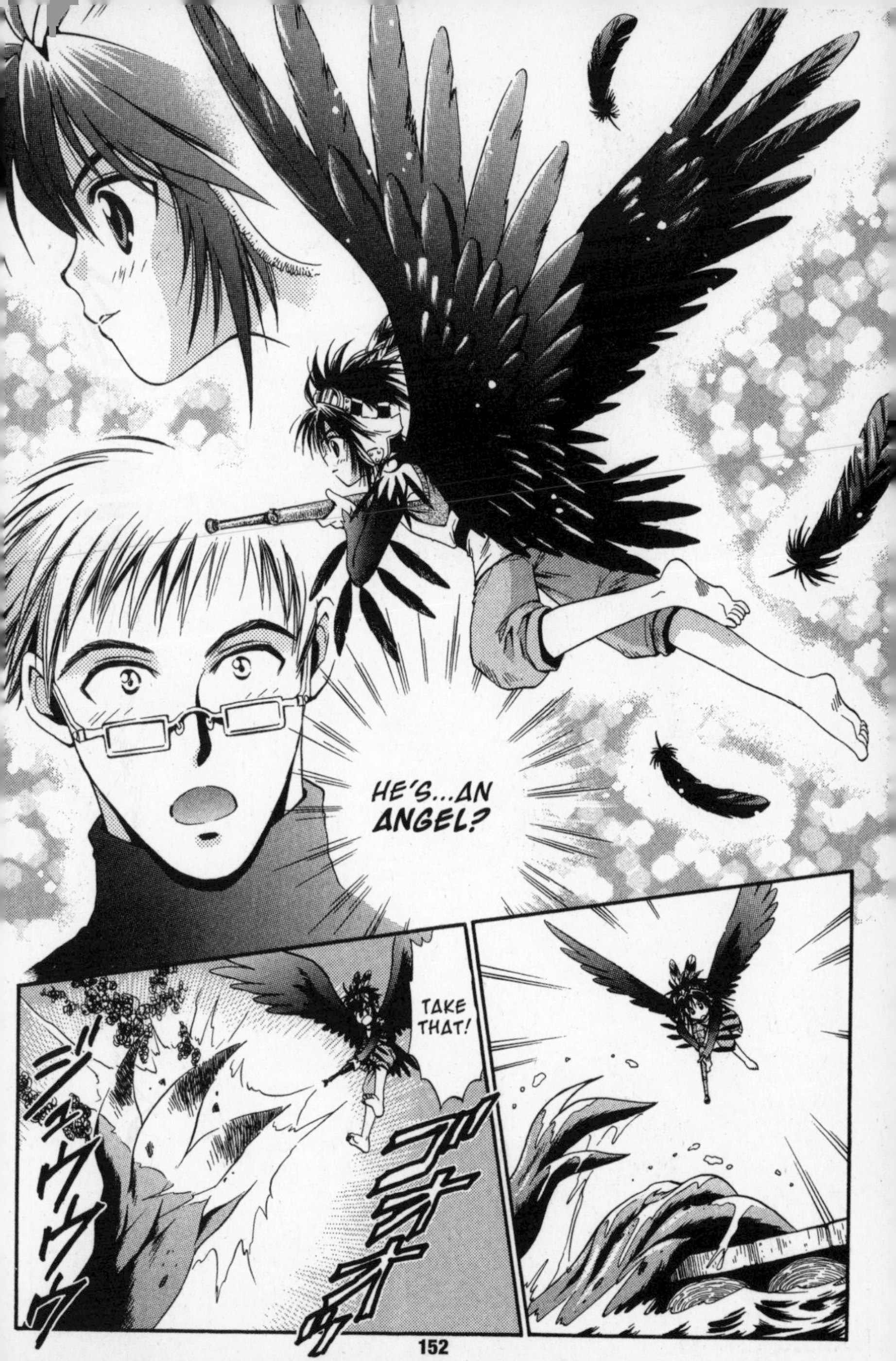
HE'S...AN ANGEL?
TAKE THAT!
ジュウウウウ

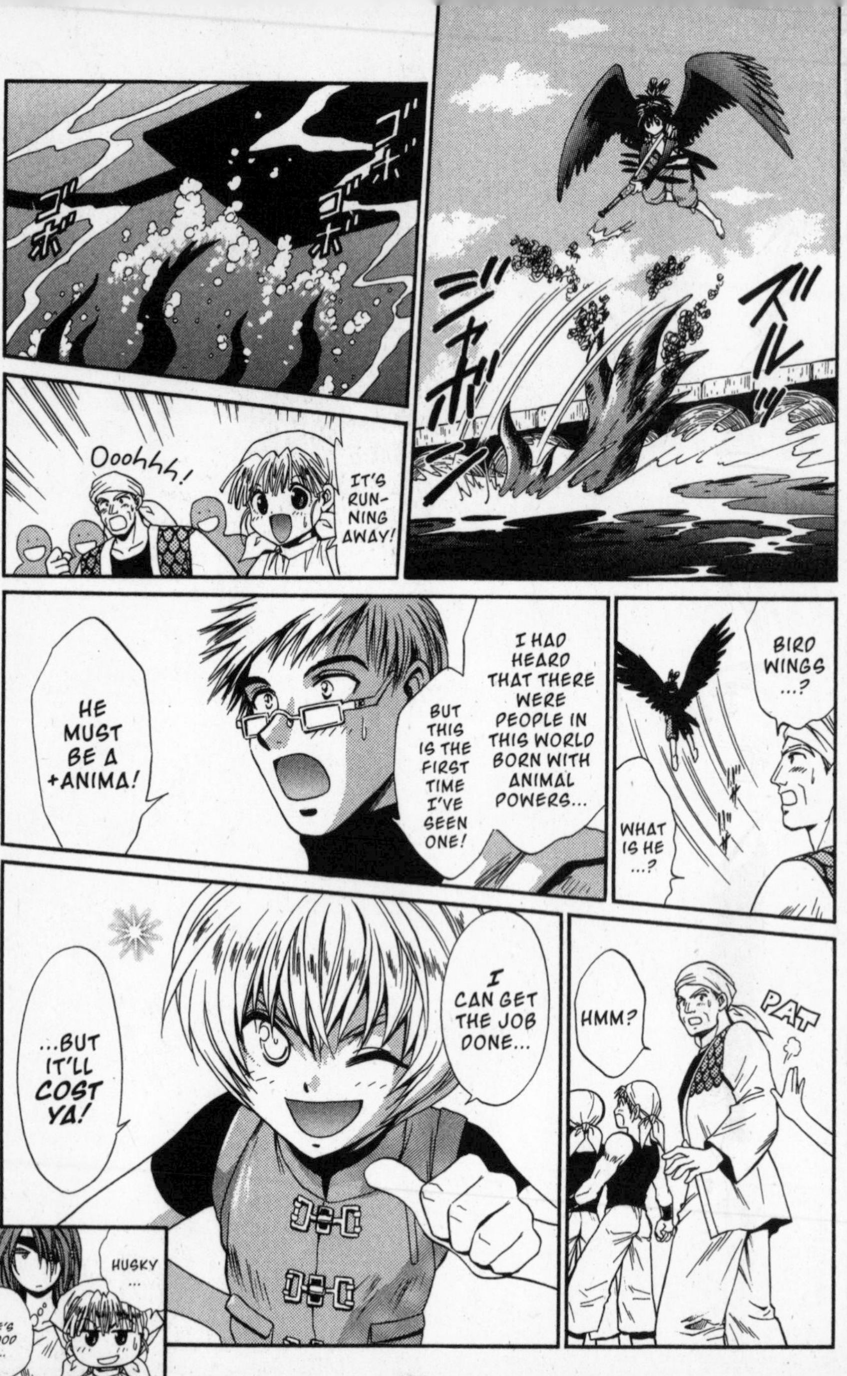
ズルッ
ジャボン
ゴボ
ゴボ
ゴボ
IT'S RUN-NING AWAY!
Ooohhh!
BIRD WINGS ...?
WHAT IS HE ...?
I HAD HEARD THAT THERE WERE PEOPLE IN THIS WORLD BORN WITH ANIMAL POWERS...
BUT THIS IS THE FIRST TIME I'VE SEEN ONE!
HE MUST BE A +ANIMA!
PAT
HMM?
I CAN GET THE JOB DONE...
...BUT IT'LL COST YA!
HUSKY ...
HE'S GOOD ...

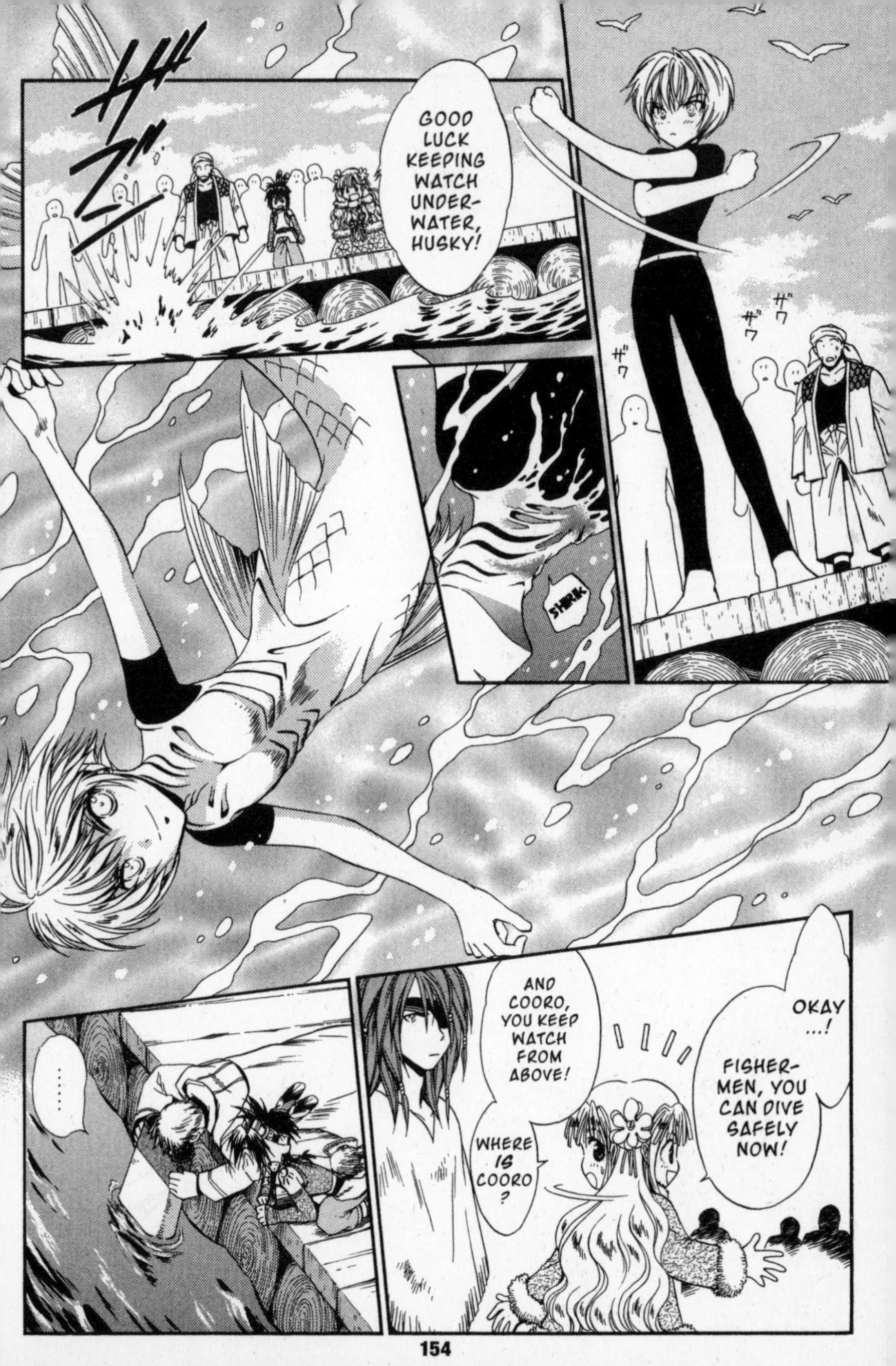
GOOD LUCK KEEPING WATCH UNDER-WATER, HUSKY!
SHRK
OKAY ...!
FISHER-MEN, YOU CAN DIVE SAFELY NOW!
AND COORO, YOU KEEP WATCH FROM ABOVE!
WHERE IS COORO?
......

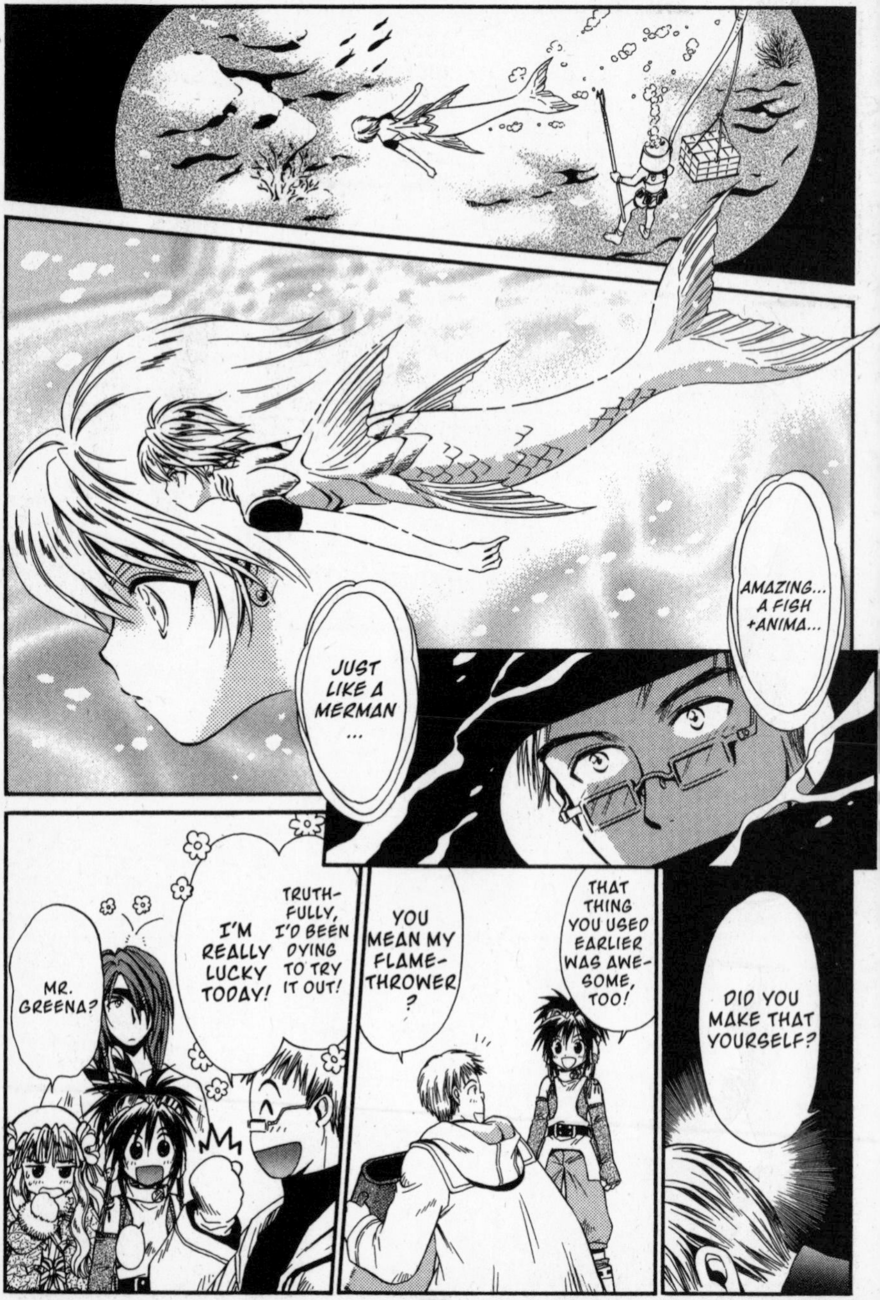
AMAZING... A FISH +ANIMA...
JUST LIKE A MERMAN...
DID YOU MAKE THAT YOURSELF?
THAT THING YOU USED EARLIER WAS AWE-SOME, TOO!
YOU MEAN MY FLAME-THROWER?
TRUTH-FULLY, I'D BEEN DYING TO TRY IT OUT!
I'M REALLY LUCKY TODAY!
MR. GREENA?

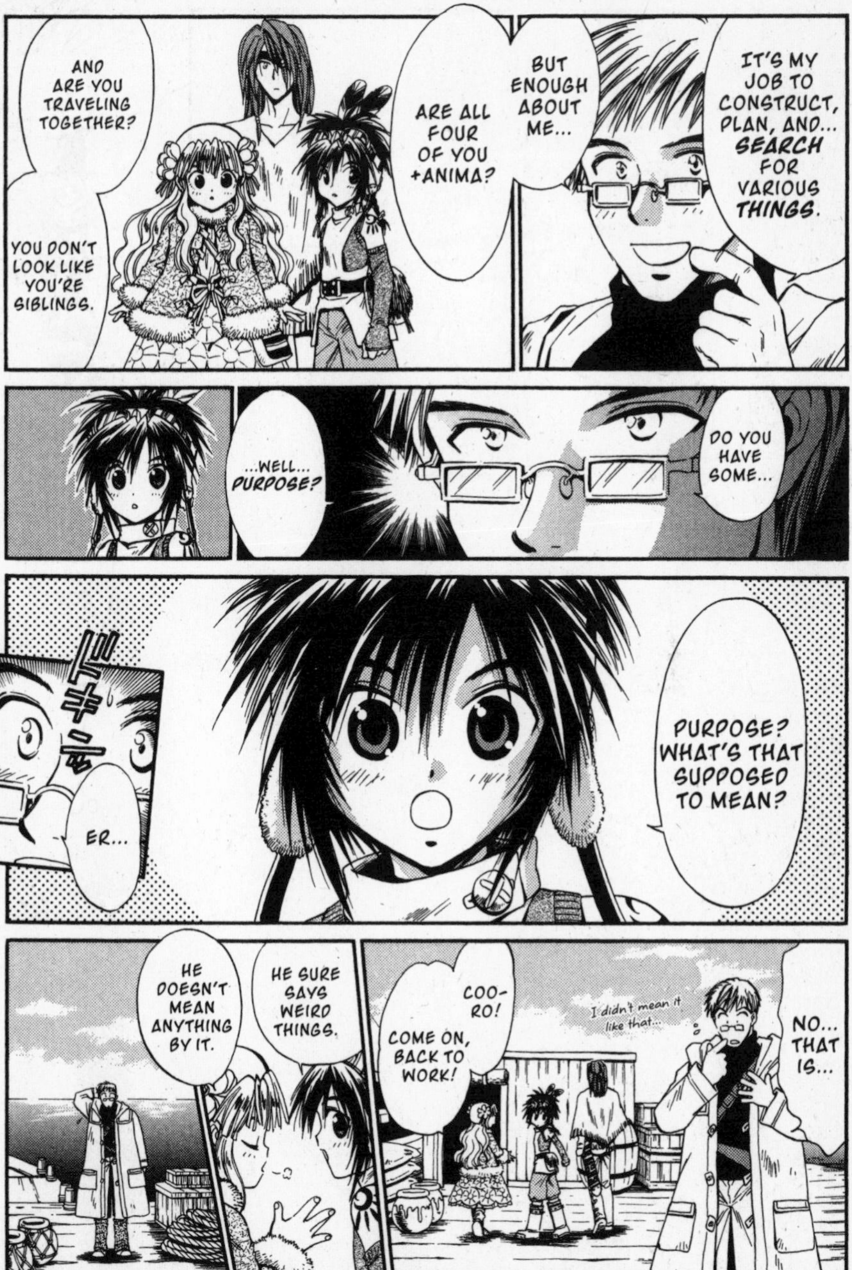
IT'S MY JOB TO CONSTRUCT, PLAN, AND... SEARCH FOR VARIOUS THINGS.
BUT ENOUGH ABOUT ME...
ARE ALL FOUR OF YOU +ANIMA?
AND ARE YOU TRAVELING TOGETHER?
YOU DON'T LOOK LIKE YOU'RE SIBLINGS.
DO YOU HAVE SOME...
...WELL... PURPOSE?
PURPOSE? WHAT'S THAT SUPPOSED TO MEAN?
ER...
NO... THAT IS...
I didn't mean it like that...
COO-RO!
COME ON, BACK TO WORK!
HE SURE SAYS WEIRD THINGS.
HE DOESN'T MEAN ANYTHING BY IT.

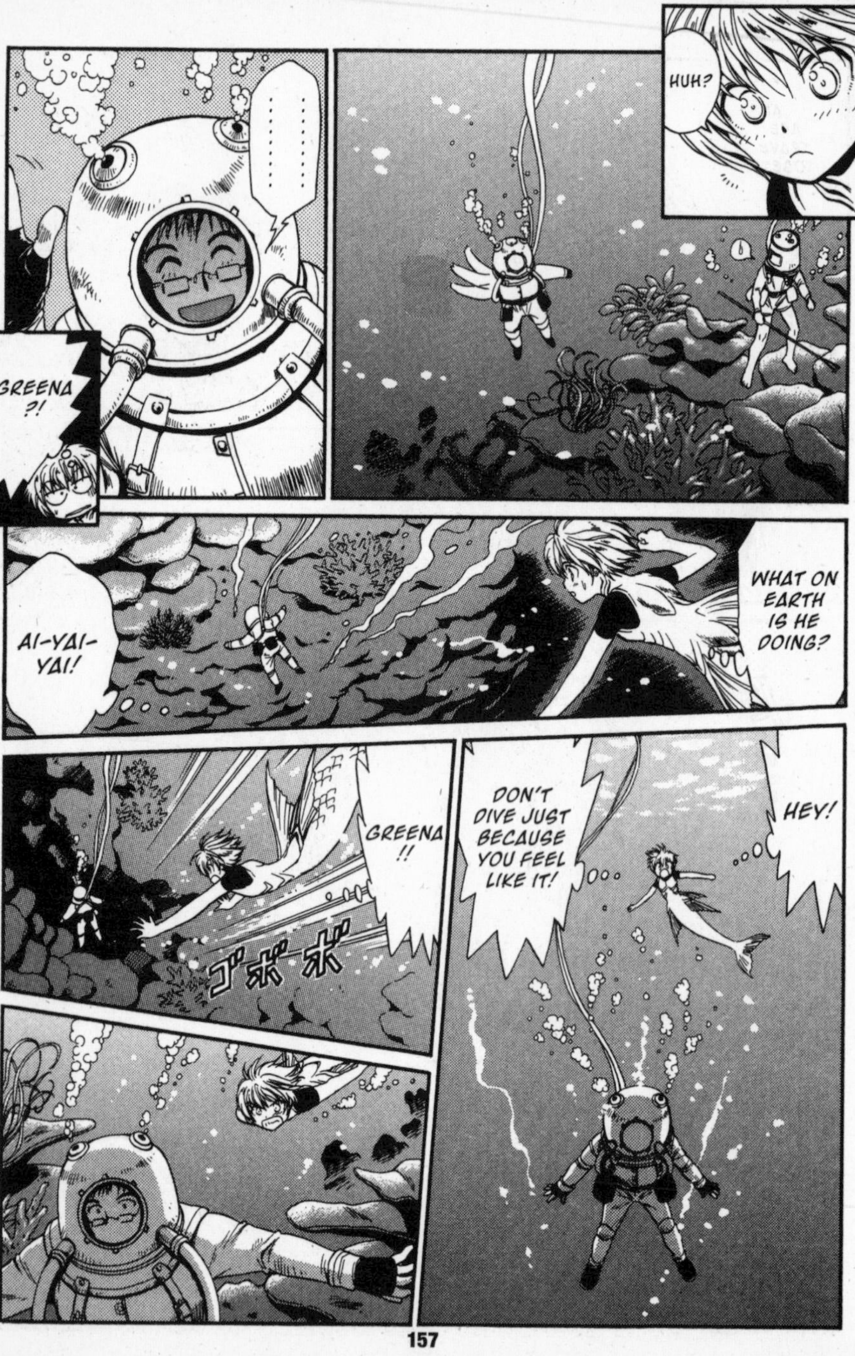
HUH?
......
GREENA ?!
WHAT ON EARTH IS HE DOING?
AI-YAI-YAI!
HEY!
DON'T DIVE JUST BECAUSE YOU FEEL LIKE IT!
GREENA !!
ゴボボ

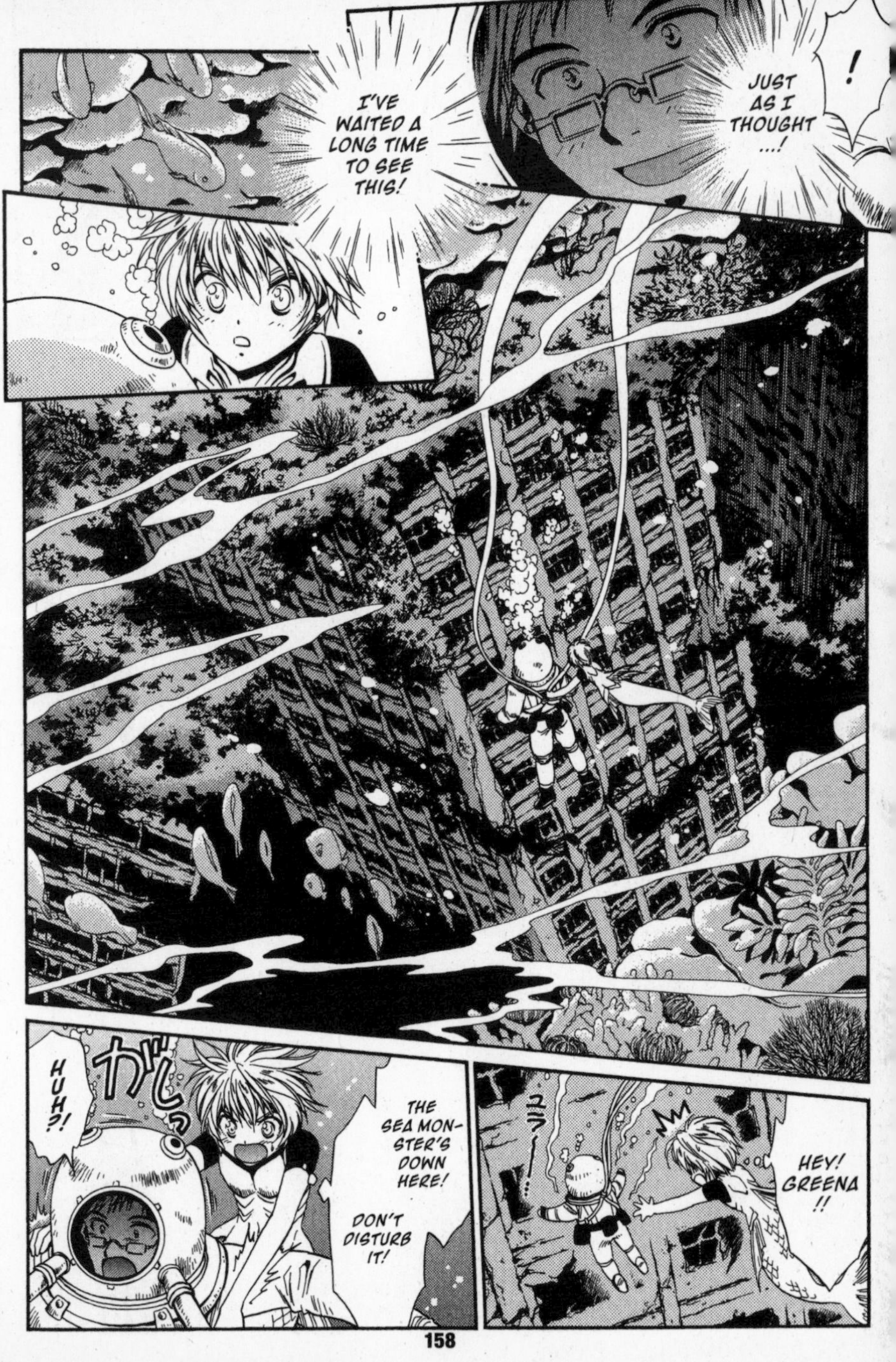
!
JUST AS I THOUGHT ...!
I'VE WAITED A LONG TIME TO SEE THIS!
HEY! GREENA !!
THE SEA MONSTER'S DOWN HERE!
DON'T DISTURB IT!
HUH?!

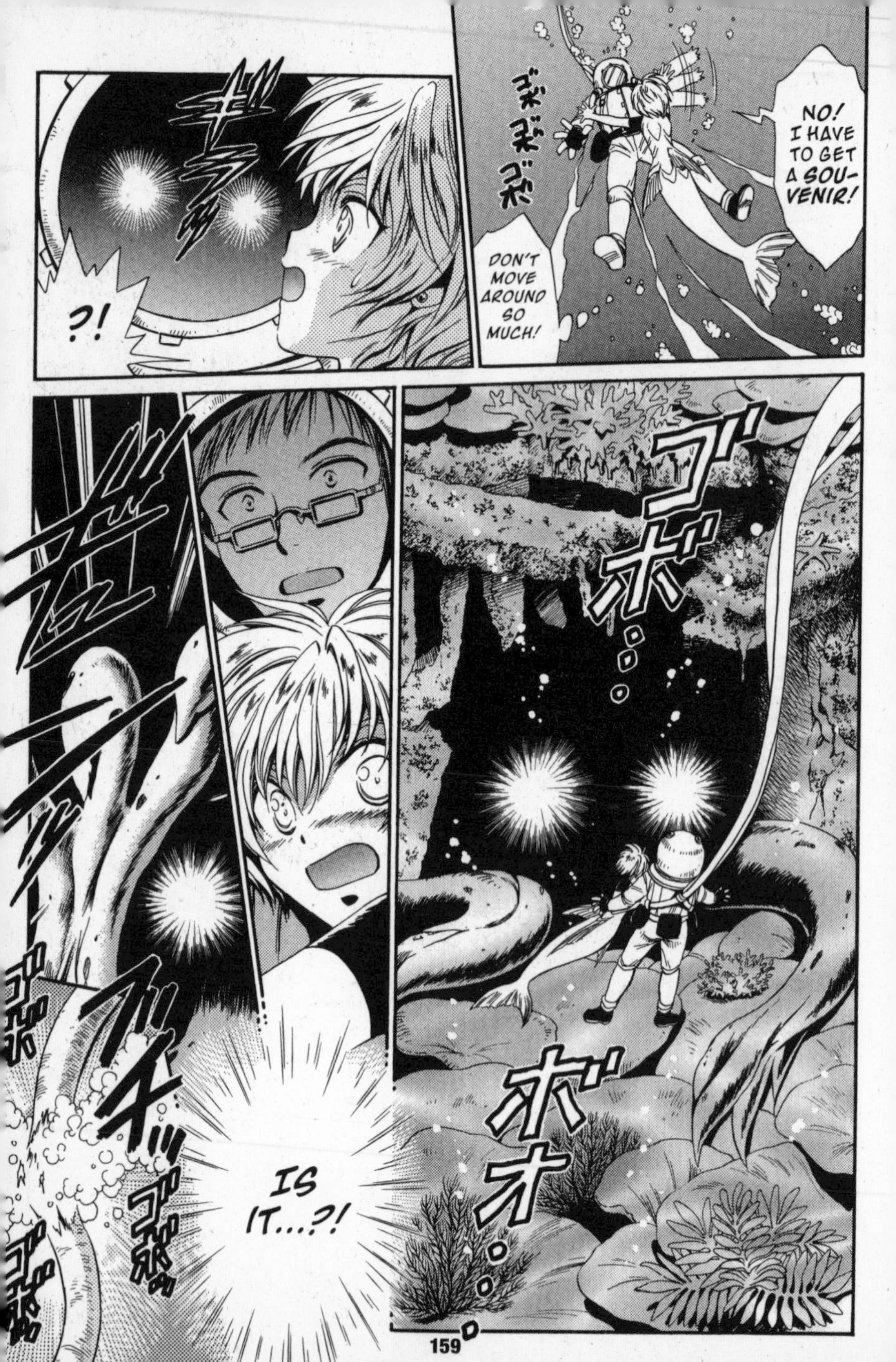
NO! I HAVE TO GET A SOUVENIR!
DON'T MOVE AROUND SO MUCH!
?!
IS IT...?!

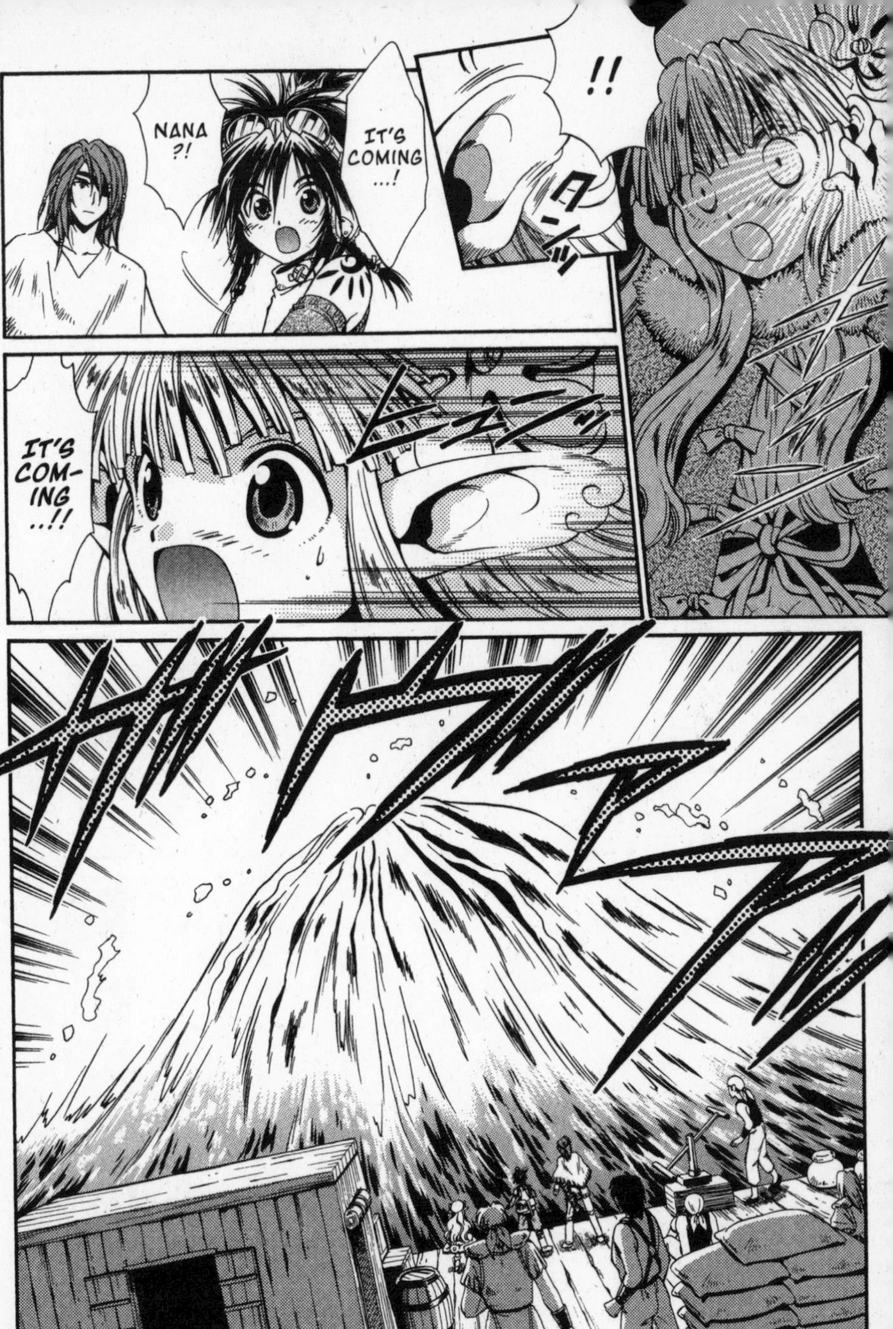
!!
IT'S COMING ...!
NANA ?!
IT'S COM-ING ...!!

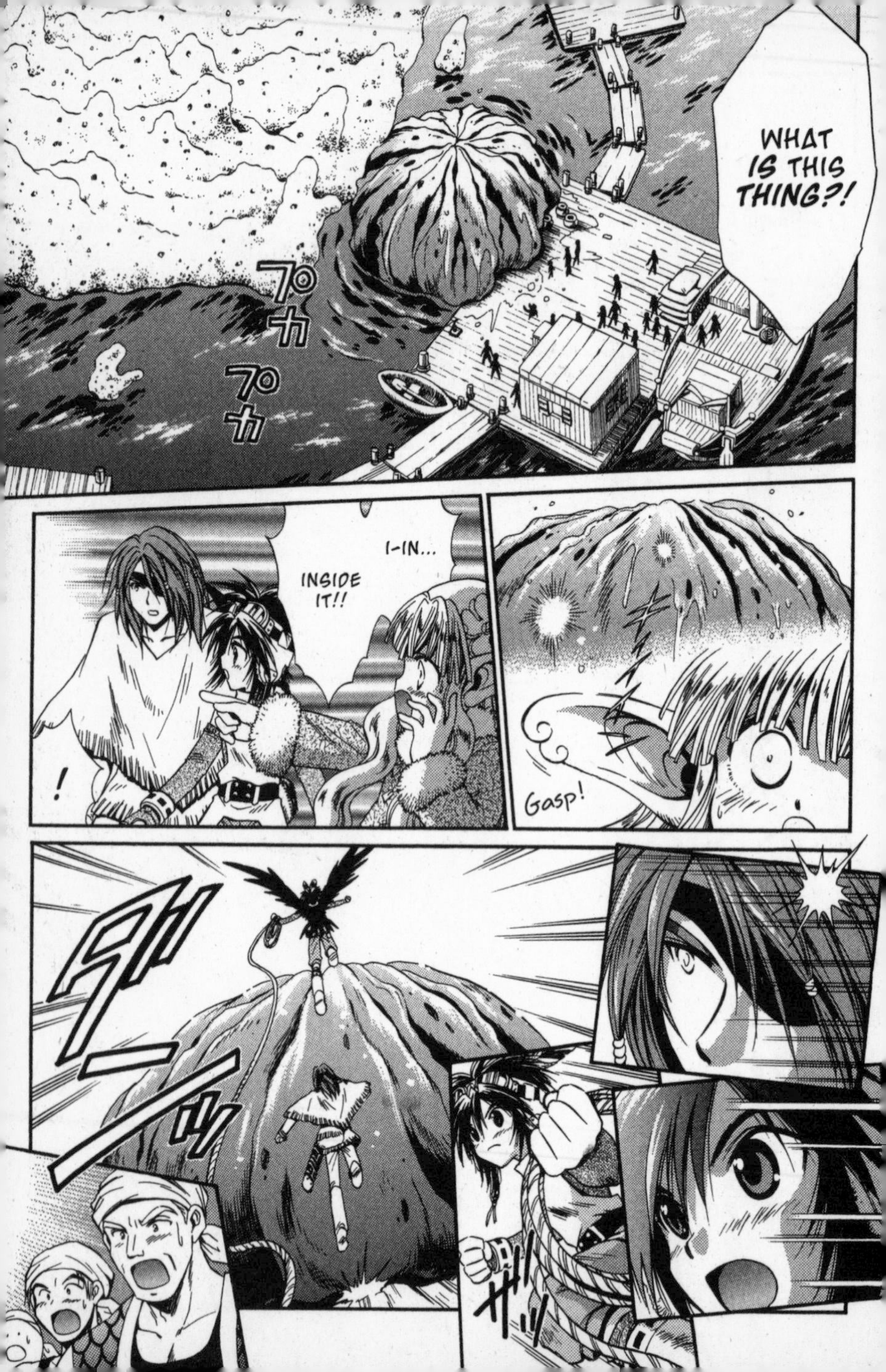
WHAT IS THIS THING?!
プカ
プカ
Gasp!
I-IN...
INSIDE IT!!
!

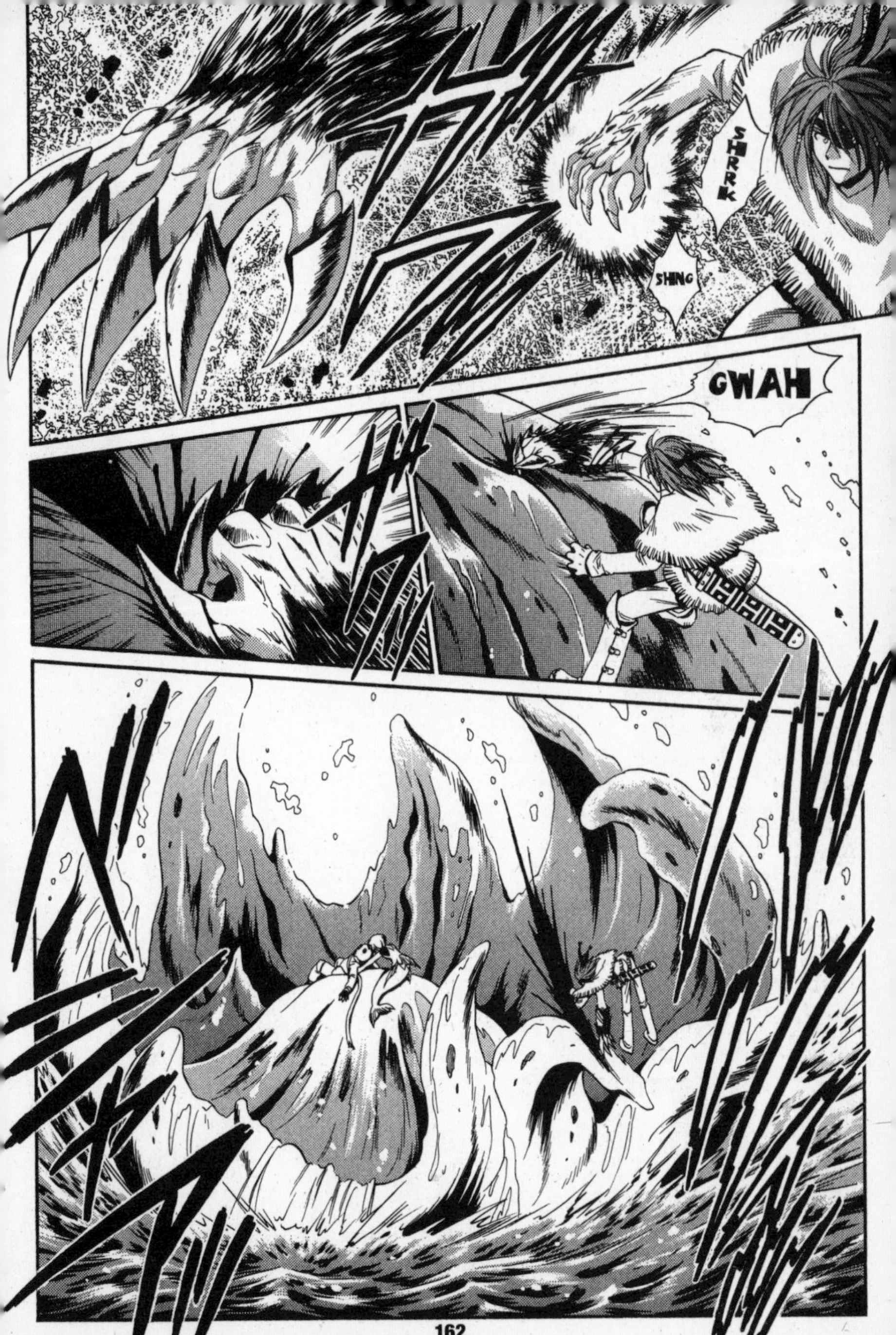
SHRRK
SHING
GWAH

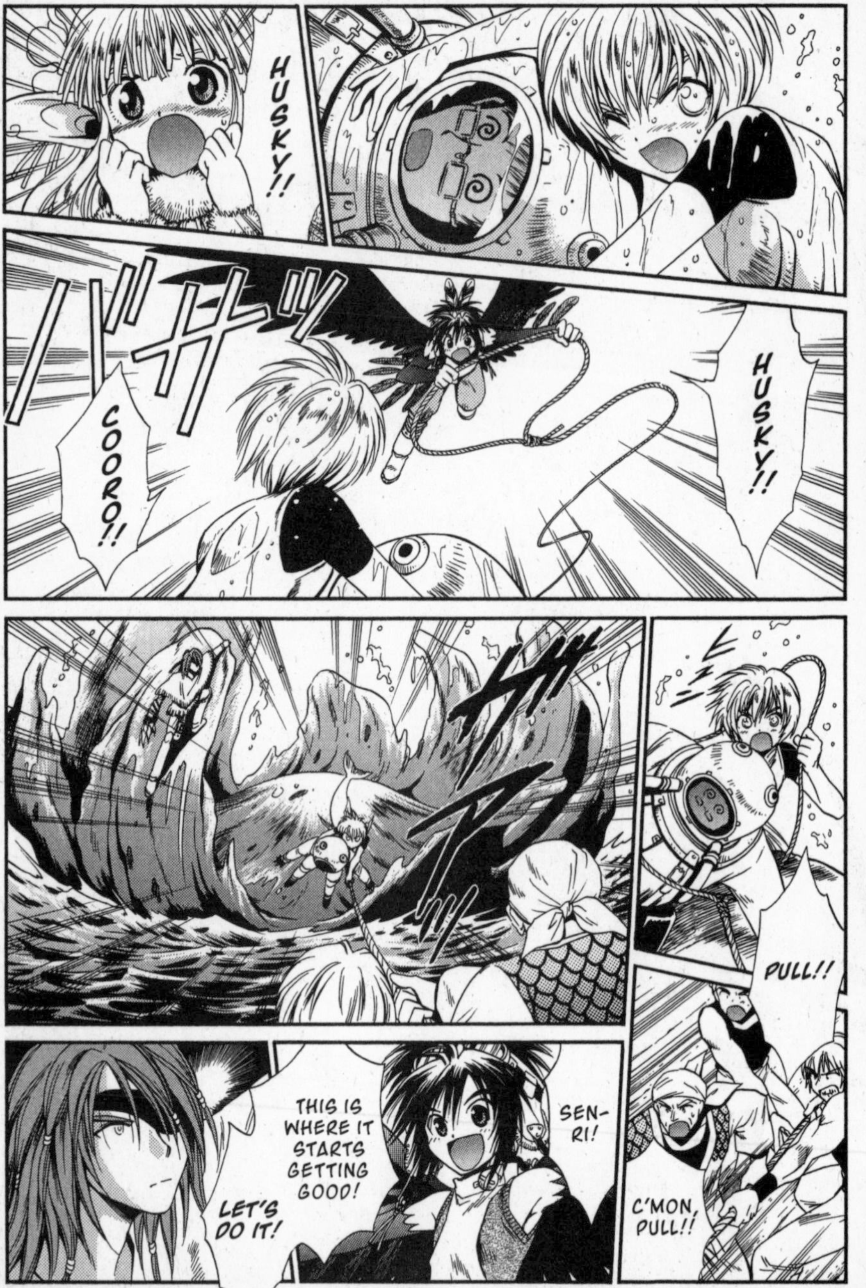
HUSKY!!
HUSKY!!
COORO!!
PULL!!
C'MON, PULL!!
SEN-RI!
THIS IS WHERE IT STARTS GETTING GOOD!
LET'S DO IT!

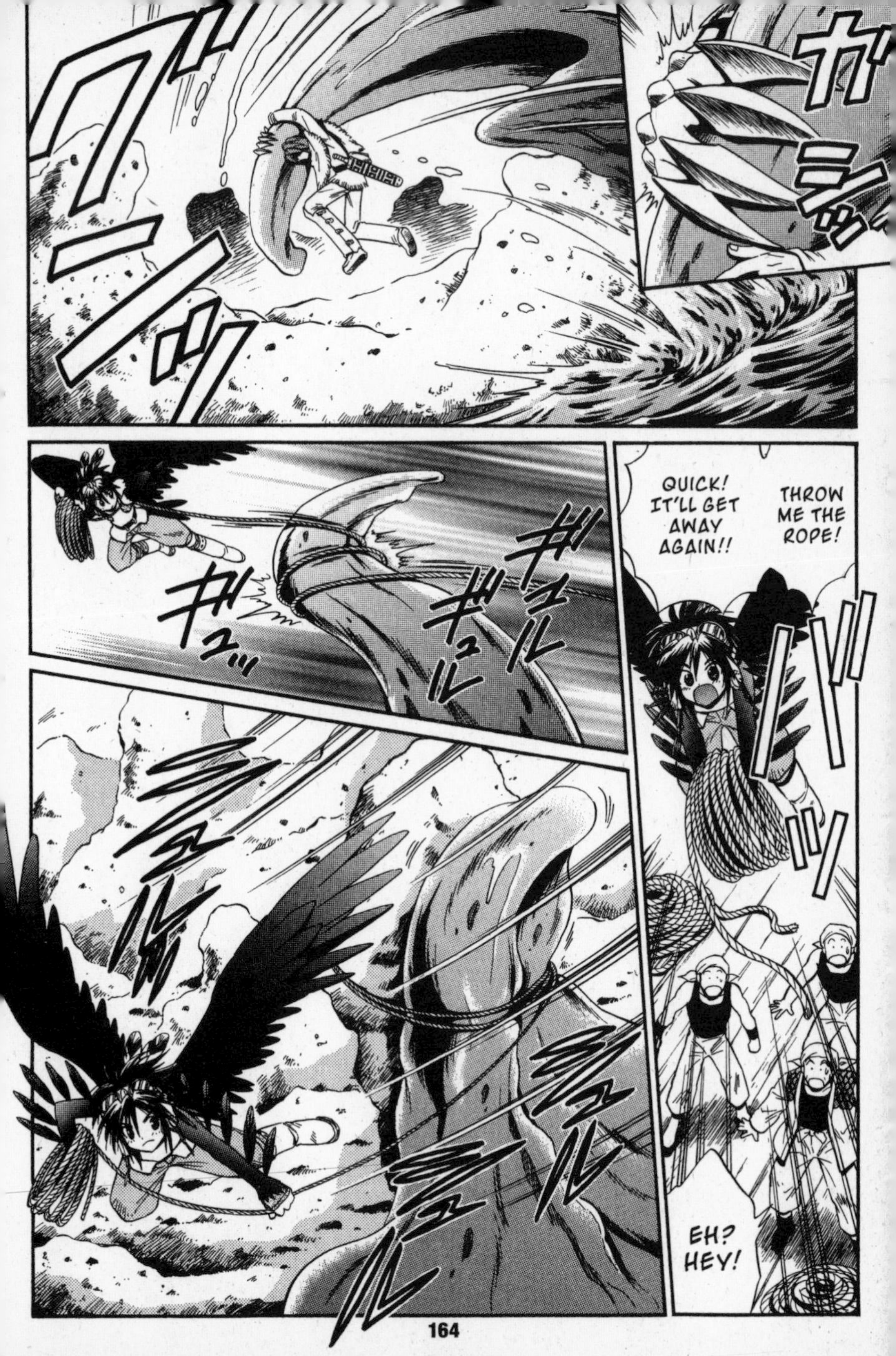
THROW ME THE ROPE!
QUICK! IT'LL GET AWAY AGAIN!!
EH? HEY!

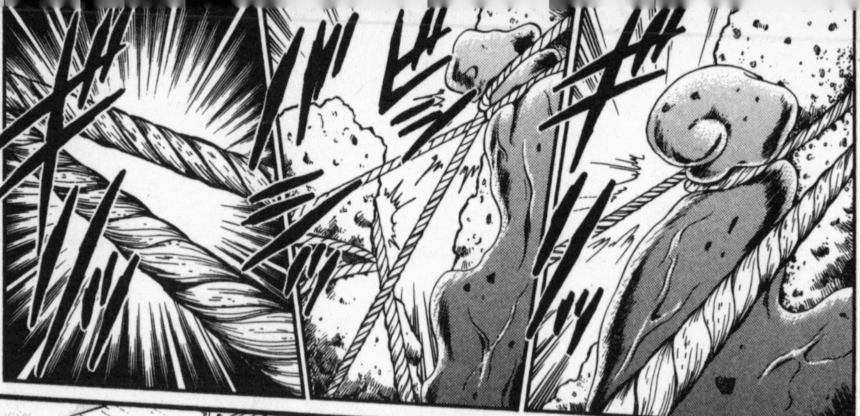
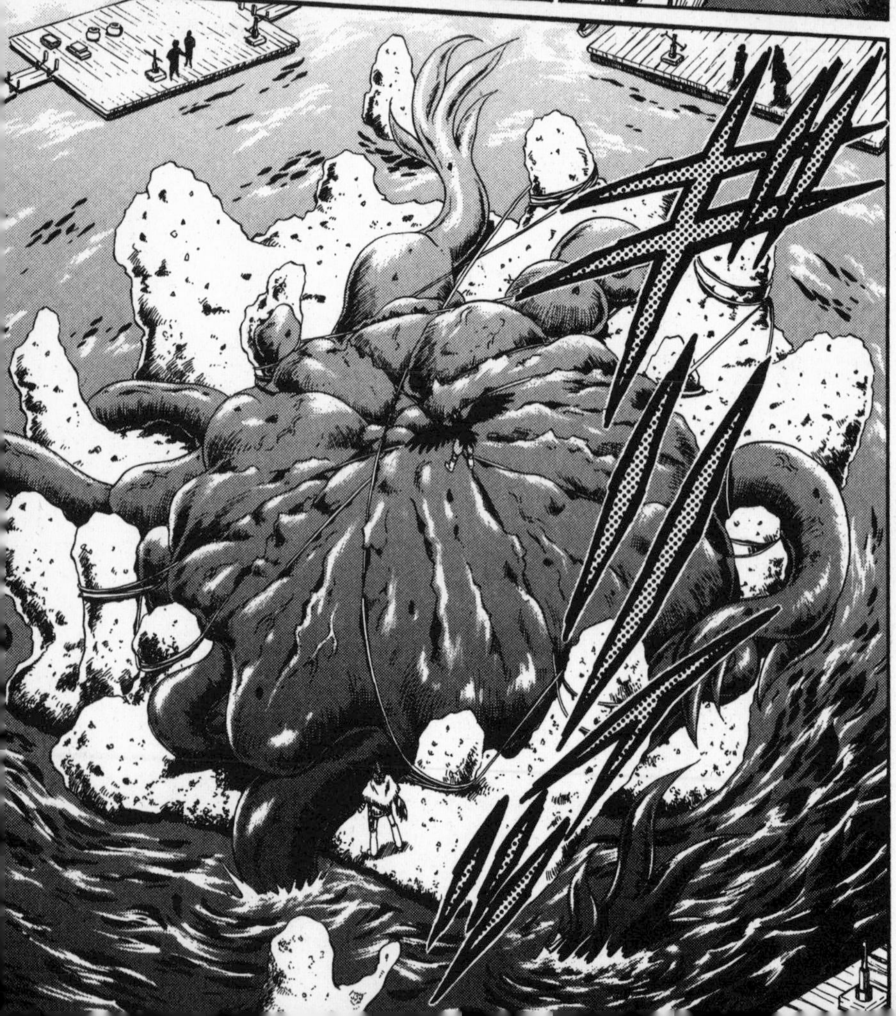

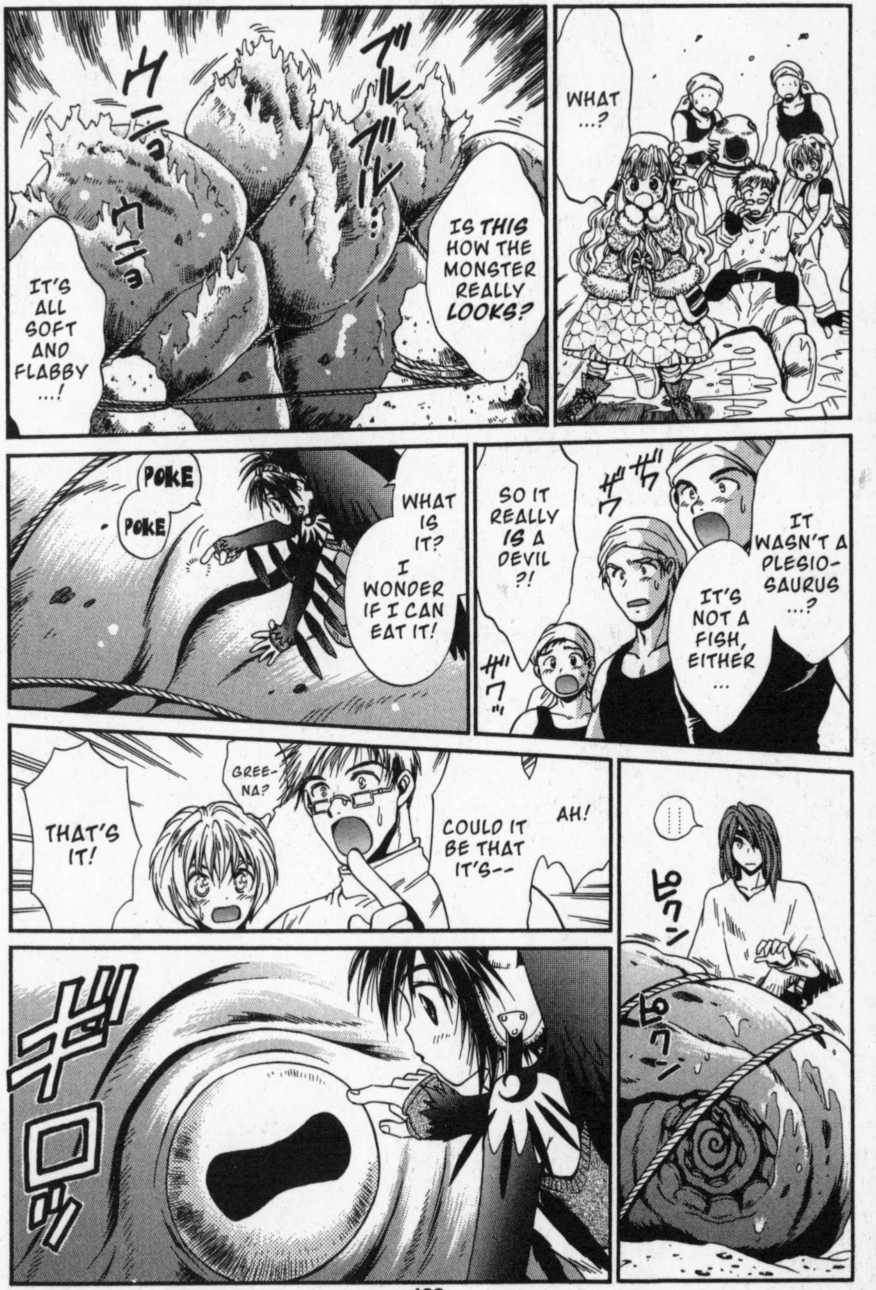
WHAT ...?
IS THIS HOW THE MONSTER REALLY LOOKS?
ブルブル…
ウニョウニョ
IT'S ALL SOFT AND FLABBY ...!
IT WASN'T A PLESIOSAURUS ...?
IT'S NOT A FISH, EITHER ...
SO IT REALLY IS A DEVIL ?!
ザワザワ
WHAT IS IT? I WONDER IF I CAN EAT IT!
POKE
POKE
......
ピクン
AH!
COULD IT BE THAT IT'S--
GREE-NA?
THAT'S IT!
ピクン
ギョロッ

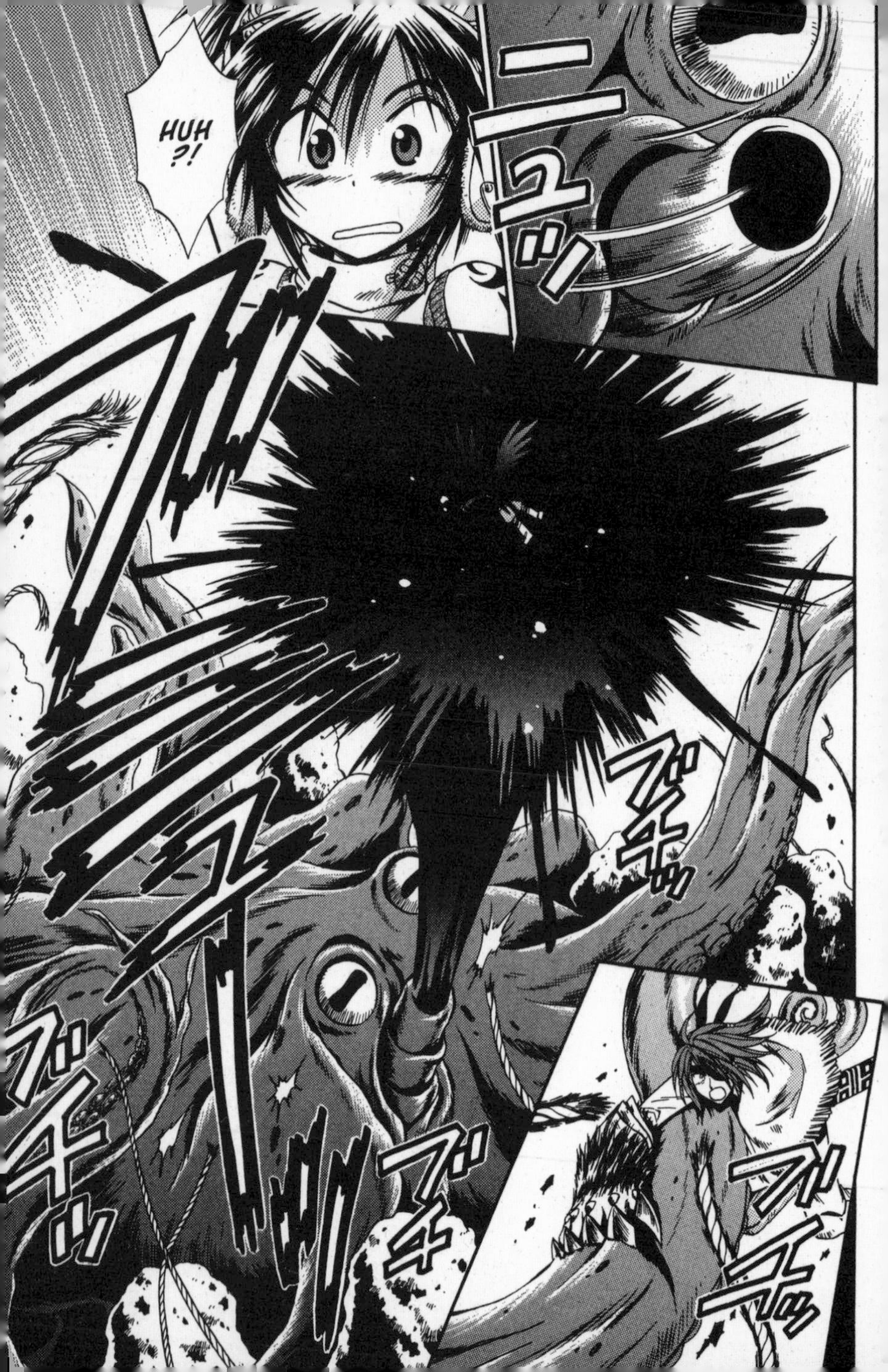
HUH ?!

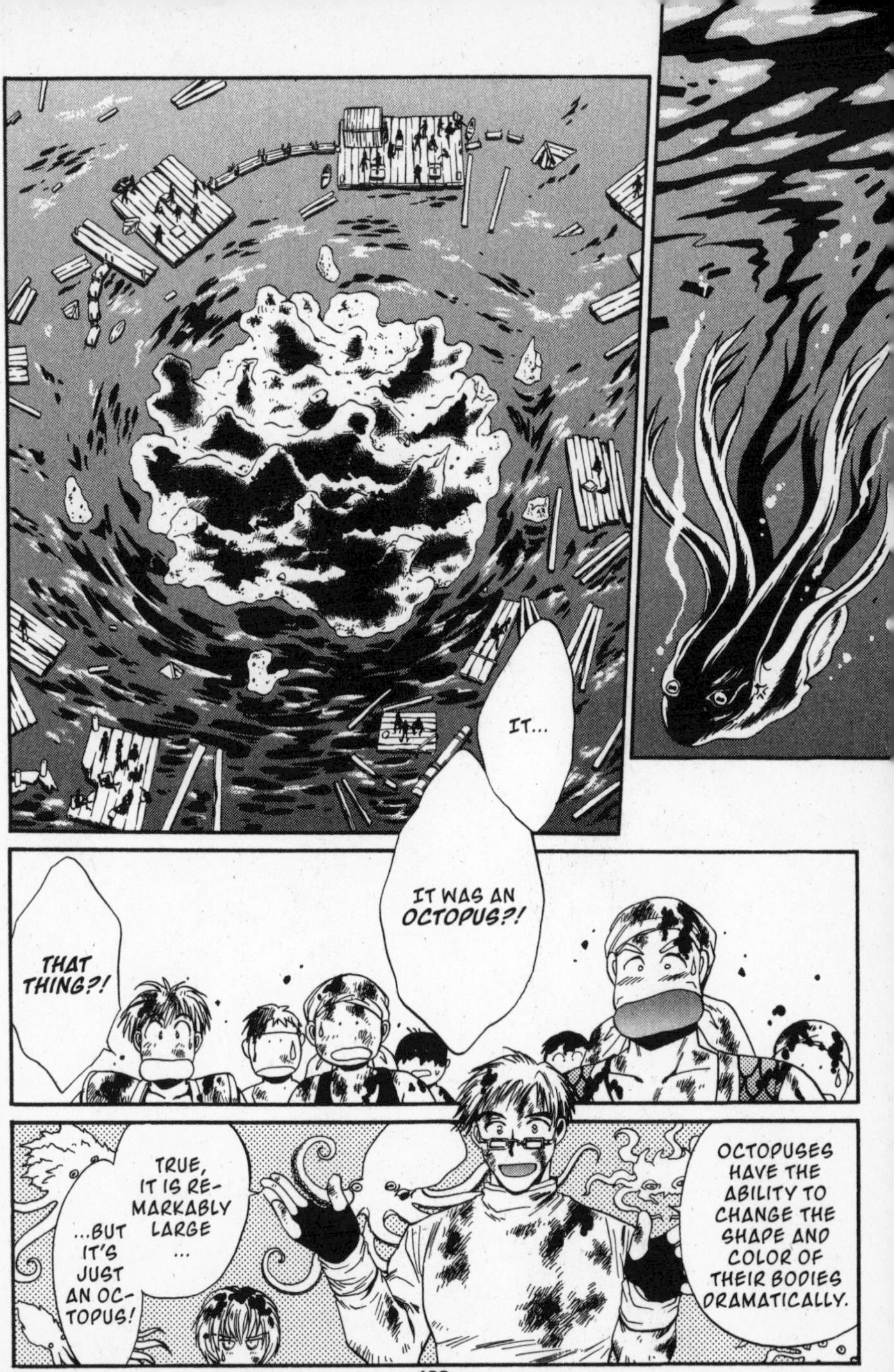
IT...
IT WAS AN OCTOPUS?!
THAT THING?!
OCTOPUSES HAVE THE ABILITY TO CHANGE THE SHAPE AND COLOR OF THEIR BODIES DRAMATICALLY.
TRUE, IT IS RE-MARKABLY LARGE ...
...BUT IT'S JUST AN OC-TOPUS!

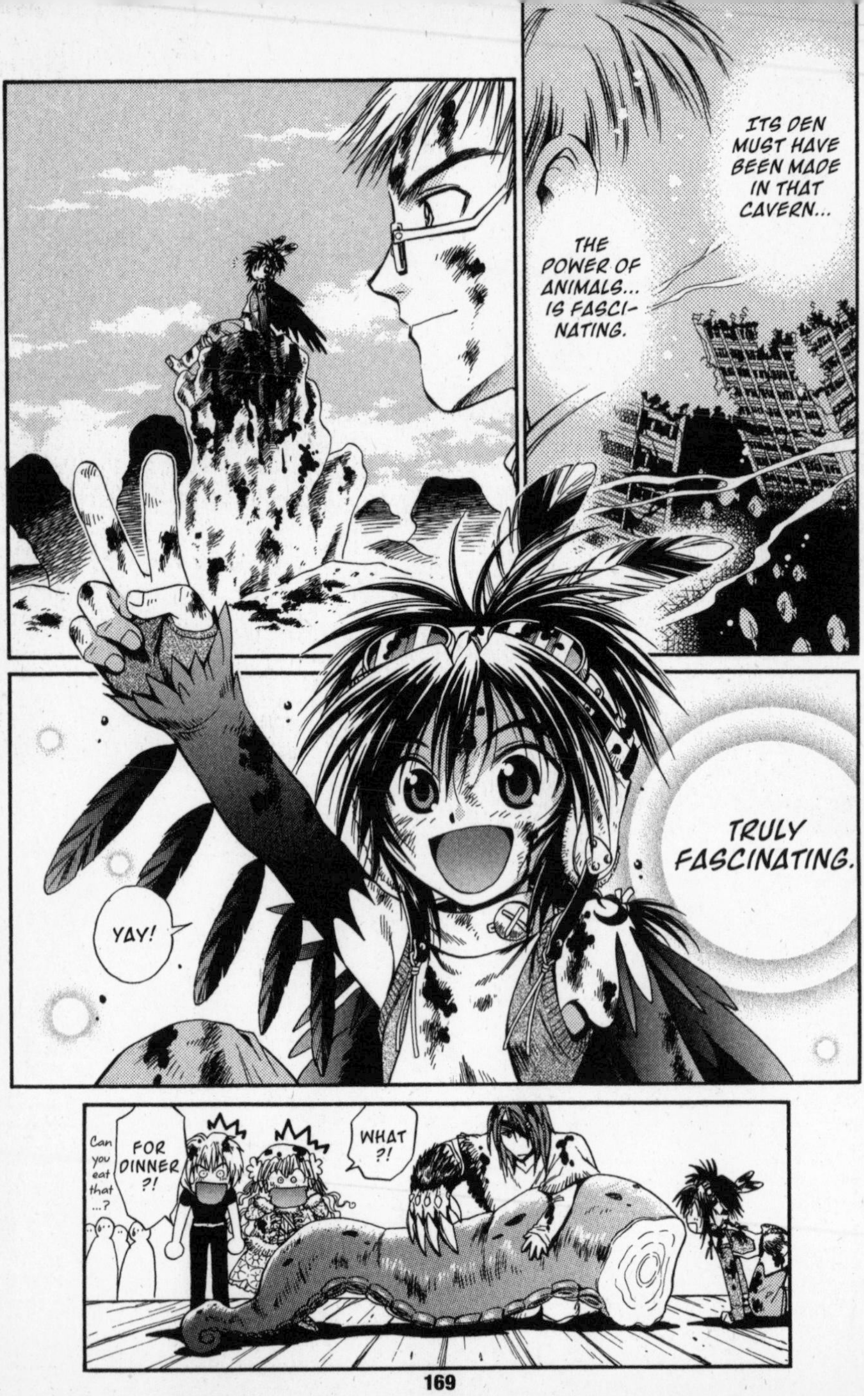
ITS DEN MUST HAVE BEEN MADE IN THAT CAVERN...
THE POWER OF ANIMALS... IS FASCI- NATING.
TRULY FASCINATING.
YAY!
WHAT ?!
FOR DINNER ?!
Can you eat that ...?

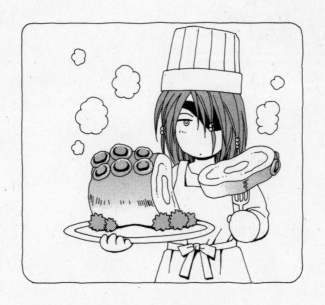

The steak of a big octopus!

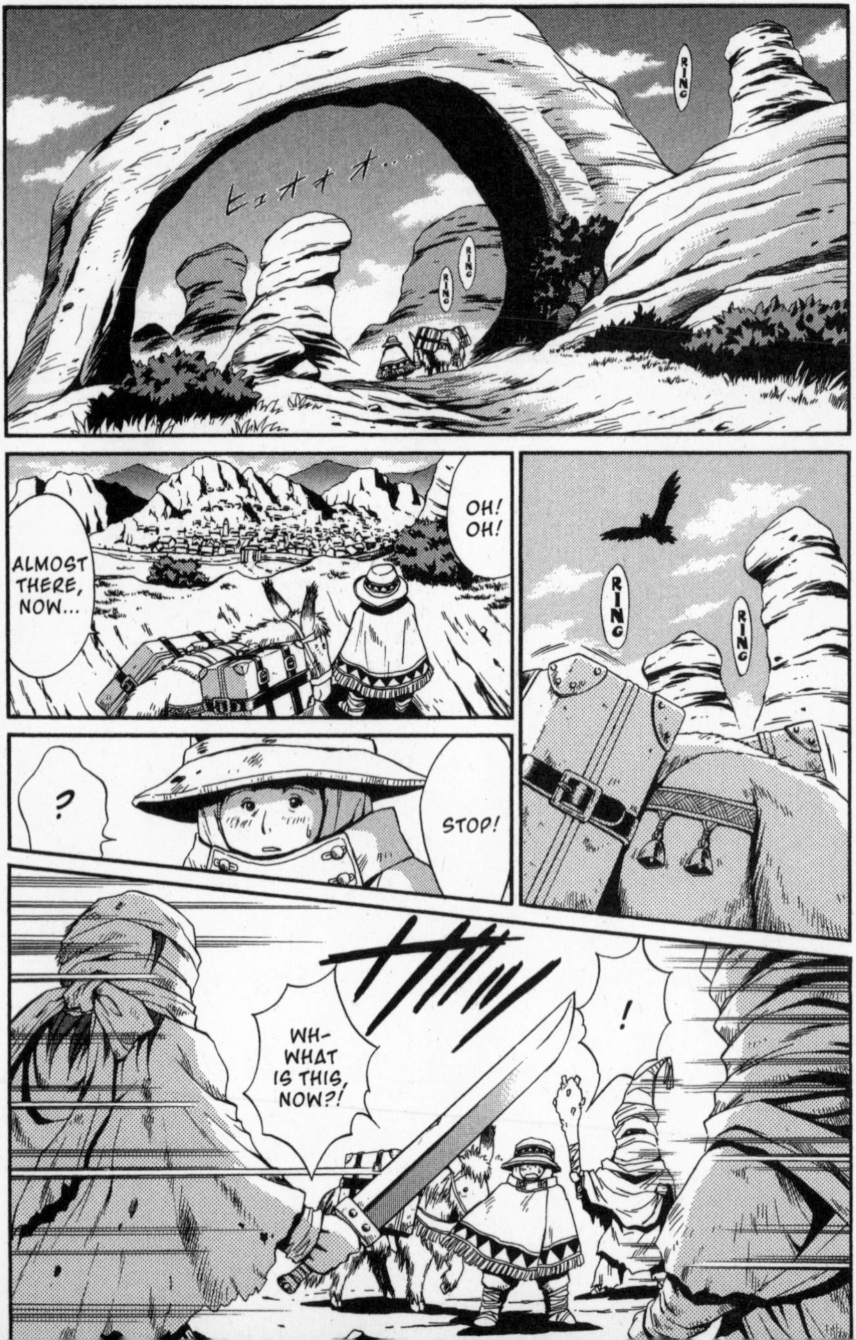
RING
RING
RING
ヒュオォオ……
RING
RING
OH! OH!
ALMOST THERE, NOW...
STOP!
?
!
WH-WHAT IS THIS, NOW?!

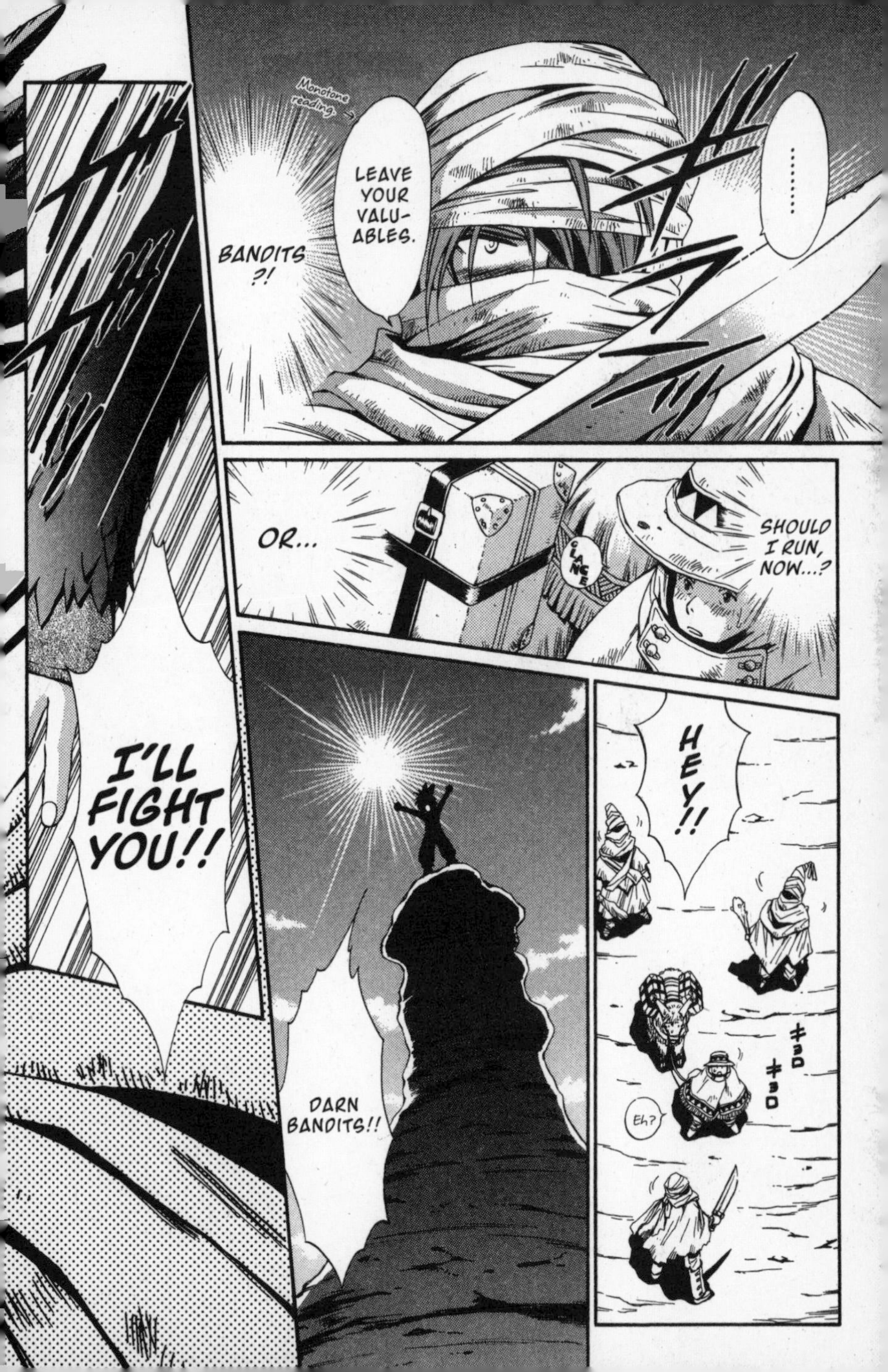
......
Monotone reading.
LEAVE YOUR VALUABLES.
BANDITS ?!
SHOULD I RUN, NOW...?
CLANG
OR...
HEY!!
キョロ
キョロ
Eh?
DARN BANDITS!!
I'LL FIGHT YOU!!

Parallel 3
Shining in the Darkness

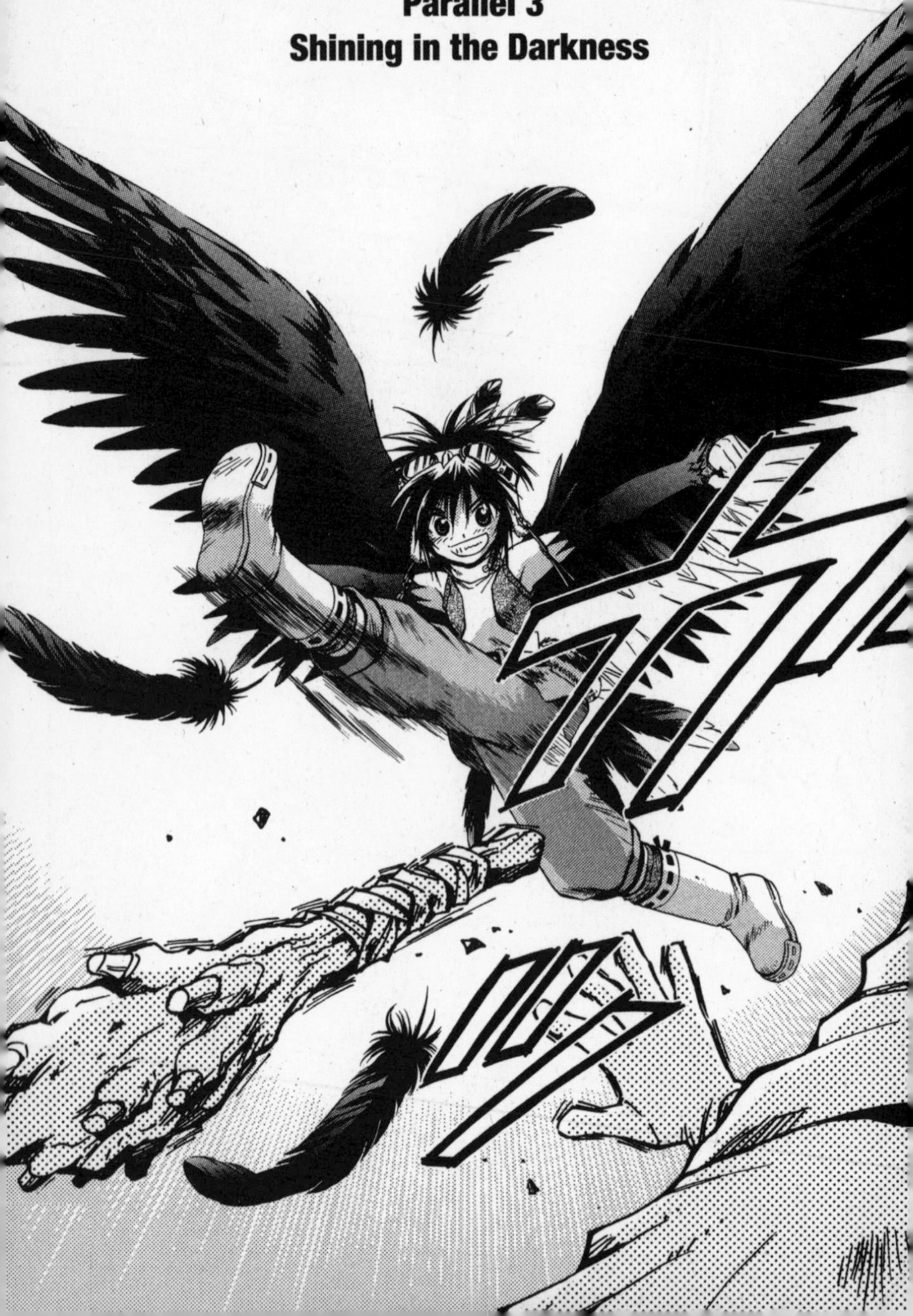

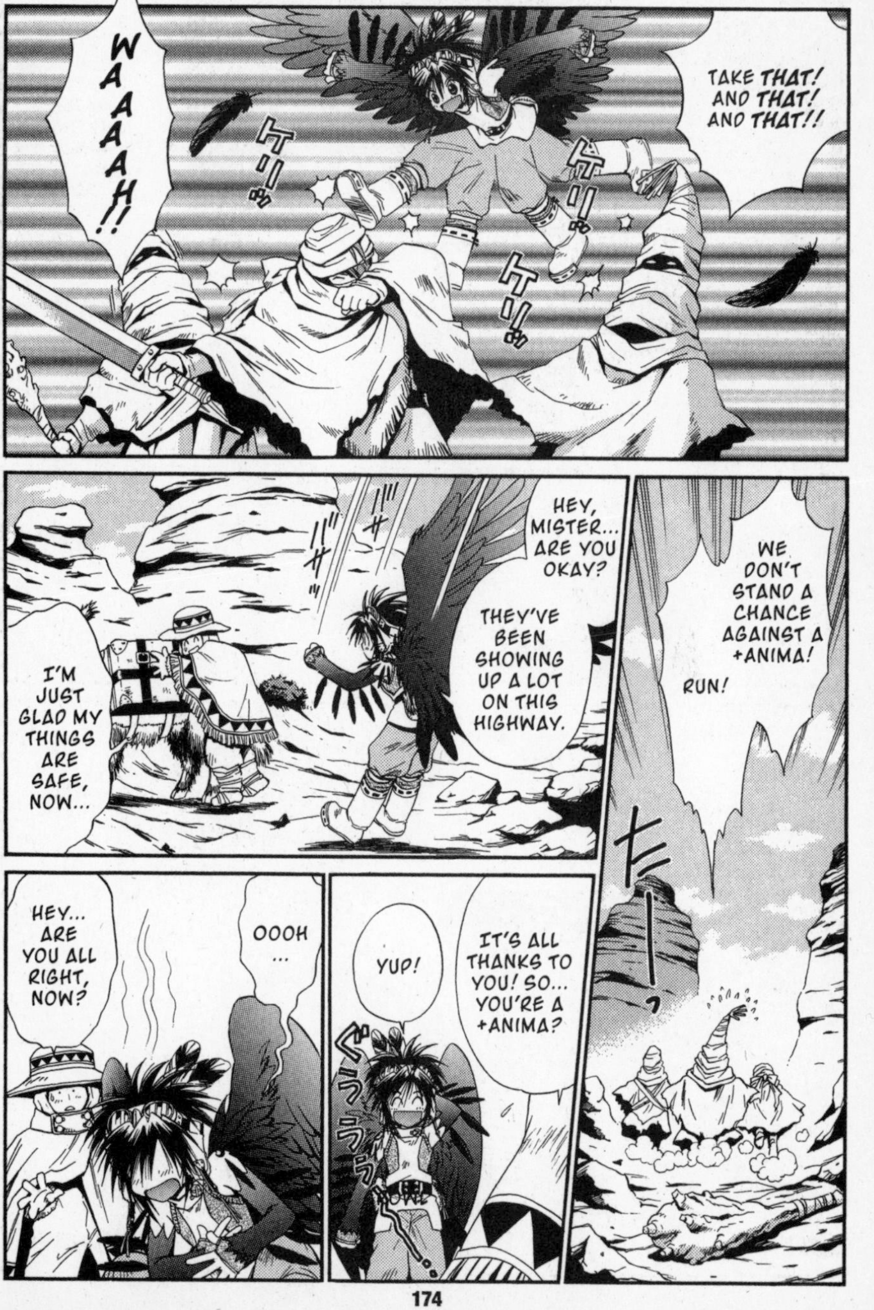
TAKE THAT! AND THAT! AND THAT!!
WAAAAAH!!
WE DON'T STAND A CHANCE AGAINST A +ANIMA!
RUN!
HEY, MISTER... ARE YOU OKAY?
THEY'VE BEEN SHOWING UP A LOT ON THIS HIGHWAY.
I'M JUST GLAD MY THINGS ARE SAFE, NOW...
IT'S ALL THANKS TO YOU! SO... YOU'RE A +ANIMA?
YUP!
OOOH ...
HEY... ARE YOU ALL RIGHT, NOW?

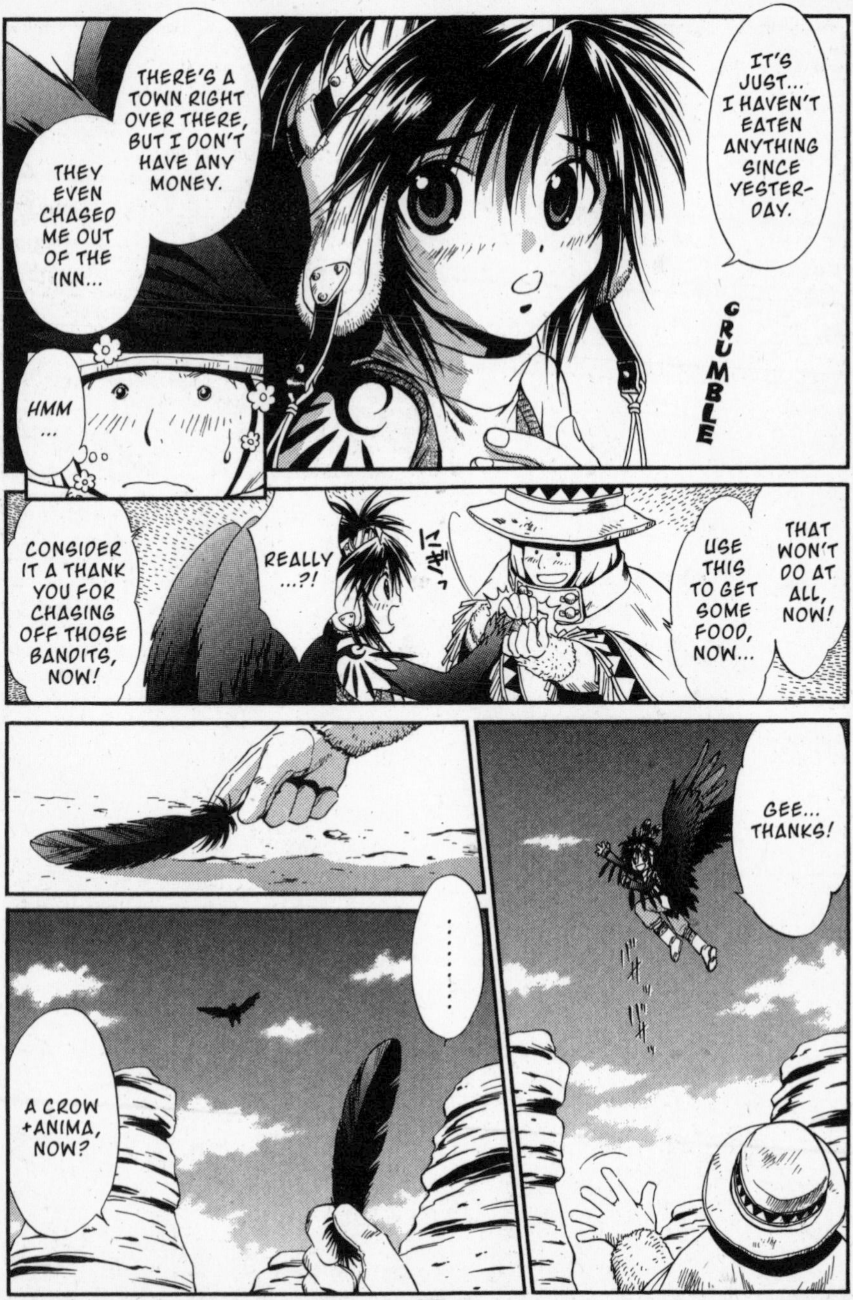
IT'S JUST... I HAVEN'T EATEN ANYTHING SINCE YESTER-DAY.
THERE'S A TOWN RIGHT OVER THERE, BUT I DON'T HAVE ANY MONEY.
THEY EVEN CHASED ME OUT OF THE INN...
GRUMBLE
HMM ...
THAT WON'T DO AT ALL, NOW!
USE THIS TO GET SOME FOOD, NOW...
REALLY ...?!
CONSIDER IT A THANK YOU FOR CHASING OFF THOSE BANDITS, NOW!
GEE... THANKS!
......
A CROW +ANIMA, NOW?

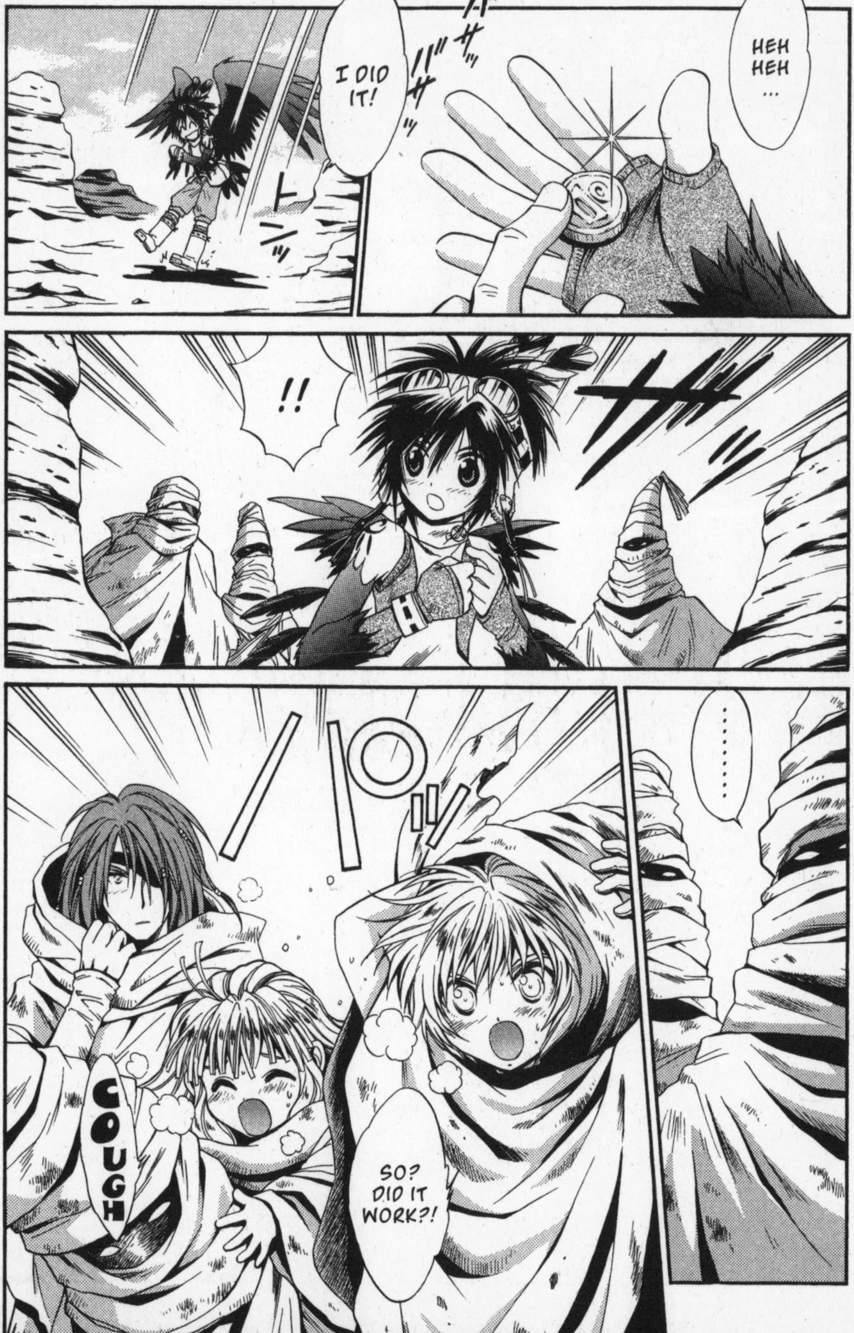
HEH HEH ...
I DID IT!
!!
......
SO? DID IT WORK?!
COUGH

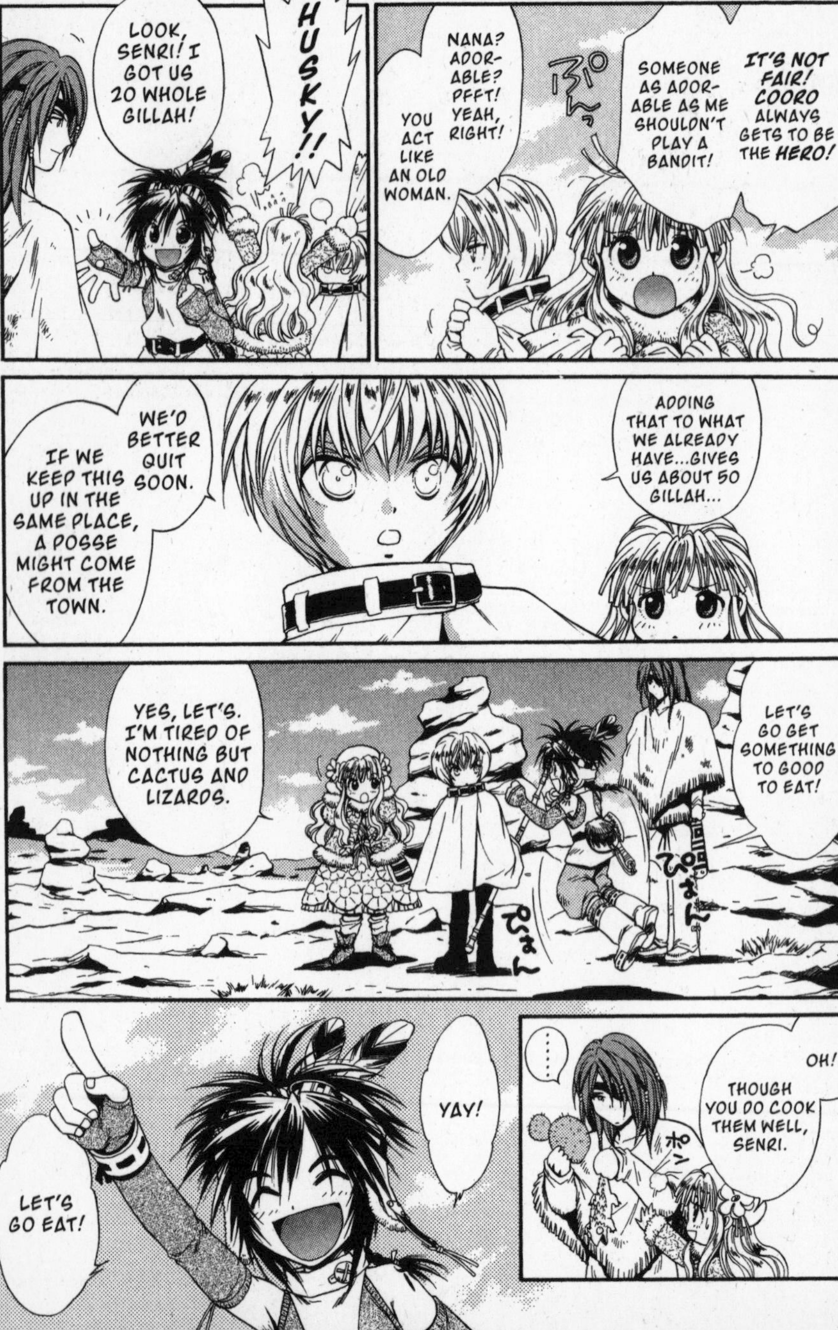
IT'S NOT FAIR! COORO ALWAYS GETS TO BE THE HERO!
SOMEONE AS ADORABLE AS ME SHOULDN'T PLAY A BANDIT!
NANA? ADORABLE? PFFT! YEAH, RIGHT!
YOU ACT LIKE AN OLD WOMAN.
HUSKY!!
LOOK, SENRI! I GOT US 20 WHOLE GILLAH!
ADDING THAT TO WHAT WE ALREADY HAVE...GIVES US ABOUT 50 GILLAH...
WE'D BETTER QUIT SOON.
IF WE KEEP THIS UP IN THE SAME PLACE, A POSSE MIGHT COME FROM THE TOWN.
LET'S GO GET SOMETHING TO GOOD TO EAT!
ぴょん
ぴょん
YES, LET'S. I'M TIRED OF NOTHING BUT CACTUS AND LIZARDS.
OH!
THOUGH YOU DO COOK THEM WELL, SENRI.
......
ポン
YAY!
LET'S GO EAT!

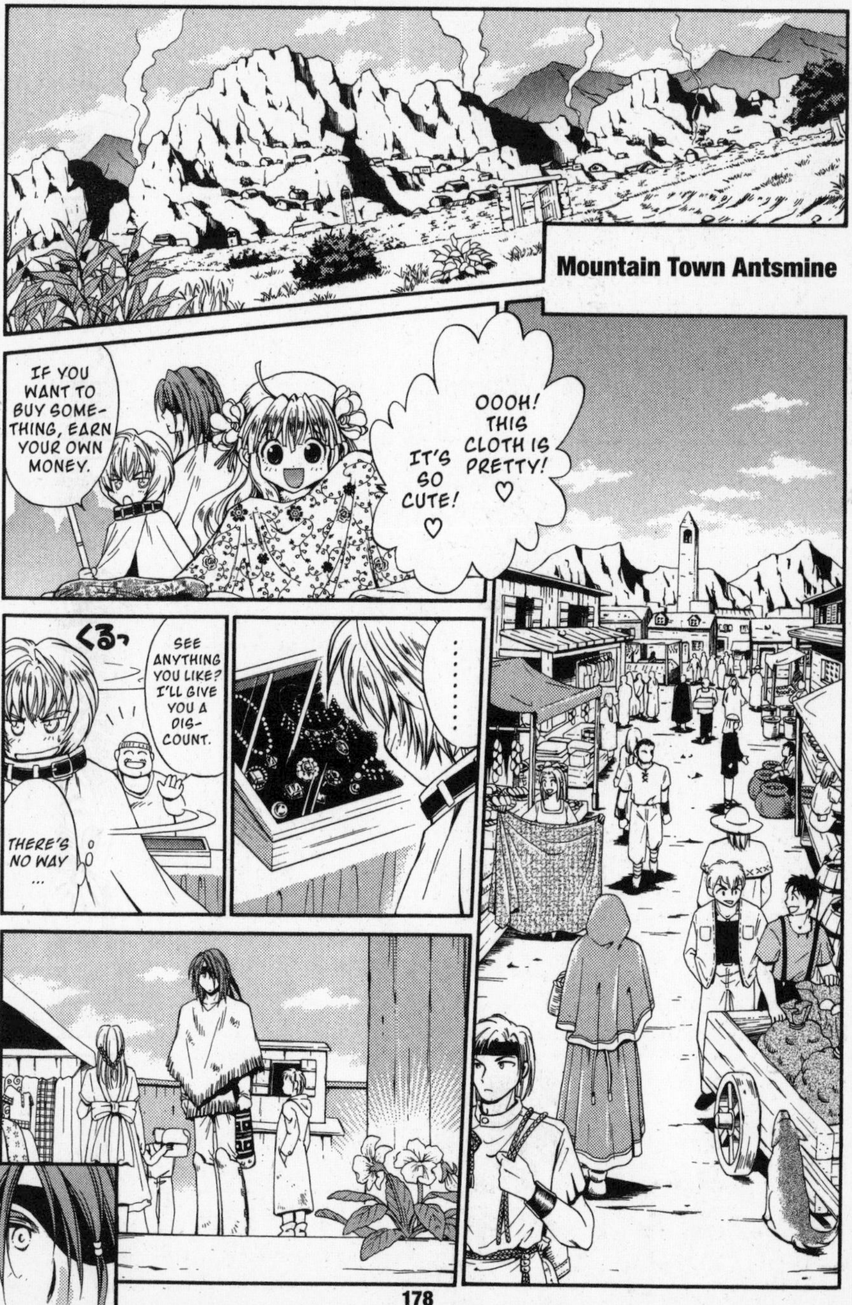
Mountain Town Antsmine
OOOH! THIS CLOTH IS PRETTY! ♡
IT'S SO CUTE! ♡
IF YOU WANT TO BUY SOMETHING, EARN YOUR OWN MONEY.
......
くるっ
SEE ANYTHING YOU LIKE? I'LL GIVE YOU A DISCOUNT.
THERE'S NO WAY ...

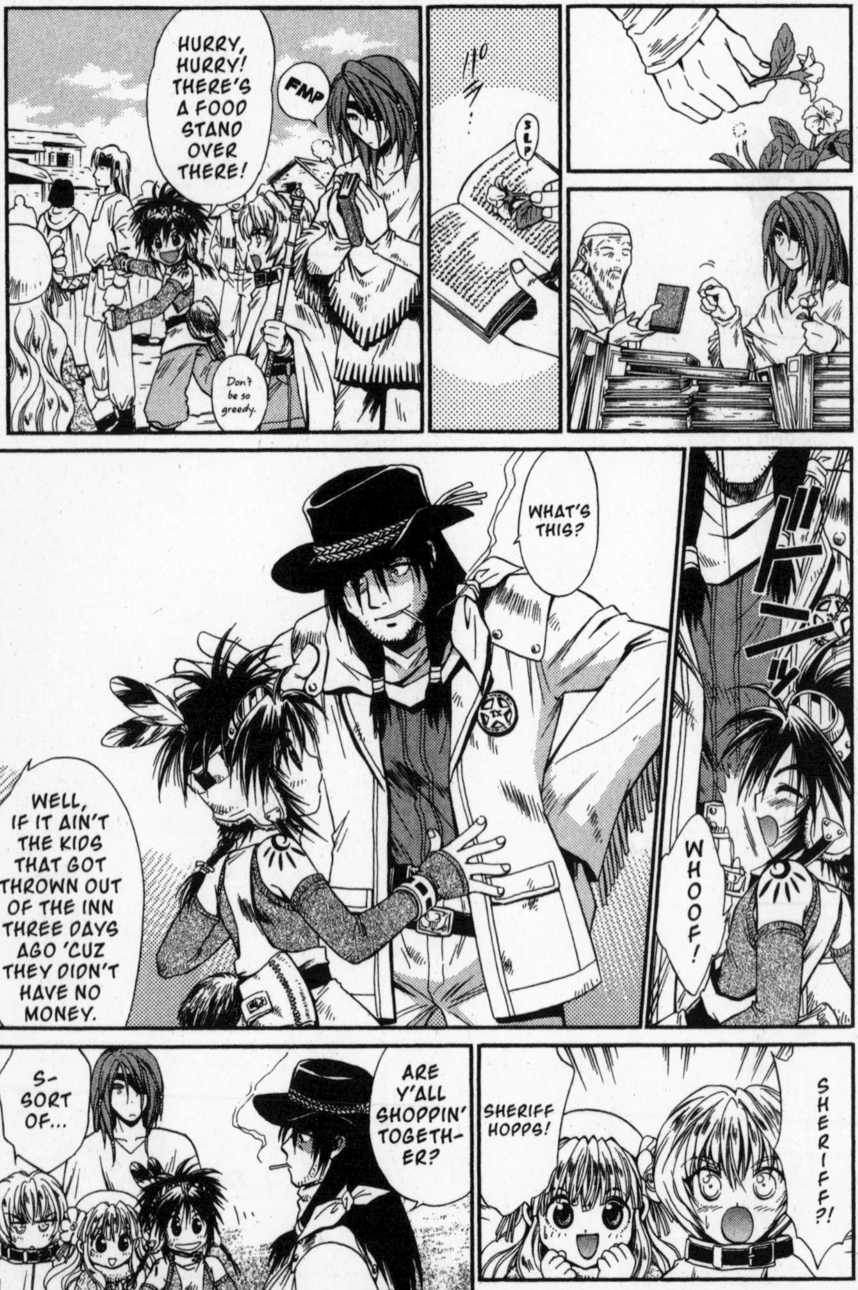

SLP
FMP
HURRY, HURRY! THERE'S A FOOD STAND OVER THERE!
Don't be so greedy.
WHOOF!
WHAT'S THIS?
WELL, IF IT AIN'T THE KIDS THAT GOT THROWN OUT OF THE INN THREE DAYS AGO 'CUZ THEY DIDN'T HAVE NO MONEY.
SHERIFF?!
SHERIFF HOPPS!
ARE Y'ALL SHOPPIN' TOGETH-ER?
S-SORT OF...

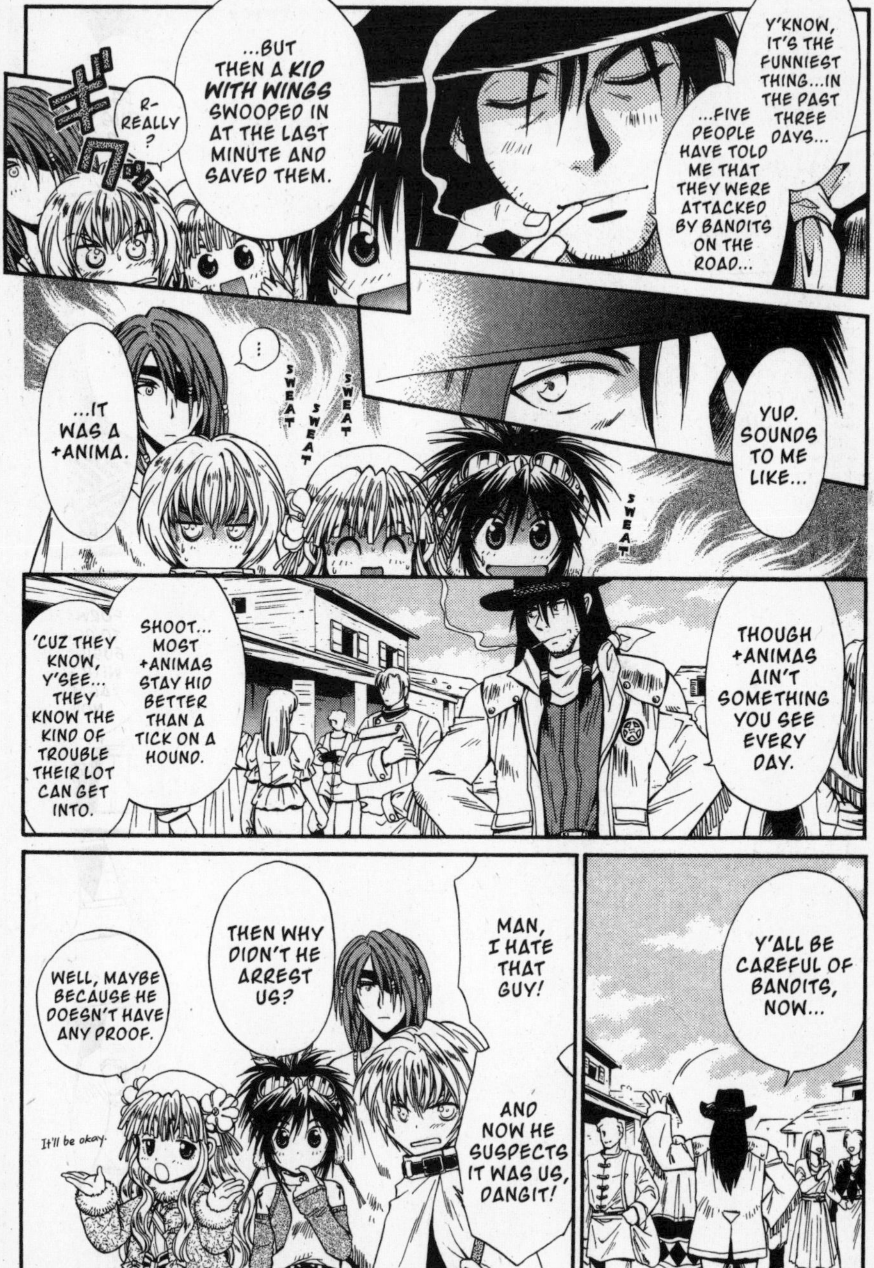
Y'KNOW, IT'S THE FUNNIEST THING...IN THE PAST THREE DAYS...
...FIVE PEOPLE HAVE TOLD ME THAT THEY WERE ATTACKED BY BANDITS ON THE ROAD...
...BUT THEN A KID WITH WINGS SWOOPED IN AT THE LAST MINUTE AND SAVED THEM.
ギクッ
R-REALLY?
YUP. SOUNDS TO ME LIKE...
...IT WAS A +ANIMA.
...
SWEAT
SWEAT
SWEAT
SWEAT
THOUGH +ANIMAS AIN'T SOMETHING YOU SEE EVERY DAY.
SHOOT... MOST +ANIMAS STAY HID BETTER THAN A TICK ON A HOUND.
'CUZ THEY KNOW, Y'SEE... THEY KNOW THE KIND OF TROUBLE THEIR LOT CAN GET INTO.
Y'ALL BE CAREFUL OF BANDITS, NOW...
MAN, I HATE THAT GUY!
AND NOW HE SUSPECTS IT WAS US, DANGIT!
THEN WHY DIDN'T HE ARREST US?
WELL, MAYBE BECAUSE HE DOESN'T HAVE ANY PROOF.
It'll be okay.

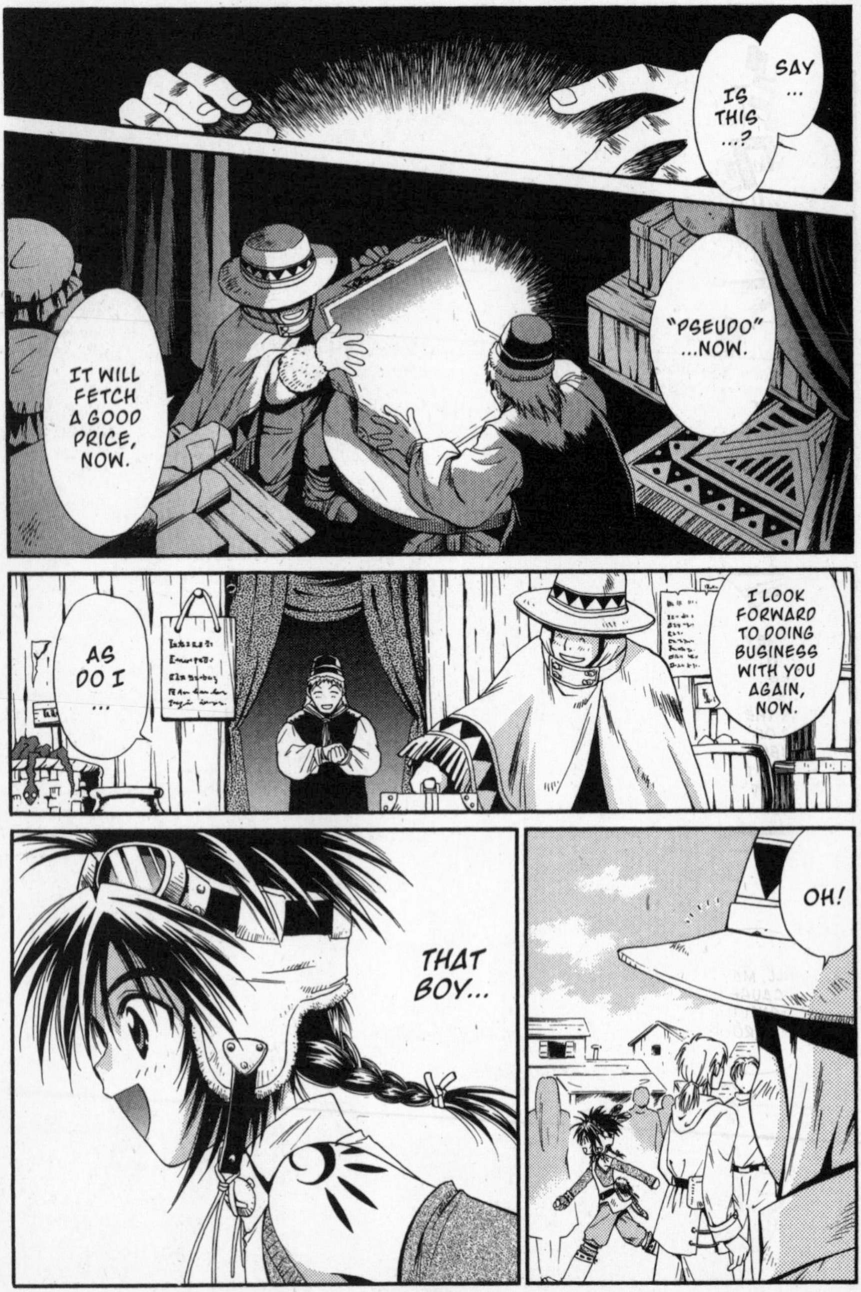
SAY ...
IS THIS ...?
"PSEUDO" ...NOW.
IT WILL FETCH A GOOD PRICE, NOW.
I LOOK FORWARD TO DOING BUSINESS WITH YOU AGAIN, NOW.
AS DO I ...
OH!
THAT BOY...

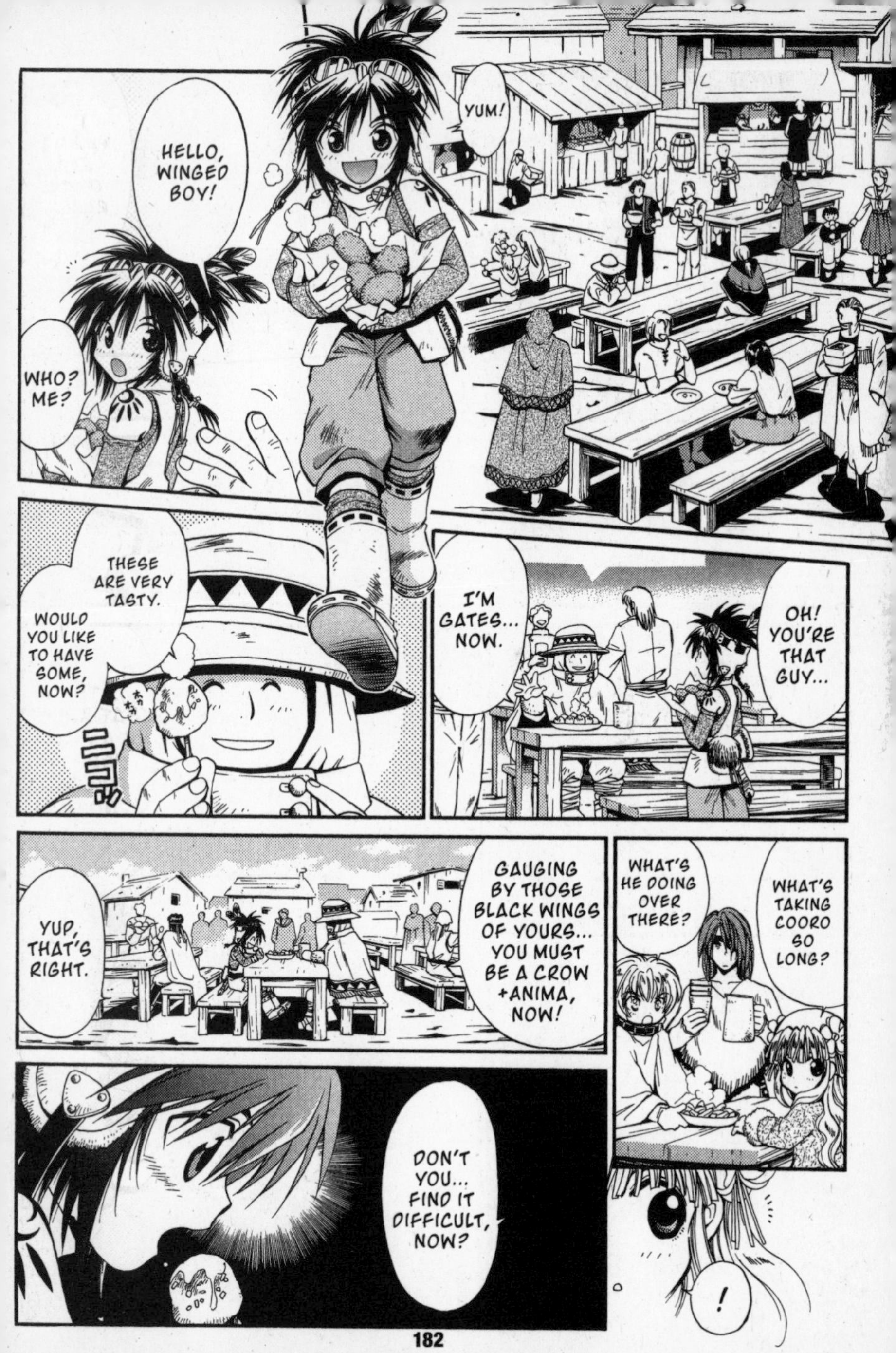
YUM!
HELLO, WINGED BOY!
WHO? ME?
OH! YOU'RE THAT GUY...
I'M GATES... NOW.
THESE ARE VERY TASTY.
WOULD YOU LIKE TO HAVE SOME, NOW?
WHAT'S TAKING COORO SO LONG?
WHAT'S HE DOING OVER THERE?
!
GAUGING BY THOSE BLACK WINGS OF YOURS... YOU MUST BE A CROW +ANIMA, NOW!
YUP, THAT'S RIGHT.
DON'T YOU... FIND IT DIFFICULT, NOW?

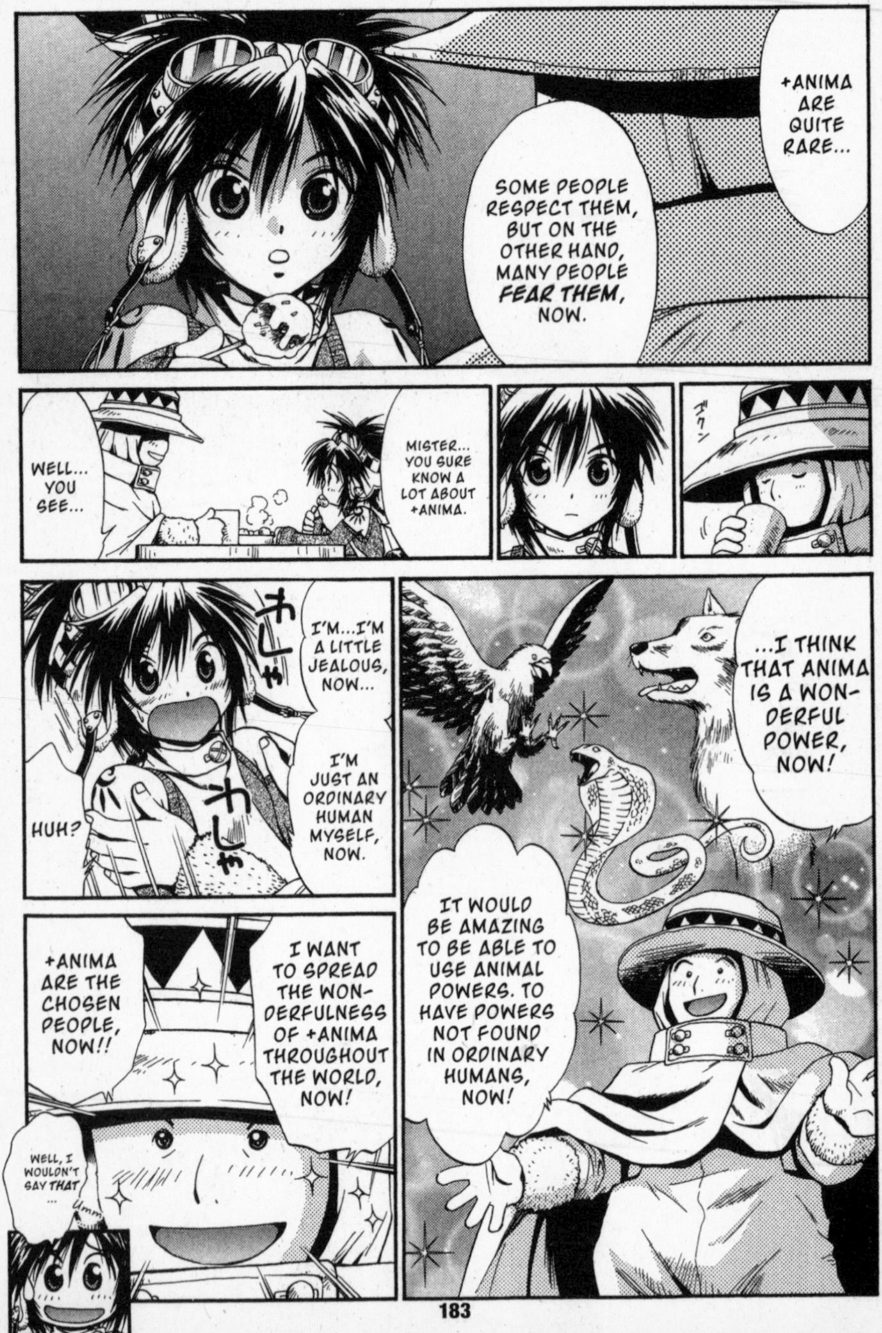
+ANIMA ARE QUITE RARE...
SOME PEOPLE RESPECT THEM, BUT ON THE OTHER HAND, MANY PEOPLE **FEAR THEM**, NOW.
ゴクン
MISTER... YOU SURE KNOW A LOT ABOUT +ANIMA.
WELL... YOU SEE...
...I THINK THAT ANIMA IS A WON-DERFUL POWER, NOW!
IT WOULD BE AMAZING TO BE ABLE TO USE ANIMAL POWERS. TO HAVE POWERS NOT FOUND IN ORDINARY HUMANS, NOW!
わしゃ わしゃ
I'M...I'M A LITTLE JEALOUS, NOW...
I'M JUST AN ORDINARY HUMAN MYSELF, NOW.
HUH?
I WANT TO SPREAD THE WON-DERFULNESS OF +ANIMA THROUGHOUT THE WORLD, NOW!
+ANIMA ARE THE CHOSEN PEOPLE, NOW!!
WELL, I WOULDN'T SAY THAT ...
Umm

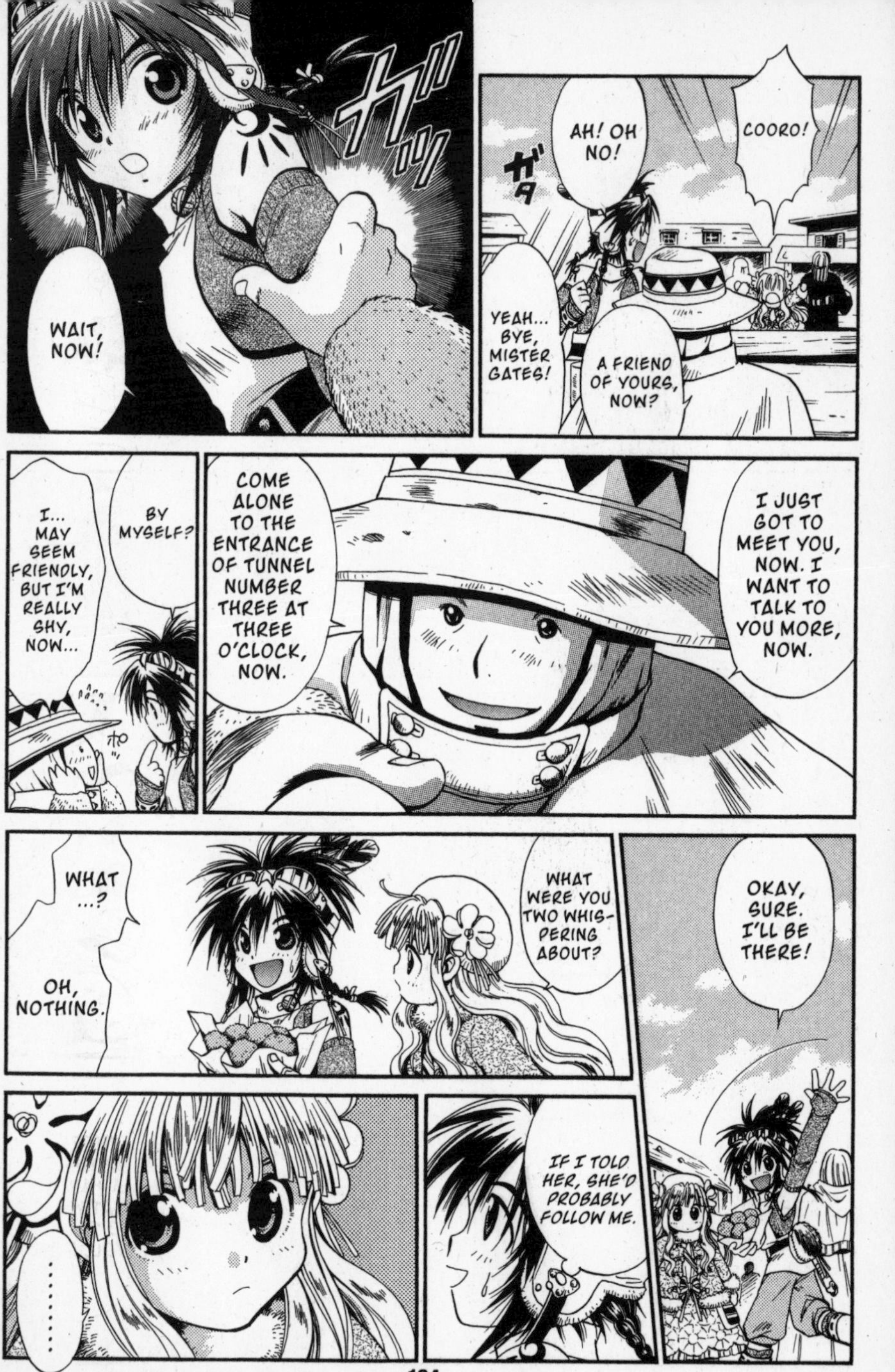

COORO!
AH! OH NO!
ガタ
A FRIEND OF YOURS, NOW?
YEAH... BYE, MISTER GATES!
ガッ
WAIT, NOW!
I JUST GOT TO MEET YOU, NOW. I WANT TO TALK TO YOU MORE, NOW.
COME ALONE TO THE ENTRANCE OF TUNNEL NUMBER THREE AT THREE O'CLOCK, NOW.
BY MYSELF?
I... MAY SEEM FRIENDLY, BUT I'M REALLY SHY, NOW...
OKAY, SURE. I'LL BE THERE!
WHAT WERE YOU TWO WHIS-PERING ABOUT?
WHAT ...?
OH, NOTHING.
IF I TOLD HER, SHE'D PROBABLY FOLLOW ME.
....

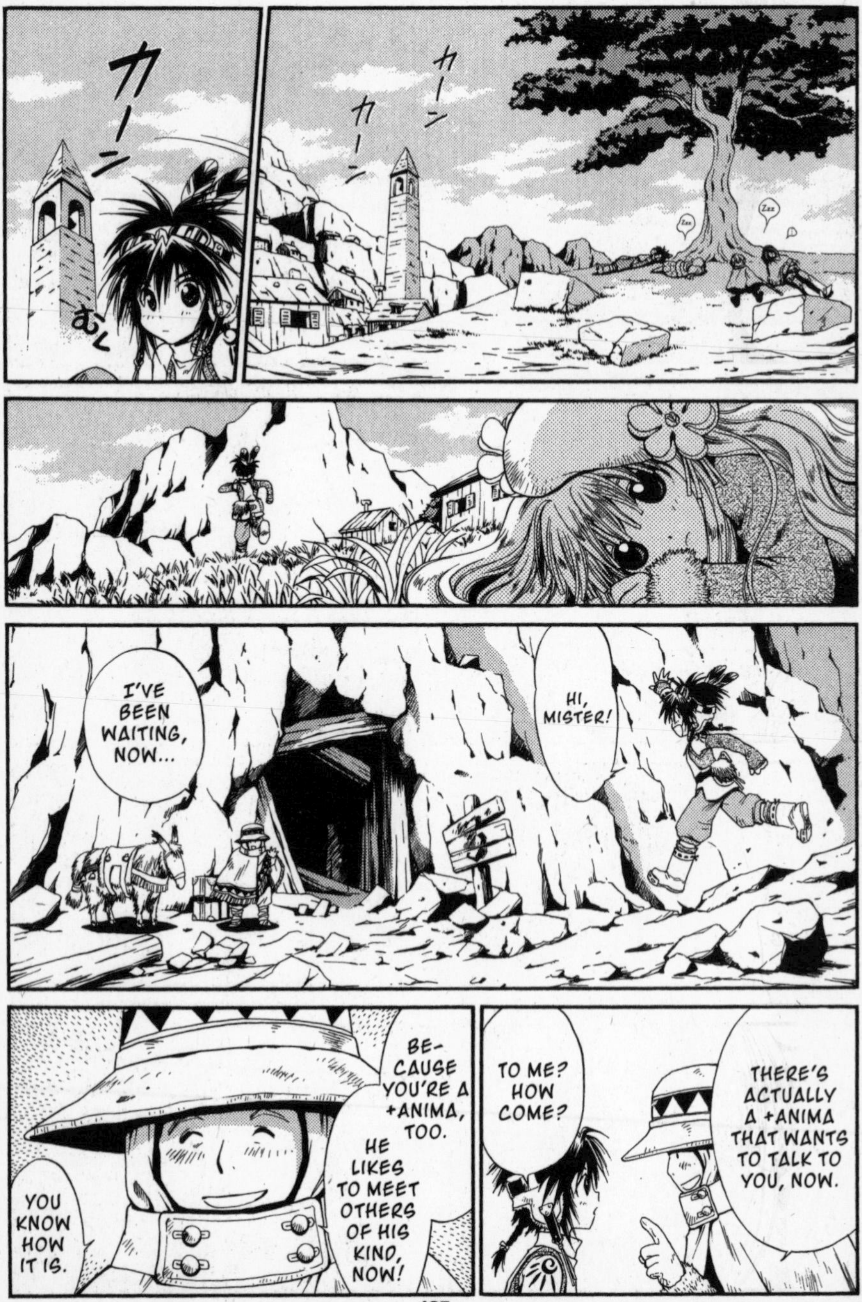
カーン
カーン
Zzz
Zzz
カーン
むく
HI, MISTER!
I'VE BEEN WAITING, NOW...
THERE'S ACTUALLY A +ANIMA THAT WANTS TO TALK TO YOU, NOW.
TO ME? HOW COME?
BE-CAUSE YOU'RE A +ANIMA, TOO.
HE LIKES TO MEET OTHERS OF HIS KIND, NOW!
YOU KNOW HOW IT IS.

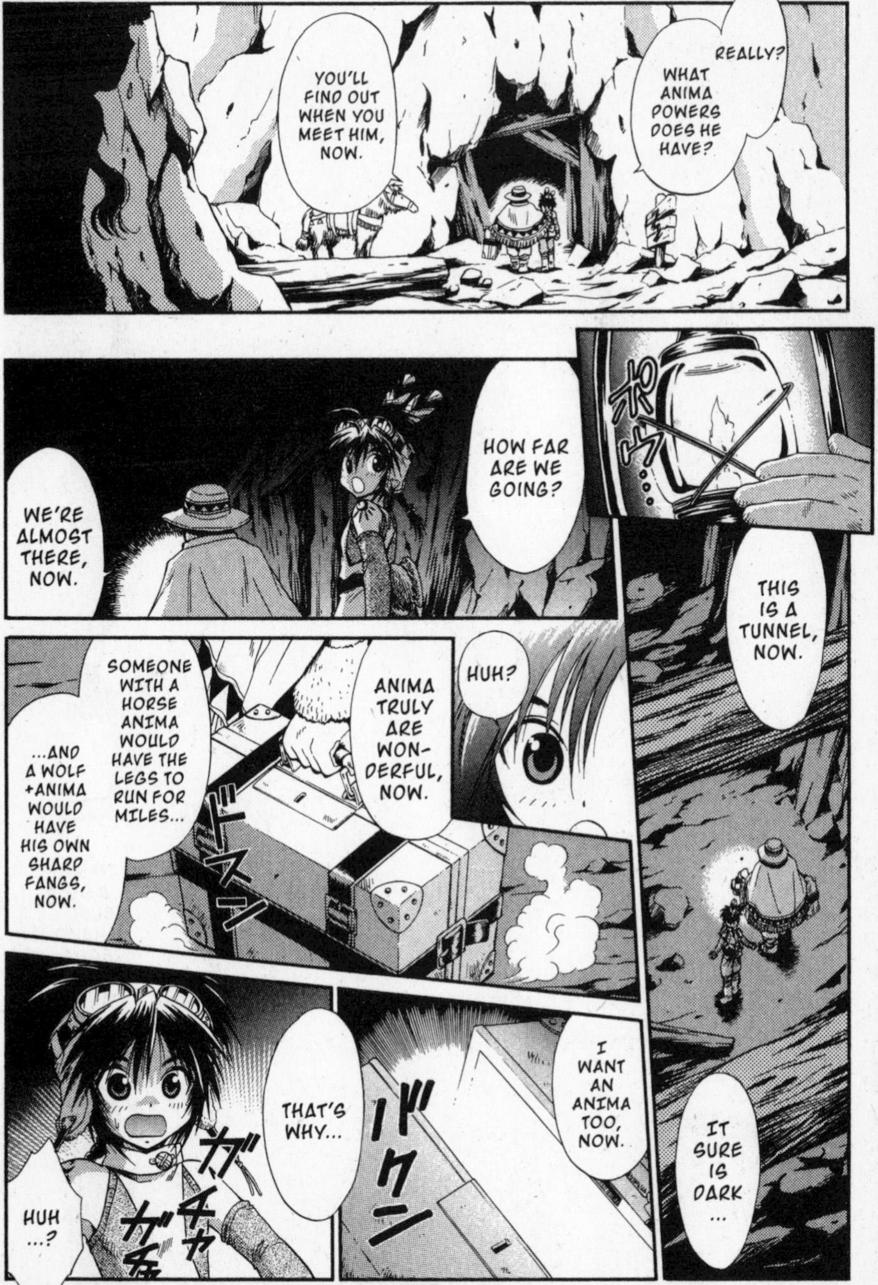
REALLY? WHAT ANIMA POWERS DOES HE HAVE?
YOU'LL FIND OUT WHEN YOU MEET HIM, NOW.
HOW FAR ARE WE GOING?
WE'RE ALMOST THERE, NOW.
THIS IS A TUNNEL, NOW.
IT SURE IS DARK ...
HUH?
ANIMA TRULY ARE WON-DERFUL, NOW.
SOMEONE WITH A HORSE ANIMA WOULD HAVE THE LEGS TO RUN FOR MILES...
...AND A WOLF +ANIMA WOULD HAVE HIS OWN SHARP FANGS, NOW.
I WANT AN ANIMA TOO, NOW.
THAT'S WHY...
HUH ...?

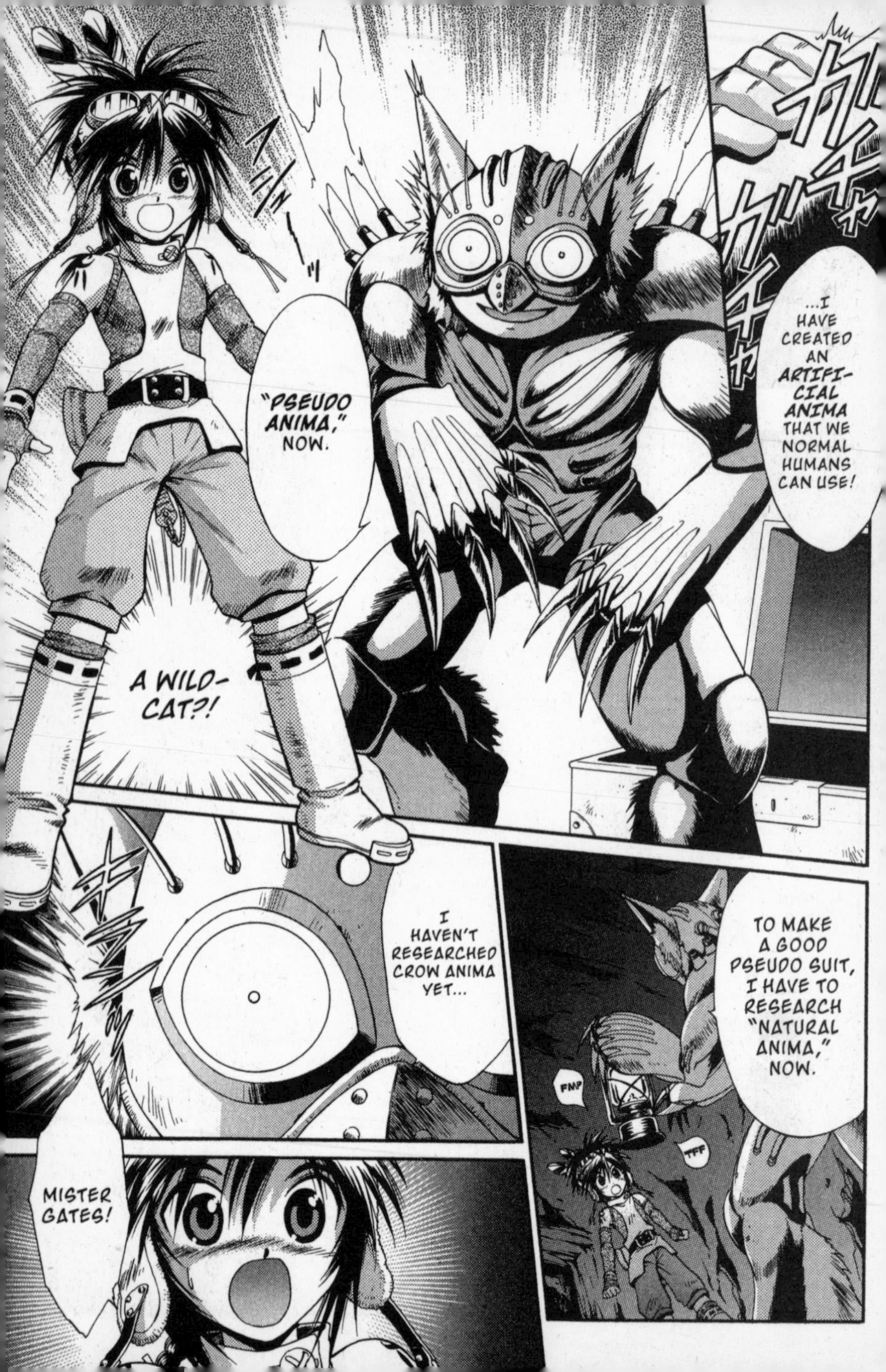
...I HAVE CREATED AN ARTIFICIAL ANIMA THAT WE NORMAL HUMANS CAN USE!
"PSEUDO ANIMA," NOW.
A WILD-CAT?!
TO MAKE A GOOD PSEUDO SUIT, I HAVE TO RESEARCH "NATURAL ANIMA," NOW.
FMP
TFF
I HAVEN'T RESEARCHED CROW ANIMA YET...
MISTER GATES!

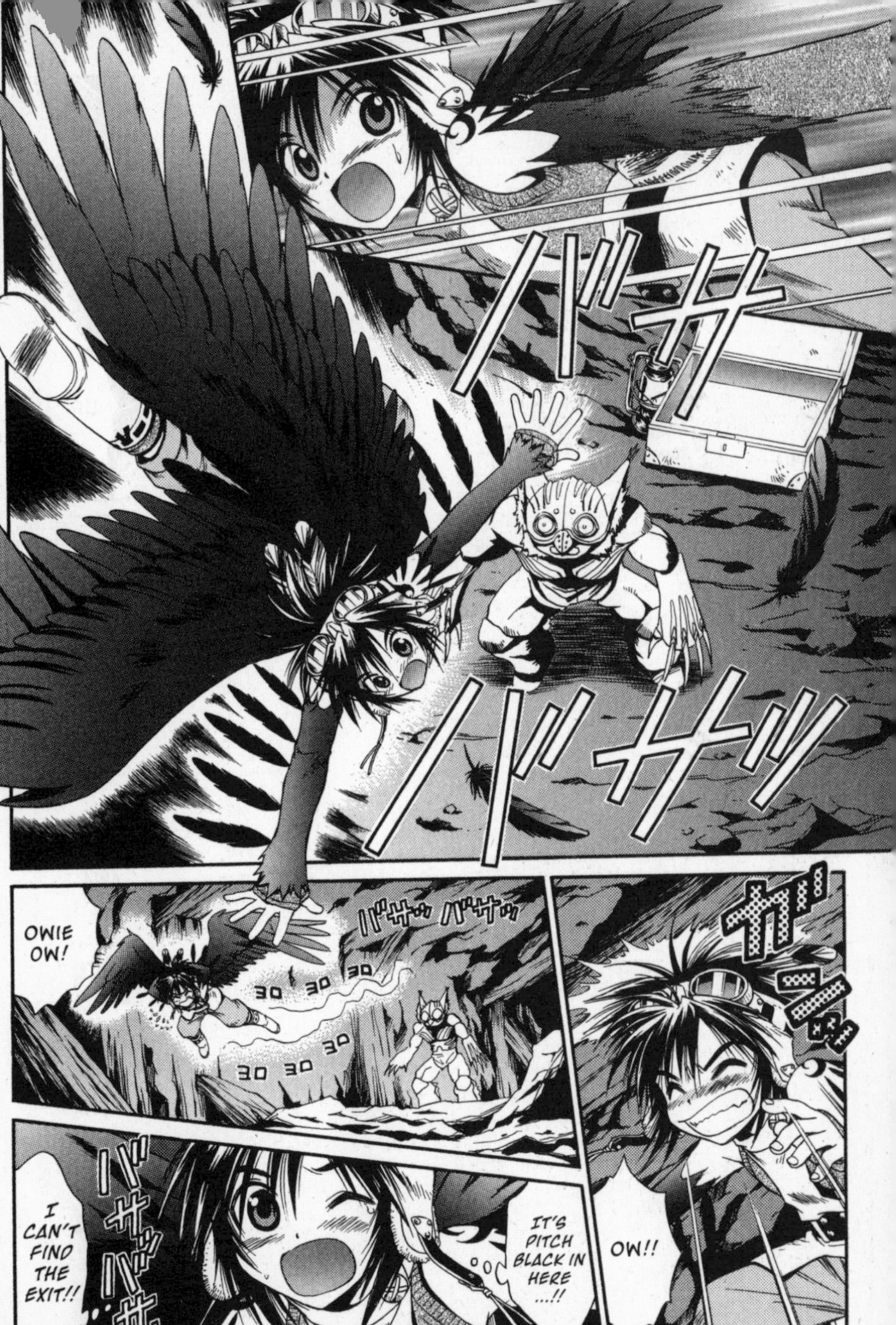

バサ
バサッ
OW!!
OWIE OW!
IT'S PITCH BLACK IN HERE ...!!
I CAN'T FIND THE EXIT!!

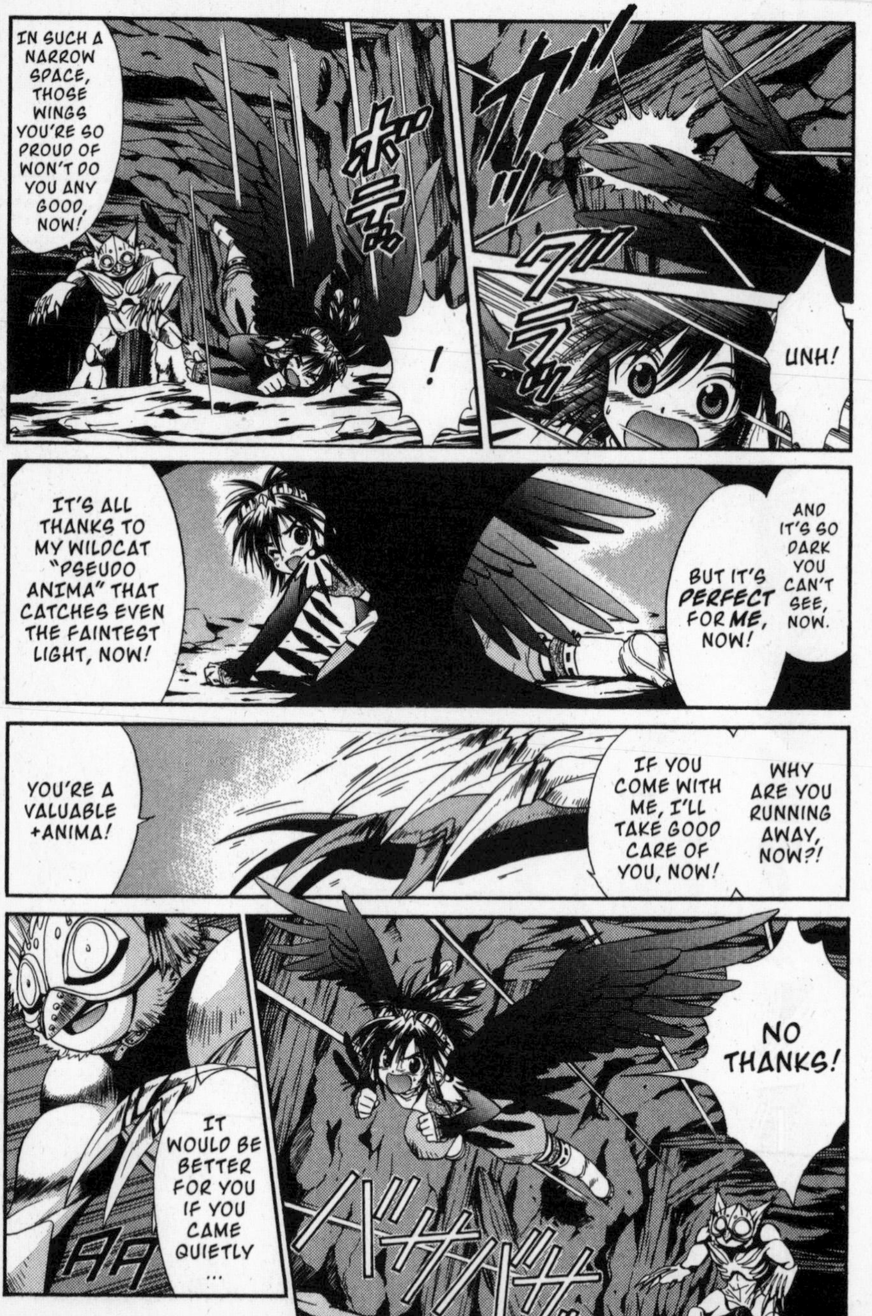
UNH!
IN SUCH A NARROW SPACE, THOSE WINGS YOU'RE SO PROUD OF WON'T DO YOU ANY GOOD, NOW!
!
AND IT'S SO DARK YOU CAN'T SEE, NOW.
BUT IT'S PERFECT FOR ME, NOW!
IT'S ALL THANKS TO MY WILDCAT "PSEUDO ANIMA" THAT CATCHES EVEN THE FAINTEST LIGHT, NOW!
WHY ARE YOU RUNNING AWAY, NOW?!
IF YOU COME WITH ME, I'LL TAKE GOOD CARE OF YOU, NOW!
YOU'RE A VALUABLE +ANIMA!
NO THANKS!
IT WOULD BE BETTER FOR YOU IF YOU CAME QUIETLY ...

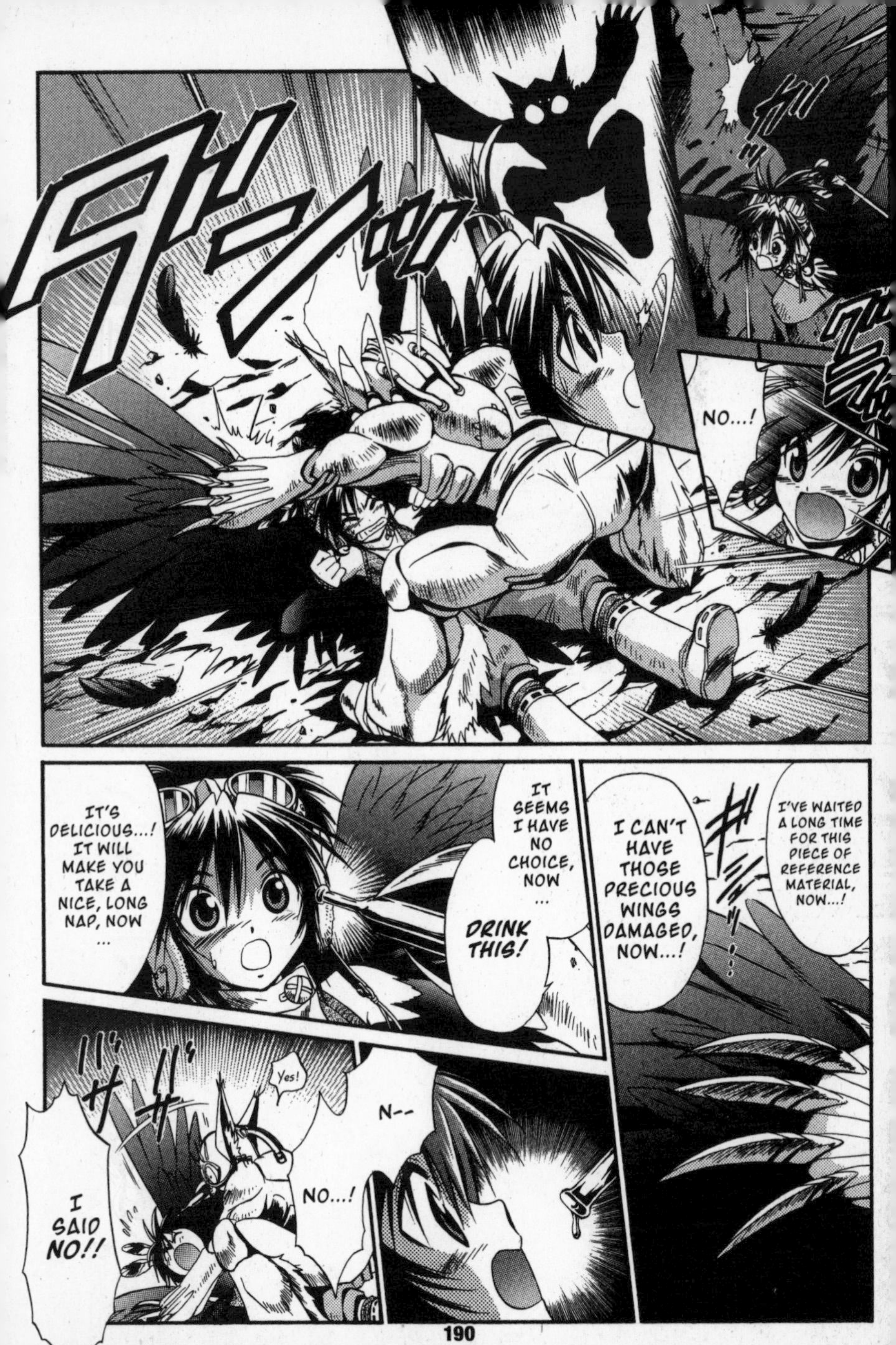
NO...!
I'VE WAITED A LONG TIME FOR THIS PIECE OF REFERENCE MATERIAL, NOW...!
I CAN'T HAVE THOSE PRECIOUS WINGS DAMAGED, NOW...!
IT SEEMS I HAVE NO CHOICE, NOW ...
DRINK THIS!
IT'S DELICIOUS...! IT WILL MAKE YOU TAKE A NICE, LONG NAP, NOW ...
N--
Yes!
NO...!
I SAID NO!!

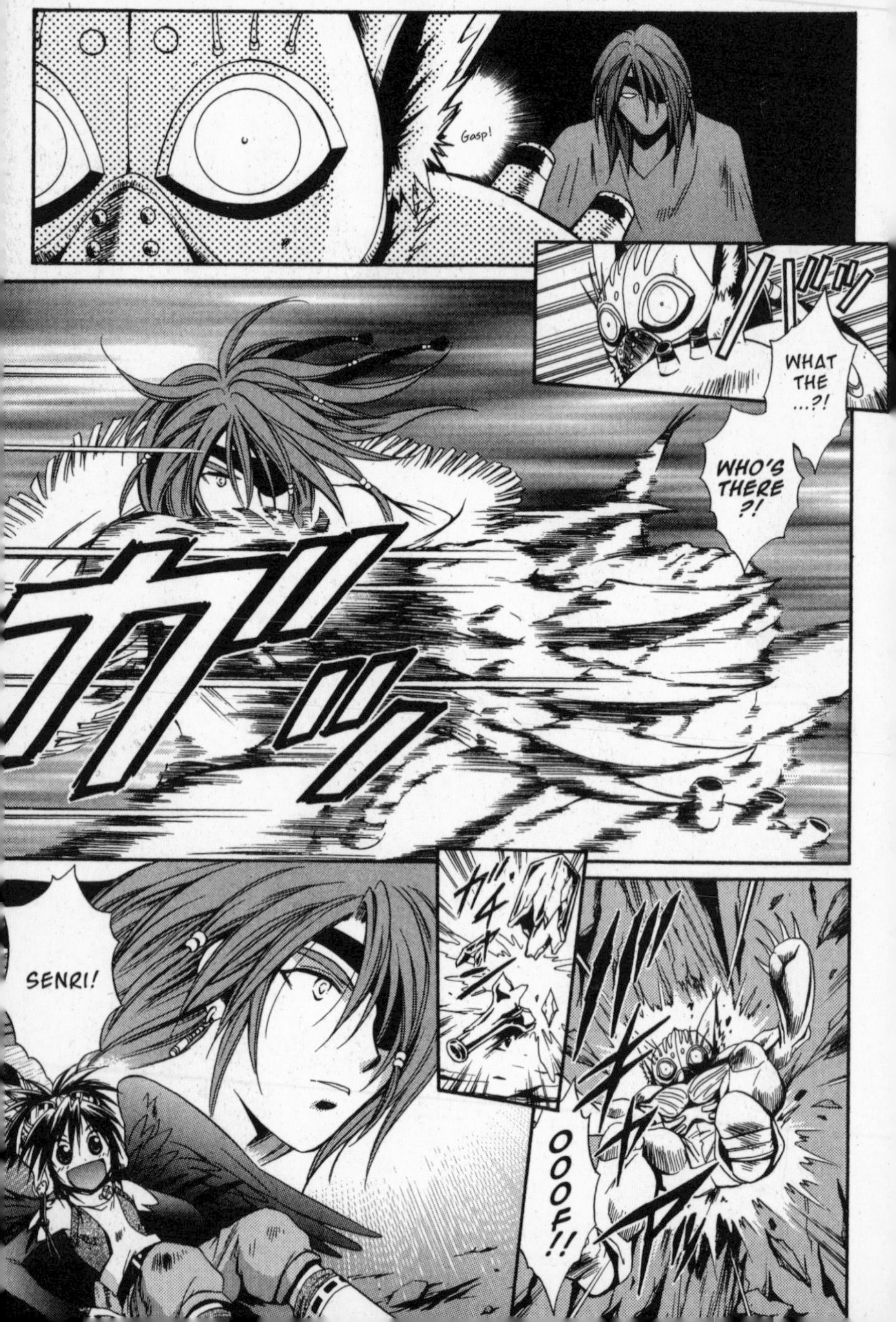
Gasp!
WHAT THE ...?!
WHO'S THERE ?!
OOOF!!
SENRI!

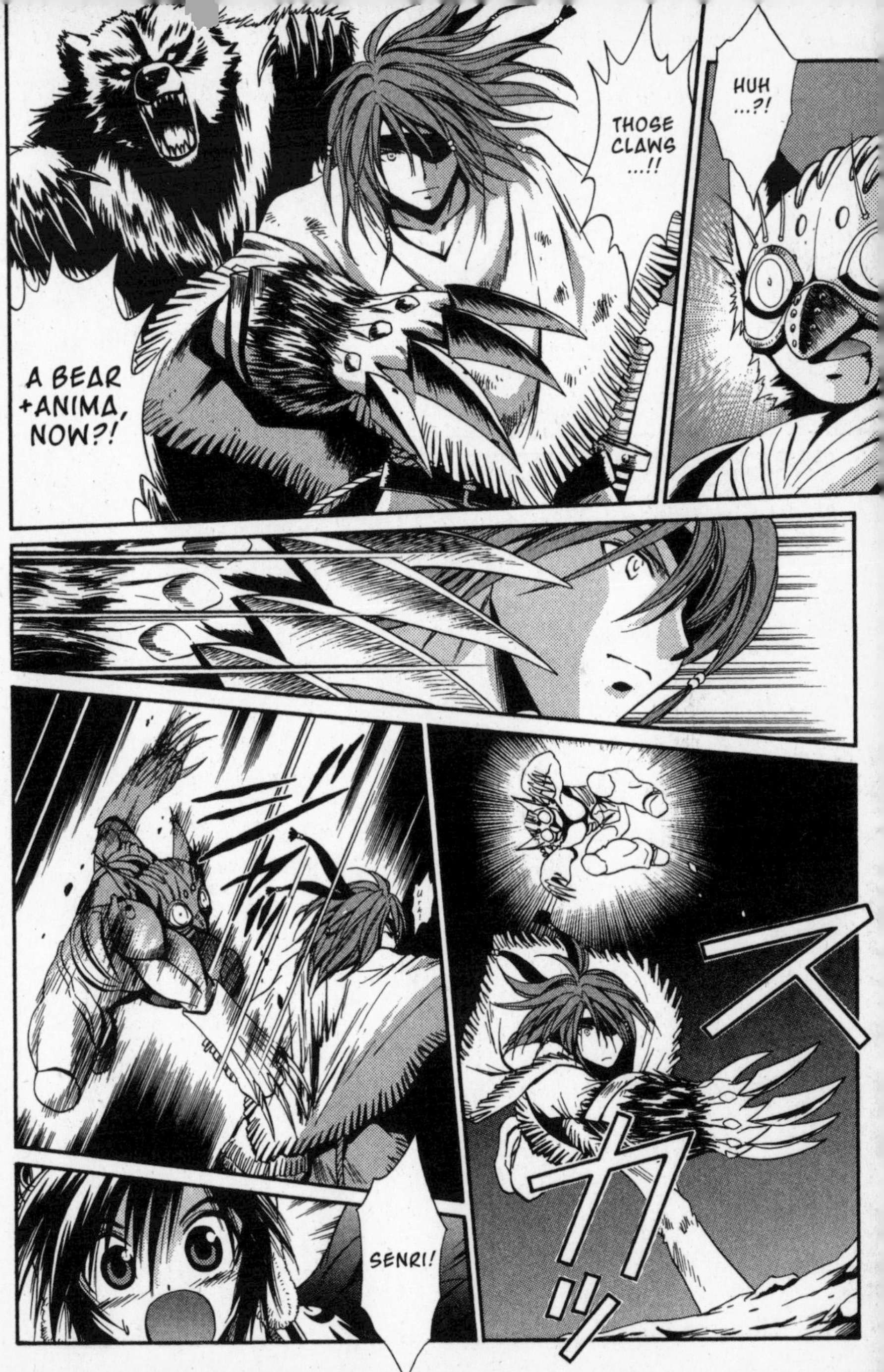
HUH ...?!
THOSE CLAWS ...!!
A BEAR ANIMA, NOW?!
Urk!
SENRI!

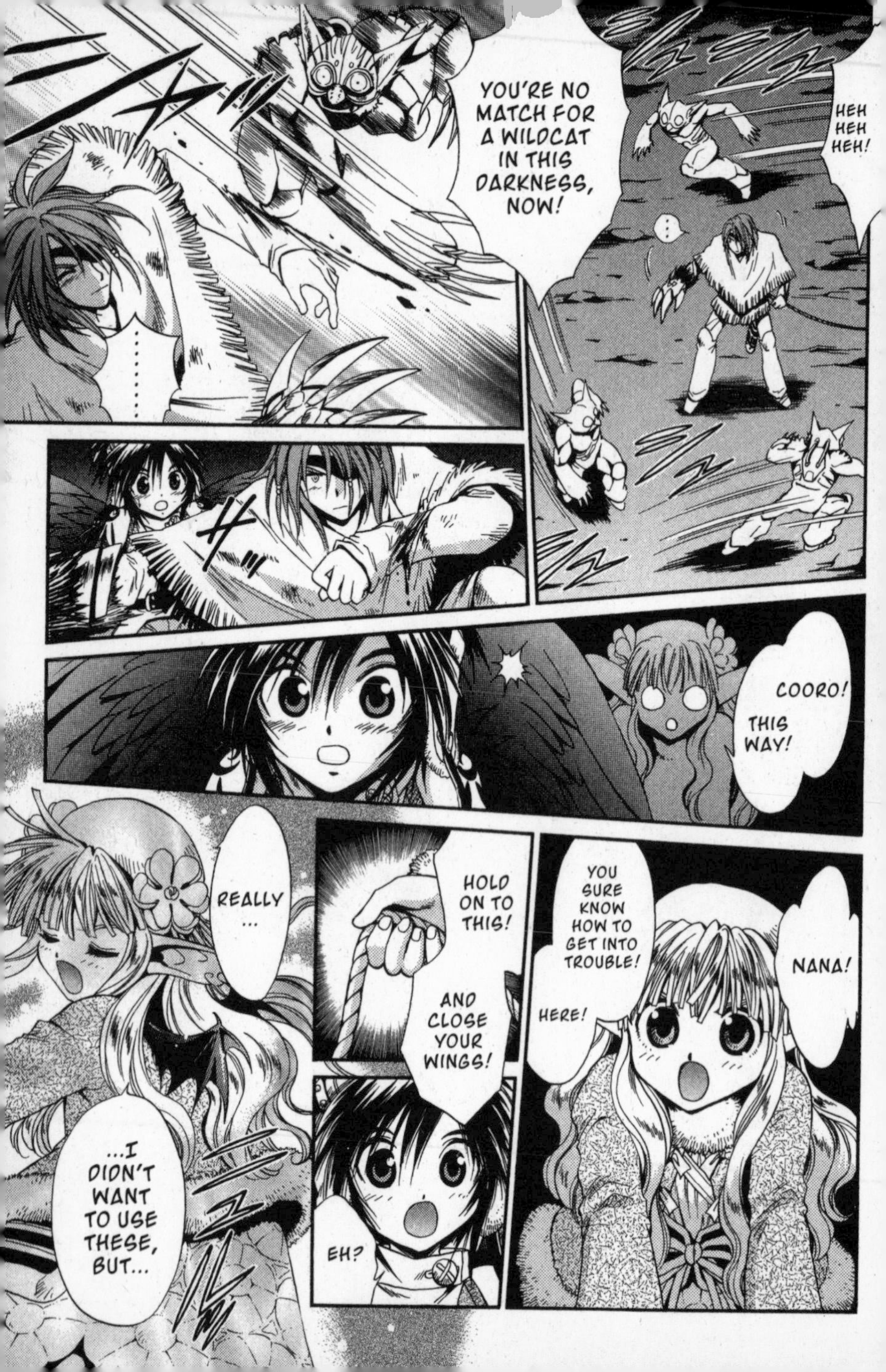

YOU'RE NO MATCH FOR A WILDCAT IN THIS DARKNESS, NOW!
HEH HEH HEH!
...
COORO!
THIS WAY!
NANA!
YOU SURE KNOW HOW TO GET INTO TROUBLE!
HERE!
HOLD ON TO THIS!
AND CLOSE YOUR WINGS!
EH?
REALLY ...
...I DIDN'T WANT TO USE THESE, BUT...

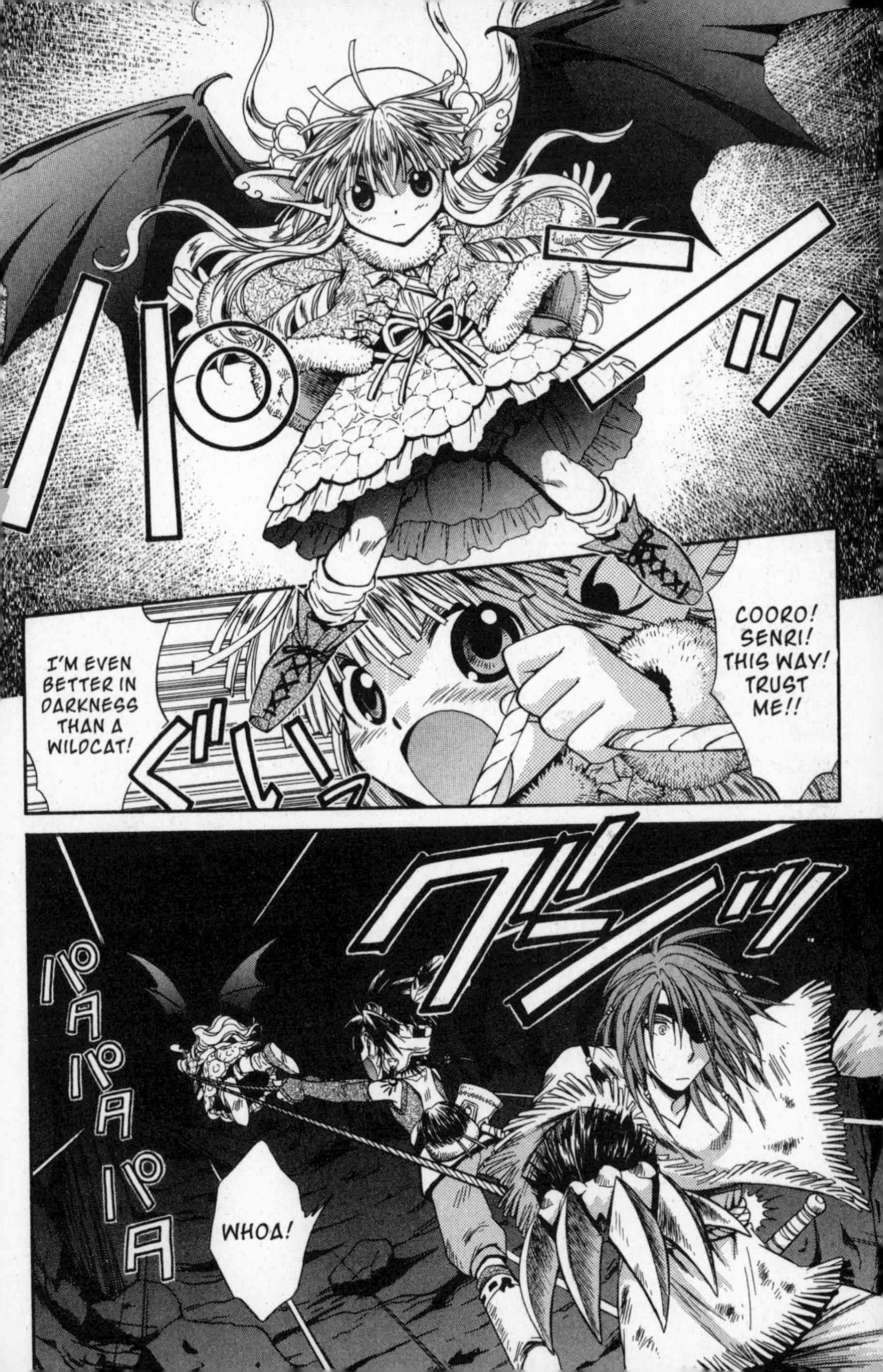
COORO! SENRI! THIS WAY! TRUST ME!!
I'M EVEN BETTER IN DARKNESS THAN A WILDCAT!
WHOA!

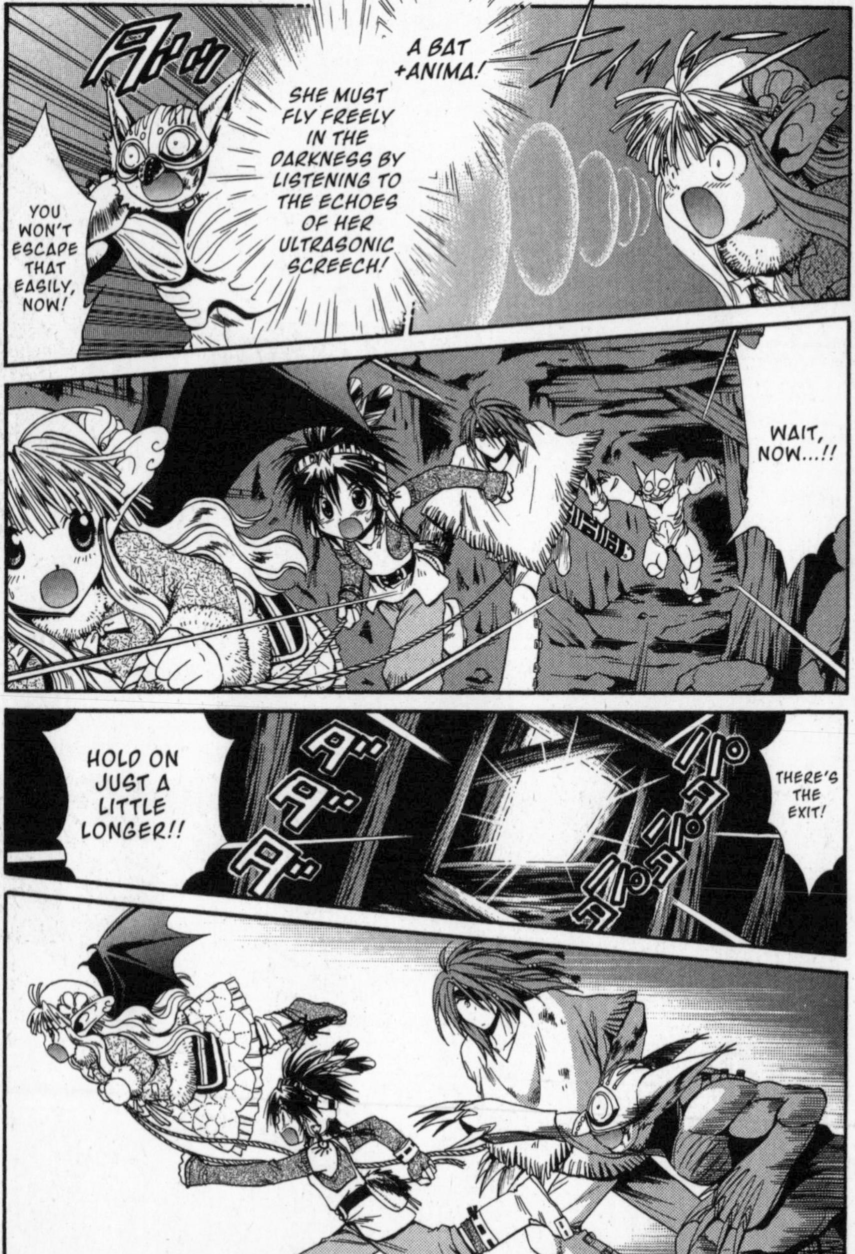
A BAT +ANIMA!
SHE MUST FLY FREELY IN THE DARKNESS BY LISTENING TO THE ECHOES OF HER ULTRASONIC SCREECH!
YOU WON'T ESCAPE THAT EASILY, NOW!
WAIT, NOW...!!
THERE'S THE EXIT!
HOLD ON JUST A LITTLE LONGER!!

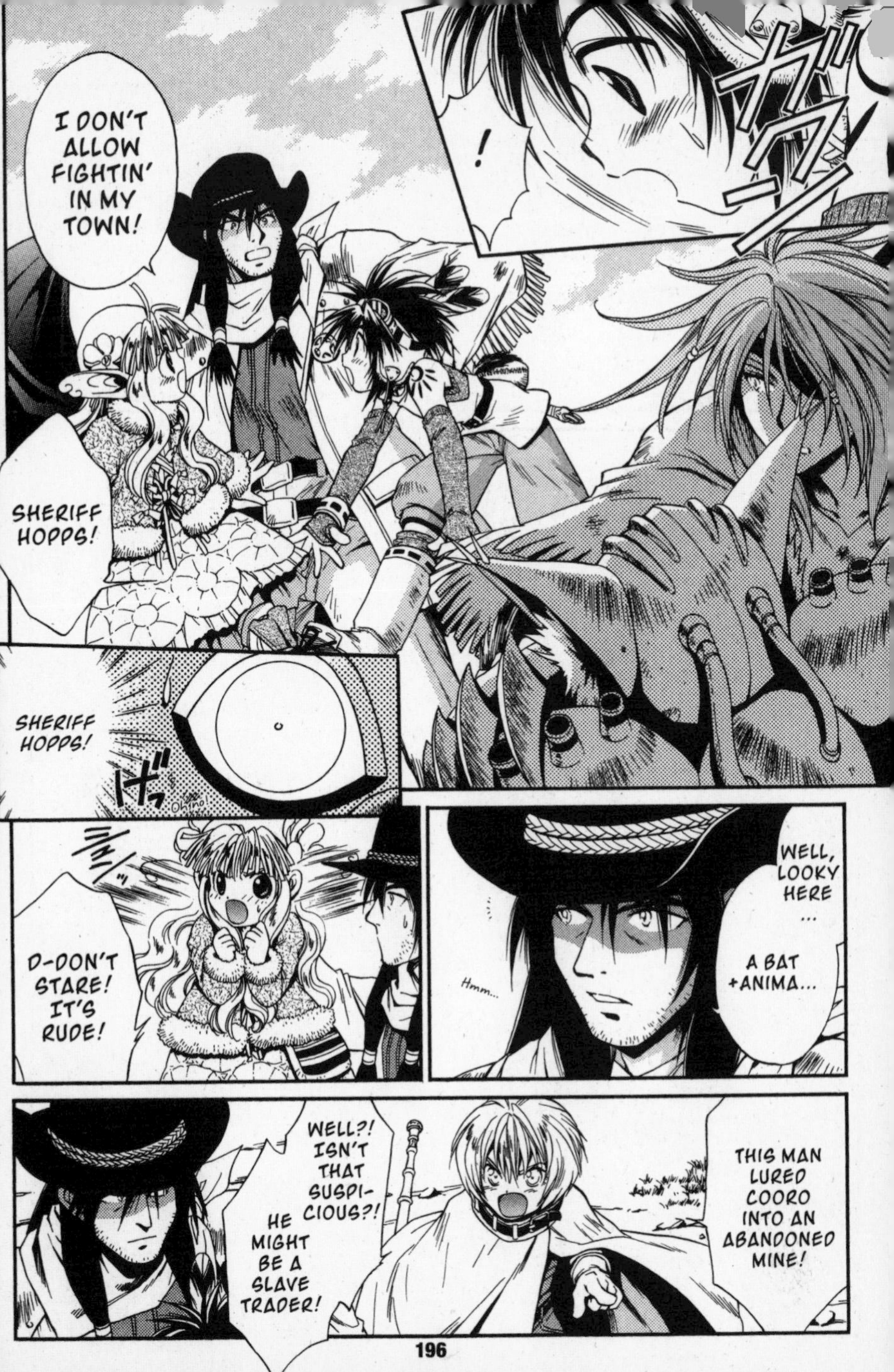
!
I DON'T ALLOW FIGHTIN' IN MY TOWN!
SHERIFF HOPPS!
SHERIFF HOPPS!
Oh no!
WELL, LOOKY HERE ...
A BAT +ANIMA...
Hmm...
D-DON'T STARE! IT'S RUDE!
THIS MAN LURED COORO INTO AN ABANDONED MINE!
WELL?! ISN'T THAT SUSPICIOUS?!
HE MIGHT BE A SLAVE TRADER!

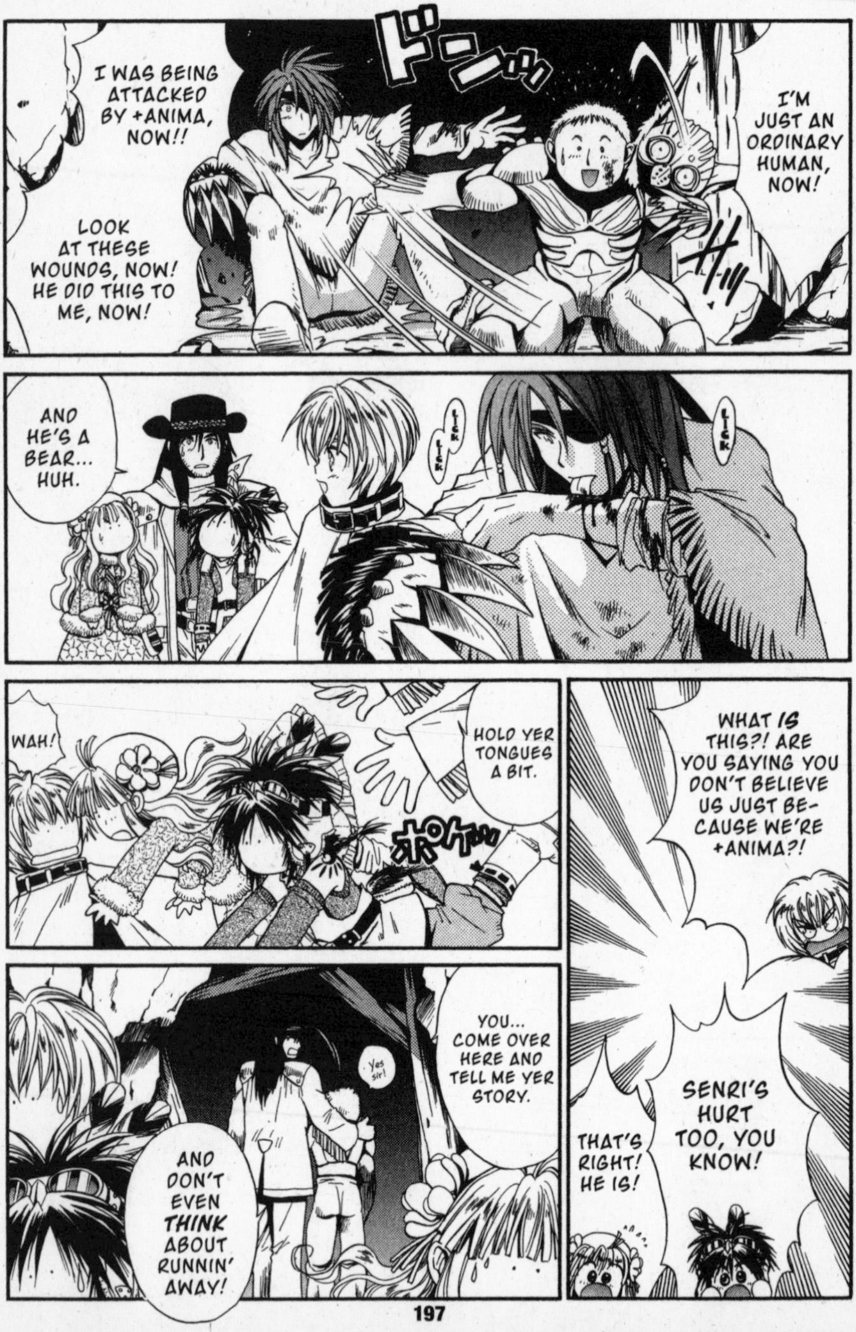
ドーン
I'M JUST AN ORDINARY HUMAN, NOW!
I WAS BEING ATTACKED BY +ANIMA, NOW!!
LOOK AT THESE WOUNDS, NOW! HE DID THIS TO ME, NOW!
LICK
LICK LICK
AND HE'S A BEAR... HUH.
WHAT *IS* THIS?! ARE YOU SAYING YOU DON'T BELIEVE US JUST BE-CAUSE WE'RE +ANIMA?!
SENRI'S HURT TOO, YOU KNOW!
THAT'S RIGHT! HE IS!
HOLD YER TONGUES A BIT.
WAH!
YOU... COME OVER HERE AND TELL ME YER STORY.
Yes sir!
AND DON'T EVEN **THINK** ABOUT RUNNIN' AWAY!

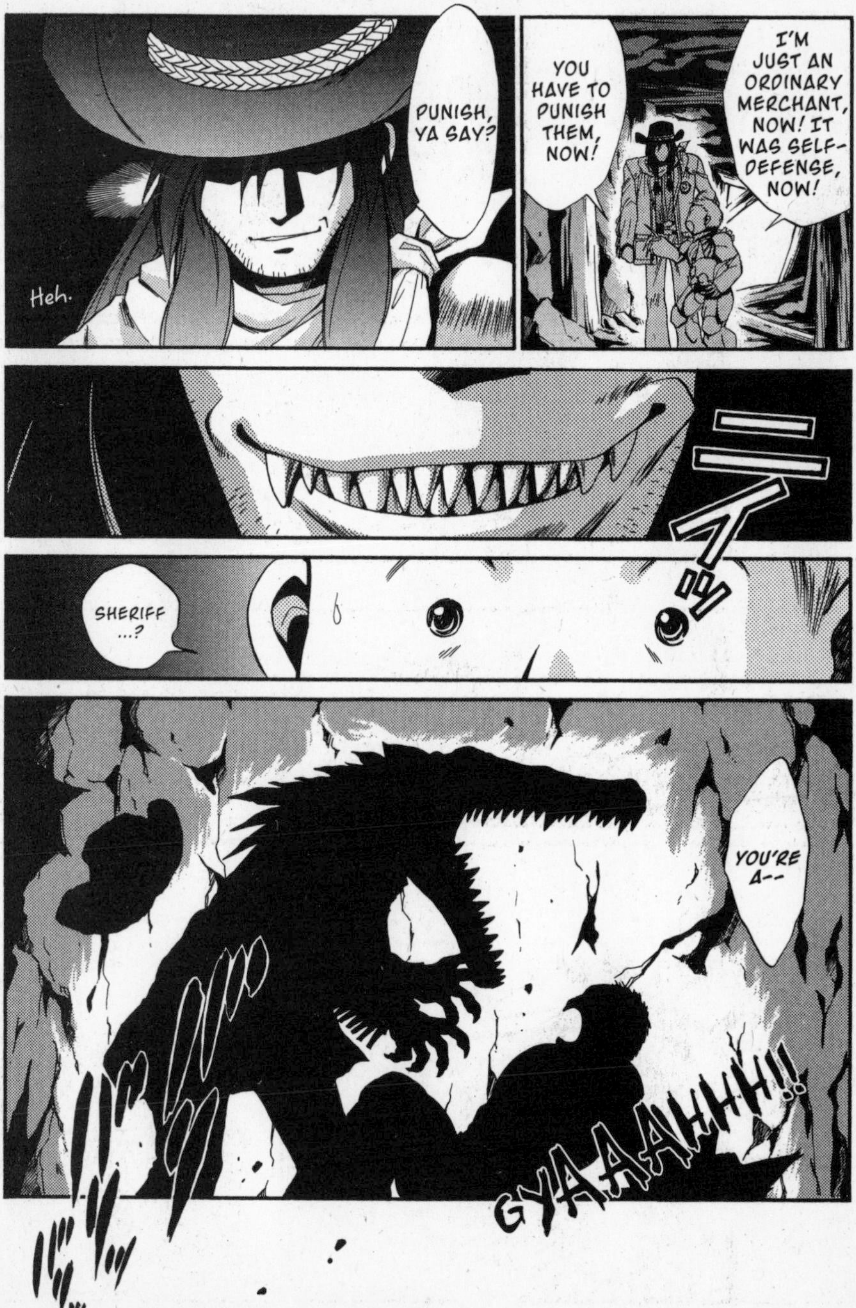
I'M JUST AN ORDINARY MERCHANT, NOW! IT WAS SELF-DEFENSE, NOW!
YOU HAVE TO PUNISH THEM, NOW!
PUNISH, YA SAY?
Heh.
SHERIFF ...?
YOU'RE A--
GYAAAAHHH!!

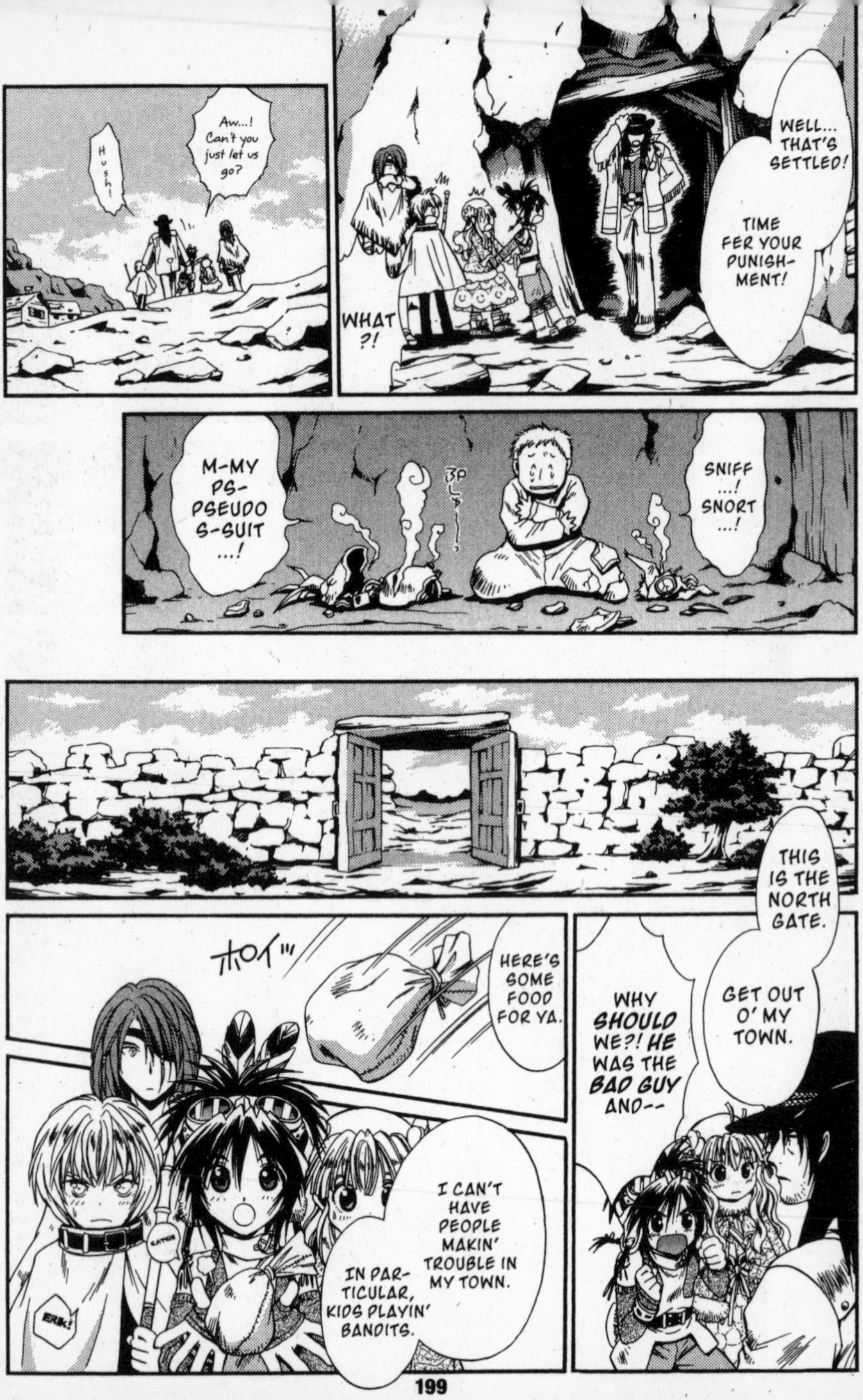
WELL... THAT'S SETTLED!
TIME FER YOUR PUNISHMENT!
WHAT ?!
Aw...! Can't you just let us go?
Hush!
SNIFF ...! SNORT ...!
M-MY PS-PSEUDO S-SUIT ...!
THIS IS THE NORTH GATE.
GET OUT O' MY TOWN.
WHY **SHOULD** WE?! **HE** WAS THE **BAD GUY** AND--
HERE'S SOME FOOD FOR YA.
I CAN'T HAVE PEOPLE MAKIN' TROUBLE IN MY TOWN.
IN PARTICULAR, KIDS PLAYIN' BANDITS.
CATCH
ERIK!

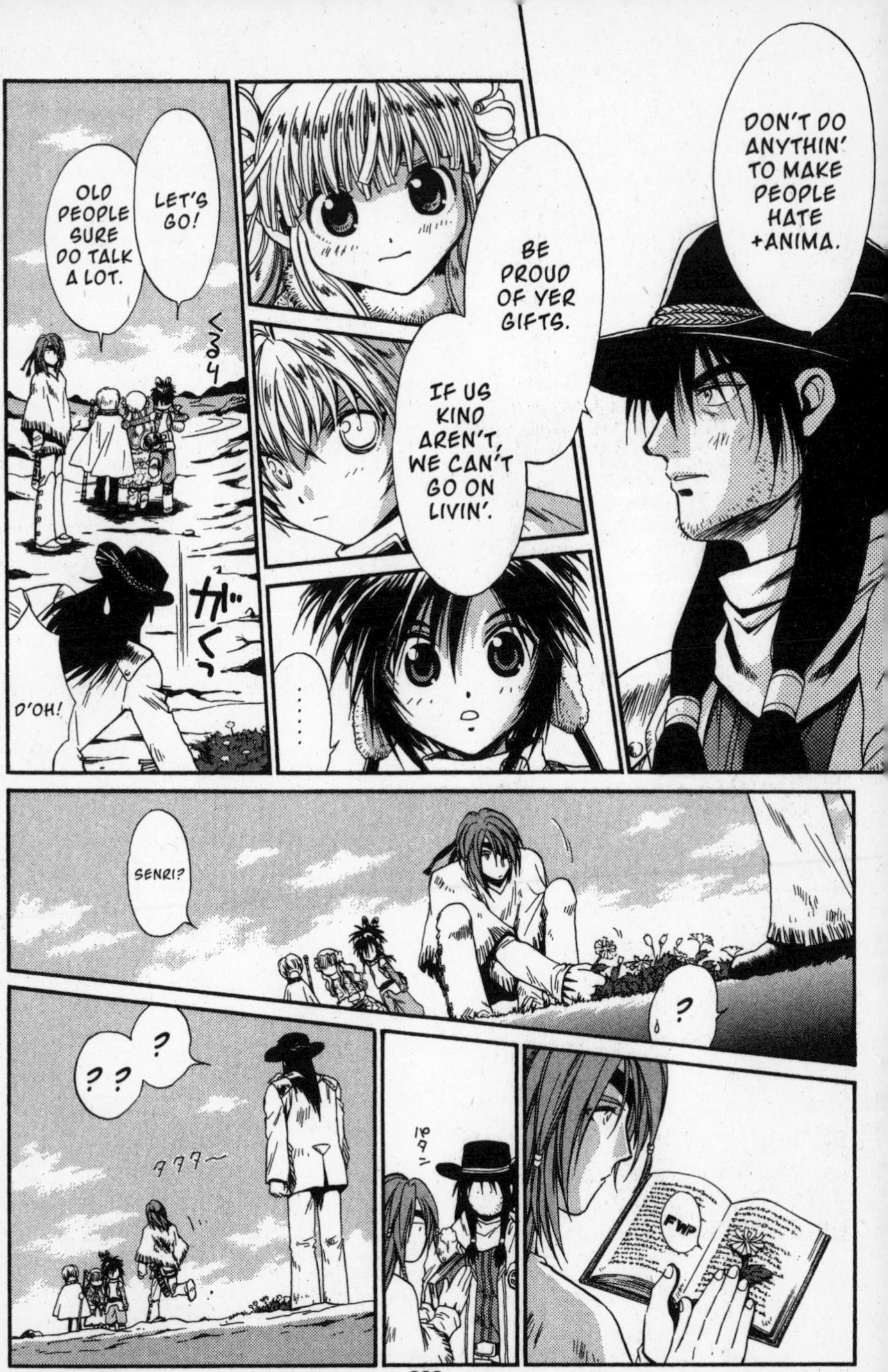
DON'T DO ANYTHIN' TO MAKE PEOPLE HATE +ANIMA.
BE PROUD OF YER GIFTS.
IF US KIND AREN'T, WE CAN'T GO ON LIVIN'.
......
LET'S GO!
OLD PEOPLE SURE DO TALK A LOT.
くるり
がくっ
D'OH!
SENRI?
?
FWP
?
??
タタタ～

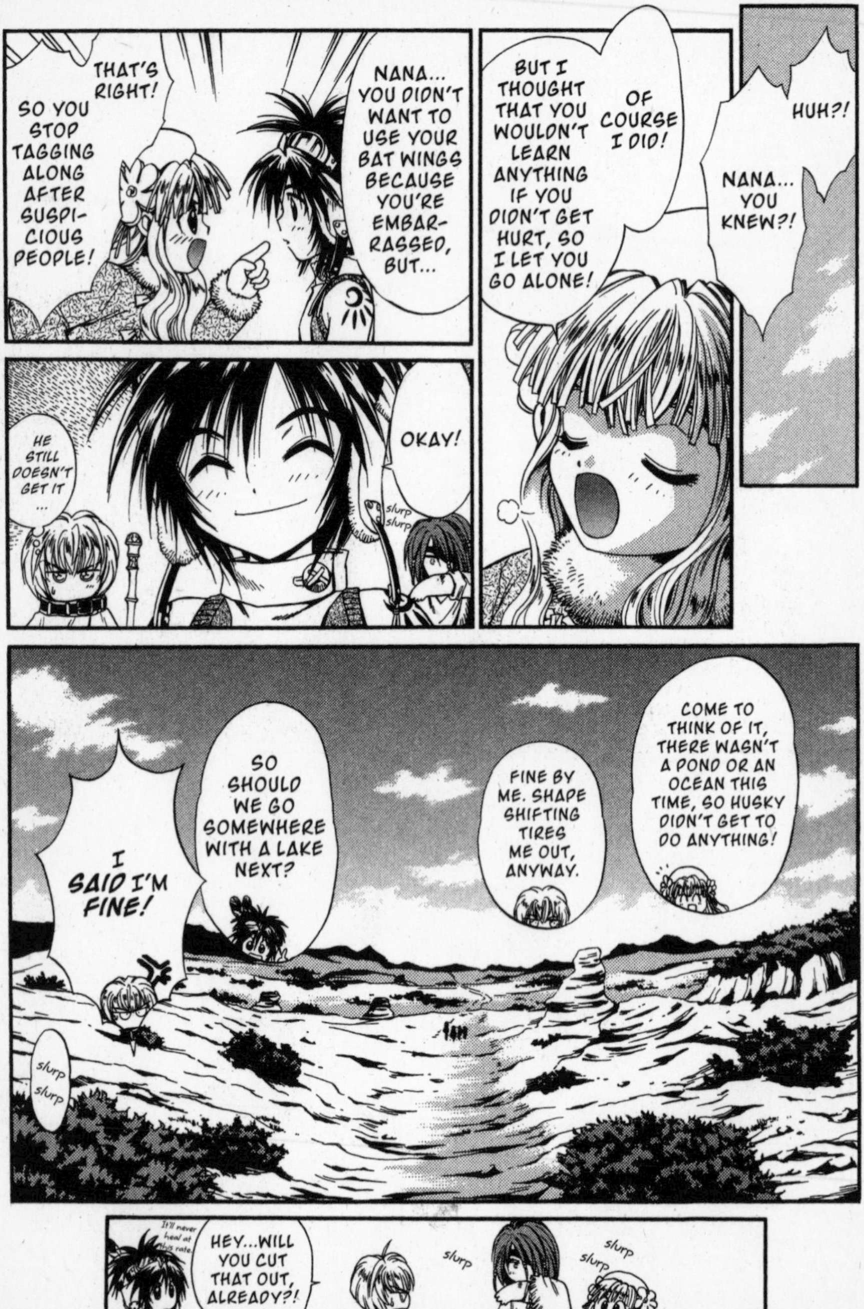
HUH?!
NANA... YOU KNEW?!
OF COURSE I DID!
BUT I THOUGHT THAT YOU WOULDN'T LEARN ANYTHING IF YOU DIDN'T GET HURT, SO I LET YOU GO ALONE!
NANA... YOU DIDN'T WANT TO USE YOUR BAT WINGS BECAUSE YOU'RE EMBARRASSED, BUT...
THAT'S RIGHT!
SO YOU STOP TAGGING ALONG AFTER SUSPICIOUS PEOPLE!
OKAY!
slurp slurp
HE STILL DOESN'T GET IT ...
COME TO THINK OF IT, THERE WASN'T A POND OR AN OCEAN THIS TIME, SO HUSKY DIDN'T GET TO DO ANYTHING!
FINE BY ME. SHAPE SHIFTING TIRES ME OUT, ANYWAY.
SO SHOULD WE GO SOMEWHERE WITH A LAKE NEXT?
I SAID I'M FINE!
slurp slurp
slurp slurp
slurp
HEY...WILL YOU CUT THAT OUT, ALREADY?!
It'll never heal at this rate.

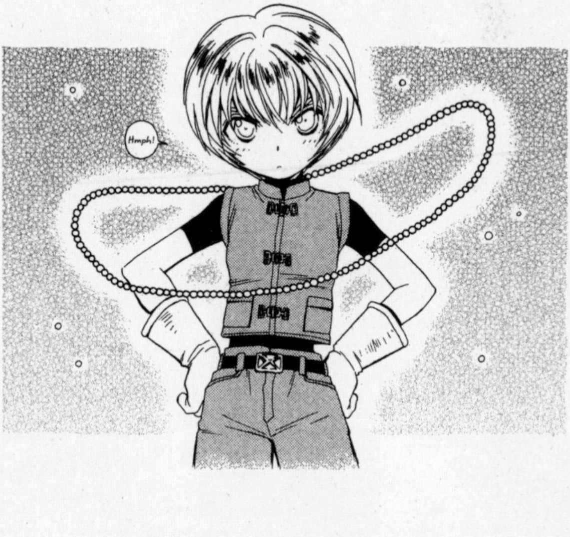
Hmph!

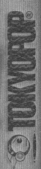

✠ANIMA

COORO BEFRIENDS A MAN IN A GLIDER NAMED SHADOW, WHO LONGS TO FLY SO HE CAN TAKE MEDICINE TO HIS FAMILY'S REMOTE FARM. BUT WHEN HE DISCOVERS THAT COORO IS A +ANIMA WITH WINGS, ENVY TEARS A RIFT BETWEEN THEM. CAN COORO SHOW HIS FEATHERLESS FRIEND THE ERROR OF HIS WAYS? LATER, COORO AND COMPANY RUN INTO COMMANDER IGNEOUS AND HIS TROOPS AT A NEARBY TOWN, WHO ORDERS THE LOCAL BLACKSMITH TO STRENGTHEN THEIR WEAPONS. WHEN THE BLACKSMITH REFUSES, IT'S UP TO COORO AND THE OTHERS TO STAND UP TO IGNEOUS. HUSKY'S PAST IS ALSO EXPLORED, AND WE LEARN WHY HE HATES GIRLS SO MUCH.

IT'S ALL IN THE NEXT ACTION-PACKED VOLUME!

③

Natsumi Mukai

WARCRAFT
THE SUNWELL TRILOGY

RICHARD A. KNAAK · KIM JAE-HWAN

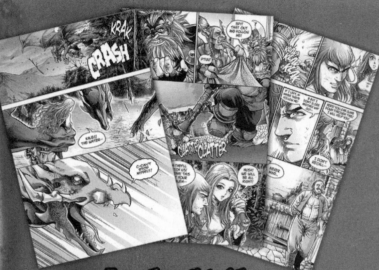

From the artist of the
best-selling *King of Hell* series!

It's an epic quest to save the entire High Elven Kingdom from the forces of the Undead Scourge! Set in the mystical world of Azeroth, *Warcraft: The Sunwell Trilogy* chronicles the adventures of Kalec, a blue dragon who has taken human form to escape deadly forces, and Anveena, a beautiful young maiden with a mysterious power.

EXPERIENCE THE MANGA

T
TEEN
AGE 13+

TOKYOPOP

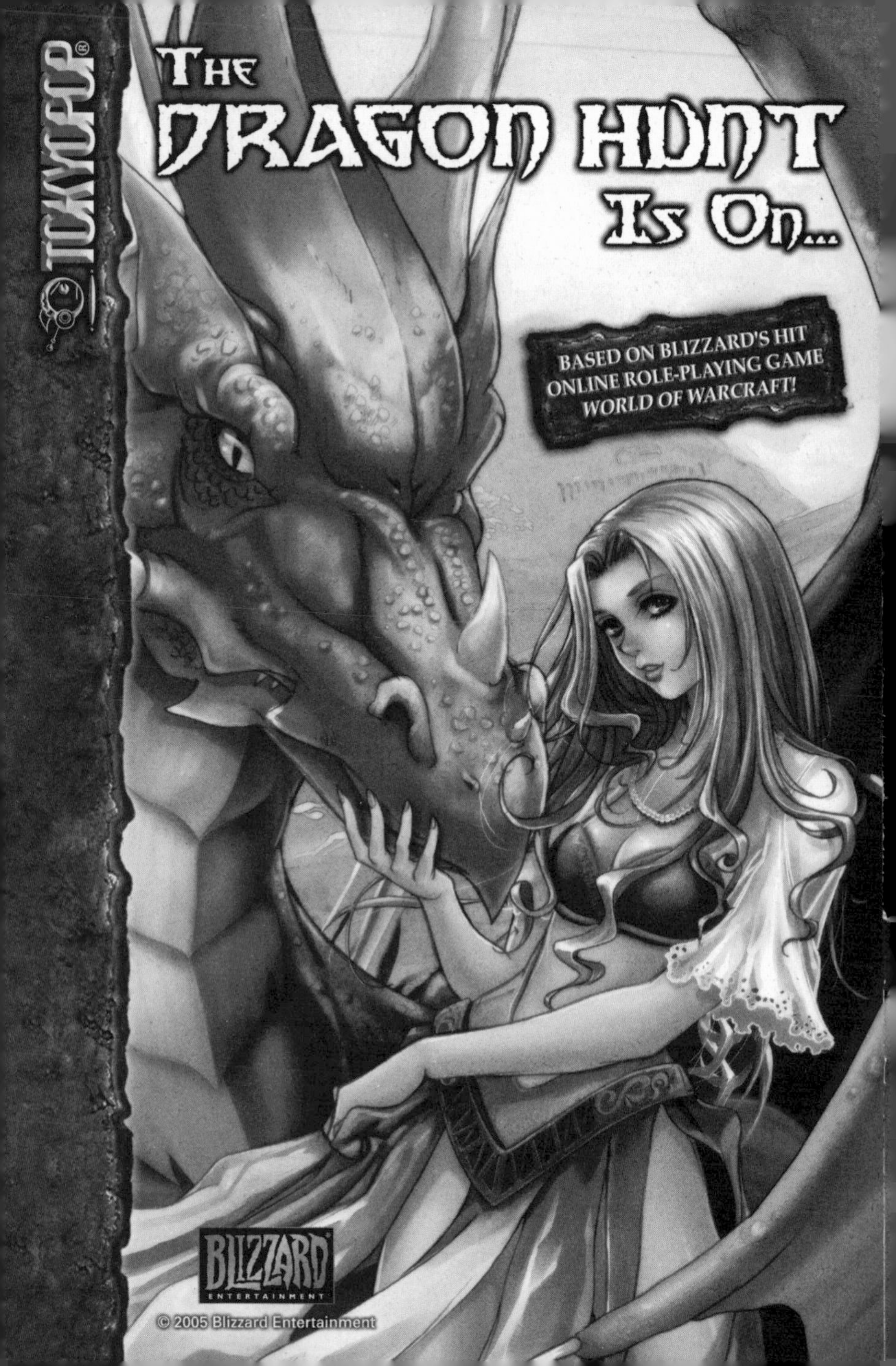
TOKYOPOP
The Dragon Hunt Is On...
BASED ON BLIZZARD'S HIT ONLINE ROLE-PLAYING GAME *WORLD OF WARCRAFT!*
BLIZZARD ENTERTAINMENT
© 2005 Blizzard Entertainment

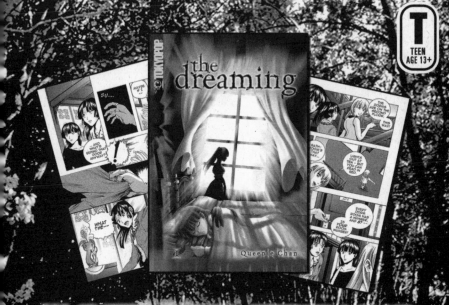

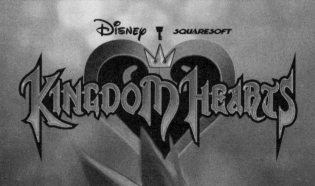

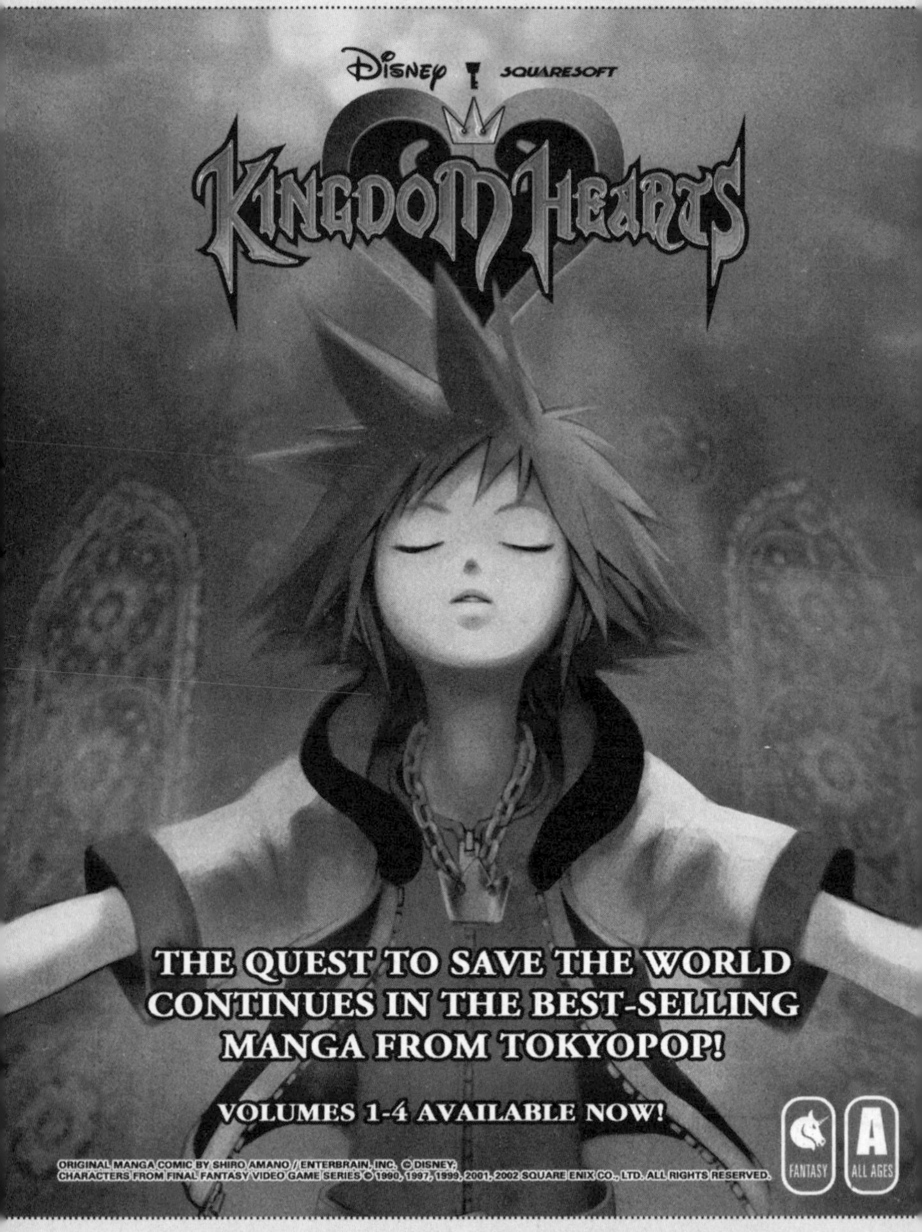

STOP!

This is the back of the book.
You wouldn't want to spoil a great ending!

This book is printed "manga-style," in the authentic Japanese right-to-left format. Since none of the artwork has been flipped or altered, readers get to experience the story just as the creator intended. You've been asking for it, so TOKYOPOP® delivered: authentic, hot-off-the-press, and far more fun!

DIRECTIONS

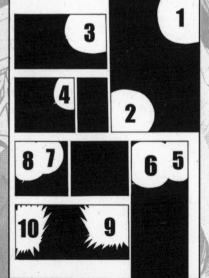

If this is your first time reading manga-style, here's a quick guide to help you understand how it works.

It's easy... just start in the top right panel and follow the numbers. Have fun, and look for more 100% authentic manga from TOKYOPOP®!

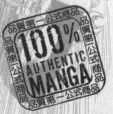